Montréal & Québec City

"All you've got to do is decide to go
and the hardest part is over.

So go!"

THIS EDITION WRITTEN AND RESEARCHED BY

Timothy N Hornyak
Gregor Clark

Contents

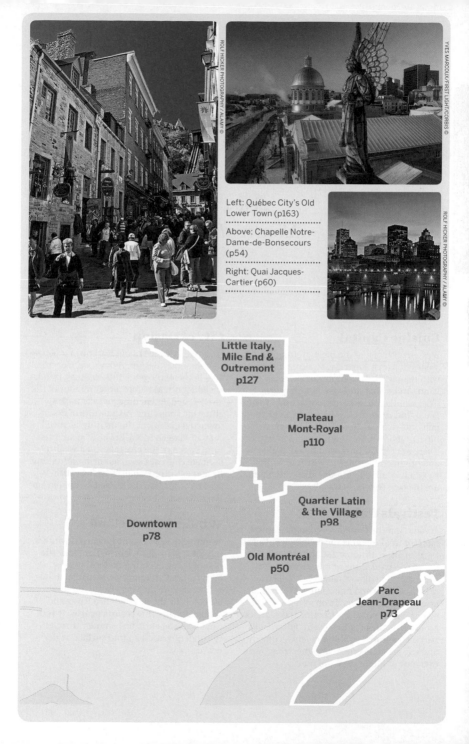

Left: Québec City's Old Lower Town (p163)

Above: Chapelle Notre-Dame-de-Bonsecours (p54)

Right: Quai Jacques-Cartier (p60)

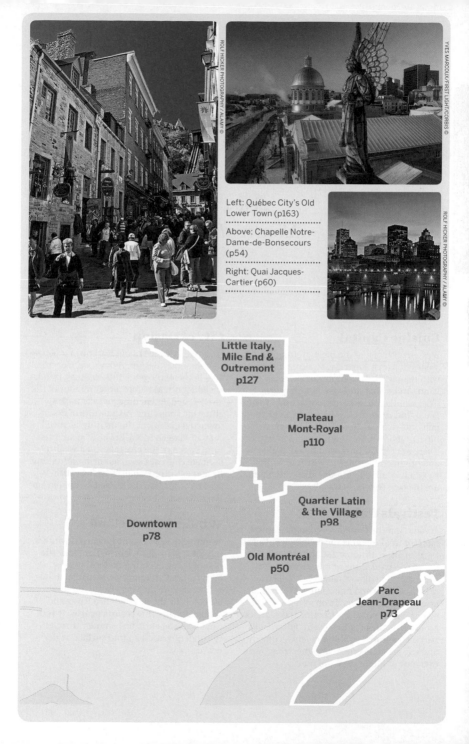

Little Italy, Mile End & Outremont p127

Plateau Mont-Royal p110

Quartier Latin & the Village p98

Downtown p78

Old Montréal p50

Parc Jean-Drapeau p73

Welcome to Montréal

Few cities can compete with Montréal's mouthwatering mix of food, festivals and fun-centric living.

Cuisine Capital

Blessed with one of the most exciting food scenes in North America, Montréal brims with temples dedicated to Kamouraska lamb, Arctic char and, of course, *poutine* (fries smothered in cheese curds and gravy). You'll find irresistible patisseries, English pubs, 80-year-old Jewish delis and magnificent food markets reminiscent of Paris. There are hipster bars with bowling alleys and innumerable cafes in which to while away a lazy afternoon. And above all, there are the best bagels on the planet.

Festivals Galore

Toronto may be Canada's economic capital, but Montréal remains the country's cultural juggernaut, with some 250 theater and dance companies, over 90 festivals and a fascinating medley of neighborhoods where artists, writers and musicians have helped cement the city's reputation as a great arts center. The Festival International de Jazz de Montréal is the headline event, followed by parties dedicated to world cinema, comedy and gay pride. There's truly something for everyone at all times of the year.

City of Design

Montréal is a slice of old Europe in a pie of contemporary design. A day's wander might take in the photogenic 18th-century facades of Old Montréal before a cycling tour of the lovely Canal de Lachine, or take in the glittering shops and restaurants of downtown and ending at the inviting terraced cafes of Plateau Mont-Royal. The architectural sweep of the city takes in a wealth of heritage churches such as the breathtaking Basilique Notre-Dame, as well as 20th-century icons like the Stade Olympique and Habitat 67.

Winter Wonderland

Montréal does get some long, cold winters. But the natives have learned to make the best of them, cheering on local hockey legends Les Canadiens de Montréal, tobogganing in Parc du Mont-Royal, building ice hotels by the St Lawrence River and skiing at many fine resorts nearby. If you can't bear the chill, just wander through the underground city and surface at the nearest pub.

Why I Love Montréal

By Timothy N Hornyak, Author

I was born and raised in Montréal, but after living in Tokyo I'm always astonished at the breadth of culture in my hometown. Despite its modest size, Montréal packs a mighty foodie punch with its myriad restaurants and devotion to good food. I could spend hours wandering through the Marché Jean-Talon and then devouring its offerings at restaurants like Kitchen Galerie, or simply spending a warm summer evening drinking on a rooftop patio in Old Montréal. But if I were exiled to a desert island, I would insist on bringing as many bagels from St-Viateur Bagel as possible.

For more about our authors, see p300.

Top: Montréal skyline

Montréal's
Top 10

Old Montréal *(p50)*

1 The old city is where Montréal began and where its heart lies still. Stroll the old-world cobblestone streets and grand plazas, and learn about local history in the museums. The neighborhood also has fine churches, 19th-century (and earlier) buildings juxtaposed with contemporary constructions, excellent shops and boutiques, numerous art galleries and cafes for your inner bohemian, and some of Montréal's finest dining and accommodations options. Old Montréal is like traveling in time without leaving the best of modernity behind.

⊙ *Old Montréal*

Musée des Beaux-Arts de Montréal *(p80)*

2 This recently expanded gem in the heart of Montréal is one of the best museums in the country. And entry to its permanent collection – spanning everything from the Old Masters to contemporary artists – is free. The new Bourgie Pavilion is in a gorgeous 19th-century church adjacent to the original neoclassical building, while the modern Desmarais Pavilion across the street reflects its engagement with contemporary art. Temporary exhibitions range from Chinese terracotta warriors to pop artist Tom Wesselmann.

⊙ *Downtown*

IMAGEBROKER / ALAMY ©

Musical Montréal (p236)

3 Montrealers are justly proud of their passion for cultivating and appreciating good music. What else would you expect from a city that has turned out everything from Leonard Cohen to Arcade Fire? That's part of the reason why thousands gather downtown every summer for the sizzling sounds of the Festival International de Jazz de Montréal, the city's main party. Free outdoor shows, star performers and a wide variety of genres make it one of the best reasons to visit.

☆ *Music & the Arts*

Basilique Notre-Dame (p52)

4 The pride of Montréal and one of the most beautiful churches on the continent, the Basilique Notre-Dame is a 19th-century Gothic Revival masterpiece with spectacular craftsmanship. Originally it was a humble building dating from 1683; it was rebuilt in 1829. Everything from the great bell (12 tons) in the western tower to the 1891 organ with its 7000 pipes and the stained-glass windows depicting the city's history speaks of the strong faith of the congregations of yesteryear.

◉ *Old Montréal*

Parc du Mont-Royal (p113)

5 The lungs of Montréal, Parc du Mont-Royal is the large green space covering much of Mont-Royal, the mountain at the heart of the city. Montrealers grow up sledding down its slopes and skiing on its ponds in winter, while the rest of the year presents perfect opportunities for looking out over the city from its belvederes, jogging, biking or simply walking its forested paths. An abundance of fauna and flora make it a nature-lover's paradise.

◉ *Plateau Mont-Royal*

Rue St-Denis (p100)

6 Few parts of Montréal have as bohemian and laid-back a vibe as Rue St-Denis in the Quartier Latin. On a few blocks below Rue Sherbrooke Est, students from the nearby Université du Québec à Montréal (UQAM) sip beer in brasseries, artists hobnob in cafes and everyone else seems to just watch the world go by. No wonder it was at the heart of the student protest movement that erupted in the city in 2012. It's also home to some excellent theaters, cinemas, churches and restaurants.

⊙ *Quartier Latin & the Village*

Canal de Lachine (p143)

7 This old industrial waterway that powered Canada's industrialization has been cleaned up, spruced up and made ready to welcome thousands of bikers, joggers and amateur sailors every summer. The best way to enjoy it is to rent a Bixi bike and pedal to the Marché Atwater, where you can browse farm produce, artisanal cheeses and freshly baked goods. The canal's banks are a perfect spot for picnicking with your purchases.

⊙ *Southwest & Outer Montréal*

YVES MARCOUX / GETTY IMAGES ©

Old Port (p60)

8 There's always something fun happening at Montréal's Old Port, whatever your pleasure. Take in a circus at Cirque du Soleil, bring the kids to a science museum, hop on a boat cruise to the Lachine Rapids, pamper yourself in a floating spa or simply park yourself in a cafe along Rue de la Commune and do some serious people-watching. The latest attraction is the Plage de l'Horloge, an artificial beach on the riverfront with everything except swimming.

⊙ *Old Montréal*

Parc Jean-Drapeau *(p73)*

9 You might not have a ticket to the Grand Prix du Canada here, but this collection of island parks in the St Lawrence River is a great spot to get a view of the city and plenty of fresh air. The Musée Stewart is a rare, authentic British garrison that tells the history of the city. After walking the forested paths, you can go thrill-seeking at the La Ronde amusement park or, for adults, the Casino de Montréal. Just save enough for the subway ride back. RICHARD BUCKMINSTER FULLER'S BIOSPHÈRE

◉ *Parc Jean-Drapeau*

RONALD SANTERRE / GETTY IMAGES ©

GUYLAIN DOYLE / GETTY IMAGES ©

Marché Jean-Talon *(p129)*

10 Where to begin? This farmers market in Little Italy has hundreds of vendors hawking fresh vegetables, fruit, seafood and baked goods, as well as seemingly endless restaurants and shops selling everything from Québec jams and wine to maple products, goat cheese, honey, microbrewed beers, crepes, European and Middle Eastern pastries, and artisanal deli meats. Nearby restaurants such as Kitchen Galerie take full advantage, to the delight of foodies.

◉ *Little Italy, Mile End & Outremont*

What's New

Quartier des Spectacles

This massive redevelopment is transforming downtown Montréal into an even greater center for festivals, with new venues and added seating capacity. When complete, the Quartier des Spectacles will take up about 1 sq km of the city, 28,000 seats in 30 performance halls and over 80 cultural venues. It should be fully complete around 2015. The most noticeable changes are happening around Place des Arts (p81), with added capacity, clubs and restaurants. (www.quartierdesspectacles.com)

Musée des Beaux-Arts de Montréal Expansion

The city's centrepiece museum has expanded into a neighboring 1894 church, where 600 Canadian artworks are on display. The Claire and Marc Bourgie Pavilion also features a beautiful new concert hall. (p80)

Village des Neiges

This delightful new snow festival features construction of an ice hotel. If that's too chilly for you, the ice restaurant does lunch and dinner. (p75)

Plage de l'Horloge

Montréal's Old Port seemed to have it all, but it didn't have a beach – until now. The newly opened Plage de l'Horloge has sand, Adirondack chairs, a bar, and plenty of sun. Unfortunately, though, there's no swimming. (p71)

L'Astral

As part of the Quartier des Spectacles, the century-old Blumenthal Building has been renovated and now hosts the L'Astral concert hall as well as jazz club Le Balmoral. (p91)

Revamped Place d'Armes

Old Montréal's main square has had a $14-million face lift, allowing better access to its main attraction, the Monument Maisonneuve honoring the city's founder. (p53)

Better Bixi

With more than 5000 bikes and over 400 docking stations, Montréal's popular bike-rental system has expanded to more suburbs, including Notre-Dame-de-Grâce and Verdun. (p91)

New Airport Link

Montréal's Pierre Elliott Trudeau Airport now has a direct, 24-hour bus link to downtown. The 747 bus brings travelers to the Gare d'Autocars and the Berri-UQAM metro station in less than an hour. (p250)

For more recommendations and reviews, see **lonelyplanet.com/montreal**

Need to Know

Currency
Canadian dollar ($)

Language
French and English

Visas
Not required for citizens of Australia, New Zealand, United Kingdom and the United States, among others. See www.cic.gc.ca.

Money
ATMs widespread. Major credit cards widely accepted.

Cell Phones
Buy local prepaid SIM cards for use with international phones

Time
Eastern Time (GMT/UTC minus five hours, minus four hours March to November)

Tourist Information
Tourisme Montréal (☑877-266-5687; www.tourisme-montreal.org); Centre Infotouriste (Map p288; www.bonjourquebec.com; 1255 Rue Peel, ☺9am-7pm late Jun-late Aug, closes earlier rest of year; ⓜPeel)

Your Daily Budget
The following are average costs per day.

Budget under $75
➡ Dorm bed $25
➡ Supermarkets, markets, fast-food restaurants $30
➡ Bixi bike rental, 24 hours $7
➡ Movie tickets $11

Midrange $75–$250
➡ Double room $150
➡ Two-course dinner with glass of wine $60
➡ Theater ticket $35

Top end over $250
➡ Boutique hotel room $200
➡ Table d'hôte in deluxe restaurant with wine $80
➡ Canadiens de Montréal hockey ticket $200

Advance Planning
Two months before Book tickets for hockey games, major festivals like the Festivale International de Jazz de Montréal, and top restaurants.

Three weeks before Scan web listings for festivals and events; book hotels and rental bikes. Be sure to have adequate clothing for winter.

A few days before Check the weather at www.weatheroffice.gc.ca.

Useful Websites
➡ **Lonely Planet** (www.lonelyplanet.com/montreal) Destination information, hotel bookings, traveler forum and more.

➡ **Montreal Gazette** (www.montrealgazette.com) Montreal's English-language daily newspaper covers everything from politics to sports.

➡ **Midnight Poutine** (www.midnightpoutine.ca) A good source for local eateries and dining trends.

➡ **Ville de Montréal** (http://ville.montreal.qc.ca) The city's official website has some useful travel info, especially on its blogs.

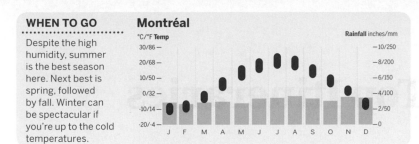

WHEN TO GO

Despite the high humidity, summer is the best season here. Next best is spring, followed by fall. Winter can be spectacular if you're up to the cold temperatures.

Arriving in Montréal

Pierre Elliott Trudeau Airport Buses and taxis run to downtown Montréal around the clock; buses $8, taxis $40.

Gare Centrale Trains pulling in to Montréal arrive at this downtown terminus, within easy reach of many parts of the city by taxi.

 For much more on **arrival**, see p250.

Getting Around

Bus Buses cover central parts of the island with well-marked routes. They run from 5am to 1am, with separate night services.

Metro There are four lines, blue trains and unique rubber wheels. Trains run approximately from 5am to midnight.

Bicycle The city's popular Bixi bike-rental system has more than 400 stations, covering central and outlying areas. There is an extensive network of bike paths too.

Boat Good for day trips to Parc Jean-Drapeau and cruises on the St Lawrence River.

Walking Subway stations are fairly close in the city centre; save a little cash by walking if you only need to go one stop.

For much more on **getting around**, see p252.

Sleeping

Finding a place to bunk in Montréal is easy thanks to the many hotels that have opened in the past d333ecade or so. Summer is a peak season, so if you're traveling to see the jazz fest and other festivals, be sure to book well in advance.

Boutique hotels set in historic surroundings such as Old Montréal have some of the most sought-after rooms in the city, but a cultural experience can also be had at some of the B&Bs housed in heritage buildings in other neighborhoods.

Accommodations range from cheap, no-frills hostels and generic hotels to charming B&Bs, boutique hotels and deluxe suites.

Useful Websites

➡ **Tourisme Montréal** (www.tourisme-montreal.org) The city's excellent tourism website.

➡ **Experience Old Montreal** (www.experienceoldmontreal.com) The Antonopoulos Group's collection of hotels, bars and restaurants in the old city.

 For much more on **sleeping** see p208.

Top Itineraries

Day One

Old Montréal (p50)

Take the subway to Place-d'Armes and make a beeline for the stunning **Basilique Notre-Dame**. Explore the cobblestone streets of the old town, winding your way to the sailors' church, **Chapelle Notre-Dame de Bonsecours**. Stroll up **Place Jacques-Cartier** with its many buskers and artists, into the **Château Ramezay** museum.

 Lunch Le Gros Jambon (p62) for *poutine* and other Québecois comfort food.

Old Montréal (p50)

Deepen your understanding of the city's history at the excellent **Musée d'Archéologie Pointe-à-Callière** before crossing Place d'Youville to **Fonderie Darling** for its innovative contemporary-art installations and irresistible **Cluny Artbar**, which has some most unusual seating choices.

Dinner Toqué! (p61) for its superlative cuisine and unforgettable service.

Old Montréal (p50)

If you're not dining in style, grab a quick pizza at **Bevo** before catching a show at **Cirque du Soleil** in the Old Port. You might also consider watching the sky turn various colors at sunset while downing a gin and tonic on the rooftop patio at **Terrasse Nelligan**. Dance the night away at scenester magnets **Velvet** and **Garde Manger**, which will rock you until 3am.

Day Two

Downtown (p78)

Start your tour of downtown Montréal at **Musée des Beaux-Arts de Montréal** for its excellent collection of Old Masters and contemporary art. Architecture aficionados will dig the contemporary Desmarais pavilion as well as the newly added wing in an 1890s church. Next stroll down **Rue Sherbrooke Ouest**, home to tony shops and heritage mansions, toward **McGill University**.

 Lunch m:brgr (p87) along Rue Drummond is a good spot for carnivores.

Canal de Lachine (p143)

Hop on the metro to Lionel-Groulx and walk down to **Marché Atwater** for a look at the farmers' produce, croissants and cheese. If you have the energy, rent a Bixi bike from a nearby station and pedal the **Canal de Lachine**. If not, consider a **cruise** on the canal.

Dinner For incredible Québécois fare, try Joe Beef (p85) if you can get in.

Downtown (p78)

Upstairs has nightly jazz performances, or better yet the **jazz festival** will be rocking the blocks around **Place des Arts** if your timing is right. Otherwise grab a postdinner glass at the pubs along **Rue Crescent** or some laughs at **Comedyworks**.

Day Three

Little Italy, Mile End & Outremont (p127)

 Make for Little Italy to explore the mouthwatering **Marché Jean-Talon**. Stroll down to the local church, the **Église Madonna della Difesa**, and be sure to spot Mussolini on the ceiling. Browse the old-world shops along Blvd St-Laurent before hopping a bus to Mile End.

> **Lunch** St-Viateur Bagel & Café (p119) for the best dough rings in the world.

Little Italy, Mile End & Outremont (p127)

 Ramble down to **Avenue Laurier**, pausing at the excellent art purveyor **Galerie Simon Blais** and hipster curiosities at **Monastiraki**. The top of Ave Laurier will put you within striking distance of **Parc du Mont-Royal**, but you'll still need to hop in a taxi to get close to the **Kondiaronk lookout**.

> **Dinner** Le Filet (p115) for its innovative local seafood with Japanese hints.

Plateau Mont-Royal (p110)

Bus it down to **Casa del Popolo** and see what the hipster kids are cheering for on stage – it could be jazz, electronica, folk or cabaret pop. To indulge your inner child, **Candi** is a syrupy-sweet bar with all manner of eye and mouth candy. **Gogo Lounge** is another good spot to kick back with a nightcap.

Day Four

Parc Jean-Drapeau (p73)

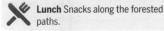 A river runs through it, dividing Parc Jean-Drapeau into two isles. Begin at **Île Ste-Hélène** with a tour of remarkable buildings from yesteryear. Learn about the environment and our impact on it at the **Biosphère**, housed in Buckminster Fuller's geodesic dome built for Expo '67. Not far away, the **Musée Stewart** is the site of an authentic British garrison.

> **Lunch** Snacks along the forested paths.

Parc Jean-Drapeau (p73)

Wander the island's walking paths, taking in the outdoor sculptures before kicking up your heels at **Piknic Électronik**, a summertime electronica dancefest. If it's not on, try for some thrills on the world's tallest wooden roller coaster at **La Ronde**. You can grab panoramic but decidedly slower views of the city from 45m up on the Ferris wheel.

> **Dinner** Ttry the excellent Québecois cuisine at Hélène de Champlain (p76).

Parc Jean-Drapeau (p73)

The island is a perfect spot to watch the sky explode with fireworks during **L'International des Feux Loto-Québec**. If not, the **Casino de Montréal** has everything you need for a good time; just bring luck. Or take a long walk or quick taxi ride to **Habitat '67**, the block-city also left over from Expo '67. The winking lights of the Old Port will be beckoning you back across the water.

If You Like...

Café Culture

Caffè Italia This very unpretentious coffee shop in Little Italy really feels like the old country. (p132)

Cluny Artbar A former industrial space with former bowling lanes for tables, it's irresistible. (p63)

1000 Grammes Probably the Village's most bubbly daytime hangout, with great cakes to boot. (p104)

Juliette et Chocolat How many ways can one enjoy chocolate? This beautiful café tries to find out. (p132)

Café Santropol Towering sandwiches and a fantastic patio make this a local favorite. (p118)

St-Viateur Bagel & Café You can't do better than Montréal's best bagels and some great coffee. (p119)

Pikolo Espresso Bar The signature drink in this stylish space is the Pikolo *ristretto,* which goes down smooth. (p90)

Olive + Gourmando With its baked loaves and yummy sandwiches, this bakery-café in the heart of Old Montréal is easy to love. (p64)

Old Buildings

Basilique Notre-Dame Dating from the 19th century, this Gothic Revival masterpiece wows from inside and out. (p52)

Château Ramezay This well-preserved 18th-century governors' home was used as a meeting place by Benjamin Franklin. (p53)

Parc La Fontaine (p112)

THOMAS SBAMPATO /IMAGEBROKER / ALAMY ©

Chapelle Notre-Dame de Bonsecours Originally founded in 1773, this sailors' chapel commands spectacular views over the harbor. (p54)

Hôtel de Ville Rebuilt in 1926, the city's gorgeous city hall displays local art by the legislative chamber. (p55)

Bank of Montréal Canada's oldest bank was erected in 1847. It stunning marble interior and vaulted ceiling still houses tellers. (p53)

Vieux Séminaire de St-Sulpice The clock on this 1680s seminary was a present from Louis XIV. (p53)

Cathédrale Marie-Reine-du-Monde This landmark was built from 1870 to 1894 as a symbol of Catholic power in the heart of Protestant Montréal. (p81)

Live Music

Place des Arts With the new Maison Symphonique venue, the city's festival nerve center is better than ever. (p81)

L'Astral This new jazz venue in a century-old building is a favorite for the jazz festival. (p91)

Casa del Popolo From folk guitarists to spoken-word poets, Casa does artsy like nowhere else. (p124)

Le Piano Rouge This piano bar in the old city is small enough to be intimate yet never dull. (p67)

Metropolis From raves to David Bowie, this former cinema has seen it all and keeps delivering. (p92)

Upstairs Slide into this downtown basement space for succulent ribs and jazz. (p90)

Pollack Concert Hall McGill University's music hall stages recitals by the McGill Chamber Orchestra. (p93)

Quaint Backstreets

Mile End Roam streets that are home to bagel bakeries, funky cafés and bars, and hipster hangouts in this multiethnic district. (p127)

Plateau Mont-Royal From Ave du Mont-Royal to Carré St-Louis, the Plateau is the city's bohemian quarter, with artsy cafes, plentiful parks and unusual boutiques. (p110)

Westmount The newly named national historic site is awash in Victorian homes, leafy parks and its heritage city hall. (p94)

Festivals

Festival International de Jazz de Montréal With over 400 concerts and nearly two million visitors every year, North America's hippest music fest just gets bigger and better. (p23)

La Fête des Neiges Montréal's Snow Festival features some ice-sculpting contests, dogsled races, snow games and costumed characters. (p21)

L'International des Feux Loto-Québec Thousands camp out on rooftops and on the Pont Jacques-Cartier for the planet's hottest pyrotechnics. (p23)

Divers/Cité Montréal's Gay Pride parade is *the* event on the Village calendar, drawing more than a million people. (p23)

Osheaga Festival Musique et Arts Some 70,000 fans typically turn up here for performers like Coldplay and Rufus Wainwright. (p23)

For more top Montréal spots, see
➡ Eating (p30)
➡ Drinking & Nightlife (p34)
➡ Entertainment (p38)
➡ Festivals (p42)
➡ Shopping (p44)

Museums

Musée des Beaux-Arts de Montréal The only museum in Canada that presents Old Masters to contemporary works free of charge as part of its permanent collection. (p80)

Musée d'Art Contemporain A weighty collection of 6000 permanent works includes Québécois legends Jean-Paul Riopelle, Paul-Émile Borduas and Geneviève Cadieux. (p81)

Musée Stewart This old British garrison where troops were stationed in the 19th century displays relics from Canada's past. (p76)

Château Ramezay A home of French governors in the early 18th century, this mansion is one of the finest examples from the ancien régime. (p53)

Musée d'Archéologie Pointe-à-Callière Built on the spot where European settlers set up their first camp, this underground space provides a good overview of Montréal's beginnings. (p54)

Fur Trade at Lachine National Historic Site This 1803 stone depot in Lachine is now an engaging little museum telling the story of the fur trade in Canada. (p143)

PLAN YOUR TRIP IF YOU LIKE...

Parks

Parc du Mont-Royal The lungs of the city, the mountain park has sledding and skating in winter, with forest biking and jogging in summer. (p113)

Parc La Fontaine In summer weary urbanites flock to leafy La Fontaine to enjoy the walking and bicycle paths; it has a popular skating rink in winter. (p112)

Parc des Rapides This space on the St Lawrence River is the spot to view the Lachine Rapids (and the jet boats that ride them). (p143)

Canal de Lachine Closed to shipping in 1970, the canal has been transformed into a 14km-long cycling and pedestrian pathway. (p143)

Jardin Botanique Since its 1931 opening, the 75-hectare garden has grown to include tens of thousands of species in about 30 thematic gardens. (p144)

City Cycling

Canal de Lachine One of the most popular bike paths in the city, the canal and its locks are a great spot for picnics. (p96)

Boulevard de Maisonneuve Much of this one-way street cutting through the heart of downtown has its own bike lanes. (p94)

Parc Jean-Drapeau The two islands in this park in the middle of the St Lawrence River have winding forest trails for hiking and cycling. (p73)

Parc du Mont-Royal It's a slog to pedal up here if you're not hauling your bike in a car, but the wooded trails make it well worth the effort. (p113)

Markets

Marché Atwater This canal-side market overflows with flowers, cheeses, meats and croissants. A great place for picnic supplies. (p82)

Marché Jean-Talon The quintessential city farmers market, Jean-Talon has over 400 stalls selling everything from maple syrup to seafood. (p129)

Marché Bonsecours Browse clothing boutiques, dine alfresco

or take in an auction or a fashion show in this heritage mall. (p70)

Marché St-Jacques The city's oldest public market has reopened as a group of luxury butchers and fishmongers, and is still finding its feet. (p109)

Marché Maisonneuve In the east end, this small market has Québécois cheese, fresh corn and lots of crab. (p109)

Art

Musée d'Art Contemporain Quebec's finest contemporary artworks, in a sleek museum right in the heart of the Quartier des Spectacles. (p81)

Galerie Simon Blais This prestigious gallery in Mile End features some of Québec's finest contemporary art. (p138)

DHC Art Features mind-bending contemporary works by artists such as Ryoji Ikeda, Jenny Holzer and Marc Quinn. (p70)

Month by Month

TOP EVENTS

La Fête des Neiges, January

Grand Prix du Canada, June

L'International des Feux Loto-Québec, June

Festival International de Jazz de Montréal, July

Montréal World Film Festival, August

January

Montréal kicks off the year with a bang, with New Year's Eve parties at restaurants and clubs throughout the city. Temperatures start to really plummet and ski season begins.

La Fête des Neiges

Featuring ice-sculpting contests, dogsled races, snow games and costumed characters like mascot polar bear Boule de Neige., Montréal's Snow Festival is held over three consecutive weekends in late January and early February. (www.fetedesneiges.com)

Village des Neiges

From early January through the end of March, visitors to Parc Jean-Drapeau can feast in a restaurant made of ice and, if they're brave enough, even sleep in an ice hotel. The ice buildings are a must-see. (www.fetedesneiges.com)

February

Amid the deep freeze, snow piles up and Montrealers do their best to beat the blahs by cheering on the Canadiens hockey club. Temperatures can fall below -20°C.

Montréal en Lumière

Created to help locals shake off the late-winter doldrums, the Montréal Highlights Festival is a kind of wintry Mardi Gras with most events taking place downtown. There are classical-music and dance performances, exhibitions, fireworks and celebrity chefs. (www.montrealhighlights.com)

April

One sign that winter may be over is when the Bixi rental bicycles are deployed and bike lanes are reinstated. Spring is here.

Blue Metropolis – Montréal International Literary Festival

This festival brings together 200-plus writers from all over the globe for five days of literary events in English, French, Spanish and other languages in the middle weeks of April. (http://bluemetropolis.org)

May

With the snow gone, rainy, windy weather sets in but doesn't last. A few weeks of mild weather preface rising temperatures, which can soon reach the high 20s.

Biennale de Montréal

One of Montréal's most creative events showcases the best and the brashest on the Canadian art scene, including conferences and seminars on contemporary art. (www.biennalemontreal.org)

Montréal Beer Festival

Here's your chance to quaff brews from around the globe, Held inside the old Windsor Station, this five-day event starts late May or early June. (www.festivalmondialbiere.qc.ca)

June

Amid this hot, festival-packed month, Quebecers celebrate their 'national' day, the Fête Nationale du Québec, on June 24. Everyone is out for a drink, some good food and fireworks.

Tour de l'Île

Also known as the Montréal Bikefest, the Tour de l'Île draws 30,000 cycling enthusiasts for a 50km spin around the island of Montréal and a big party in the city afterward. It's staged on the first Saturday in June, with preregistration required. (www.velo.qc.ca)

Grand Prix du Canada

Formula One is going strong in Montréal despite a hiatus in 2009. It's usually held in mid-June on the Circuit Gilles-Villeneuve. Don't forget your earplugs. (www.grandprixmontreal.com)

(Top) A street performer at the Just for Laughs festival

(Bottom) Place des Arts during the Festival International de Jazz de Montréal (p238)

✴ L'International des Feux Loto-Québec

Thousands camp out on rooftops and on the Pont Jacques-Cartier for the planet's hottest pyrotechnics. The 10 shows last 30 minutes each and are held on Saturday nights and a few Wednesday nights from late June to the end of July. (www.internation aldesfeuxloto-quebec.com)

July

The heat is on in July, humidity sets in and Montrealers long for surrounding lakes and distant beaches. Tourists throng the city for the jazz fest and other major festivals.

✴ Festival International de Jazz de Montréal

With over 400-plus concerts and nearly two million visitors every year, North America's hippest music fest just gets bigger and better, with world music, rock and even pop music sharing the program with jazz legends and upstarts over 13 days from late June to mid-July. See also p238. (www.montreal jazzfest.com)

✴ Just for Laughs

More than 650 artists perform in over 1000 shows at this comedy festival which runs for two weeks in mid-July. Past events have featured The Muppets, Lewis Black, Bob Saget and Bill Hader. See also p40. (www .hahaha.com)

✴ Divers/cité

Montréal's Gay Pride parade is *the* event on the Village calendar, drawing more than a million people, even in slow years. The streets around Pl Émilie-Gamelin pulse with dancing, art exhibits, concerts and parades. It's held over one week starting in late July. (www.diverscite.org)

August

Steamy days, heat and thunderstorms mark August, when many Montrealers leave town for seaside resorts. It's high season for travel.

☆ Osheaga Festival Musique et Arts

In early August, Parc Jean-Drapeau is transformed into a giant stage for one of the city's grand rock festivals. Some 70,000 music fans typically turn up to witness the powerhouse lineup of performers, which in recent years has included heavy hitters like the Flaming Lips, Franz Ferdinand and the Black Keys. (www.osheaga.com)

✴ Montréal World Film Festival

One of the most prestigious film events in Canada, attracting 400,000 visitors to screenings from 70 countries. The stars come out, as well as the directors, producers and writers of the big screen. It's held over 10 days in late August and early September. (www.ffm -montreal.org)

October

Temperatures begin to fall quickly in October as trees put on a spectacular display of color. It's a perfect time to see the Laurentians and the Eastern Townships.

✴ Festival du Nouveau Cinéma de Montréal

This festival highlights who is up-and-coming in feature films, documentaries, experimental shorts, videos, narrative features and electronic art forms during 10 days in early October. (www.nouveau cinema.ca)

✴ Black & Blue Festival

One of the biggest events for the gay community, with major dance parties, cultural and art shows as well as a killer megaparty in the Olympic Stadium, all in the second week of October. Tickets $75 to $120. (www.bbcm.org)

With Kids

Montréal has many sights for younger visitors. Depending on the season, you can go boating, biking, skating or get some thrills at an amusement park or skydiving center.

Cirque du Soleil (p67)

This world-renowned circus combines dance, theater and circus in powerpacked shows that will thrill the kids, but are truly for all ages

Hands-On Activities

Skyventure (p151) Children aged four and above can try their hand at flying in this unique skydiving simulator.

Old Port (p60) Hop into a paddleboat, go jet boating on the St Lawrence or tootle along in a minitrain for a grand tour.

Centre des Sciences de Montréal (p60) Technological wonders, unusual games and an IMAX cinema.

Biosphère (p75) Make a dam and walk on water at this hands-on multimedia museum in Parc Jean-Drapeau.

Kid-Friendly Museums

Biodôme (p145) A giant indoor zoo with forest, river and marine habitats.

Insectarium (p144) With 144,000 specimens creeping, crawling or otherwise on display, this is heaven for kids at Jardin Botanique.

Musée Ferroviaire Canadien (p147) Stationary, moving, new, old...trains of every type that thrill adults as much as children.

Cosmodôme (p147) Take your tots on a virtual mission to Mars in this engaging space center.

Musée Stewart (p76) Oversized cannons, military parades and guides in period costumes inside an old British garrison.

Canadiens de Montréal (p97) The local hockey legends have their own **Hall of Fame** (www.hall.canadiens.com) at the Bell Centre.

Outdoor Fun

La Ronde (p75) Chills and thrills galore – plus fireworks some nights – at Québec's largest amusement park.

Parc du Mont-Royal (p113) This enormous park in the heart of the city is especially fun for kids in winter, with tobogganing, skiing and ice skating.

Parc Nature du Cap-St-Jacques (p147) Verdant park with trails, a beach, a sugar shack and a working farm.

Need to Know

Babysitting
➤ **Parentheses Montréal** (www.parenthesesmontreal.com)
➤ **Denise Miller Babysitting Services** (☎514-365-1704; denise.miller@videotron.ca).

Kid-friendly Restaurants
➤ **Resto Montréal** (www.restomontreal.ca)

Specialty Resources
➤ **Exploring Montreal with Kids** (www.montrealwithkids.com)

Like a Local

Local Hangouts

Montréal often ranks as one of the most liveable cities in the world. A devotion to culture, the arts, good food and drink, as well as green spaces and outdoor fun makes it very easy to blend in here.

Parc du Mont-Royal

This giant park centered on Mont-Royal, 'the Mountain' at the heart of the city, is both collective backyard and workout zone. Walk the forested paths to the lookouts or take a horse-drawn sleigh ride in winter. (p113)

Terraces

Known as patios everywhere else, alfresco terraces are the best way to imbibe with friends, according to Montrealers. Some of the best spots are rooftop terraces in Old Montréal.

Canal de Lachine

You can bike it, sail it, fish it and tan by it. Just don't swim in it. This former industrial waterway has been transformed into an unlikely hot spot with a long bike path and plenty of grass to picnic or lounge on. (p96)

Local Obsessions

Food

Montrealers put lots of love and time into eating. Whether it's getting the freshest ingredients from local markets, or queuing for bagels in Mile End, or fine dining downtown, there's an embarrassment of riches in this city that makes it very special.

Hockey

Les Canadiens de Montréal is more than just a hockey team – it's the local religion. If you're lucky enough to get a ticket, sign up for conversion at the Bell Centre and say 'hallelujah!'. (p97)

Winter

Most Montrealers hate it, some love it, but you can't avoid it for four to five months of the year. So lace up those skates, hit the slopes outside the city, or dine in the riverside ice restaurant and make the best of it!

Get Festive

Summer Celebrations

One of the best ways to take the pulse of Montréal is to get out into a big-time summer festival like the jazz fest. You'll see the city at its best.

For Free

Montréal is already known as an affordable city compared to Toronto or Vancouver. Besides its many parks, churches, markets and art galleries, you'll find free festivals and events, especially in the summer months.

Art Galleries

Montréal museums usually charge admission, but not always. Following is a list of some excellent collections with free entry. There's also the Montréal Museums Pass for discounts (see p255).

Musée des Beaux-Arts (p80) There's never a charge to visit the permanent collection of Montréal's stellar art museum.

Centre Canadien d'Architecture (p81) The fascinating exhibits of this beautifully designed museum are free on Thursday nights (from 6pm to 9pm).

Musée d'Art Contemporain (p81) Wednesday nights (6pm to 9pm) are free at this showcase of modern art.

Fonderie Darling (p54) This avant-garde art gallery offers free admission on Thursdays, when it's open until 10pm. Keep an eye out for summertime events on the street in front.

Science & History Museums

Musée Redpath (p81) Check out a full-sized dinosaur skeleton, Egyptian mummies and tons of other curiosities at this free natural history museum.

Musée des Soeurs-Grises (p58) This small museum offers free tours, by appointment only, of exhibits related to Canada's first homegrown saint.

Musée de Lachine (p143) Follow the canal path far enough (14km) and you reach the oldest house in Montréal, now a cozy museum depicting early colonial days among settlers and fur traders.

Other Attractions

Oratoire St-Joseph (p142) The world's largest shrine to Jesus' dad offers captivating views over Mont-Royal.

Cinémathèque Québécoise (p108) This homage to Québec's film and TV industries has interesting permanent collections on both that are always free.

Tam-tam jam (p115) Dance, pound your drums or simply gawk at this Sunday-afternoon bongo-banging bash held all summer long.

Need to Know

For more information on free events or discounts taking place during your visit, see the following websites:

➡ **Tourisme Montréal** (www.tourisme -montreal.org)

➡ **Resto Montréal** (www.restomontreal .ca)

➡ **Board of Montréal Museum Directors** (www.museesmontreal.org)

Visiting Québec City

With colorful festivals, rambling streets and a cliff-top setting overlooking the St Lawrence River, North America's oldest French-speaking city is a gorgeous, seductive place. An easy excursion from Montréal, Québec City has enough magnetism to be the centerpiece of your vacation.

Statue of Samuel de Champlain, with Château Frontenac (p156) in the background

Getting to Québec City

Two superhighways link Québec City with Montréal: Hwy 40 north of the St Lawrence River and Hwy 20 south of the river. Both routes are arrow-straight and easy (if boring) to drive, and each takes just over three hours.

A nicer way to travel between the two cities is by rail; VIA Rail (www.viarail .ca) runs four trains daily from Montréal's Gare Centrale to Québec's Gare du Palais (three to 3½ hours, one way/return from $63/126). Frequent and economical bus service (three to 3½ hours, at least hourly, one way/return $57/91) is also offered by Greyhound (www.greyhound.com) and Orléans Express (www.orleansexpress.com).

When to Go

Summer is the liveliest time to visit, with a jam-packed events calendar and crowds overflowing the Old Town's narrow lanes.

Québec's other peak season coincides with Winter Carnival in February. To avoid the crowds, visit in spring or fall.

Québec City Festivals & Events

Winter Carnival (www.carnaval.qc.ca) Spanning 17 days in January/February, the world's biggest winter carnival features parades, ice sculptures, boat races, music and lots of drinking.

Fête Nationale du Québec (www.fete nationale.qc.ca) Québec City parties hard on June 24, honoring John the Baptist, the patron saint of French Canadians.

Le Grand Rire (www.grandrire.com) This big June/July comedy fest features everything from stand-up shows to street performances.

Festival d'Été (www.infofestival.com) This 11-day July festival attracts musicians from all over the world.

Les Grands Feux Loto-Québec (www.lesgrandsfeux.com) A spectacular three-week fireworks and international music show in July/August.

Fêtes de la Nouvelle-France (www.nouvelle france.qc.ca) This fab five-day festival in August commemorates Québec's colonial period with historical reenactments and period costumes.

Fête Arc-en-Ciel (www.glbtquebec.org/fete _aec.html) September Gay Pride celebrations.

Festival International des Musiques Sacrées de Québec (www.imsq.ca) This sacred music festival in September showcases everything from gospel to Gregorian chants.

Top Sights

In Québec City, just walking down the street is an aesthetic treat. The city's historic core is unlike anyplace else in North America, with hundreds of gorgeous mansard-roofed old stone buildings clustered inside a perfect frame of crenellated town walls. Québec's dramatic cliffside setting enhances its appeal, with picture-postcard views of the St Lawrence River unfolding from the Terrasse Dufferin boardwalk (p158), and scenic stairways connecting the Upper and Lower Towns.

The most memorable sight for first-time visitors is the castlelike Château Frontenac (p156), dominating the Upper Town from its lofty perch. The city also boasts a fine collection of museums, most notably the Musée des Beaux-Arts (p166) and the eclectic Musée de la Civilisation (p163). History buffs will love Québec's 19th-century hilltop Citadelle (p155) and two museums offering graphic representations of the battles between France and Britain for control of the city (p159 and p164). Just outside the town walls, the vast Parc des Champs de Bataille (Battlefields Park; p164) is ideal for cycling, cross-country skiing, snowshoeing and other outdoor activities.

Québec City for Kids

Youngsters go giddy over the ubiquitous street performers and guides in period costume, the uniformed soldiers beating the retreat at the Citadelle (p155) and the antique cannons sprinkled around Parc des Champs de Bataille (Battlefields Park; p164). Walking the Fortifications (p158) or rampaging down the pedestrian-friendly Terrasse Dufferin (p158) helps get the wiggles out, while a slow tour of the Old Town

in a calèche (horse-drawn carriage; p190) appeals to the whole family. In winter, children will be mesmerized by the superfast slides and whimsically decorated rooms at the ice hotel (p196), the outdoor ice-skating rink at Place d'Youville (p190) and the engaging historical dress-ups at the Centre d'Interpretation de Place-Royale (p163). Outside the center, kids also love the polar-bear, walrus and sea-lion shows at the Aquarium du Québec (p171).

Eating

Dozens of *boulangeries* (bakeries) and patisseries, such as Paillard (p172) and Le Croquembouche (p179), dazzle the eyes and taste buds with perfect croissants and abundant, beautiful displays of éclairs, strawberry tarts and chocolatines. For other affordable French-inspired treats, sample the quiches and savory snacks at *traiteurs* (delis) along Ave Cartier (such as Picardie, p178) or the *crêperies* along Rue St-Jean (including Casse-Crêpe Breton, p173), or head to the lively Marché du Vieux Port (p187), where purveyors of artisanal cheeses and sausages mingle with farmers selling fresh produce from nearby Île d'Orléans. If it's fine cuisine you're after, prepare to be spoiled at top-of-the-line restaurants such as Le Saint-Amour (p172), classy brunch hangouts like Café du Clocher Penché (p178), or trendy bistros like L'Échaudé (p174) and Bistro B (p178).

Drinking & Nightlife

From top-notch microbreweries to outdoor stalls selling the potent wintertime elixir known as caribou, Québec City is a fine place to drink up some local color. Raise a frosty glass (literally, it's made of ice!) beside the roaring fireplace at the city's incomparable ice hotel (p196), quench your midsummer thirst with a ridiculously tall 'yard' of beer at Aux Vieux Canons (p181), get cozy in an ancient stone cellar at Le Pape-Georges (p180) or L'Oncle Antoine (p180), or sunbathe on the outdoor terraces at Le Sacrilège (p180) and La Barberie (p182). When it's time to move on, dance the night away at a cluster of renovated mansions-turned-discos on Grande-Allée

The Glissade de la Terrasse (p190)

(p181) or make a beeline for Le Drague (p181), the lively center of Québec City's gay and lesbian scene.

Entertainment

Entertainment here is a year-round proposition, spilling onto the streets in an endless succession of festivals. Jugglers, acrobats, fire-eaters and street musicians perform on every corner in summertime, while winter brings death-defying downhill ice-skating competitions and ice-canoe races.

Le Grand Théâtre de Québec (p183) and Le Théâtre Capitole (p183) offer venerable settings for drama, classical music and other high culture, while bars around town host everything from Québécois ballads with fiddle and accordion to live rock, alternative music and jazz. In summer outdoor music venues pop up like mushrooms, including Kiosque Edwin Bélanger (p183) on the Plains of Abraham and Agora (p183) by the riverfront.

Shopping

In keeping with the city's historic nature, Québec is an antique-lover's paradise. Rue St-Paul in the Lower Town is crammed with shops offering one-of-a-kind items with a distinctly French-Canadian flavor. Striking an equally retro note, North America's oldest grocery store, JA Moisan (p188), is another browser's delight. On the cobblestone sidewalks below Château Frontenac, local artisans spread out jewelry, leather goods and other handicrafts, while trendy homegrown boutiques abound in the less touristy St-Jean Baptiste, Montcalm and St-Roch neighborhoods. Kids will love the miniature entryway built especially for them at the jam-packed toy emporium Benjo (p189), and fashionistas will swoon over everything from designer shoes to the outrageous glasses frames produced by Québécois designer Anne-Marie Faniel (p187).

Sleeping

Québec City is loaded with atmospheric places to spend the night. Top draws include the upper-floor rooms with river views inside the iconic Château Frontenac (p193), and the plethora of mansions-turned-B&Bs lining the Jardin des Gouverneurs park next door, including Manoir Sur le Cap (p193). Other peak sleeping experiences include chilling out in a fur-lined sleeping bag on a bed of ice at the city's famous Ice Hotel (p196), bedding down above a sumptuous century-old theater (p196), immersing yourself in Van Gogh–inspired decor at trendy boutique hotel Auberge Le Vincent (p197), living it up in a riverfront luxury hotel with an award-winning restaurant (p195) or economizing at two excellent hostels (p194 and p194) inside the Old City walls.

Parlez-Vous Français?

Quebecers, like Montrealers, grow up studying English, but because the anglophone minority in Québec is so tiny, they rarely use it outside the major tourist areas. Most city residents are fully bilingual, but if you stray into the surrounding countryside, you'll quickly find that French is the province's official language.

STEPHEN SAKS / GETTY IMAGES ©

L'Express bistro (p116)

 **Eating**

Montréal is one of the great foodie destinations of the north. Here you'll find an outstanding assortment of classic French cuisine, hearty Québécois fare and countless ethnic restaurants from 80-odd nationalities. Today's haute cuisine is as likely to be conjured by talented young Italian, Japanese or British chefs as graduates from the Académie Culinaire du Québec.

Neighborhoods

Montréal has more eating choices per capita than anywhere in North America except for New York City, and boasts more than 5000 restaurants. The dining scene is marked by dazzling variety and quality, and brash chefs who attack their creations with innovative gusto. Life in Montréal revolves around food, and it's as much about satisfying your sensual fantasies as it is about nourishment.

Nearly every neighborhood has its culinary stars, which makes for rewarding dining no matter where you wander. The challenge, however, is knowing where to begin. A few good entry points into Montréal's dining scene follow.

Downtown and Plateau Mont-Royal are a diner's nirvana, linked by arteries Blvd St-Laurent and Rue St-Denis. 'The Main,' as locals call Blvd St-Laurent, teems with trendy establishments but shades into the alternative as you move north. Still in the Plateau, Rue Prince-Arthur Est and Ave Duluth Est are popular for their good-time BYOB (bring your own bottle) places. Mile End and Outremont also have a great selection of bistros and ethnic fare, with new places popping up all the time. The key streets here are Ave Laurier, Ave St-Viateur and Rue Bernard. Little Italy has great Italian trattorias along Blvd St-Laurent and Rue Dante. Old Montréal, meanwhile, is the latest setting for the city's culinary showdown, with a number of award-winning restaurants hidden in the old streets, particularly west of Blvd St-Laurent.

Specialties

Montrealers enjoy an enormous variety of locally produced ingredients and delicacies: raw cheeses, foie gras, game and maple syrup, to name a few. The outdoor markets carry exotic foodstuffs that weren't available even a decade ago alongside the tasty produce from local farms. Marché Atwater and Marché Jean-Talon (see the boxed text, p109) are the city's two biggest markets, and are great places to assemble a picnic.

Residents argue heatedly over which places serve the best of anything – chewy bagels, espresso, comfort soup, fluffy omelet or creamy cakes. Montréal smoked meat and bagels, of course, have a formidable reputation that stretches across the country and is a constant source of friendly rivalry with New Yorkers. Montréal loyalists insist the secret to the hometown bagel's success is all in the time-tested preparation.

More Than Poutine

Traditional Québécois cuisine is classic comfort food, heavy and centered on meat dishes. The fact that the ingredients are basic is said to be a historical legacy, as French settlers only had access to limited produce. A classic Québécois meal might center on game meat (caribou, duck, wild boar) or the *tourtière,* a meat pie usually made with pork and another meat like beef or veal along with celery and onions. Another favorite lowbrow staple is *poutine* (fries smothered in cheese curds and gravy), with many inventive versions served across the city (see the boxed text, p120).

There's also a fine choice of French food in the city, with bistros and brasseries of all types and price ranges. Many of them incorporate the best of Québec's produce and market ingredients, and you'll find everything from no-nonsense French food to experimental takes on the classics.

PLAN YOUR TRIP EATING

NEED TO KNOW

Price Range

In our listings we've used the following price codes to represent the cost of a meal:

$	under $16
$$	$16 to $30
$$$	over $30

Opening Hours & Meal Times

Standard opening hours for restaurants are 11:30am to 2:30pm and 5:30pm to 11pm. Many places close on Monday. Breakfast cafes open around 8am (9am on Sundays). On weekends two dinner sittings are common at 5:30pm to 6pm and 8pm to 8:30pm. Places fill up from 8pm onwards.

Reservations

Reserve on weekends to avoid disappointment. During the week you needn't book a table unless the place is quite popular (or formal). Most budget eateries don't take reservations.

Paying

Credit cards and debit cards are widely accepted. Some restaurants accept cash only, which is noted in the reviews.

Tipping

A tip of 15% of the pretax bill is customary in restaurants. Note that your bill will show the total with tax in bold numbers. Some waiters may add a service charge for large parties; in these cases, no tip should be added unless the service was extraordinary.

Websites

➡ **Midnight Poutine** (www.midnight poutine.ca)

➡ **Montreal For Insiders** (http://montrealforinsiders.blogspot.ca)

➡ **Shut Up And Eat** (www.shutup andeat.ca)

For local recipes and tips on mastering the great dishes of the province, pick up the cookbook *The Art of Living According to Joe Beef,* by Frederic Morin et al.

How Much?

Depending on where you go (and sometimes what time you go), dining out in Montréal doesn't have to be a costly venture. On average, a multicourse dinner for two (including a glass of wine and taxes and tip) at a midrange place will set you back about $80 to $120. At the city's more famous establishments, expect to pay about twice that for a multicourse meal. At the other end of the scale, it's possible to eat some delicious fare at casual spots – vegetarian cafes, Jewish delis and downmarket ethnic eateries (like a number of places in Chinatown) – for under $40 for two.

Keep an eye out for the table d'hôte, a fixed-price meal – usually three or four courses – that can be a good way to sample the chef's top dishes of the day. Prices start at around $20. Some restaurants offer a discount menu for late dining (usually starting at 10pm), while others have a policy of *apportez votre vin*, or bring your own wine. There's rarely a corkage fee, so take advantage of this. Pick up your tipple from an outlet of the government's alcohol retailer, Société des Alcools du Québec (SAQ).

Taxes amounting to 15% apply at all restaurants. Most don't include the taxes in their menu prices, but check the fine print.

Groceries

In Plateau Mont-Royal, the section of Blvd St-Laurent between Ave des Pins and Ave Mont-Royal is renowned for its ethnic food shops. Little Italy has a multitude of small groceries and deli shops on Blvd St-Laurent, a few blocks south of Rue Jean-Talon.

There are several open-air food markets where farmers, butchers and cheese makers sell their produce directly. Most sites also have indoor sections that stay open all winter.

Eating by Neighbourhood

➡ **Old Montréal** (p61) The old-world setting, the rooftop patios, and some of the best eateries in town make this irresistible. Chinatown is next door.

➡ **Park Jean-Drapeau** (p76) Has very limited eating options. Plan to eat meals elsewhere or bring a picnic with you.

➡ **Downtown** (p85) With an emerging Chinatown around Concordia University, eating downtown is back on the foodie circuit.

➡ **Quartier Latin & The Village** (p101) Best for brasseries and bohemian cafes, as well as great budget eats.

➡ **Plateau Mont-Royal** (p115) Cosmopolitan and hip, with excellent dining options in all price ranges.

➡ **Little Italy, Mile End & Outremont** (p129) One of the best food destinations in the city, with everyting from bagels to market-based fine dining.

➡ **Southwest & Outer Montréal** (p150) The city's outer districts are off the beaten path for foodies, but have a few distant gems.

Lonely Planet's Top Choices

Toqué! (p61) Innovative cuisine, a fantastic tasting menu and superb foie gras.

Garde-Manger (p61) Tiny atmospheric restaurant gets noisy, but pork chops and lobster *poutine* make up for that.

Joe Beef (p85) Creative seafood, excellent wine list and knowledgeable staff.

Kazu (p85) Ramen noodles and Japanese comfort food in this budget hole in the wall.

Le Filet (p115) Creative seafood with hints of Japanese.

Au Pied de Cochon (p116) Decadent offerings such as foie gras *poutine*.

Lawrence (p131) Chic hangout with excellent braised kid on toast.

Best by Budget

$

Schwartz's (p116)

Le Gros Jambon (p62)

Kazu (p85)

Cuisine Szechuan (p85)

Dépanneur Le Pick Up (p131)

$$

L'Express (p116)

Le Petit Alep (p132)

Pintxo (p116)

Kitchenette (p101)

$$$

Toqué! (p61)

Joe Beef (p85)

Queue de Cheval (p85)

L'Orignal (p61)

Best for Breakfast

Beauty's (p116)

Toi, Moi & Cafe (p137)

La Croissanterie Figaro (p137)

Best for Bagels

St-Viateur Bagel (p131)

Fairmount Bagel (p136)

St-Viateur Bagel & Cafe (p119)

Bagels on Greene (p94)

Best for Atmosphere

Garde-Manger (p61)

Le Filet (p115)

Au Pied de Cochon (p116)

Boris Bistro (p62)

Best for C

Pikolo Espresso

Café Différance

Café Santé Ver

Toi, Moi & Caf

Best Old-Fashioned Eats

Schwartz's (p116)

Wilensky's Light Lunch (p133)

Lester's (p133)

Dunn's (p87)

Caffè Italia (p132)

Best for Fine Dining

Toqué! (p61)

Queue de Cheval (p85)

Beaver Club (p85)

Le Club Chasse Et Pêche (p62)

Le St-Sulpice bar (p104)

 Drinking & Nightlife

Montrealers love to drink. Maybe it's the European influence: this is a town where it's perfectly acceptable, even expected, to begin cocktail hour after work and continue well into the night. On a sunny Friday afternoon, the cinq-à-sept (traditional 5pm to 7pm happy hour) often becomes 5-à-last-call.

Nightlife

Montréal nightlife is the stuff of legend; it's a vibrant, exciting and ever-evolving scene on the cutting edge of international trends. That's why touring bands and DJs rave about Montréal audiences: crowds here aren't afraid to let loose and really get into the musical experience. At live shows, they hoot, holler and sing along, and even in cooler-than-thou clubs people get down and dirty on the dance floor.

Its worldwide party-town reputation may make Montréal a bachelor-party and frat-weekend destination, but beyond such mainstream titillation is the real deal.

From underground dance clubs to French hip-hop, dub reggae to breakbeat; comedy shows to supper clubs and the still-exciting Anglo indie rock so hyped in the recent past, Montréal after dark holds something for everyone. You just have to know where to look.

Bars

Montrealers treat their bars like a second home, unwinding after work for the legendary *cinq à sept* happy hour on Thursdays and Fridays, quaffing wine, beer and cocktails until the wee hours. Preferably on a rooftop patio as temperatures rise in late spring and summer. Come wintertime, Montrealers are undaunted by snowstorms and long, frigid nights. In fact, that's when there's not much else to do but find yourself a warm, cozy bar and drink and laugh the night away.

Cafes

As in Europe, espresso coffee is big here, and most locals start the day with strong, espresso-based drinks at their neighborhood cafes. It's not uncommon for artists, students and self-employed types to spend days hanging out at their favorite cafes, laptops in tow. Many cafes roast their own beans, and fair trade and specialty blends to brew at home are sold in shops around town.

Clubbing & After-hours

While established events and club nights have their followings, when it comes to one-off concerts and parties (including raves), an event's appeal has little to do with where it's happening and everything to do with who is putting it on. (And, of course, the talent on the bill!) Beloved party brands throw events regularly, while indie concert promoters book shows of all musical genres virtually every night. You can catch big names and local up-and-comers before they top the charts.

Blvd St-Laurent and Rue St-Denis are the two main club strips, with Rue Ste-Cathcrine in the Village housing a strip of gay clubs. Blvd St-Laurent, known as 'the Main', is traditionally more English and St-Denis more French, though the lines have blurred. Fancier clubs have selective door policies and cover charges, but anything goes at most underground spots. Things tend to start late (after midnight) and close at 3am, but Montréal's after-hours scene is very happening, with clubs and private warehouse and loft parties; they don't serve alcohol but are made for dancing and all-night club experiences. The scene on the sidewalk of Blvd St-Laurent at 3am is pretty interesting, as revelers pour onto the street, in search of 99-cent pizza (the late-night snack of choice) and after-parties.

NEED TO KNOW

Practicalities

➡ The legal drinking age in the province of Québec is 18.

➡ To buy alcohol to drink at home, Societé des Alcools du Québec (SAQ) are government-run liquor stores all over town. Their opening hours vary, but *dépanneurs* (corner stores) sell a selection of wine and beer until 11pm. Some supermarkets also sell alcohol.

Opening Hours

Bars usually open around 4pm or 5pm and must close by 3am, so last call is usually about 15 minutes prior. Clubs can open anywhere from 7pm to 11pm or later (some open only Thurday to Saturday), with some continuing into the late morning the following day. Pubs, bistros, cafes and other establishments have opening hours that vary widely, check reviews or websites.

Tipping

Generally, you're expected to tip your server or bartender the greater of 15% of your bill, or between $1 and $2 for each drink you order.

Costs

You can often find midweek specials; some will waive cover before 11pm. Admission can be as low as $5 or free, but expect to pay $10 to $15 in larger clubs.

Tickets & Guest Lists

Lining up in freezing temperatures can be a real drag, so check club websites for the chance to get on their guest list, to reserve tables, or get advance tickets to events.

Dress Code

Nearly all clubs and bars in the city have a relaxed dress code.

Websites

➡ **Nightlife.ca** (www.nightlife.ca)

➡ **Montreal Nightlife** (http://montreal nightlife.ca)

➡ **Crescent Montreal** (www.crescent montreal.com)

Drinking & Nightlife by Neighbourhood

➡ **Old Montréal** (p65) The old city's nightspots attract a 30s and 40s crowd who have more money to spend. Its chichi boutique hotels and the new media industry boom centered around the Old Port have resulted in posh new lounges, wine bars and upscale restos where international celebrities canoodle with local scenesters and the fashion crowd.

➡ **Downtown** (p90) Downtown's many bars, clubs and cafes tend to cater to tourists and students. In particular, the busy strip of Rue Crescent between Rue Ste-Catherine and Blvd de Maisonneuve is très touristy, especially weekend nights. However, hidden among these more mainstream establishments are some vibrant taverns and quirky little pubs that are part of the city's cultural energy. A satellite downtown scene centers on the bars and restaurants, such as Burgundy Lion, on Notre-Dame Ouest at Rue Charlevoix.

➡ **Quartier Latin & the Village** (p104) Frenetic Rue St-Paul below Rue Sherbrooke Est packs in the students with pubs and patio beer pitchers. To the northeast alone Rue Ste-Catherine Est, the Village's buzzing bars can get the night started before hitting local gay clubs. You'll find a mix of gay and straight, French and English, and many other backgrounds in this giant melting pot.

➡ **Plateau Mont-Royal** (p119) This sprawling area mixes Downtown's edge with Mile End's relaxed residential vibe. The blocks along Blvd St-Laurent above Rue Sherbrooke are, along with Rue Crescent, a major anglophone bar scene, with myriad drunk 20-somethings (and police to keep order). Watering holes get more sophisticated and interesting along Ave Roy and Ave Mont-Royal.

➡ **Little Italy, Mile End & Outremont** (p136) From hipster cafes to whiskey lounges, this trio of residential neighborhoods has some of the city's most interesting drink options. They're widely spaced but several cluster around Ave Laurier, and make for an excellent nightcap after a bite at the superb local restos.

Lonely Planet's Top Choices

Philémon (p65) Rip it up with great club beats and a huge bar in a heritage space.

Terrasse Nelligan (p65) One of the best rooftop terraces in the city.

La Buvette Chez Simone (p136) Low-lit Mile End wine bar with tapas and laid-back vibe.

Garde-Manger (p65) After dinner, this infectiously atmospheric restaurant kicks up the volume.

Baldwin Barmacie (p136) Mile End hipsters mix it up in this pharmacy-themed lounge.

Velvet (p65) Hopping, candlelit fashionista club nestled in the bowels of an 18th-century inn.

Best Pubs

McKibbin's (p90)

Burgundy Lion (p90)

Dominion Square Tavern (p90)

Taverne Gaspar (p66)

Hurley's Irish Pub (p90)

Le Saint-Bock (p104)

Sir Winston Churchill (p91)

Best Terraces

Terrasse Nelligan (p65)

Terrasse Place d'Armes (p66)

Le Magellan Bar (p105)

Le St-Sulpice (p104)

Best Clubs

Philémon (p65)

Velvet (p65)

UN (p67)

Tokyo Bar (p124)

Electric Avenue (p91)

Best Bars

Philémon (p65)

L'Assomoir (p67)

Garde-Manger (p61)

La Buvette Chez Simone (p136)

Whiskey Café (p136)

L'Île Noire (p104)

Best Cafes

Pikolo Espresso Bar (p90)

Café Différence (p66)

Café Santé Veritas (p66)

Cluny Artbar (p63)

Olive + Gourmando (p64)

1000 Grammes (p104)

Best Gay Bars & Clubs

Apollon (p105)

Sky Pub & Club (p105)

Circus (p105)

Unity (p105)

1000 Grammes (p104)

Best Lounges

Baldwin Barmacie (p136)

Whiskey Café (p136)

Wunderbar (p67)

Gogo Lounge (p121)

Best Brewpubs

Dieu du Ciel (p136)

Les Soeurs Grises (p66)

Brutopia (p90)

Best for Sport

Café Olimpico (p137)

Chez Serge (p136)

McKibbin's (p90)

Le St-Sulpice (p104)

Hurley's Irish Pub (p90)

PLAN YOUR TRIP DRINKING & NIGHTLIFE

Musicians perform at the Festival International de Jazz de Montréal (p238)

☆ Entertainment

Montréal is definitely Canada's unofficial arts capital, with both French-and English-language theater, dance, classical and jazz music and all sorts of interesting blends of the above on stage virtually every night of the week. The city's bilingualism makes it creatively unique and encourages opportunity for creative collaborations and cross-pollinations that light up the performing arts scene.

Live Rock, Pop, Jazz & Blues

It's no secret that Montréal is a music power-house, fostering an incredible variety of talent from cabaret pop stars like Patrick Watson to Leonard Cohen and jazz legends such as Oscar Peterson. The underground and indie music community has many venues to catch rising stars, such as Casa del Popolo (p124), while major acts from elsewhere in Canada and overseas perform at the Bell Centre or occasionally at special venues like the Stade Olympique and the Hippodrome,

a former race track where U2 wowed fans in 2011.

There are dozens of concerts happening every week at bars, clubs, live houses and summer festivals like Osheaga. Check local listings for details and try to buy tickets in advance.

Performance Power

While the city may be small compared to other artistic capitals (like New York and London), Montréal boasts some world-class companies that are renowned on the international circuit: a symphony orchestra, the Orchestre Symphonique de Montréal (p92); an opera, Opéra de Montréal (p93); and a ballet company, Les Grands Ballets Canadiens (p124). And don't forget Cirque du Soleil (see the boxed text, p241), the magical, Québec-born circus of dance, music and acrobatics that forever changed the art form.

Film Hub

The presence of Québec's large French-language film and TV industry, and US productions that shoot here, have made the picturesque city a hotbed of film and TV production. Especially during spring and summer, you're likely to see movie shoots taking place on downtown streets and Hollywood stars nonchalantly roaming around. They may show up in unexpected places. The present author, for instance, was surprised when actor Neil Patrick Harris walked unaccompanied into an obscure new Asian restaurant in the suburb of Westmount. He was in town shooting the sequel to *The Smurfs*.

Cinemas

Montréal has its share of multiplex cinemas, but many also include foreign or independent films in their repertoire. More interesting are the several independent movie houses and repertory theaters. The website www.cinemamontreal.com is excellent, with reviews and details of discount admissions. The repertory houses offer double bills and midnight movies on weekends. These cinemas are sometimes cheaper than the chains showing first-run films.

Film Festivals

Montréal has so many film festivals that it's hard to keep track. In addition to the Montréal World Film Festival (p23) and Festival du Nouveau Cinéma de Montréal (p23) check out the following festivals.

Festival International du Film sur l'Art
(www.artfifa.com) A March festival devoted to films and documentaries about art from all over the world.

Vues d'Afrique (www.vuesdafrique.org) Held
in late April and early May, this growing festival celebrates film about Africa.

Les Rendez-Vous du Cinéma Québecois
(www.rvcq.com) Also in April and early May, this event showcases the best of Québécois film.

NEED TO KNOW
••
Tickets
➡ Book tickets well in advance for live performances. Prices vary widely depending on the performer. To purchase tickets for concerts, shows and festivals, go to the venue box office or call **Admission** (☎514-790-1245; www.admission.com) or **Ticketmaster** (☎514-790-1111; www.ticketmaster.ca) or **Evenko** (www.evenko.ca).

➡ Beware of buying from touts outside event venues on the night of a performance. Try to check with other attendees whether you're buying a genuine ticket and not a forgery.

➡ General admission to mainstream movie theaters like Cineplex is $10 to $13. Some arthouse theaters like Excentris have discount Mondays, as well as lower prices for tickets other days of the week before 6pm.

➡ The *Montreal Gazette* and French-language *La Presse* daily newspapers are great resources for arts and culture listings, as is the city's free weekly, *Voir* (in French).

Websites
➡ **Nightlife.ca** (www.nightlife.ca)
➡ **Festival International de Jazz de Montréal** (www.montrealjazzfest.com)
➡ **Cirque du Soleil** (www.cirquedusoleil.com)
➡ **La Scena** (www.scena.org)
➡ **Tourisme Montréal** (www.tourisme-montreal.org/What-To-Do/Events)
➡ **33mag** (www.33mag.com)

Fantasia (www.festivalfantasia.com) This leading genre festival in July and August features works from Asia and appeals to the manga-loving *otaku* (geek) set.

Montreal Stop-motion Film Festival
(www.stopmotionmontreal.com) In October, fans of stop-motion animation gather to see painstakingly crafted works in this genre.

Cinemania (www.cinemaniafilmfestival.com) This November festival features films from French-speaking countries, all subtitled in English for non-native speakers.

Dance

Considered Canada's dance capital, Montréal has always boasted an avant-garde and extremely vibrant dance scene. These days styles like ballet, modern, jazz, hip-hop, Latin social dancing and tango exist side by side with cutting-edge contemporary dance that fuses various styles and incorporates theater, music and digital art. As such, Montréal is home to many internationally renowned companies, such as **Les Grands Ballets Canadiens de Montréal** (www.grandsballets.com), **La La La Human Steps** (www.lalalahumansteps.com), **O Vertigo Danse** (www.overtigo.com), **Tangente** (www.tangente.qc.ca), **Les Ballets Jazz De Montréal** (www.bjmdanse.ca) and the popular theatrical touring dance company **Cirque Eloize** (www.cirque-eloize.com). The fact that Canada's **National Circus School** (www.nationalcircusschool.ca) is based here certainly helps feed fresh, unconventional talent into the dance and performing-arts scene.

Comedy

With so many potholes in its roads, long winters and its multiethnic brew, humor comes naturally to Montréal. It's no wonder that in July, the city plays host to the largest comedy festival in the world – the home-grown **Just For Laughs** (www.hahaha.com). The laugh-fest has being going strong for 30 years, attracting top comics such as Lewis Black, Jerry Seinfeld, Dave Chappelle, John Cleese and Jon Stewart, and even exporting itself to Toronto, Chicago and Sydney. See also p23.

When Just For Laughs isn't on, you can still get knee-slapping laughs at dedicated venues in the city. Comedyworks (p93) hosts regular improv nights and up-and-coming local talent, while **Comedy Nest** (www.comedynest.com) specializes in stand-up and open-mic nights. Improv specialty venue **Montreal Improv** (www.montrealimprov.com) has free classes for those who want to be funnier.

Coffeehouses & Spoken Word

The spoken-word scene is quite popular in Montréal, often linked to the hip-hop community. Some of the most exciting and interesting stuff is being done on university campuses. Since these events tend to move around from bar to bar, it's best to check out the bulletin boards or flyers at McGill or Concordia Universities where new and underground performances are regularly announced. Bars such as Barfly (p120) also hold spoken-word events, and hip-hop crews and improvisational music collectives like **Kalmunity** (www.kalmunity.com) organize special spoken-word and improv events.

Lonely Planet's Top Choices

Place des Arts (p81) Performing arts complex, home to everything from jazz to ballet and opera.

L'Astral (p91) A new venue for the jazz festival and other events.

Casa del Popolo (p124) One of the best indie music venues in the city.

Usine C (p108) Former industrial space hosting innovative avant-garde theater and dance.

Théâtre St-Denis (p108) Century-old venue hosting everything from comedy to rock and theater.

Best Classical Music Ensembles

Orchestre Symphonique de Montréal (p92)

Orchestre Métropolitain (p93)

McGill Chamber Orchestra (p93)

Opéra de Montréal (p93)

I Musici de Montréal (p93)

Best Venues for Classical Music

Salle Wilfred-Pelletier (p81)

Maison Syphonique de Montréal (p81)

Pollack Concert Hall (p93)

Basilique Notre-Dame (p52)

Best for Jazz

Place des Arts (p81)

L'Astral (p91)

Upstairs (p90)

House of Jazz (p92)

St James United Church (p84)

Club Soda (p92)

Best Cinemas

Cinéma Excentris (p92)

Le Nouveau Cinéma Du Parc (p92)

Cinéma Banque Scotia Montréal (p92)

Cinéma Quartier Latin (p108)

Cinéma Imax du Centre des Sciences de Montréal (p70)

Théâtre Outremont (p137)

Best Live Rock & Pop Venues

Bell Centre (p97)

Metropolis (p92)

Club Soda (p92)

Le Divan Orange (p124)

Foufounes Électriques (p93)

Best Theater

Centaur Theater (p70)

Théâtre St-Denis (p108)

Théâtre du Nouveau Monde (p92)

Usine C (p108)

Cabaret Mado (p108)

Théâtre Ste Catherine (p108)

Théâtre Outremont (p137)

Best Street Music

Festival International de Jazz de Montréal (p238)

Parc du Mont-Royal (p115)

PLAN YOUR TRIP ENTERTAINMENT

◉ Festivals

Described by some as the city of festivals, Montréal has a packed calendar of lively events when entire blocks get closed to traffic, and stages appear across town for free concerts, improv and cinema. Public holidays are also usually marked with massive downtown parades and raucous concerts. Winter events tend to have fewer out-of-town visitors but Montrealers themselves come out in droves.

For Music Lovers

You can't go wrong with the fantastic Festival International de Jazz de Montreal (p238). As the city's signature summer party, it has a range of genres, stars and venues to suit all tastes. Just be sure to book tickets early, and show up early for free outdoor concerts, which get packed out quickly.

For Fashionistas

One event that fashion fiends won't want to miss is the biannual **Montréal Fashion Week** (www.montrealfashionweek.ca), held in February and Septempber. It used to be a purely Canadian affair, but nowadays is filled with as many buyers from around the world as local fashion writers, and the **Montréal Fashion and Design Festival** (www.festivalmodedesign.com), a free fashion show held in August (open to the public) where you can see Québécois, Canadian and international designers show off their collections outdoors, usually on stages set up on Ave McGill College.

For Foodies

Montréal itself is a moveable feast due to the quality of its cuisine, but if you want true celebrations, check out The **Montreal Festival en Lumière** (www.montrealenlumiere.com), held in February and March, has fine-dining events and guest chefs hosting special events at local restaurants. To get really local, try Blvd St-Laurent's **food fairs** (http://boulevard saintlaurent.com), from June to August, when restaurants expand their patios and street food becomes legal. Finally, get sudsy with samples of beer from around the world at the **Mondiale de la Bière** (http://festivalmondial biere.qc.ca) in June.

Lonely Planet's Top Choices

Festival International de Jazz de Montréal (p238) The city's main music event keeps getting better. Has some free events.

Just For Laughs (p23) Top comics from around the world at the largest event of its kind.

Montréal World Film Festival (p23) Screens works from all over the world.

Osheaga Festival Musique et Arts (p23) Rock out in the great outdoors of Parc Jean-Drapeau.

Best Music Festivals

Festival International de Jazz de Montréal (www.montreal jazzfest.com; ☺Jul)

Osheaga Festival Musique et Arts (www.osheaga.com; ☺Aug)

FrancoFolies (www.francofolies .com; ☺Jun)

Festival de Lanaudière (http:// lanaudiere.org; ☺Jul-Aug)

Pop Montreal (http://pop montreal.com; ☺Sep)

Montreal Chamber Music Festival (www.festivalmontreal .org; ☺May-Jun)

Best Film Festivals

Montréal World Film Festival (www.ffm-montreal.org; ☺Aug-Sep)

Rendez-vous du Cinéma Québé- cois (www.rvcq.com; ☺Feb)

Fantasia Film Fest (www.festival fantasia.com; ☺Jul-Aug)

Vues d'Afrique (www.vues dafrique.org; ☺Apr-May)

Montreal International Black Film Festival (www.montreal blackfilm.com; ☺Sep)

Best Festivals with Free Events

Festival International de Jazz de Montréal (www.montrealjazz fest.com; ☺Jul)

L'International des Feux Loto- Québec (www.internation aldesfeuxloto-quebec.com; ☺Jun-Jul)

Divers/Cité (www.diverscite.org; ☺July)

Festival International Montréal en Arts (www.festivaldesarts .org; ☺Jun/Jul)

Best Unknown Festivals

Mutek International Festival of Digital Creativity and Electronic Music (www.mutek.org; ☺May-Jun)

Art Tattoo Montreal (www.art tattoomontreal.com; ☺Sep)

Montreal Anarchist Book Fair (www.anarchistbookfair.ca; ☺May)

Otakuthon (www.otakuthon. com; ☺Aug)

The Magic of Lanterns (www2.ville.montreal.qc .ca/jardin/jardin.htm; ☺Sep-Nov)

Best Community Festivals

St. Patrick's Day Parade (www.montrealirishparade.com; ☺Mar)

Italian Week (www.italianweek .ca; ☺Aug)

Montreal Highland Games & Festival (www.montreal highlandgames.qc.ca; ☺Aug)

Matsuri Japon (http://festival japon.com; ☺Aug)

NEED TO KNOW

Access

Many of the city's festivals have cheap or free shows that can be accessed on the day of the event, but crowds can be a killer if you don't show up early. The famous free outdoor concerts at the Festival International de Jazz de Montréal attract so many fans that you might find it hard to get within a block of the stage. Plan early and get there early to secure good spots.

Websites

➡ **Tourisme Montréal** (www.tourisme -montreal.org)

➡ **Festival Interna- tional de Jazz de Montréal** (www .montrealjazzfest.com)

➡ **Fesitvals in Montreal** (www.mon treal.com/tourism/ festivals/index.html)

➡ **Ville de Montréal** (ville.montreal.qc.ca)

Best Performance Festivals

Festival TransAmériques (www.fta.qc.ca; ☺May-Jun)

Montréal Completement Cirque (http://montrealcompletement cirque.com; ☺Jul)

Le Festival St-Ambroise Fringe de Montréal (www.montreal fringe.ca; ☺Jun)

Montreal Burlesque Festival (www.montrealburlesque festival.ca; ☺Sep)

Shakespeare in the Park (www.repercussiontheatre.com; ☺Jul-Aug)

Shopping

Style is synonymous with Montréal living. The city itself is beautiful and locals live up to the standard it sets. Maybe it's that much-touted European influence, but most Montrealers seem to instinctively lead stylish lives regardless of income level, enjoying aesthetic pleasures like food, art and, of course, fashion.

Fashion City

Montréal is Canada's unofficial fashion capital and many of the country's most talented and internationally successful designers have roots here. Gorgeous locally based lines to look for include Denis Gagnon, Nadya Toto, Christian Chenail and up-and-comer Travis Taddeo. For more information, check out Québec fashion magazines like *Clin d'Oeil*, *Lou Lou* and *Elle Québec*. Better still, visit during **Montreal Fashion Week** (www.montrealfashionweek.ca), which takes place every February and September to showcase new collections.

Something for Everyone

Even beyond fashion, Montréal is an ideal shopping city, full of goods you'll want to take home. You'll find the cream of the crop in this shopping paradise – from big international department stores to high-fashion designers, vintage clothing boutiques to weird one-of-a-kind antique shops, used music- and booksellers, chic home decor and more. As well, many international megastore chains have set up shop here, but with a local or European flair.

Shopping Tours

For a professionally guided shopping tour of local fashions, try **Montreal Shopping Tours** (www.montrealshoppingtours.com). *Flare* magazine contributor Janna Zittrer's regular tours feature luminaries such as accessories maker Charlotte Hosten and elegant draped attire by renowned designer Marie Saint Pierre.

Shopping by Neighborhood

➡ **Old Montréal** Upscale Rue St-Paul in is home to galleries, designer furnishings and clothing shops, while nearby Rue Amherst is full of retro-chic antiques and knickknacks.

➡ **Downtown** Busy Rue Ste-Catherine has all the big names, department stores, and some specialty shops and local fashion boutiques. For antiques, head southwest to Rue Notre-Dame Ouest, between Rue Atwater and Rue Guy.

➡ **Plateau Mont-Royal** Full of hip clothing and home-decor boutiques, many located on Blvd St-Laurent and Rue St-Denis.

➡ **Little Italy, Mile End & Outremont** Terrific for grocery shopping and cooking items. Prices and style quotient soar on Rue Laurier and Ave Bernard, as well as in elegant Westmount Square.

PLAN YOUR TRIP SHOPPING

Lonely Planet's Top Choices

Ogilvy (p95) Noontime bagpipe performances celebrate this grand department store's Scottish roots.

Monastiraki (p137) Vintage comic books to eclectic antiques: this hipster retro shrine fascinates.

Les Touilleurs (p138) The best kitchenware and cookbooks, plus workshops by local chefs.

Galeries d'Art Contemporain du Belgo (p94) Art of every description huddles in this building.

Holt Renfrew (p93) Holt's department store stands out for its fashion collections and basement cafe.

Best Markets

Marché Jean-Talon (p109)

Marché Atwater (p82)

Marché St-Jacques (p109)

Marché de Maisonneuve (p109)

Best Art

Galerie Simon Blais (p138)

Galeries d'Art Contemporain du Belgo (p94)

DHC Art (p70)

Parisian Laundry (p95)

Galerie Le Chariot (p70)

Best Retro

Monastiraki (p137)

Zéphyr (p109)

Boutique Spoutnik (p109)

Les Antiquités Grand Central (p95)

Style Labo (p138)

Best Department Stores & Malls

Ogilvy (p95)

Holt Renfrew (p93)

Hudson Bay Co (p94)

Les Cours Mont-Royal (p94)

Marché Bonsecours (p70)

NEED TO KNOW

Opening hours

Most stores are open from 9:30am or 10am to 6pm Monday to Wednesday; clothing boutiques usually open their doors at 11am. Thursday and Friday are late opening days, usually until 9pm; Saturday hours are 10am to 5pm. Opening hours on Sunday afternoon (noon to 5pm) are standard along Rue Ste-Catherine and Blvd St-Laurent as well as in the malls.

Taxes

In Québec, there is a provincial sales tax of 9.5% (aka Taxe de vente du Québec, TVQ) as well as a federal goods and services tax of 5% (GST, or TPS in French). Canada had a GST refund scheme for visitors, but it was abolished in 2007.

Prices

While Montréal can't compare to the US in terms of bargain prices or the glamour of the many high-end brand stores in New York, visitors to the city appreciate the variety of shops and products.

Websites

➡ **Tourisme Montréal** (www.tourisme -montreal.org/What -To-Do/Shopping)

➡ **Montreal Fashion Blog** (http://themon trealfashionblog.com)

➡ **Smart Shopping Montreal** (www.smart shoppingmontreal.com)

Explore Montréal & Québec City

MONTRÉAL &
QUÉBEC CITY'S
TOP SIGHTS

Neighborhoods at a Glance

❶ Old Montréal (p50)

On the edge of the St Lawrence River, Old Montréal is the city's birthplace, composed of picturesque squares, grand old-world architecture and a dense concentration of camera-toting tourists. The narrow Rue St-Paul, the old main street, teems with art galleries, shops and eateries, while the broad concourse of the Old Port is lined with green parkland and cafes along Rue de la Com-mune. The nearby Chinatown is small but packed with cheap, yummy eats.

❷ Parc Jean-Drapeau (p73)

Worlds away from the city bustle, this park stretches across two leafy islands in the midst of the mighty St Lawrence, about 1km east of the Old Port. The prime draws are outdoor activities such as cycling and jogging, though you'll also find some noteworthy museums,

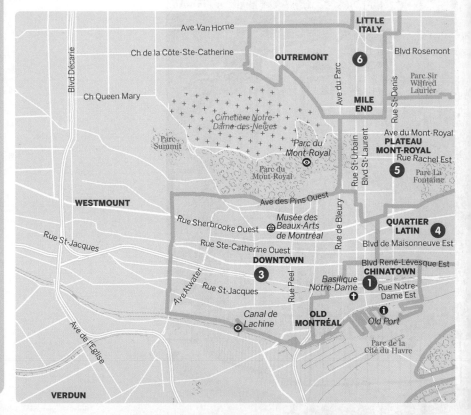

architectural remnants of the landmark Expo '67, plus lake swimming and weekly dance parties in the summer.

❸ Downtown (p78)

At the feet of its modern skyscrapers and condo developments lie heritage buildings and old-time mansions, top-notch museums and numerous green spaces. The two most common species here are businesspeople, and students from McGill and Concordia Universities. The city's major shopping district is downtown, as is the performing-arts complex, Place des Arts. This is the epicenter of the city's jazz festival in summer.

❹ Quartier Latin & the Village (p98)

The Quartier Latin is a gateway to theaters, lively cafes and low-key bars packed with students from the French-speaking Université du Québec à Montréal. Continue west to reach the Village, a major icon for gay travelers. Shops, restaurants and bars proudly fly the rainbow colors here, and the nightlife and cafe scene rarely slows down.

❺ Plateau Mont-Royal (p110)

This former immigrant neighborhood now houses a wealth of sidewalk cafes, excellent restaurants, clubs and boutiques. For many Montrealers and visitors alike, exploring the Plateau is what Montréal is all about. The Plateau is handily located next to Montréal's beloved 'mountain', Mont-Royal, home to walking and biking trails, a pretty lake and great views over the city.

❻ Little Italy, Mile End & Outremont (p127)

Just up from the Plateau are Mile End and Outremont, two leafy neighborhoods with upscale boutiques and restaurants; nearby, Little Italy is a slice out of the old world, with classic Italian trattorias and espresso bars, plus neighborhood churches and the sprawling Marché Jean-Talon, the city's best market.

❼ Southwest & Outer Montréal (p140)

This grab bag of districts takes in the Canal de Lachine, one of the best biking paths in the city, as well as working-class districts like Petite-Bourgogne and St-Henri. The highlight, however, is the majestic Oratoire St-Joseph, the iconic hillside church. The eastern part of the city also has some popular attractions, including Olympic Park, which is home to botanical gardens, a kid-friendly ecosystems museum and an eye-popping stadium.

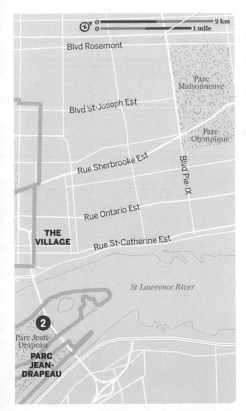

Old Montréal

OLD MONTRÉAL | OLD PORT | CHINATOWN

Neighborhood Top Five

1 Soaking up the beautiful craftsmanship and soaring architecture of the **Basilique Notre-Dame** (p52), the city's spiritual jewel.

2 Taking in a circus performance, river cruise, or a waterfront stroll at the storied **Old Port** (p60).

3 Taking your bearings amid the heritage architecture of **Place d'Armes** (p53) and its monument to Montréal's founder.

4 Learning about the city's history in the **Château Ramezay** (p53), a timeless 18th-century residence.

5 Visiting the sailors' chapel in the charming **Chapelle Notre Dame de Bonsecours** (p54), immortalized by Leonard Cohen.

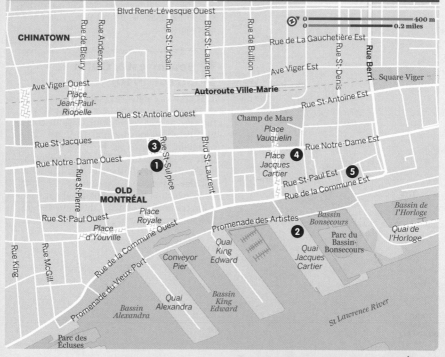

For more detail of this area, see Map p280 ➡

Explore Old Montréal

Begin your tour of Vieux-Montréal (Old Montréal) in its heart, historic Place d'Armes. Admire the recently renovated square, with its statue of city founder Paul Chomedy de Maisonneuve, and then head inside the iconic Basilique Notre-Dame. Take your time viewing its finely crafted interior before crossing the square and visiting the Bank of Montreal's 1847 headquarters, with its neoclassical facade and vaulted marble interior.

Next head down Rue St-Sulpice past the basilica to Rue St-Paul Ouest and turn left. It's lined with art galleries, plush boutiques and eateries, but these give way to tacky souvenir shops before you reach Place Jacques-Cartier, a grand square dedicated to the French explorer that's full of artists and buskers. At one end is the photogenic Hôtel de Ville (City Hall) while one block to the north, along Rue St-Paul Est, is the equally pretty Marché Bonsecours with its silver dome. Just past it is the beautiful Chapelle Notre Dame de Bonsecours, a humble sailors' church that's the perfect counterpoint to the basilica.

One block east is Rue de la Commune Est, a breezy waterfront street that gives you access to the Old Port and its museums, Cirque du Soleil big top and river cruises. Then proceed northwest up Blvd St-Laurent for 15 minutes to reach Montréal's small Chinatown. It's an excellent place to grab a cheap but satisfying plate of dumplings.

Local Life

➡ **Happy hour** In summer Montrealers love to enjoy *cinq à sept* (happy hour) on rooftop patios in Old Montréal.

➡ **Fine dining** Locals flock here both for its high-end eateries in Old Montréal and cheapie dumplings and noodles in Chinatown (p64).

➡ **Biking** Rent a Bixi bike and ride from the Old Port to the Canal de Lachine bike path.

Getting There & Away

➡ **Metro** To reach Old Montréal or Chinatown, take the metro to Square-Victoria, Place-d'Armes or Champ-de-Mars.

➡ **Bus** Bus 14 runs along Rue Notre-Dame in Old Montréal between Rue Berri and Blvd St-Laurent; bus 55 stops on Blvd St-Laurent.

➡ **On foot** While it is expansive, the area can be easily explored on foot, and accessed from downtown via streets such as Rue de Bleury.

➡ **Biking** The Old Port is an entry point to a bike path that leads to the Canal de Lachine, which connects to the fringes of downtown at Rue Charlevoix.

Lonely Planet's Top Tip

As with many streets in the city, east and west (*est* and *ouest* in French) labels on street signs don't reflect true compass orientations. Remember that 'east–west' streets like Rue Notre-Dame actually run closer to north–south, and this can be confusing if you like orienteering with maps.

Best Places to Eat

➡ Garde-Manger (p61)
➡ L'Orignal (p61)
➡ Toqué! (p61)
➡ Le Gros Jambon (p62)

For reviews, see p61 ➡

Best Places to Drink

➡ Philémon (p65)
➡ Terrasse Nelligan (p65)
➡ Les Soeurs Grises (p66)
➡ Terrasse Place d'Armes (p66)

For reviews, see p65 ➡

Best Activities

➡ Ça Roule Montréal (p71)
➡ Bota Bota (p71)
➡ Saute-Moutons (p71)

For reviews, see p71 ➡

JEAN-PIERRE LESCOURRET / GETTY IMAGES ©

TOP SIGHTS
BASILIQUE NOTRE-DAME

The grand dame of Montréal's ecclesiastical treasures, this basilica is a must-see when exploring the city. The looming Gothic Revival church can hold up to 3200 worshippers and houses a collection of finely crafted artworks, including an elaborately carved altarpiece, vibrant stained-glass windows and an intricate pulpit.

The Sulpicians commissioned James O'Donnell, a New York architect and Irish Protestant, to design what would be the largest church north of Mexico. He converted to Catholicism so he could have his funeral in the basilica, and is buried in the basement.

Opened in 1829, the basilica has a spectacular interior with a forest of ornate wood pillars and carvings made entirely by hand (and constructed without the aid of a single nail). Gilt stars shine from the ceiling vaults and the altar is backlit in evening-sky blues. The massive **Casavant organ** with 7000 pipes provides the powerful anthem at the famous Christmas concerts; the church bell, the Gros Bourdon, is the largest on the continent.

The **Chapelle du Sacré Coeur** (Sacred Heart Chapel), located behind the main hall, is nicknamed the Wedding Chapel. The curious mix of styles emerged after a 1978 fire, when the chapel was rebuilt with a brass altar with abstract-modern motifs.

An evening **sound and light display** (adult/child $10/5; ⊘6:30pm Tue-Thu, 6:30pm & 8:30pm Fri, 7pm & 8:30pm Sat) uses cutting-edge technology to tell the story of the church and the city.

DON'T MISS
➡ Casavant organ
➡ Chapelle du Sacré Coeur
➡ Sound and light display

PRACTICALITIES
➡ Map p280
➡ ☎514-842-2925
➡ www.basiliquenddm.org
➡ 110 Rue Notre-Dame Ouest
➡ adult/7-17yr/child $5/4/free
➡ ⊘8am-4:30pm Mon-Fri, 8am-4pm Sat, 12:30-4pm Sun; sometimes closed for weddings
➡ Ⓜ Place-d'Armes

 SIGHTS

◉ Old Montréal

BASILIQUE NOTRE-DAME   CHURCH
See p52.

PLACE D'ARMES   SQUARE
Map p280 (ⓂPlace-d'Armes) This recently renovated square is framed by some of the finest buildings in Old Montréal, including its oldest bank, first skyscraper and Basilique Notre-Dame. The square's name references the bloody battles that took place here as religious settlers and First Nations tribes clashed over control of what would become Montréal. At its center stands the **Monument Maisonneuve**, dedicated to city founder Paul de Chomedey, *sieur* de Maisonneuve.

The red sandstone building on the north side of the square is the **New York Life Insurance Building** (Map p280), Montréal's first skyscraper (1888). It's said to be built with the blocks used for ballast on ships bringing goods to Montréal. Next door, the **Aldred Building** (Map p280) is made of limestone and was designed to emulate the Empire State Building. Completed in 1931, it has an opulent, L-shaped, art-deco lobby. On the west side of the square, the Bank of Montréal was Canada's first permanent bank.

Near the south side of the square, you'll find horse-drawn carriages (p71) waiting to take you for a ride.

BANK OF MONTRÉAL   HISTORIC BUILDING
Map p280 (119 Rue St-Jacques; ☺9am-5pm Mon-Fri; ⓂPlace-d'Armes) Modeled after the Pantheon in Rome, the grand colonnaded edifice of Canada's oldest chartered bank, built in 1847, dominates the north side of Place d'Armes and is still a working bank. The imposing interior has 32 marble columns and a coffered 20m ceiling in Italian Renaissance style over a long row of tellers behind glass partitions. The helmeted marble lady is Patria, representing a minor Roman god of patriotism to honor the war dead.

A snoozy **money museum** (admission free; ☺9am-4pm Mon-Fri) inside the bank has a replica of a cashier's window, old banknotes and an account of early banking in Canada.

VIEUX SÉMINAIRE DE ST-SULPICE   HISTORIC BUILDING
Map p280 (116 Rue Notre-Dame Ouest; ⓂPlace-d'Armes) The seminary by the Basilique Notre-Dame and its grounds are closed to the public, but you can look at them through the gate. The Catholic order of Sulpicians was given title to the entire Island of Montréal in 1663. The order built the seminary in 1684 and the 3rd-floor apartments of the old seminary have been occupied ever since. The clock on the facade was a gift from French king Louis XIV in 1701; it is believed to be the oldest working clock in North America. Ancient oaks shade the rear garden laid out in 1715.

RUE ST-JACQUES   STREET
Map p280 (ⓂPlace-d'Armes) Known as the Wall St of Canada into the 1930s, Rue St-Jacques was lined with the head offices of insurance companies and banks that proclaimed Montréal's prosperity for the best part of a century. In those days it was known as St James Street.

Some great edifices are veritable temples to capitalism. The 1902 **Guardian Trust Building** (Map p280; 240 Rue St-Jacques) has helmeted women guarding the entrance while lions and mermaids watch over on the 2nd floor. The Molson beer-brewing dynasty had its own bank, but the **Molson Bank Building** (Map p280; 278-288 Rue St-Jacques) looks more like a royal residence; heads of founder William and his two sons grace the doorway.

The most glamorous of the lot is the **Royal Bank Building** (Map p280; 360 Rue St-Jacques), the city's tallest building (22 stories) when it was built in 1928. Pass under the royal coat of arms into a banking hall that resembles a Florentine palace; the coffered ceilings are of Wedgwood and the walls display insignias of eight provinces, Montréal (St George's Cross) and Halifax (a yellow bird).

CHÂTEAU RAMEZAY   MUSEUM
Map p280 (www.chateauramezay.qc.ca; 280 Rue Notre-Dame Est; adult/child $10/5; ☺10am-6pm Jun-Oct, to 4:30pm Tue-Sun rest of year; ⓂChamp-de-Mars) A home of French governors in the early 18th century, this mansion is one of the finest examples from the ancien régime. It was built for the 11th governor, Claude de Ramezay, and includes 15 interconnecting rooms with a ballroom of mirrors, as well as mahogany galore.

Ramezay went broke trying to maintain it. American generals used it as a headquarters during the revolution, and Benjamin Franklin held conferences here when attempting (and failing) to convince the Canadians to join the cause. In 1903 turrets were added to give the 'château' its fanciful French look.

The building is a repository of Québec history with a collection of 20,000 objects, including valuable Canadian art and furniture. The **Governor's Garden** (open June to October) in the rear re-creates a horticultural garden from the 18th century, including many original varieties of fruit trees and vegetables.

CHAPELLE NOTRE-DAME-DE-BONSECOURS
CHURCH

Map p280 (www.marguerite-bourgeoys.com; 400 Rue St-Paul Est; admission to chapel free, museum adult/child $10/5; ☺10am-6pm Tue-Sun May-Oct, 11am-4pm Tue-Sun rest of year but closed Jan 14-Feb 28; ⓂChamp-de-Mars) Known as the Sailors' Church, this enchanting chapel derives its name from the sailors who left behind votive lamps in the shapes of ships in thanksgiving for safe passage. The restored interior has stained-glass windows and paintings depicting key moments in the life of the Virgin Mary (for whom Montréal – aka Ville-Marie – was originally named).

The **Musée Marguerite-Bourgeoys**, which is attached to the chapel, relates the story of Montréal's first teacher and the founder of the Congregation of Notre-Dame order of nuns. The crypt has artifacts dating back 2000 years and foundations of the original chapel from 1773. The **observation tower** offers grand views of the Old Port.

MUSÉE D'ARCHÉOLOGIE ET D'HISTOIRE POINTE-À-CALLIÈRE
MUSEUM

Map p280 (www.pacmuseum.qc.ca; 350 Pl Royale; adult/child $16/6.50; ☺10am-6pm Mon-Fri, 11am-6pm Sat & Sun late Jun-early Sep, 10am-5pm Tue-Fri, 11am-5pm Sat & Sun rest of year; ⓂPlace-d'Armes) Built on the spot where European settlers set up their first camp, the Pointe-à-Callière Museum of Archaeology and History provides a good overview of Montréal's beginnings. Visitors should start with *Yours Truly, Montréal,* a 20-minute multimedia show that takes visitors back through the centuries.

For the most part the museum is underground. Head to the archaeological crypt in the basement where you can explore the remains of the city's ancient sewage and river system and the foundations of its first buildings and first public square. Interactive exhibits allow visitors to hear what life was like in the 17th and 18th centuries from characters on video screens.

The **lookout** at the top of the tower provides an excellent view of the Old Port.

FONDERIE DARLING
ARTS CENTER

Map p280 (www.fonderiedarling.org; 745 Rue Ottawa; ☺noon-7pm Wed & Fri-Sun, to 10pm Thu; admission $5, Thu free; ⓂSquare-Victoria) Tucked away in a little-visited corner of Old Montréal, the Darling Foundry hosts avant-garde, often large-scale exhibitions in its two sizable showrooms. The brick industrial building, which dates back to the early 1900s, once housed a prosperous iron foundry and is today home to the gallery and live-work studios for artists. The space also houses the Cluny Artbar (p63); entrance around the corner on Rue Prince), a fine spot for coffee, desserts or light lunch fare. In the summertime the foundry hosts occasional Thursday-night street events (when admission is free). Check the website for upcoming exhibitions.

CENTRE D'HISTOIRE DE MONTRÉAL
MUSEUM

Map p280 (http://ville.montreal.qc.ca; 335 Pl d'Youville; adult/child $6/4; ☺10am-5pm Tue-Sun; ⓂSquare-Victoria) In a handsome old fire hall on Pl d'Youville, the Montréal History Center has 300-plus artifacts that illustrate the city's eventful past while focusing on its social history. You can listen to the tales of long-lost neighborhoods, or travel back in time while watching archival footage from the '40s and '60s.

PLACE JACQUES-CARTIER
SQUARE

Map p280 (ⓂChamp-de-Mars) The liveliest spot in Old Montréal, this gently inclined square hums with performance artists, street musicians and the animated chatter from terrace restaurants linings its borders. A public market was set up here after a château burned down in 1803.

At its top end stands the **Colonne Nelson**, a monument erected to Admiral Lord Nelson after his defeat of Napoleon's fleet at Trafalgar.

LOCAL KNOWLEDGE

THE GREY NUNS

Born in Varennes, Quebec, in 1701, Marguerite d'Youville was initially known as the wife of a bootlegger, Francois d'Youville, who had a bad reputation for selling liquor to Indians on the black market. When he died of illness at age 30, Marguerite decided to dedicate her life to help the poor in an age where there was no social welfare. Fired by a religious devotion, her work drew other women to her cause. In those days, drunks were described as being *grisé par l'alcool* (grey from alcohol) and memories of Francois' profiteering earned the sisters the derisive nickname Les Soeurs Grises (The Grey Nuns). Undaunted, they founded a religious order in 1737 and 10 years later were granted a charter to run the General Hospital of Montréal, caring for orphans, prostitutes, the elderly and the poor. Marguerite, who died at the hospital in 1771, retained the name Grey Nuns to remind the sisters of their humble beginnings. She was canonized in 1990, becoming Canada's first homegrown saint.

OLD MONTRÉAL SIGHTS

Nelson's presence is a thorn in the side of many French Quebecers, and there have been many attempts to have it removed. Francophones later installed a statue of an obscure French admiral, Jean Vauquelin, in the nearby **Place Vauquelin**, just west of Hôtel de Ville on Rue Notre-Dame.

HÔTEL DE VILLE   HISTORIC BUILDING
Map p280 (http://ville.montreal.qc.ca; 275 Rue Notre-Dame Est; ⊘8:30am-5pm Mon-Fri; ⋒Champ -de-Mars) Montréal's handsome City Hall was built between 1872 and 1878, then rebuilt after a fire in 1926. Far from being a humdrum administrative center, it's actually steeped in local lore. Most famously, it's where French leader Charles de Gaulle took to the balcony in 1967 and yelled to the crowds outside *'Vive le Québec libre!'* ('Long live a free Québec!'). Those four words fueled the fires of Québécois separatism and strained relations with Ottawa for years. Peer into the **Great Hall of Honor** for some scenes of rural Québec and busts of Jacques Viger, the first French-speaking mayor (1833–36), and Peter McGill, the first English-speaking mayor (1840–42).

MARCHÉ BONSECOURS   HISTORIC BUILDING
Map p280 (www.marchebonsecours.qc.ca; 350 Rue St-Paul Est; ⊘generally 10am-6pm, to 9pm late Jun-early Sep; ⋒Champ-de-Mars) Opened in 1847, this sprawling neoclassical building has been everything from a farmers market to a concert theater, and even served briefly as Montréal's city hall (1852–78). It's also where the government of United Canada retreated, in order to continue the legislative session after the parliament buildings nearby were burned down by an angry Anglo mob in 1849. Today's *marché* (market) plays a somewhat less heroic role. The restored building reopened in 1992 as a gallery for shops selling arts and crafts, leather goods and garments. The upstairs hall hosts fashion shows and art auctions. Restaurants line the facade on Rue St-Paul.

LIEU HISTORIQUE DE SIR
GEORGE-ÉTIENNE-CARTIER   MUSEUM
Map p280 (www.parkscanada.gc.ca/cartier; 458 Rue Notre-Dame Est; adult/child $4/2; ⊘10am-5pm daily late Jun-early Sep, 10am-5pm Wed-Sun early Sep to late Dec & early May to late Jun) The Sir George-Étienne Cartier National Historic Site consists of two historic houses owned by the Cartier family. Exhibitions in the first detail the life of Sir George-Étienne Cartier, one of the founders of the Canadian Confederation, and illustrate the changes that society saw in his lifetime. The other house is a faithful reconstruction of his home during the Victorian era. Staff in period costume run guided tours throughout the day and hold dramatic presentations on etiquette and a servant's life. In season the program includes a Victorian Christmas.

COURS LE ROYER   SQUARE
Map p280 (⋒Place-d'Armes) Montréal's first hospital was founded on this narrow lane by Jeanne Mance in 1644. Later on a huge commercial complex was built here, leaving several beautiful 19th-century warehouses behind. The buildings caught the eyes of developers in the 1970s and were converted into apartments and offices. Today the buildings line this quiet pedestrian mall pocked with lush greenery.

1. Chapelle Notre-Dame-de-Bonsecours (p54)
'The Lady of the Harbor' statue atop this enchanting little chapel, which also houses Musée Marguerite-Bourgeoys.

2. Hôtel de Ville (p55)
Montréal's handsome City Hall is both an administrative center and an icon of the separatist movement.

3. Autumn in Montréal
Promenade du Vieux-Port (p61) is a favorite recreation spot for joggers, in-line skaters and cyclists, plus those seeking a little relaxation.

4. Quai Jacques-Cartier (p60)
The heart of the Old Port area, it hosts shows, exhibits and performances by Cirque du Soleil.

FREE MUSÉE DES SOEURS-GRISES MUSEUM
Map p280 (☎514-842-9411; www.sgm.qc.ca; 138
Rue St-Pierre; ◎appointment only; Ⓜ Square-
Victoria) Dedicated to Saint Marguerite
d'Youville, founder of the community of
the Sisters of Charity, better known as the
Grey Nuns (see box p55), this museum has
a small but wonderfully presented set of ex-
hibits. Tours of the museum in French and
English are available by appointment only.

RUE ST-PAUL STREET
Map p280 This narrow cobblestone street,
the oldest in Montréal, was once a dirt road
packed tight by horses laden with goods
bound for the Old Port. Today it's a shopping street with galleries, boutiques and
restaurants, touristy in spots but undeni-
ably picturesque and enjoyable to wander.

PLACE ROYALE SQUARE
Map p280 (Ⓜ Place-d'Armes) This little square
in the west of Old Montréal marks the
spot where the first fort, Ville-Marie, was
erected. Defense was a key consideration
due to lengthy fighting with the Iroquois.
In the 17th and 18th centuries this was a
marketplace; it's now the paved forecourt
of the 1836 **Old Customs House** (Vieille
Douane; Map p280) and linked to the Musée
d'Archéologie Pointe-à-Callière by an underground passage. The neoclassical building
looks much the same today as when it was
built, but now serves as the museum's gift
shop.

RUE DE L'HÔPITAL & AROUND NEIGHBORHOOD
Map p280 (Ⓜ Place-d'Armes) Named for a
hospice set up by nuns in the 17th century,
the Rue de l'Hôpital and adjoining streets
are full of architectural quirks and highlights. On the corner of Rue St-François-
Xavier, the **Canadian Pacific Telegraph
Chambers** (Map p280) was the 19th-century
equivalent of a national internet provider. It
houses condominiums today but the wild-
eyed keystone over the entrance remains.
The **Lewis Building** (Map p280) was built
as the head office of the Cunard Shipping
Lines. One mischievous character on the
facade is holding a bag full of loot; a more
scholarly colleague is taking notes.

The Centaur Theatre (p70) performs
English-language plays in the old **Mon-
tréal Stock Exchange Building** (Map p280).
Opened in 1903, the huge columns recall

imperial Rome while the interior has sumptuous marble and wood paneling.

COURTHOUSES NOTABLE BUILDINGS
Map p280 (Ⓜ Place-d'Armes) Along the north
side of Rue Notre-Dame Est near Pl Jacques-
Cartier, three courthouses stand bunched
together. The most fetching is the neoclassical **Vieux Palais de Justice**, Montréal's
old justice palace and oldest courthouse
(1856) that's now an annex of the Hôtel de
Ville. It's a popular backdrop for wedding
photos. The **Édifice Ernest Cormier** from
the 1920s was used for criminal trials before being turned into a conservatory and
later a court of appeal. The ugly stepsister
is the oversized **Palais de Justice**, built in
1971 when concrete and smoked glass were
all the rage.

PLACE JEAN-PAUL-RIOPELLE SQUARE
Map p280 (cnr Ave Viger Ouest & Rue de Bleury;
◎ring of fire every hour 6:30-10:30pm mid-May–
mid-Oct; Ⓜ Place-d'Armes) The big draw of
this square by the Palais Des Congrès is the
fountain that releases a ring of fire (and
an ethereal mist) at certain times of year.
The fountain and sculpture by Jean-Paul
Riopelle (1923–2002), called La Joute (The
Joust), was inaugurated here in 2003. During the day this area is filled with nearby
office workers having lunch, but summer
nights are a big draw – that's when the pyrotechnics take place.

SQUARE VICTORIA SQUARE
Map p280 (Ⓜ Square-Victoria) In the `19th
century this was a Victorian garden in a
swanky district of Second Empire homes
and offices. Today Square Victoria is a tri-
angle of manicured greenery and water
jets in the midst of modern skyscrapers.
The only vestige of the period is a statue
of Queen Victoria (1872). The art-nouveau
entrance railing to the metro station was a
gift from the city of Paris for Expo '67.

PALAIS DES CONGRÈS NOTABLE BUILDING
Map p280 (www.congresmtl.com; 201 Ave Viger
Ouest; Ⓜ Place-d'Armes) Entering the hall of
this convention center with its facade of
popsicle-colored panes is akin to strolling
through a kaleidoscope. Day brings out the
colors, night the transparency. The cutting-
edge Palais integrates several historic buildings: a 1908 fire station, the art-deco Tram-
ways building from 1928 and a Victorian-
era office complex. Immediately east of the

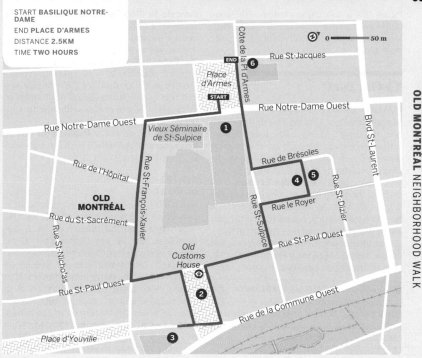

START **BASILIQUE NOTRE-DAME**
END **PLACE D'ARMES**
DISTANCE **2.5KM**
TIME **TWO HOURS**

Neighborhood Walk
Reliving History in Old Montréal

Wigged colonists, top-hatted financiers and scheming spies are just some of the characters you'll run into in Old Montréal. It's a treasure trove of period sets for visiting film crews and there's a historic building at every turn. You can recall what you've seen in the atmospheric cafes and restaurants of this very walkable district.

On the southeast side of Place d'Armes plaza, you'll see the city's most celebrated cathedral, the magnificent **1 Basilique Notre-Dame**. Go inside for a look at the spectacularly carved pulpit and richly hued stained-glass windows relating key events from the city's founding.

Head southwest along Rue Notre-Dame, turn left down Rue St-François-Xavier and then left again on Rue St-Paul Ouest, where you then cut past the Old Customs House to **2 Place Royale**, the square believed to be where the first settlers landed. In the 17th and 18th centuries, this was the city's marketplace.

The Old Customs House is connected by underground tunnel to the **3 Musée d'Archéologie et d'Histoire Pointe-à-Callière**, a fascinating museum devoted to the city's history and archaeology. Head inside for a look at the city's ancient foundations. On the top floor is a fine vantage point over the Old Port.

Exiting the museum, walk north to Rue St-Sulpice. Turn right onto Rue le Royer – this leads to the lovely **4 Cours Le Royer**, a tranquil pedestrian mall with fountains and lush greenery. The passageway on the north side features a **5 stained-glass window of Jérôme Le Royer**, one of the founders of Montréal.

Continue through the passage to Rue de Brésoles and take a left, walking up to Rue St-Sulpice, where you'll make a right to return to Place d'Armes. Before leaving the area, note the **6 New York Life Insurance Building**, Montréal's first skyscraper, eight storeys tall and built in 1888.

Palais lies a landscape garden with stone pathways linking 31 heaps of earth, each topped off with Montréal's official tree, the crab apple.

◉ Old Port

QUAI ALEXANDRA & AROUND   PIER
Map p280 (ⓂPlace-d'Armes) This easternmost pier in the port is home to the Iberville Passenger Terminal, the dock for cruise ships that ply the St Lawrence River as far as the Magdalen Islands out in the Gulf of St Lawrence. Nearby, the **Parc des Écluses** (Park of Locks; Map p280) holds exhibitions of landscape architecture, shows and concerts. A bicycle path starts here and runs southeast along the pretty Canal de Lachine (p143).

The abandoned 17-story-tall concrete silo on the south side of the locks is the last big relic of Montréal's heyday as a grain port.

QUAI JACQUES-CARTIER & AROUND   PIER
Map p280 (ⓂChamp-de-Mars) This pier is the anchor of the Old Port area, home to restaurants, an open-air stage and a handicraft center. Every year the port stages a number of temporary exhibits, shows and events.

Montréal's world-renowed Cirque du Soleil (p67) performs under its eye-catching big top here; recent shows have included the new production *Amaluna*.

Tours of the port area also depart from the pier, and a ferry can take you to Parc Jean-Drapeau. The ferry can also stop at

Parc de la Cité-du-Havre, where there's a restaurant and picnic tables, as well as the nearby Habitat 67 building (p76).

Just north of Quai Jacques-Cartier is the **Parc du Bassin Bonsecours**, a grassy expanse enclosed by a waterway and crisscrossed with footbridges. In summer you can rent paddleboats ($6.50 per half-hour) or remote-control model sailboats; in winter the ice-skaters take over.

There's a cafe at the **Pavilion du Bassin Bonsecours** (Map p280) with outdoor seating in the summer.

CENTRE DES SCIENCES
DE MONTRÉAL   MUSEUM
Map p280 (www.centredessciencesdemontreal. com; Quai King-Edward; adult/child $11.50/8.50; ⊙9am-4pm Mon-Thu, 10am-9pm Fri & Sat, 10am-5pm Sun; ⓂPlace-d'Arme) This sleek, glass-covered science center houses virtual and interactive games, technology exhibits and an 'immersion theater' that puts a video game on giant screens. Note that there is a huge range of different admission prices depending on which combinations of films and/or exhibits you want to take in. The center includes an IMAX cinema (p70) that shows vivid nature and science films.

RUE DE LA COMMUNE   STREET
Map p280 (ⓂChamp-de-Mars) Set back from the waterfront, 'the Common' is a showcase of the rejuvenation that has swept Old Montréal. Compare it with old photos and you'll

A CAPITAL EXPERIMENT

Montréal would have a very different place in history but for a boozy rabble and a few newspaper articles. When the city became the capital of the United Provinces of Canada in 1844, the government moved into a two-story limestone building on the elongated **Place d'Youville** (Map p280), which at the time was a public market. It was here that Canada's first prime minister, John A Macdonald, made his inaugural speech to a joint French-English parliament.

Montréal's tenure as capital came to an abrupt end in 1849. Egged on by inflammatory editorials in the *Gazette*, an anglophone mob set fire to the assembly and the building burned to a crisp. The crowd was protesting a law that would require the Crown to compensate French Canadians for damages inflicted by the British army in the rebellion of 1837. As a consequence Montréal lost its status as capital, and the seat of government shifted back and forth between Québec City and Toronto until 1858, when Queen Victoria declared Ottawa the new capital.

Nothing was saved from the flames except a legislative mace and a portrait of Queen Victoria; the latter now hangs in the federal parliament building in Ottawa. The location of the first Canadian parliament (the east end of the square) is today a parking lot.

see the warehouses and factory buildings haven't changed much on the outside, but the tenants are upmarket hotels, restaurants and converted condos. Though the street has lost its raw, industrial feel, the original stone walls can still be viewed inside many buildings.

SAILORS' MEMORIAL CLOCK TOWER
MONUMENT

Map p280 (Quai de l'Horloge; ⊘10am-7pm; ⓂChamp-de-Mars) At the eastern edge of the historic port stands the striking white Tour de l'Horloge. This notable clock commemorates all of the sailors and shipmen who died in the world wars. Visitors can climb the 192 steps for a view over Old Montréal and the river.

✖ EATING

Vieux-Montréal has experienced a culinary renaissance in recent years, with a number of acclaimed restaurants winning over discerning diners and food critics alike. Here you'll find top-notch Québécois and fusion fare, among some of the city's most atmospheric dining rooms (it's hard to beat the 18th-century backdrop). That said, Old Montréal still has plenty of touristy restaurants (mostly along Pl Jacques-Cartier) where quantity not quality is the name of the game. The touristy-local divide is roughly Blvd St-Laurent, with the better restaurants lying to the west of this iconic street.

Billowy steam and scrumptious odors waft out of kitchens and into the streets of Montréal's tiny but lively Chinatown. Cantonese, Szechuan and Vietnamese restaurants dominate Blvd St-Laurent and the pedestrian Rue de la Gauchetière.

✖ Old Montréal

TOP CHOICE GARDE-MANGER   INTERNATIONAL $$$

Map p280 (☑514-678-5044; http://crownsalts .com/gardemanger; 409 Rue St-François-Xavier; mains $25-35; ⊘6pm-3am Tue-Sun; ⓂPlace-d'Armes) The buzz surrounding Garde-Manger has barely let up since its opening in

2006. This tiny upscale restaurant, recently expanded with a back room seating an extra 20 people, attracts a mix of local scenesters and haute-cuisine-loving out-of-towners who come for the lobster risotto, short ribs, succulent snow crab and other changing chalkboard specials. If you're looking for an intimate dinner, this is not the place: it can get so loud here that waitstaff have to shout to be heard. After midnight the soundtrack gets cranked up a notch and the candlelit dining room becomes a party place for the A-list. Reservations essential.

TOP CHOICE L'ORIGNAL   QUÉBÉCOIS $$$

Map p280 (☑514-303-0479; www.restaurant-lorignal.com; 479 Rue St-Alexis; mains $28-38; ⊘dinner; ⓂPlace-d'Armes) This cozy chalet-style restaurant specializes in exquisitely prepared game meat and fresh seafood. Start off with oysters before moving on to braised wild boar or poached turbot in a lobster bisque. The service is excellent here. On weekend nights, L'Orignal gets packed and attracts a festive crowd when the kitchen closes. Its modest bar makes a great spot for a drink, but the official policy is customers have to be dining as well.

TOP CHOICE TOQUÉ!   FRENCH $$$

Map p280 (☑514-499-2084; www.restaurant-toque.com; 900 Pl Jean-Paul-Riopelle; mains $48-96; ⊘dinner Tue-Sat; ⓂPlace-d'Armes) Chef Normand Laprise has earned rave reviews for his innovative recipes based on products sourced from local farms. Even his desserts excite, created around fresh fruit with surprises like basil highlights. The bright, wide-open dining room has high ceilings accented by playful splashes of color, with a glass-enclosed wine cave with suspended bottles looming front and center. The seven-course *menu dégustation* ($98) is the pinnacle of dining in Montréal – allow three hours for the feast.

LE GROS JAMBON   DINER $

Map p280 (http://legrosjambon.com; 286 Rue Notre-Dame Ouest; mains $8-18; ⊙8am-3pm Mon, 8am-11pm Tue-Thu, 8am-4:30am Fri, 10am-4:30am Sat, 10am-3:30pm Sun; Ⓜ Square-Victoria) From Travis Champion of local favorite l'Orignal, just around the corner, this faux-retro snack bar serves up yummy hipster comfort food with homemade ingredients. It's high-calorie food, but just try to resist: smoked meat-topped hot dogs (aka the Montréal), mac 'n' cheese duck confit, smoked-meat and grilled cheese sandwiches, fish tacos and olive oil–bathed *poutine* (fries smothered in cheese curds and gravy)bathed in truffle oil. Vintage Montréal kitsch adorns the wall along the bar.

LE CLUB CHASSE ET PÊCHE   FRENCH $$$

Map p280 (☎514-861-1112; www.leclubchasse etpeche.com; 423 Rue St-Claude mains $29-31;;⊙lunch Tue-Sat early Jun-Sep, dinner Tue-Sat; Ⓜ Champ-de-Mars) One of the pillars of Old Montréal's grand dining scene, this elegant restaurant serves fantastic new-wave French fare, including grilled Wagyu beef, sautéed scallops with fennel and succulent lamb. Given the prices, it's a favorite among lunching execs and Montrealers celebrating a special occasion. In the summer at lunchtime, dine alfresco in the historical Château Ramezay garden over the road.

LE LOCAL   FRENCH $$$

Map p280 (☎514-397-7737; http://resto-lelocal .com; 740 Rue William; mains $22-68; ⊙lunch Mon-Fri, dinner nightly; Ⓜ Square-Victoria) On the western edge of Old Montréal, this captivating addition to the dining scene serves delectable fare in an architecturally stunning dining room. Well-moneyed 20- and 30-somethings feast on inventive (critics say overly complicated) dishes with rich, market-fresh ingredients to the backdrop of unobtrusive electronica. There's an outdoor terrace and an extensive wine list (and an award-winning sommelier). Reservations recommended.

CHEZ L'ÉPICIER   FRENCH $$$

Map p280 (☎514-878-2232; www.chezlepicier .com; 311 Rue St-Paul Est; mains $28-40; ⊙dinner; Ⓜ Champ-de-Mars) Helmed by chef Laurent Godbout, Chez L'Épicier is a perennial favorite. Inside the bright and cozy dining room with big windows overlooking the street, you'll find a menu that changes regularly, but features handsomely presented dishes like maple-syrup glazed pork, lobster and wild mushroom crispy roll, or seared filet mignon. For dessert, try the famous chocolate club sandwich with pineapple fries.

BEVO   ITALIAN $$

Map p280 (☎514-861-5039; 410 Rue St-Vincent; mains $13-31; ⊙dinner; Ⓜ Place-d'Armes) In a smartly renovated 1850s stone building, this new pizzeria delivers reliably tasty pies from its wood-fired oven including pizzas topped with all manner of prosciutto and pepperoni. Braised veal *poutine*, red snapper and pastas round out the menu, while the interior old-world stone and brick contrast with a snazzy red bar and suspended bubble chairs. The scene spills out onto Rue St-Vincent in the summer for al fresco dining.

CHEZ QUEUX   FRENCH $$

Map p280 (☎514-866-5194; www.chezqueux .com; 158 Rue St-Paul Est; mains $30-50; ⊙dinner Tue-Sun; Ⓜ Champ-de-Mars) Housed in a historic warehouse dating from 1862, with stone walls, polished paneling and Third Empire furnishings, this gem offers the epitome of old-fashioned French cuisine. Settle into a thronelike chair, order the delicious chateaubriand and prepare for a pampering. The little-known rear terrace overlooking the Old Port is a lovely dining spot in summer. The wine list features 300-plus varieties.

BORIS BISTRO   BISTRO $$

Map p280 (☎514-848-9575; www.borisbistro .com; 465 Rue McGill; mains $16-24; ⊙lunch & dinner daily mid-May to end Aug, lunch Mon-Fri, dinner Tue-Sat rest of year; Ⓜ Square-Victoria) You'll be elbowing your way through everyone from Armani-clad executives to disheveled artists to get a table at this popular bistro. Once settled, however, you can feast on a mouthwatering assortment of dishes, including artfully presented salads, a much-touted duck risotto with mushrooms or uncomplicated favorites such

MONTRÉAL'S LITERARY STAR

Émile Nelligan (1879–1941) is one of Québec's literary icons, a star like Oscar Wilde or Lord Byron whose mix of talent and tragedy keeps them in the public consciousness long after their era is over. A poetic genius, Nelligan created most of his famous works by the age of 20 before being committed and spending the rest of his life in mental institutions.

Born in Montréal to an Irish father and a Québécois mother, his bohemian traits were in evidence from the time he was a teenager. He sailed in and out of school to the dismay of his parents and seemed interested in little other than romantic poetry. After submitting two samples of his work, he was accepted by the l'École Littéraire de Montréal (Literary School of Montréal); public readings followed and his poems exploring love and loneliness were regularly published in French-language magazines around Montréal. Nelligan had always marched to a different drum but by 1899 it was apparent his problems were more than just those of a temperamental artist and there was something seriously wrong.

His father had him committed to a mental institution that year. Though he tried briefly to rejoin society in 1925, he was back in care within days. What was wrong with him? Historians who've examined his hospital records believe he may have suffered from schizophrenia.

Though there has been both a movie and play about Nelligan's life, and he was immortalized in a painting by master Québec artist Jean-Paul Lemieux, there is no museum devoted to his work or life. Hunting his ghost around town is the best you'll be able to do. The Château Ramezay (p53) is where l'École Littéraire de Montréal used to meet and where Nelligan's poems were first read in public. Nelligan lived in a house on the west side of Carré St-Louis (p112). The square is also the setting for the famous Lemieux painting. Further along, St Patrick's Basilica (p84) is where Nelligan was baptized; there's a plaque at the back commemorating this event, along with a plaque devoted to Montréal's other famous Irishman, D'Arcy McGee.

as pasta mahi mahi on crispy vegetables. Whether you want to eat inside or in the gorgeous outdoor courtyard, it's a good idea to reserve ahead.

RESTAURANT HOLDER — BISTRO $$

Map p280 (☑514-849-0333; http://restaurant holder.com; 407 Rue McGill; mains $18-28; ⏰11:30am-11pm Mon-Fri, 10am-3pm & 5:30-11pm Sat & Sun; Ⓜ Square-Victoria) High ceilings, a warm color scheme and beautifully turned-out dishes are just part of the appeal of this classic bistro on busy Rue McGill. It's a buzzing place (sometimes quite noisy), where the crowd – good-looking media and corporate types – dines on tuna niçoise, grilled hangar steak, pan-seared tilapia and other bistro classics.

DA EMMA — ITALIAN $$

Map p280 (☑514-392-1568; 777 Rue de la Commune Ouest; mains $18-45; ⏰lunch & dinner Mon-Fri, dinner Sat; Ⓜ Square-Victoria) The old stone walls and beamed ceiling of this atmospheric place – a former women's prison– today provide the backdrop to delicious

Italian cooking. Osso buco, fresh grilled fish, agnolotti with stuffed veal and satisfying homemade pastas are the top picks from the changing menu. Reservations are recommended.

GIBBY'S — STEAKHOUSE $$$

Map p280 (☑514-282-1837; www.gibbys.com; 298 Place d'Youville; mains $30-45; ⏰dinner; Ⓜ Square-Victoria) A purveyor of the good old-fashioned steak, Gibby's serves excellent grilled meats and seafood, including a respected rack of lamb. A mix of corporate types clink glasses inside the elegant stone building (former stables, actually) dating back to the 1700s. There's an open courtyard in the back.

CLUNY ARTBAR — CAFE $

Map p280 (www.fonderiedarling.org; 257 Rue Prince; mains $6-13; ⏰8am-5pm Mon-Fri, to 10pm Thu; Ⓜ Square-Victoria) Industrial style dominates at this renovated factory shared with the Fonderie Darling art space. Tables are made of recycled bowling lanes, while exposed beams and pipes snake overhead.

The menu features a daily special, along with reliably good deli sandwiches, soups, salads and antipasti. The breakfast menu includes flaky croissants and heartier *huevos rancheros* (fried eggs, tortillas and salsa).

OLIVE + GOURMANDO
BAKERY-CAFE $

Map p280 (http://oliveetgourmando.com; 351 Rue St-Paul Ouest; mains $9-12; ⊘8am-6pm Tue-Sat, to 8pm summer; MSquare-Victoria) Named after the owners' two cats, this bakery-cafe is legendary in town for its sandwiches and baked goods. Excellent choices include the smoked trout with herbed cream cheese and the Cuban (ham, roast pork, Swiss cheese and house-made chipotle mayo). You'll also find good coffee, tempting desserts and fresh loaves for takeout (including olive and rosemary bread). Try to avoid the busy weekday lunch rush (11:30am to 1:30pm).

SOUPESOUP
CAFE $

Map p280 (www.soupesoup.com, in French; 649 Rue Wellington; mains $3-6; ⊘8am-4pm Mon-Fri, 11am-3pm Sat & Sun; MSquare-Victoria) The brainchild of chef, writer and all-around soup-lover Caroline Dumas, this warm cafeteria-like eatery housed in a former factory offers over 200 varieties of soup, as well as sandwiches and salads. It's one of six locations in the city.

STASH CAFÉ
POLISH $$

Map p280 (✆514-845-6611; www.stashcafe.com; 200 Rue St-Paul Ouest; mains $11-17; ⊘1:30am-10pm Mon-Thu, 11:30am-11pm Fri, noon-11pm Sat, noon-10pm Sun; MPlace-d'Armes) Hearty Polish cuisine is served up with good humor in a dining room with seats made of church pews and daringly low red lights illuminating the tables. Staff range from warm and gregarious to completely standoffish, but the food is consistent, with quality fare like pierogy (dumplings stuffed with meat or cheese, with sour cream) and potato pancakes with apple sauce. An enthusiastic pianist hammers away from time to time.

GANDHI
INDIAN $$

Map p280 (✆514-845-5866; www.restaurant gandhi.com; 230 Rue St-Paul Ouest; mains $16-27; ⊘lunch & dinner Mon-Fri, dinner Sat & Sun; MSquare-Victoria) Gandhi has a core of loyal fans who come here for classics like tandoori chicken as well as the extensive curry menu with adventurous fare such as

malaya, a curry of pineapple, lychees and cream. Appetizers such as *pakoras* or vegetable samosas are finely spiced, and faves such as tandoori duck, butter chicken and lamb *korahi* also go down nicely. Reservations are recommended.

TITANIC
CAFE $

Map p280 (www.titanicmontreal.com; 445 Rue St-Pierre; mains $7-12; ⊘8am-4:30pm Mon-Fri; MSquare-Victoria) The sandwiches here have office workers scurrying to these cramped basement quarters from all over Old Montréal on their lunch breaks. The varieties are endless and can include pepper pâté, smoked mackerel or spicy Calabrese sausage. Excellent salads, pastas, quiche and antipasto misto are popular takeouts that round out the mix.

✖ Chinatown

MAI XIANG YUAN
CHINESE $

Map p280 (1084 Blvd St-Laurent; mains $6-10; ⊘11am-9pm Mon-Sun; MPlace-d'Armes) You'd be hard-pressed to find better dumplings in Montréal than the perfect little bits of heaven, pan-fried or steamed, that come out of the kitchen in this humble hole in the wall. Each plate comes with 15 dumplings and fillings include everything from lamb and onion to pork and leek, as well as tomato and egg for vegetarians.

LA MAISON KAM FUNG
CHINESE $$

Map p280 (✆514-878-2888; www.restaurant lamaisonkamfung.com; 1111 Rue St-Urbain; mains $8-15; ⊘7am-3pm & 4:30-10pm; MPlace-d'Armes) This is generally considered the best place in town for dim sum, and is especially popular for Saturday and Sunday brunch. Waiters circle the tables with carts of dim sum ($3 to $6 each) – you pick and choose from tender dumplings, spare ribs, mushrooms, spicy shrimp and much more. The entrance is hidden in the rear of a shopping passage up an escalator. Reservations recommended.

NOODLE FACTORY
CHINESE $

Map p280 (www.restonoodlefactory.com; 1018 Rue St-Urbain; mains $5-11; ⊘11am-10pm; MPlace-d'Armes) Noodle fanatics roll up to this bustling hole in the wall for chef Lin Kwong Cheung's famed homemade noodles. You can watch him in the open kitchen whacking and kneading the dough into fine strips before devouring it yourself. Cash only.

PHO BANG NEW YORK   VIETNAMESE $

Map p280 (1001 Blvd St-Laurent; mains $10-15; ⊙10am-9:30pm; MPlace-d'Armes) Near the gateway to Chinatown, Pho Bang New York has decor and service geared more toward Westerners who want to have their *pho* (noodle soups) in swisher digs. The food here is still good and regularly turns up on people's 'top' lists, but it lacks the kind of manic energy that makes the other Vietnamese places on this drag so atmospheric. The *pho* here tends to be leaner than at other Chinatown spots.

BEIJING   CHINESE $

Map p280 (www.restaurantbeijing.net; 92 Rue de la Gauchetière Ouest; mains $8-18; ⊙11:30am-3am; MPlace-d'Armes) Every Montrealer has a favorite Chinatown restaurant, a familiar place where a warm welcome awaits when turning up in the neighborhood. The unassuming and always-buzzing Beijing tops many lists, with a reputation built on tasty, fresh Cantonese and Szechuan dishes, friendly service and its late-night hours.

JARDIN DE JADE   CHINESE $

Map p280 (67 Rue de la Gauchetière Ouest; buffet $9-14; ⊙11am-11pm; MPlace-d'Armes) The chaotic, free-for-all Jardin de Jade buffet should be a must on your list if only to see it in action. Vegetarian, sushi, dumplings, fish, ribs, desserts and even pizza. To see it in its full elbow-bumping glory, try weekdays when locals, business people and students battle it out over the stir-fry. One of the town's best deals. Prices vary depending on day and time.

PHO CALI   VIETNAMESE $

Map p280 (1011 Blvd St-Laurent; mains $6-12; ⊙10am-10pm; MPlace-d'Armes) Cali is a decent hole-in-the-wall place, with friendly, good-humored waitstaff no matter how busy things get. The deal with this place is to get you in and out as quickly as possible, so don't be surprised if your order lands in front of you, piping hot, moments after you order it.

HOANG OANH   VIETNAMESE $

Map p280 (1071 Blvd St-Laurent; sandwiches $3-4; ⊙9:30am-7pm; MPlace-d'Armes) The Vietnamese baguette sandwiches here are the very best in Chinatown. There's an endless choice of fillings but the grilled chicken or the tofu varieties topped with mayonnaise, veggies and coriander are pretty much unbeatable.

🍷 DRINKING & NIGHTLIFE

TOP CHOICE PHILÉMON   CLUB

Map p280 (http://philemonbar.com; 111 Rue St-Paul Ouest; MPlace-d'Armes) A major stop for local scenesters rotating between watering holes in the old city, Philémon was carved out of stone, brick and wood with large windows looking out over Rue St-Paul. Twenty-somethings fill the space around a huge central bar that doles out basic cocktails and menus with light offerings such as duck confit salad.

TOP CHOICE TERRASSE NELLIGAN   TERRACE BAR

Map p50 (www.terrassenelligan.com; Rue 100 St-Paul Ouest, ⊙11:30am-11:30pm summer; MPlace-d'Armes) Above heritage Hôtel Nelligan, this delightful patio is the perfect spot to down a mojito while the sun sinks. There's a full menu for lunch and dinner, and splendid views over the St Lawrence River and the Old Port. It's less of a scene than Terrasse Place d'Armes but equally enjoyable.

GARDE-MANGER   BAR

Map p280 (http://crownsalts.com/gardemanger; 409 Rue St-Francois-Xavier; ⊙Tue-Sun; MPlace-d'Armes) After midnight this tiny, upmarket restaurant becomes party central as scenesters, actors and gourmands-turned-merrymakers gyrate around. You'll probably find yourself dancing on the bar, or in the kitchen making out with some hottie. Be warned: the music is loud and getting in on weekends is tough – unless you're a close pal with the cool, beautiful staff.

VELVET   CLUB

Map p280 (426 Rue St-Gabriel; ⊙Thu-Sat; MChamp-de-Mars) Who knew that an inn dating from 1754 could be so hip? Beneath restaurant Auberge St-Gabriel, walk through a long, candlelit stone passageway to this grooving grotto of electronic beats done up like a speakeasy of yore. Fashionistas, scenesters and models flock here, and there's often a long lineup outside.

QUÉBEC'S TOP ARTISANAL BEERS

McAuslan Brewing Keep an eye out for its apricot wheat ale and especially its St-Ambroise oatmeal stout and St-Ambroise Pale Ale.

Boréale Everything from black beer to blond, but the red variety is by far the preferred.

Unibroue Fin du Monde (End of the World) is a triple-fermented monster with 9% alcohol that more than lives up to its name; La Maudite (the Damned) is a rich, spicy beer that clocks in a close second at 8%; Blanche de Chambly is a light wheat ale.

L'Alchimiste This Joliette-based brewer (about 60km northeast of Montréal) turns out a stable of different brews but its Bock de Joliette, an amber beer, is the star of the bunch.

Les Trois Mousquetaires Based in Brossard (across the St Lawrence River to the southeast of Montréal), this small brewery's Baltic Porter has won awards overseas for its bold taste.

Lion d'Or This Lennoxville brewer (see p207) is one of the best in the province and does an outstanding, *very* bitter, bitter beer. For some reason, finding the label in Montréal these days is a bit like searching for a needle in a haystack (you know it's there somewhere but...) so if you come across this particular mark, be sure to scoop it up fast.

LES SOEURS GRISES PUB

Map p280 (www.bblsg.com, in French; 32 Rue McGill; ⊙11am-midnight or later Mon-Fri, from 3pm Sat & Sun; MSquare-Victoria) Named after the famous Montreal religious order of nuns founded by St Marguerite d'Youville, this swanky new bistro-brasserie near the Old Port bike path is a good spot to unwind after cycling the Canal de Lachine. Food is served on planks of wood. Grab some *ailes de lapin* (rabbit wings), a pulled pork sandwich, or trout filet smoked in-house and wash it down with Quebec beers like Dominus from MicroBrasserie Charlevoix and house brew La Marguerite.

TERRASSE PLACE D'ARMES TERRACE BAR

Map p280 (www.terrasseplacedarmes.com; 8th fl, 710 Côte de la Place d'Armes; ⊙11am-3am summer; MPlace-d'Armes) The rooftop terrace above the boutique Hôtel Place-d'Armes is a requisite stop on the nightlife circuit if you're around during the summer. Nicely mixed cocktails, eclectic cuisine and a fantastic view over Place d'Armes and the Basilique Notre-Dame never fail to bring in the beautiful crowd.

TAVERNE GASPAR PUB

Map p280 (www.tavernegaspar.com; 89 Rue de la Commune Est; MChamp-de-Mars) Facing the Old Port, this cozy watering hole in the Auberge du Vieux Port has delicious faux-retro decor, a long zinc bar, and a menu with lobster sliders, oysters, fish and chips, and a delish mac 'n cheese. The house brew is the Gaspar lager, and other local beers include St-Ambroise suds.

CAFÉ DIFFÉRANCE CAFE

Map p280 (http://cafedifferance.ca; 449 Ave Viger Ouest; ⊙7:15am-5pm Mon-Fri, 9am-4pm Sat, 10am-4pm Sun; MSquare-Victoria) With hipster baristas in wool caps and a great variety of African and local coffees, this espresso bar is helping to bring great brews to Montréal. It has occasional weekend coffee workshops to educate drinkers about the finer points of the bean.

CAFÉ SANTÉ VERITAS CAFE

Map p280 (www.cafesanteveritas.com; 480 Blvd St-Laurent; ⊙7:30am-7pm Mon-Fri, 10am-6pm Sat & Sun; MPlace-d'Armes) Serving coffee brewed from beans from Vancouver's 49th Parallel Roasters and prepared with a sleek Synesso Cyncra espresso machine, this chic cafe-bistro is very serious about gourmet joe. The health-oriented kitchen menu features low-fat, low-carb choices such as Cajun chicken salad, as well as veggie sandwiches and mouth-watering breakfast crepes.

CLUNY ARTBAR
CAFE

Map p280 (www.fonderiedarling.org; 257 Rue Prince; ☺8am-5pm Mon-Wed & Fri, to 10pm Thu; Ⓜ️Square-Victoria) Tucked into the loft-like Fonderie Darling gallery is this charmingly hip cafe that serves breakfast, lunch and coffee to an artsy-chic, bilingual, Old Montréal clientele. It's open later Thursdays for dinner and drinks, and can be rented for private parties, but Cluny's is really a daytime scene. It doesn't get more Montréal than this.

L'ORIGNAL
BAR

Map p280 (www.restaurantlorignal.com; 479 Rue St-Alexis; Ⓜ️Place-d'Armes) While you can't drink at 'The Moose' unless you're having dinner or dessert, this cozy chalet restaurant is a convivial spot to clink glasses. Nearing midnight, things get crazy as pretty people dance and flirt the night away.

L'ASSOMMOIR
PUB

Map p280 (http://assommoir.ca; 211 Rue Notre-Dame Ouest; ☺11am-3am Mon-Fri, 5pm-3am Sat & Sun; Ⓜ️Place-d'Armes) Like its sister pub in Mile-End (p136), L'Assomoir is home to a beautiful long bar that makes a great place to start the night with a house cocktail like the Dragon Vert (gin and kiwi) or snacks like lamb keftas. At L'Assomoir Cabaret next door, acoustic bands, burlesque performers and artists like famed Québec poet Gilles Vigneault take the stage Wednesday nights, while the Bayou Swing Trio gets your toes tapping during Sunday brunch.

UN
CLUB

Map p280 (http://clubunmontreal.com; 390 Notre-Dame Ouest; ☺Thu-Sat; Ⓜ️Square-Victoria) With its shiny hardwood floors and chic lighting, this basement club reels in the Old Montréal kids for its electro-house, hopping beats, and many sofas in the relaxing lounge. Enter on Rue Ste-Hélène.

WUNDERBAR
LOUNGE

Map p280 (www.wunderbarmontreal.com; 901 Square Victoria; ☺Wed-Sat; Ⓜ️Square-Victoria) This modern room in the W Hotel is among the city's safest bets for a soiree on the town. Wunderbar was developed by New York–based nightlife impresarios, who blended local and international culture with the ease of a dry martini. Weekly DJ nights attract a dancey, trendy crowd.

PUB ST-PAUL
PUB

Map p280 (www.pubstpaul.com, in French; 124 Rue St-Paul Est; ☺11am-3am; Ⓜ️Champ-de-Mars) In the heart of Old Montréal's most touristy drag is this rock pub, a hit among students, jocks and passersby. A lunch and dinner menu of upscale pub fare is served, live bands rock out weekend nights, and drink specials complete the Top 40 formula.

TIME SUPPERCLUB
CLUB

Map p280 (www.timesupperclub.com; 997 Rue St-Jacques Ouest; ☺Thu-Sat; Ⓜ️Square-Victoria) Dress to impress at this Miami-inspired supper club, where models and wannabes shake their booty on a lit-up catwalk. Events with international DJs and celebrities attract paparazzi-seekers who dig the high-energy house music and overall gorgeousness.

BAINS DOUCHES
CLUB

Map p280 (www.bainsdouches.ca; 390 Rue St-Jacques Ouest; ☺Thu-Sun; Ⓜ️Square-Victoria) Celebrity guests, house, trance and techno DJs, and sexy 20-somethings make this very hyper nightclub the go-to spot of thousands. Don't forget the monstrous 100,000-watt sound system. If you're ready for bottle service, book a table in advance.

☆ ENTERTAINMENT

CIRQUE DU SOLEIL
CIRCUS

Map p280 (☎800-450-1480; www.cirquedusoleil.com; 145 rue de la Commune Est, Quai Jacques-Cartier; adult/child from $43/33; Ⓜ️Place-d'Armes) Globally famous Cirque du Soleil, one of the city's most famous exports, puts on a new production of acrobats and music in this marvelous tent complex roughly once every two years in summer; one of the most recent shows is *Amaluna*, a re-imagining of Shakespeare's *The Tempest* that is directed by Diane Paulus of the American Repertory Theatre.

LE PIANO ROUGE
LIVE MUSIC

Map p280 (www.pianorougelounge.com; 22 Rue St-Paul Est; ☺7pm-late, Tue-Sun; Ⓜ️Champ-de-Mars) This intimate, brick-walled bistro-lounge centers on its titular red piano, where jazz, soul and R&B artists raise the temperature and bodies start swaying to the music. Before the show starts, it's a very laid-back spot for a glass of wine and jerk chicken. Seating is limited.

Top Five Parks & Gardens

Montreal is an especially leafy city, with extensive green spaces and one of the world's largest botanical gardens. Locals especially love skating, walking, and banging drums on the mountainous centerpiece of the island, Parc du Mont-Royal. Here are five spots to soak up some rays.

Parc Jean-Drapeau

1 These islands (p73) in the St Lawrence River offer walking paths with spectacular views of Montréal, as well as plenty of unique sights along the way, like the leftovers of Expo '67.

Parc du Mont-Royal

2 Montréal's green-space gem, 'the Mountain' (p113) has sweeping views of the city below, skating and tobogganing in winter, miles of forested paths and a weekly all-you-can-drum get-together in the spirit of the 1960s.

Parc Outremont

3 This little-known neighborhood park (p130) has a picturesque pond, yarmulke-wearing tots and a great little ice-cream shop a few blocks away.

Jardin Botanique

4 This exceptional collection of plants (p144) from all over the world takes in everything from bonsai trees to orchids, set in dozens of thematic gardens to make for some memorable meandering.

Parc LaFontaine

5 This is the perfect year-round park (p112) with performances at the bandstand in summer and ice-skating on the pond in winter. Set in a neighborhood that's home to artsy types, it always has interesting characters.

Clockwise from top left
1 Autumn foliage, Parc Jean-Drapeau **2** View of Montréal from Parc du Mont-Royal **3** Parc Outremont

MEGAPRESS / ALAMY ©

CINÉMA IMAX DU CENTRE DES SCIENCES DE MONTRÉAL CINEMA

Map p280 (Quai King-Edward; www.montreal sciencecentre.com; MPlace-d'Armes) Located in the Centre des Sciences de Montréal, this theater brings specially produced adventure, nature and historical films to oversized screens. Watch Cirque du Soleil, dinosaurs or marine life come tumbling into your lap with the aid of 3-D glasses and translation headsets. Great for kids.

CENTAUR THEATRE THEATER

Map p280 (514-288-3161; http://centaurthea tre.com; 453 Rue St-François-Xavier; MPlace-d'Armes) Montréal's chief English-language theater presents everything from Shakespearean classics to works by experimental Canadian playwrights. It occupies Montréal's former stock exchange (1903), a striking building with classical columns.

🛍 SHOPPING

MARCHÉ BONSECOURS SHOPPING MALL

Map p280 (www.marchebonsecours.qc.ca; 350 Rue St-Paul Est; generally 10am-6pm, to 9pm late Jun-early Sep; MChamp-de-Mars) This majestic old building has housed the Canadian parliament, city hall and, now, a collection of cute boutiques selling Québec-made goodies like fashion, accessories, jewelry and crafts. Restaurants and terraces are also on-site, and the *marché* is often used for trade shows and art events.

LE CARTET FOOD & DRINK

Map p280 (http://lecartet.com; 106 Rue McGill; 7am-7pm Mon-Fri, 9am-4pm Sat & Sun; MSquare-Victoria) Le Cartet is a boutique-restaurant with a shop in front and a dining room behind that's perfect for brunch. The store deals in artisanal chocolates, Québec jams and cheeses, and delicious brioche.

DHC ART GALLERY

Map p280 (http://dhc-art.org; 451 Rue St-Jean; noon-7pm Wed-Fri, 11am-6pm Sat & Sun; MPlace-d'Armes) Opened in 2007, this excellent contemporary art gallery in a heritage building features mind-bending works by artists such as Ryoji Ikeda, Jenny Holzer and Marc Quinn.

MY CUP OF TEA FOOD & DRINK

Map p280 (www.mcot.ca; 1057A Blvd St-Laurent; noon-7pm; MPlace-d'Armes) This stylish Chinatown tea shop has more than 50 tea varieties in loose and teabag form, including its popular blooming tea, which opens up from a ball once immersed. It also has a range of beautiful glassware and tea containers.

GALERIE 2000 GALLERY

Map p280 (www.gallery2000.ca; 45 Rue St-Paul Ouest; 10am-6pm Wed-Sat; MChamp-de-Mars) Always fresh and entertaining, this eclectic gallery has large, tasteful displays from classic landscapes to neocubist portraits, with the occasional well-charted flight into the alternative.

GALERIE LE CHARIOT GALLERY

Map p280 (446 Place Jacques-Cartier; 10am-6pm MChamp-de-Mars) This arts emporium claims to have the largest Inuit collection in Canada. Choose from First Nations art carved mainly from soapstone, as well as walrus tusks, fur hats, mountain-goat rugs and fleecy moccasins.

GALERIE ST-DIZIER GALLERY

Map p280 (www.saintdizier.com; 24 Rue St-Paul Ouest; 10am-6pm Sun-Wed, to 8pm Thu-Sat; MChamp-de-Mars) This spacious old gallery has always been at the forefront of the avant-garde scene in Montréal. Works are split between local and heavyweight artists known abroad, including Besner, Missakian and Tetro. Its forte is naïve and modernist art and sculpture.

LA GUILDE GRAPHIQUE GALLERY

Map p280 (www.guildegraphique.com; 9 Rue St-Paul Ouest; MChamp-de-Mars) This place exhibits works of more than 200 contemporary artists in a variety of media and techniques. Most works are sketches, woodcuts, etchings and lithographs on paper, and you can visit the artists working in the upstairs studio.

REBORN FASHION

Map p280 (http://reborn.ws; 231 Rue St-Paul Ouest; 11am-6pm Mon-Wed & Sat, 11am-8pm Thu & Fri, noon-6pm Sun; MPlace-d'Armes) Upscale lines like Kenzo, Assembly New York and Devoa meet accessories and a slick, old-meets-new feel at this must-see fashion laboratory.

A RIDE IN THE CALÈCHE

Horse-drawn carriages are one of the most popular (and romantic – assuming Silver didn't go overboard on the morning oats) ways to see downtown. Calèche drivers pony up in front of Place-d'Armes and next to Place Jacques-Cartier by the Old Port. You can even sometimes score sleigh rides through Parc du Mont-Royal once the winter weather arrives. Drivers have a fair bit of knowledge about the old quarters, and will happily rattle off some history along the way. A half-hour ride is $48, one hour is $80.

ROONEY   FASHION
Map p280 (www.rooneyshop.com; 395 Rue Notre-Dame Ouest; MSquare-Victoria) Jeans, jeans and more jeans are the highlight of this high-end streetwear headquarters. Coveted international brands in stock include Barbour and Levi's Vintage Clothing. Rooney also sells a range of other fashion items.

BOUTIQUE ANNE DE SHALLA   FASHION
Map p280 (www.annedeshalla.com; 350 Rue St-Paul Est, Marché Bonsecours; MChamp-de-Mars) French fashion diva Anne de Shalla studied fashion in Paris and came to Montréal in the 1970s. She now selects from up to 30 Québec designers every year for her exclusive shop collection – stretchy leathers, semi-sheer dresses, blouses and wraparound casuals.

🏃 SPORTS & ACTIVITIES

ÇA ROULE MONTRÉAL   RENTAL
Map p280 (☎514-866-0633; www.caroulemontreal.com; 27 Rue de la Commune Est; bicycle per hr/day from $8/25, in-line skates from $9/20; ☺9am-8pm Apr-Oct; MPlace-d'Armes) Near the Old Port, Ça Roule Montréal has a wide selection of bicycles, in-line skates, spare parts and a good repair shop. Each rental includes a lock, helmet, patch kit, cycling map and (in the case of in-line skates) full protective gear. Prices listed are for weekday rentals; weekend rentals cost more. You can also rent children's bikes, tandems and bike trailers for pulling the little ones along while you pedal. Tours are also available.

BOTA BOTA   DAY SPA
Map p280 (☎514-284-0333; www.botabota.ca; 358 Rue de la Commune Ouest; ☺10am-10pm; admission from $45; MSquare-Victoria) This unique floating spa is actually a 1950s ferry that's been retooled as an oasis on the water. It's permanently docked by the Old Port with great city views, offering a range of treatments on its five beautifully redesigned decks. The Water Circuit admission gives you access to saunas, hot tubs and the outdoor terraces, while treatments run the gamut from manicures and pedicures to the Tribal Journey ($125), in which your body is treated with everything from coffee to cactus wax.

SAUTE-MOUTONS   BOAT TOUR
Map p280 (☎514-284-9607; www.jetboatingmontreal.com; 47 Rue de la Commune Ouest, Old Port; jet boat tour per adult/teen/child $67/57/47, speedboat $26/21/19; ☺10am-6pm May-Oct; MChamps-de-Mars) Thrill-seekers will certainly get their money's worth on these fast, wet and bouncy boat tours to the Lachine Rapids. The aluminum jet boats take you through foaming white water, from Quai de l'Horloge, on hour-long tours. There are also speedboats that take 20-minute jaunts around the Parc des Îles from the Jacques Cartier pier. Reservations are a must.

PLAGE DE L'HORLOGE   BEACH
Map p280 (www.quaysoftheoldport.com; Old Port; adult/child $6/3; ☺10:30am-7:30pm daily mid-Jun to early Sep, Sat & Sun to late Sep; MChamp-de-Mars) Montréal opened this 'urban beach' along the Quai de l'Horloge in 2012, trucking in sand, Adirondack chairs, parasols and a bar. Unfortunately, there's no swimming, but it's a fine spot to take in views of the river and to catch some rays.

LA PATINOIRE DES QUAIS   SKATING
Map p280 (Old Port; adult/child $6/4, skate rental $7; ☺10am-9pm Mon-Wed, to 10pm Thu-Sun; MChamp-de-Mars, ⬛14) This is one of Montréal's most popular outdoor skating rinks, located on the shore of the St Lawrence

River next to the Pavilion du Bassin Bonsecours. DJs add to the festivities. At Christmas time there's a big nativity scene.

AML CRUISES
BOAT TOUR

Map p280 (☏514-842-3871; www.croisieresaml.com; Quai King-Edward; 1½hr tour adult/child $28/15; ⏰11:30am & 2pm; Ⓜ Champ-de-Mars) These 1½-hour river tours in a glassed-in sightseeing boat take in the Old Port and Île Ste-Hélène. Other options include night cruises with a band, dancing and a gourmet dinner. Early and late cruises are in high season only.

LE BATEAU MOUCHE
BOAT TOUR

Map p280 (☏514-849-9952; www.bateau mouche.ca; Quai Jacques-Cartier; 1hr tour per adult/child $24/12, 1½hr tour $28/15; ⏰1hr tour 2:30pm & 4pm, 1½hr tour 12:30pm mid-May–mid-Oct; Ⓜ Champ-de-Mars) This comfortable, climate-controlled sightseeing boat with a glass roof offers narrated cruises of the Old Port and Parc Jean-Drapeau. Dinner cruises of 3½ hours are also available. Phone ahead for reservations and make sure you board the vessel 15 minutes before departure.

LE PETIT NAVIRE
BOAT TOUR

Map p280 (☏514-602-1000; www.lepetitnavire.ca; Quai Jacques-Cartier; 45min tour per adult/child $18/8, 2hr tour $25/19; ⏰mid-May-Aug; Ⓜ Champ-de-Mars) Aside from rowing a boat yourself, this outfit offers the most ecologically friendly boat tours in Montréal. The silent, electric- powered Le Petit Navire takes passengers on 45-minute tours departing hourly around the Old Port area. Equally intriguing are the 1½-hour cruises up the Canal de Lachine (departing Fridays, Saturdays and Sundays at 2pm).

CENTRE LUNA YOGA
YOGA

Map p280 (☏514-845-1881; www.centrelunayoga.com; 231 Rue St-Paul Ouest, ste 200; 1½hr class $17; Ⓜ Square-Victoria) Conveniently located in Old Montréal, this yoga center offers a small selection of daily Vinyasa classes. Go online or stop in to find out its latest schedule.

Parc Jean-Drapeau

ÎLE STE-HÉLÈNE | ÎLE NOTRE-DAME

Neighborhood Top Five

1 Take a long breather from the hustle of the city by soaking up some sunshine and fresh air on verdant **Île Ste-Hélène** (p75).

2 Ride the world's tallest wooden roller coaster at **La Ronde** (p75). Or get eye-popping views of the city from the Ferris wheel.

3 Ever wanted to sleep in an igloo? Get seriously cool at **Village des Neiges** (p75), where everything is made of ice and snow.

4 Fight the good fight, 18th-century style, with military parades at **Musée Stewart** (p76), housed in a British garrison.

5 Learn about the environment and view the city from the unique globe that is the **Biosphère** (p75).

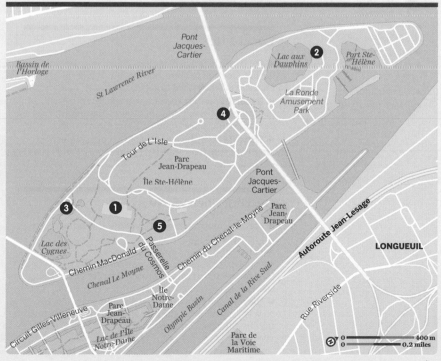

For more detail of this area, see Map p298 ➡

Lonely Planet's Top Tip

Parc Jean-Drapeau has a few snack bars and vending machines, but almost no eating options in terms of restaurants. If you're visiting in early spring, late fall, or winter, you should consider packing a lunch or snacks. In a pinch, try the restaurants at the Casino de Montréal.

☀ Best Places for Fun

➡ La Ronde (p75)
➡ Casino de Montréal (p76)
➡ Grand Prix du Canada (p77)
➡ Plage des Îles (p77)

For reviews, see p75 ➡

☀ Best Events

➡ L'International des Feux Loto-Québec (p75)
➡ Village des Neiges (p75)
➡ Grand Prix du Canada (p77)
➡ Osheaga (p75)
➡ Piknic Électronik (p75)

For reviews, see p75 ➡

Explore Parc Jean-Drapeau

In the middle of the mighty St Lawrence, this alluring green space spreads across Île Ste-Hélène and Île Notre-Dame. Together, the two islands offer a fine choice of recreational activities, along with some worthwhile museums. The park is also home to a casino, a Formula One racetrack, an old-fashioned amusement park and summer festivals (see www.parcjeandrapeau.com).

You can easily spend the better part of a day exploring Parc Jean-Drapeau. From Jean-Drapeau station on the yellow line, walk north to the Biosphère (built for Expo '67) and take in its unique superstructure and environment-themed exhibits. Continue along Chemin du Tour de l'Île, which winds its way around the center of Île Ste-Hélène, toward Musée Stewart, where you might be able to catch retro military maneuvers in action. Take in the historical pageantry and exhibits before continuing north along the chemin to the amusement park La Ronde. While you're walking through the island, note the numerous outdoor sculptures, the most famous of which is Alexander Calder's L'Homme, as well as other buildings that are leftovers from Expo '67; the western side of the island offers great views of the city. If you're looking for thrills of another kind, hop on bus 167 to the Casino de Montréal on Île Notre-Dame and try your luck at roulette, blackjack, slots, and many other games of chance.

Local Life

➡ **Festivals** Parc Jean-Drapeau comes into its own during excellent festivals and events such as the Osheaga music festival (p75).

➡ **Beach bumming** The St Lawrence River doesn't make for good swimming, but there's the decent Plage des Îles artificial beach on Île Notre-Dame (p76).

➡ **Formula One** The main event that brings most Montrealers to Parc Jean-Drapeau is the Grand Prix du Canada (p77).

Getting There & Away

➡ **Metro** Jean-Drapeau on the yellow line brings you to the heart of the park.

➡ **Ferry** In summer, catch a ferry (www.navettesmaritimes.com; one way adult/child $7.50/free) to the park from the Jacques-Cartier Pier at the Old Port.

➡ **Bicycle** The best way to get around the park is by bicycle – access is via the busy Pont Jacques-Cartier or the circuitous but far more peaceful route via Cité du Havre.

⊙ SIGHTS

⊙ Île Ste-Hélène

Walkways meander around this island, past gardens and among the old pavilions from the Expo '67. The western part of the island was transformed into an open-air stage for shows, concerts and even after-hour parties. A large metal sculpture, **L'Homme** (Humankind; Map p298), was created by American artist Alexander Calder for Expo '67.

It's also here, near the sculpture, that the fantastic **Piknic Électronik** (Map p298; www.piknicelectronik.com; Place de l'Homme; admission $12; ☺2-9pm Sun late-May–Oct) takes place. DJs spin techno and electronic music while you dance or lounge on the grass. Going strong since 2006, **Osheaga Festival Musique et Arts** (www.osheaga.com; Place de l'Homme; ☺early Aug) is the island's major music festival, showcasing local alternative bands as well as big-name international acts.

Mainly on weekends from late June to early August, the **L'International des Feux Loto-Québec** fireworks show (www.internationaldesfeuxlotoquebec.com) at the La Ronde amusement park lights up the skies with pyrotechnics from around the world.

From early January to late March, **Village des Neiges** (Map p298; www.snowvillagecanada.com; adult/child $13/6.50) presents a stunning replica of Montréal crafted out of ice and snow. If you really want to chill out, the Village also has an **Ice Hotel** (r from $259) which fortunately offers thermal sleeping bags. For those who'd simply prefer a different dining experience, the Village's **Pommery Ice Restaurant** (lunch/dinner $18/69) has multi-course Nordic gourmet cuisine, served on icy tables and fur-covered benches.

BIOSPHÈRE   NATURE CENTER

Map p298 (www.ec.gc.ca/biosphere; 160 Chemin du Tour de l'Île; adult/child $12/free; ☺10am-6pm daily Jun-Oct, 10am-5pm Tue-Sun Nov-May; ⓂJean-Drapeau) Housed in Buckminster Fuller's striking geodesic dome built for the American pavilion at Expo '67, this nature center has its own geothermal energy system and fun interactive displays involving hand-pumps and water spouts. Exhibits focus on urban ecosystems and emerging ecotechnologies; there's a model house outside built using sustainable design principles. The upstairs gallery about Fuller, and the exterior belvederes, offer spectacular river views.

LA RONDE   AMUSEMENT PARK

Map p298 (www.laronde.com; 22 Chemin Macdonald; adult/child $47/34; ☺varies, generally 11am-8pm, daily late May-late Aug, weekends only Sep-Oct; ⓂJean-Drapeau, then bus 167; Ⓟ$13) Québec's largest amusement park, La Ronde has a battery of impressive rides, including Le Monstre, the world's highest double wooden roller coaster, and Le Vampire, a corkscrew roller coaster with gut-wrenching turns. For a more peaceful experience,

---

THE LAST GOOD YEAR

For Montrealers who are old enough, there are few events in the history of the city that evoke such an emotional response as the 1967 International and Universal Exposition, fondly known as Expo '67. For six months of that year, what is now Parc Jean-Drapeau hosted 62 nations from around the world and drew 50 million visitors (more than double Canada's population), including VIPs like Queen Elizabeth II, Lyndon Johnson and Charles de Gaulle. In no small part thanks to the efforts of Mayor Jean Drapeau, Expo '67 became one of the most successful world fairs ever held. It also coincided with the centenary of Canadian confederation, and the country – and Montréal itself – seemed on top of the world (one of the fair's many legacies was the Expos, Montréal's pro baseball team from 1969 to 2004).

However, in the decades that followed the Expo, the sovereigntist political movement, an exodus of Anglophones and economic stagnation precipitated for many a period of decline for the city. And thus there is a deep longing for Expo and its glories. As historian Pierre Berton remembers it in his book *1967: The Last Good Year*, 'I fell captive to an unexpected emotion: a moistness in the eyes and a huskiness in the throat of the kind one usually experiences only in moments of national stress…It was nationalism unabashed and I discovered later that others had felt it too.'

there's a Ferris wheel and a gentle minirail that offers views of the river and city. Concerts and shows are held throughout the summer, and fireworks explode overhead on weekend evenings (when the park stays open later).

MUSÉE STEWART   MUSEUM
Map p298 (www.stewart-museum.org; 20 Chemin du Tour de l'Île; adult/child under 7/student $13/free/10; ☺11am-5pm Wed-Sun; ⓜJean-Drapeau) Inside the old Arsenal British garrison (where troops were stationed in the 19th century), this beautifully renovated museum displays relics from Canada's past in its new permanent exhibition, History and Memory. In summer, there are military parades outside by actors in 18th-century uniforms; check the website for details. It's a 15-minute walk from Jean-Drapeau metro station.

☉ Île Notre-Dame

This isle emerged in 10 months from the riverbed, atop millions of tons of earth and rock excavated from the new metro created in 1967. The planners were creative with the use of water, carving out canals and pretty garden walkways amid the parklands that stretch across the isle. The **Circuit Gilles-Villeneuve** (Map p298) continues to host the uberpopular Grand Prix du Canada in summer, while the more recent Casino de Montréal draws punters year-round.

HABITAT 67   HISTORIC BUILDING
Map p298 (www.habitat67.com; 2600 Ave Pierre-Dupuy, Cité du Havre; ⓜJean-Drapeau, then bus 167) The artificial peninsula called **Cité-du-Havre** was created to protect the port from vicious currents and ice. Here, in 1967, architect Moshe Safdie designed a set of futuristic cubelike condominiums for Expo '67 when he was just 23 years old. This narrow spit of land connects Île Ste-Hélène with Old Montréal via the Pont de la Concorde.

✖ EATING

HÉLÈNE DE CHAMPLAIN   FRENCH $$
Map p298 (☎514-395-2424; 200 Chemin du Tour de l'Île, Île Ste-Hélène; ⓜJean-Drapeau) Named after Hélène Boullé, wife of explorer Samuel de Champlain, this illustrious eatery served

as a pavilion of honor during Expo '67. The city of Montréal has spent over $16 million updating the traditional stone homestead dating from 1930. It offers a varied menu of seafood and meats. At the time of writing, it was closed, but expected to reopen in 2013.

LE BUFFET   BUFFET $$
Map p298 (www.casinosduquebec.com/montreal; 1 Ave du Casino, Île Notre-Dame; buffets from $17;☺lunch & dinner; ⓜJean-Drapeau, then bus 167) Located in the Casino de Montréal, Le Buffet is a serviceable option for decent buffets centering on fish, pasta, beef and pork as well as soups and salads. Note that the casino does not admit kids under 18.

☆ ENTERTAINMENT

CASINO DE MONTRÉAL   CASINO
Map p298 (www.casinosduquebec.com/montreal; 1 Ave du Casino, Île Notre-Dame; ☺24hr; ⓜJean-Drapeau, then bus 167) Based in the former French pavilion from Expo '67, the Montréal Casino opened in 1993 and was so popular (and earned so much money) that expansion occurred almost instantly. It remains Canada's biggest casino. You can gather your winnings at more than 3,000 slot machines and 120 gaming tables, but drinking isn't allowed on the floor. Glitzy Las Vegas–style shows are sometimes staged here too, as well as poker tournaments and other special events.

Arched footbridges link the casino to the **Jardin des Floralies** (Map p298), a rose garden that is wonderful for a stroll.

⚲ SPORTS & ACTIVITIES

AQUATIC COMPLEX   WATER SPORTS
Map p298 (www.parcjeandrapeau.com; Île Ste-Hélène; adult/child $6/3; ☺10am-8pm daily mid-Jun-late Aug, 3:30-7pm Mon-Fri, 11am-4pm Sat & Sun late Aug–mid-Sep; ⓜJean-Drapeau) This pool complex was rebuilt when Montréal scored the 2005 World Aquatic Championships. The diving pool – complete with underwater viewing windows – and competition pool are generally reserved for hosting competitions or for training competitive swimmers and athletic teams. But

RETURN OF THE MONTRÉAL MELON

In its heyday it was truly the Queen of Melons. A single specimen might easily have reached 9kg and its spicy flavor earned it the nickname 'Nutmeg Melon.' The market gardeners of western Montréal did a booming business in the fruit.

After WWII small agricultural plots in Montréal vanished as the city expanded, and industrial farms had little interest in growing a melon with ultrasensitive rind. By the 1950s the melon was gone – but not forever. In 1996 an enterprising Montréal journalist tracked down Montréal melon seeds held in a US Department of Agriculture collection in Iowa. The first new crop was harvested a year later in a new collective garden in Notre-Dame-de-Grâce, the heart of the old melon-growing district. To sample this blast from the past, visit local markets such as Marché Atwater (p82) or Marché Jean-Talon (p129) after the harvest every September.

the magnificent 55m x 44m warm-up pool is open for recreational swimming. There's also a bay-like portion of the pool with a shallow, gently sloping bottom that's great for kids and families.

OLYMPIC BASIN   WATER SPORTS

Map p298 (www.parcjeandrapeau.com; 1 Circuit Gilles-Villeneuve, Île Notre-Dame; ☺6am-8pm late April-Nov; ⓂJean-Drapeau, then bus 167) Competitive rowers and kayakers, along with other amateur athletes, train at this 2.2km-long former rowing basin built for the 1976 Olympic Games. You can take in many competitive boating events here such as the **Canadian Masters Championships** and the **Montréal International Dragon Boat Race Festival** (www.montrealdragonboat.com), held in late July.

PLAGE DES ÎLES   BEACH

Map p298 (www.parcjeandrapeau.com; Île Notre-Dame; adult/child $8/4; ☺10am-7pm mid Jun-late Aug; ⓂJean-Drapeau, then bus 167) On warm summer days this artificial sandy beach can accommodate up to 5000 sunning and splashing souls. It's safe, clean and ideal for kids; picnic facilities and snack bars serv-

ing beer are also on-site. There are also paddle-boats, canoes and kayaks for rent.

NASCAR: NAPA
AUTO PARTS 200   CAR RACING

Map p298 (www.nascar.com; Circuit Gilles-Villeneuve, Île Notre-Dame; ☺Aug; ⓂJean-Drapeau) The NASCAR Napa Auto Parts 200 at Circuit Gilles-Villeneuve is part of the Nationwide Series. Local favorite Jacques Villeneuve, son of racing great Gilles Villeneuve, also competes. The race is typically held toward the end of August.

GRAND PRIX DU CANADA   CAR RACING

Map p298 (www.circuitgillesvilleneuve.ca; Circuit Gilles-Villeneuve, Île Notre-Dame; tickets $42-557; ☺Jun; ⓂJean-Drapeau) Canada's only Grand Prix race has been held on Île Notre-Dame since 1978, though it went on hiatus in 2009 due to a dispute between the city and Formula One supremo Bernie Ecclestone; the current contract calls for races to be held annually through 2014. It remains one of the most popular motorsport events in the world, selling out and packing Montréal's hotels in early June. Be sure to reserve your tickets early.

Downtown

Neighborhood Top Five

❶ Spending nothing and getting to see an encyclopedic array of traditional and contemporary art at the **Musée des Beaux-Arts de Montréal** (p80).

❷ Getting your festival freak on with thousands of others when the jazz festival hits town at **Place des Arts** (p81).

❸ Exploring downtown's beautiful historic churches, such as the **Cathédrale Marie-Reine-du-Monde** (p81).

❹ Browsing the chichi shops and heritage buildings along **Rue Sherbrooke Ouest** (p82).

❺ Learning all about great building designers at the excellent **Centre Canadien d'Architecture** (p81).

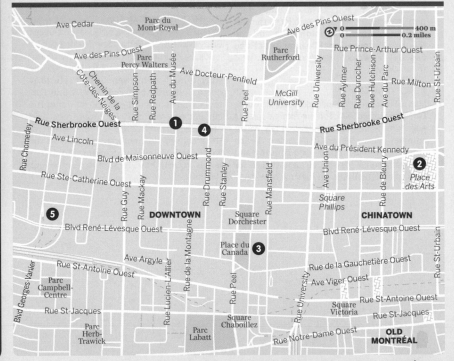

For more detail of this area, see Map p284 and p288 ➡

Explore Downtown

Downtown Montréal's wide boulevards, glass skyscrapers and shopping galleries give the area a decidedly North American flavor, while numerous green spaces, eye-catching heritage buildings and 19th-century churches add a more European character to the bustling city streets. You can explore the area easily in the better part of a day with a pause for lunch.

Begin your tour at the Musée des Beaux-Arts de Montréal, spending the morning taking in its vast collection of Old Masters and modern Canadian art, before grabbing a snack or lunch at nearby spots like the cafe in Holt Renfrew. Make your way along Rue Sherbrooke Ouest, passing the heritage houses and tony businesses en route, before reaching McGill University, a bustling haven of green with its own museums.

From the university, you can climb toward Parc du Mont-Royal if you really want to stretch your legs, or turn down Ave McGill College to reach Rue Ste-Catherine Ouest, downtown's main shopping drag. To the west, there's Rue Crescent and Rue Bishop, the traditional anglophone centers of nightlife with an array of bars and restaurants. More shopping centers and the festival-oriented Quartier des Spectacles – including Place des Arts, the performing-arts complex and hub of the jazz festival – are within a short walk to the east along Rue Ste-Catherine Ouest. From Place des Arts, it's easy to walk to Chinatown, and even Old Montréal, for dinner.

Local Life

➡ **Pedaling** Rent a Bixi bike and pedal up and down Blvd de Maisonneuve to the leafy suburb of Westmount (p94).

➡ **Hiking** Hoof it up hills such as Rue Peel to reach one of the entrances to Parc du Mont-Royal.

➡ **Get to the pint** Pubs along Rue Crescent and surrounding streets, such as the Sir Winston Churchill (p91), form a popular Anglo hangout for relaxing with a drink, preferably on a patio.

Getting There & Away

➡ **Metro** Peel and McGill are both central and convenient.

➡ **Bus** Bus 15 runs on Rue Ste-Catherine and Blvd de Maisonneuve, bus 24 on Rue Sherbrooke and bus 150 on Blvd René-Lévesque.

➡ **Bike** Bixi bikes have numerous stations in the area. If you're cycling, head to Blvd de Maisonneuve, which has separate protected bike lanes.

DOWNTOWN

✗ Best Places to Eat

➡ Joe Beef (p85)

➡ Beaver Club (p85)

➡ Queue du Cheval (p85)

➡ Kazu (p85)

For reviews, see p85 ➡

🍷 Best Places to Drink

➡ Dominion Square Tavern (p90)

➡ Burgundy Lion (p90)

➡ McKibbin's (p90)

➡ NYKS (p90)

For reviews, see p90 ➡

☆ Best Entertainment

➡ Place des Arts (p91)

➡ Théâtre du Nouveau Monde (p92)

➡ Upstairs (p90)

For reviews, see p91 ➡

TOP SIGHTS
MUSÉE DES BEAUX-ARTS DE MONTRÉAL

Montréal's Museum of Fine Arts is an accessible and beautifully updated oasis of art housed in both heritage and modern pavilions. Its recent expansion into a third building, a neighboring church, has allowed more room for Canadian and Québécois art.

Musée des Beaux-Arts de Montréal is Canada's oldest museum and the city's largest, with works from Old Masters to contemporary artists; it is also the only museum in Canada that displays its permanent collection free of charge.

The beaux-arts, marble-covered **Michal and Renata Hornstein Pavilion** at 1379 Rue Sherbrooke Ouest presents World Cultures – everything from ancient African to modern Japanese art – and an excellent **Decorative Arts and Design** wing, with over 800 works from some of the world's most influential designers.

Next door, the award-winning new **Claire and Marc Bourgie Pavilion** is situated in a renovated 1894 church and displays 600 works of Canadian and Québécois art including many recent acquisitions. The church's Bourgie Concert Hall features gorgeous Tiffany stained-glass windows and live shows.

The modern annex across the street is the **Jean-Noël Desmarais Pavilion**, home to the Old and Modern Masters, with paintings from the Middle Ages stretching through the Renaissance and classical eras up to contemporary works. It can be reached via an underground passage from the Hornstein Pavilion.

DON'T MISS

➡ Pablo Picasso's *Embrace*

➡ Jean-Paul Riopelle's *Austria*

➡ Bourgie pavilion

PRACTICALITIES

➡ Map p284

➡ www.mbam.qc.ca

➡ ☎514-285-2000

➡ 1380, 1379 & 1339 Rue Sherbrooke Ouest

➡ permanent collection free, special exhibits adult/student $15/9 (both $7.50 Wed night), child free

➡ ⊙collection 11am-5pm Tue-Fri, 10am-5pm Sat & Sun; temporary exhibitions 11am-5pm Tue, to 9pm Wed, to 7pm Thu & Fri, 10am-5pm Sat & Sun

➡ ⓂGuy-Concordia or Peel

◉ SIGHTS

MUSÉE DES BEAUX-ARTS
DE MONTRÉAL   ART GALLERY
See p80.

MUSÉE D'ART CONTEMPORAIN   ART GALLERY
Map p288 (www.macm.org; 185 Rue Ste-Catherine Ouest, Place des Arts; adult/student $12/8, 5-9pm Wed free; ☺11am-6pm Tue & Thu-Sun, to 9pm Wed, English tours 6:30pm Wed, 1pm Sat & Sun; ⓂPlace-des-Arts) This showcase of modern Canadian and international art has eight galleries divided between past greats (since 1939) and exciting current developments. A weighty collection of 6000 permanent works includes Québécois legends Jean-Paul Riopelle, Paul-Émile Borduas and Geneviève Cadieux, but also temporary exhibitions of the latest trends in current art from Canadian and international artists. Forms range from traditional to new media, from painting, sculpture and prints to installation art, photography and video. The **sculpture garden** is also worth a look.
The pleasant **restaurant** upstairs has a great dining terrace.

CENTRE CANADIEN
D'ARCHITECTURE   MUSEUM
Map p284 (www.cca.qc.ca; 1920 Rue Baile; adult/child $10/free, after 5:30pm Thu free; ☺11am-6pm Wed & Fri-Sun, to 9pm Thu; ⓂGuy-Concordia; ☎) A must for architecture fans, this center is equal parts museum and research institute. The building incorporates the **Shaughnessy House**, a 19th-century gray limestone treasure. Highlights in this section include the conservatory and an ornate sitting room with intricate woodwork and a massive stone fireplace. There's also a busy, well-stocked bookstore. The exhibition galleries focus on remarkable architectural works of both local and international scope, with a particular focus on urban design. The CCA's sculpture garden is located on a grassy lot overlooking south Montréal.

MUSÉE MCCORD   MUSEUM
Map p288 (www.mccord-museum.qc.ca; 690 Rue Sherbrooke Ouest; adult/child/student $14/free/8, Wed 5-9pm & first Sat each month free; ☺10am-6pm Tue, Thu & Fri, to 9pm Wed, to 5pm Sat & Sun; ⓂMcGill) With hardly an inch to spare in its cramped but welcoming galleries, the McCord Museum of Canadian History houses over one million artifacts and documents illustrating Canada's social, cultural and archaeological history from the 18th century to the present day.

FREE MUSÉE REDPATH   MUSEUM
Map p288 (www.mcgill.ca/redpath; 859 Rue Sherbrooke Ouest, McGill University; ☺9am-5pm Mon-Fri, 11am-5pm Sun; ⓂMcGill) A Victorian spirit of discovery pervades this old natural history museum, though you won't find anything more gruesome than stuffed animals from the Laurentians hinterland. The Redpath Museum houses a large variety of specimens, including a dinosaur skeleton and seashells donated from around the world. A highlight is the 3rd-floor **World Cultures Exhibits**, which includes Egyptian mummies, shrunken heads and artifacts from ancient Mediterranean, African and East Asian communities.

CATHÉDRALE MARIE-REINE-
DU-MONDE   CHURCH
Map p288 (www.cathedralecatholiquedemontreal.org, in French; 1045 Rue de la Cathédrale; ☺7:30am-6pm; ⓂBonaventure) The Cathedral of Mary Queen of the World is a smaller but still magnificent version of St Peter's Basilica in Rome. The architects scaled it down to one-quarter size, mindful of the structural risks of Montréal's severe winters. This landmark was built from 1870 to 1894 as a symbol of Catholic power in the heart of Protestant Montréal.
The 13 statues of saints over the entrance are sculpted in wood and covered with copper; at night they are brilliantly illuminated. The neobaroque altar canopy, a replica of Bernini's masterpiece in St Peter's, is fashioned of gold leaf and copper with swirled roof supports.

PLACE DES ARTS   ARTS CENTER
Map p288 (☎box office 514-842-2112; www.pdarts.com; 175 Rue Ste-Catherine Ouest; ⓂPlace-des-Arts) Montréal's performing-arts center is the nexus for artistic and cultural events. Several renowned musical companies call the Place des Arts home, including the Opéra de Montréal and the Montréal Symphony Orchestra, now based in the new, 1900-seat **Maison Symphonique de Montréal**. It's also center stage for the Festival International de Jazz de Montréal (p238). A key part of the **Quartier des Spectacles**, the complex embraces an outdoor plaza with fountains and an ornamental pool and is attached to the **Complexe Desjardins** shopping center via an

underground tunnel. The six halls also include the 3000-seat **Salle Wilfrid-Pelletier** and the 1500-seat **Théâtre Maisonneuve**, and there's a small experimental space called the **Cinquième Salle**.

RUE SHERBROOKE OUEST STREET

Map p288 Until the 1930s the downtown stretch of Rue Sherbrooke Ouest was home to the **Golden Square Mile**, then one of the richest residential neighborhoods in Canada. You'll see a few glorious old homes along this drag, including the **Reid Wilson House**, the **Louis-Joseph Forget House** and the **Mount Royal Club**. There are good interpretation panels outside them explaining their history. The route is also home to visit-worthy churches, some first-rate museums and strings of energetic students en route to McGill University.

CHRIST CHURCH CATHEDRAL CHURCH

Map p288 (www.montrealcathedral.ca; 1444 Ave Union; ⊙7:30am-5:45pm; ⓂMcGill) Montréal's first Anglican bishop had this cathedral built (modeled on a church in Salisbury, England) and it was completed in 1859. The church was the talk of the town in the late 1980s when it allowed a shopping center, the **Promenades de la Cathédrale**, to be built underneath it. Spectacular photos show the house of worship resting on concrete stilts while construction went on underneath.

The interior is sober apart from the pretty stained-glass windows made by William Morris' studios in London. In the rear cloister garden stands a memorial statue to Raoul Wallenberg, the Swedish diplomat who saved 100,000 Jews from the concentration camps in WWII.

MARCHÉ ATWATER MARKET

Map p284 (www.marchespublics-mtl.com; 138 Ave Atwater; ⊙7am-6pm Mon-Wed, to 7pm Thu, to 8pm Fri, to 5pm Sat & Sun; ⓂLionel-Groulx) Just off the Canal de Lachine, this fantastic market has a mouthwatering assortment of fresh produce from local farms, excellent wines, crusty breads, fine cheeses and other delectable fare. The market's specialty shops operate year-round, while outdoor stalls open from March to October. The excellent **Première Moisson** is a popular cafe and bakery. It's all housed in a 1933 brick hall, topped with a clock tower. The grassy banks overlooking the nearby Canal de Lachine make a great spot for a picnic.

MCGILL UNIVERSITY UNIVERSITY

Map p288 (www.mcgill.ca; 845 Rue Sherbrooke Ouest; ⓂMcGill) Founded in 1828 by James McGill, a rich Scottish fur trader, McGill University is one of Canada's most prestigious learning institutions, with 37,000 students. The university's medical and engineering faculties have a fine reputation and many campus buildings are showcases of Victorian architecture. The campus, at the foot of Mont-Royal, is rather nice for a stroll around and also incorporates the Musée Redpath (p81).

SQUARE DORCHESTER SQUARE

Map p288 (ⓂPeel) This leafy expanse in the heart of downtown was known until 1988 as Dominion Sq, a reminder of Canada's founding in 1867. A Catholic cemetery was here until 1870 and bodies still lie beneath the grass. Events of all kinds have taken place here over the years – fashion shows, political rallies and royal visits. The square still exudes the might of the British Empire, with statues of Boer War booster Lord Strathcona, Queen Victoria and poet Robert Burns, plus Wilfrid Laurier, Canada's first francophone prime minister, who faces off a statue of John A Macdonald, the first anglophone prime minister, in Place du Canada across Blvd René-Lévesque Ouest.

The city's main tourist office (p259) lies on the square's northwest side.

GARE WINDSOR HISTORIC BUILDING

Map p288 (1160 de la Gauchetière Ouest; ⓂBonaventure) The massive Victorian building hugging the slope west of the Marriott Château Champlain is the old Windsor Station, opened in 1889 as the headquarters of the Canadian Pacific Railway. The Romanesque structure inspired a château style for train stations across the country; its architect, Bruce Price, would later build the remarkable Château Frontenac (p156) in Québec City.

PLACE DU CANADA PARK

Map p288 (ⓂBonaventure) This park immediately southeast of Sq Dorchester is best known for its monument of John A Macdonald, Canada's first prime minister, who addressed the maiden session of parliament in Montréal. The two cannons around the base were captured in the Crimean War; if you look closely you'll see the dual-headed eagle of Czar Nicholas I. The statue was decapitated by vandals in 1992 and the head vanished for two years.

Le Château

Reid Wilson House

Rue Sherbrooke Ouest

Rue Stanley

Rue Peel

Rue Metcalfe

Brûlerie St Denis

Blvd de Maisonneuve Ouest

Peel

Rue Bishop

Rue Crescent

Rue de la Montagne

Rue Drummond

Pl Mont-Royal

Rue Peel

Rue Ste-Catherine Ouest

DOWNTOWN

Sq Dorchester

Rue Cypress

START

Square Dorchester

0   200 m
0   0.1 miles

DOWNTOWN NEIGHBORHOOD WALK

Neighborhood Walk
Delving into Downtown

Skyscrapers give downtown Montréal a distinctly North American feel, but the area is also dotted with historic buildings. Rue Ste-Catherine and Rue Sherbrooke slice through the area in a blaze of trendy boutiques and department stores, and some are attractions in their own right.

Start at ❶ **Square Dorchester**. The statue on the northeast side represents Lord Strathcona, a philanthropist who sponsored Canada's efforts in the South African Boer War. Wander south to see a statue of Sir Wilfrid Laurier (1841–1919), one of Canada's most respected prime ministers.

Cut over to Rue Metcalfe and walk northwest to the upscale shopping complex ❷ **Les Cours Mont-Royal**. The central atrium features bird sculptures with human heads and a chandelier from a Monte Carlo casino.

Head down Rue Peel and turn right onto Rue Ste-Catherine Ouest; head right again at Rue Drummond, where you'll soon come to the impressive ❸ **Emmanuel Congre-**

gation Church. The highlight here is the peaceful rear garden (turn into the little passageway leading to Rue Stanley).

In the garden, you can refuel at the pleasant Brûlerie St Denis with outdoor tables. Otherwise continue up Rue Stanley to Rue Sherbrooke Ouest. This was Montréal's most prestigious residential street in the early 20th century, and features some glorious old homes, including the ❹ **Mount Royal Club**.

Nearby is another impressive mansion, the Reid Wilson House. Continue along Sherbrooke and you'll soon reach the lavish, recently renovated ❺ **Ritz-Carlton**.

Further along Sherbrooke, you'll pass Le Château, a fortresslike apartment complex with vestiges of shell fossils in the limestone. Directly opposite, the department store with art-deco motifs is ❻ **Holt Renfrew**, an upscale department store with a long history. End your tour with a look at Québec's finest artists at the ❼ **Musée des Beaux-Arts de Montréal**.

THE UNDERGROUND CITY

Brilliant marketing that conjures up images of subterranean skyscrapers and roads has made the underground city one of the first things visitors seek out when they travel to Montréal.

The underground city doesn't actually have any of these things. What it does have is a network of some 2600 shops, 200 restaurants and 40-odd cinemas, theaters and exhibition halls, all hidden neatly beneath the surface in over 30km of tunnels and underground spaces. For most travelers, it's a major letdown, because no matter what tourism officials call it, it is basically just a kind of colossal network of interlocking shopping malls. Where it does get interesting, however, is for residents living in downtown Montréal, as it gives them a reprieve from winter – hundreds of thousands use it every day of the year.

The 60-odd distinct complexes that make up this network are linked by brightly lit, well-ventilated corridors; fountains play to maintain humidity and the temperature hovers around 20°C. Add the metro and you've got a self-contained world, shielded from the subarctic temperatures. If you move to Montréal and pick the right apartment building, it could literally be the middle of winter and you would be able to go to work, do your grocery shopping, go see a movie and take in a performance at Place des Arts and never need more than a T-shirt.

ST PATRICK'S BASILICA   CHURCH

Map p288 (www.stpatricksmtl.ca; 454 Blvd René-Lévesque Ouest; ⊙9am-6pm; MSquare-Victoria) Built for Montréal's booming Irish population in 1847, the interior of St Patrick's Basilica contains huge columns from single pine trunks, an ornate baptismal font and nectar-colored stained-glass windows. The pope raised its status to basilica in 1989, in recognition of its importance to English-speaking Catholics in Montréal. It's a sterling example of French-Gothic style and, as you might expect, is classified a national monument. The Irish-Canadian patriot D'Arcy McGee was buried here after his assassination in 1868; his pew (number 240) is marked with a small Canadian flag.

RUE STE-CATHERINE OUEST   STREET

Map p288 Lively Rue Ste-Catherine Ouest is one endless orgy of shops, restaurants, bars and cafes on the hyperactive stretch between Rue Crescent and Rue St-Urbain. Shopping malls, department stores and multiplex cinemas are sprinkled along the way. Shoppers flood the streets on weekends, slowing pedestrian traffic to a mere shuffle.

CHURCH OF ST JAMES THE APOSTLE   CHURCH

Map p284 (stjamestheapostle.ca; 1439 Rue Ste-Catherine Ouest; ⊙Wed, Sun 8am-5pm; MGuy-Concordia) Built in 1864 on a sports field for the British military, this Anglican church used to be called St Crickets in the Fields

for the matches that unfolded here. The stained glass in the east transept, the Regimental Window, was donated in memory of the WWI fallen. The Writers' Chapel honors Canadian poets and authors such as John Glassco and A.J.M. Smith.

ST JAMES UNITED CHURCH   CHURCH

Map p288 (463 Rue Ste-Catherine Ouest; ⊙11am Sun; MMcGill) The excellent acoustics at St James United are coveted for organ and choir concerts as well as performances at the international jazz festival (p238). The church was originally opened in 1889.

ILLUMINATED CROWD   MONUMENT

Map p288 (1981 Ave McGill College; MMcGill) Constructed of polyester resin, Raymond Mason's sculpture of 65 people is one of Montréal's most photographed pieces of public art. The inscription reads in part: 'A crowd has gathered...the strong light casts shadows, and as light moves toward the back and diminishes, the mood degenerates; hooliganism, disorder and violence occur.'

LE CHÂTEAU   HISTORIC BUILDING

Map p284 (1321 Rue Sherbrooke Ouest; MGuy-Concordia) This fortresslike apartment complex from 1926 was designed by the famed Montréal architects George Ross and Robert MacDonald. The style would do Errol Flynn proud: Scottish and French Renaissance with stone battlements, demons and pavilion roofs. Fossilized shells are visible in the limestone blocks.

MAISON ALCAN
HISTORIC BUILDING

Map p288 (1188 Rue Sherbrooke Ouest; Ⓜ Peel) This mélange of four carefully restored 19th- and 20th-century buildings is not only an architectural wonder, but also the symbolic headquarters of the Alcan aluminum concern. It integrates the old Berkeley Hotel and four houses, including the Atholstan House, a Québec historic monument. To the rear is an intriguing atrium with a pretty garden. Also on the property stands the **Emmanuel Congregation Church**, which belongs to the Salvation Army.

PLACE VILLE-MARIE
NOTABLE BUILDING

Map p288 (www.placevillemarie.com; 1 Pl Ville-Marie; Ⓜ McGill) Known for its rotating rooftop beacon that illuminates downtown at night, the 42-story Pl Ville-Marie tower marked the beginning of Montréal's Underground City five decades ago. Its cruciform shape was chosen to commemorate Maisonneuve's planting of a great cross on Mont-Royal in 1642. Today it houses some 80 restaurants and shops, as well as 10,000 occupants.

EATING

TOP CHOICE JOE BEEF
QUÉBÉCOIS $$$

Map p284 (☑ 514-935-6504; joebeef.ca; ◯ dinner Tue-Sat; 2491 Rue Notre-Dame Ouest; mains $22-35; Ⓜ Lionel-Groulx) In the heart of the Little Burgundy neighborhood, Joe Beef is the current darling of food critics for its unfussy, market-fresh fare. The rustic, country-kitsch setting is a great spot to linger over fresh oysters, tender Wagyu beef, fresh fish and a changing selection of hearty Québécois dishes – all served with a dollop of good humor and a welcome lack of pretension. Try to avoid being seated in the streetside window bays, which have little privacy. In summer, some of the best seats are in the backyard garden. Reserve weeks in advance.

TOP CHOICE QUEUE DE CHEVAL
STEAKHOUSE $$$

Map p284 (☑ 514-390-0090; www.queuedecheval.com; check website for new address; mains $28-46; ◯ lunch Mon-Fri, dinner nightly; Ⓜ Lucien-L'Allier) This mecca of expense-account carnivores serves up delectable prime beef that's dry-aged on the premises. Order from a dozen varieties of mammoth-sized steaks that span filet mignon, T-bone and thick slabs of marbled tenderloin, and then watch as it's char-broiled in the pyrotechnics of the open kitchen. Due to local construction, the Q will move to a new location in the neighborhood for two years from November 2012; check the website. Reserve as early as possible.

BEAVER CLUB
QUÉBÉCOIS $$$

Map p288 (☑ 514-861-3511; www.beaverclub.ca; Fairmont Le Reine Elizabeth, 900 Blvd René-Lévesque Ouest; table d'hôte $69-95; ◯ dinner Thu-Sat; Ⓜ Bonaventure) The original Beaver Club was formed in 1785 by a group of Montréal fur barons, and to join you had to have wintered in the Northwest Territories. Membership is still elite – ask to see the pic of Bill Gates in trapper's furs – but anyone with the right currency can reserve in the impeccably serviced, old-fashioned dining room to enjoy a cross-section of Canadian luxury edibles. The *menu découverte* is a multicourse meal highlighting Québec produce like Îles de la Madeleine scallops, Marieville foie gras and Île d'Orléans raspberries. Reservations and proper attire are essential.

KAZU
JAPANESE $

Map p278/ (1862 Rue Ste-Catherine Ouest; mains $10-15; ◯ lunch & dinner Sun-Fri, dinner Sat; Ⓜ Guy-Concordia) Kazuo Akutsu's frenetic hole in the wall in the Concordia Chinatown has a thrown-together air, and isn't quite an authentic *izakaya* (Japanese pub) as some claim, but the long lines of people waiting for *gyoza* (dumplings), ramen noodle soup and awesome creations such as the 48-hour pork attest to its popularity. If you don't mind a wait, a cramped table and sometimes slow service, your taste buds will love you for a long time.

CUISINE SZECHUAN
CHINESE $

Map p284 (2350 Rue Guy; mains $6-12; ◯ 10am-10pm Mon & Wed-Fri, from 5pm Tue, noon-10pm Sat & Sun; Ⓜ Guy-Concordia) One of the best-kept secrets of the Concordia Chinatown, this humble hillside eatery serves up spicily authentic Szechuan fare. Favorites include the delectable cumin beef, and the ever-popular poached fish and twice-cooked fish. You can't go wrong with the tofu braised in hot sauce, either. Just tell the staff if you want your food on the mild side.

IMADAKE   JAPANESE $
Map p284 (☎514-931-8833; www.imadake.ca; 4006 Rue Ste-Catherine Ouest; mains $6-15; ☺lunch Mon-Thu, dinner nightly; ⓂAtwater) Also on the fringes of the Concordia Chinatown, Imadake is the closest thing to an authentic *izakaya* in the city. Staff scream *irrashaimase!* (welcome!) when you walk in, and there's an excellent assortment of *izakaya* standbys like *tsukune* (chicken meatballs), *takoyaki* (grilled octopus) and *yakiika* (grilled cuttlefish). The ramen noodles are excellent. The sake selection is decent too, but avoid the Gekkeikan plonk. Students crank up the volume here on weekend nights.

THALI   INDIAN $
Map p284 (thalimontreal.com; 1409 Rue St-Marc; mains $5-16; ☺11:30am-10pm Mon-Thu, to 11pm Fri, 1pm-11pm Sat, 4pm-10pm Sun; ⓂGuy-Concordia) Another budget gem in the Concordia Chinatown, Thali offers quick plates of delish Indian fare, from $8.50 curry plates to half-tandoori chicken plates for $9. The naan bread, butter chicken and lamb kebab are particularly delectable.

FERREIRA CAFÉ   PORTUGUESE $$$
Map p288 (☎514-848-0988; www.ferreiracafe. com; 1446 Rue Peel; mains $29-46; ☺lunch Mon-Fri, dinner nightly; ⓂPeel) This warm and inviting restaurant serves some of Montréal's best Portuguese fare. The *cataplana* (a bouillabaisse-style seafood stew) is magnificent, tender morsels of grilled fish comes to the table cooked to perfection, while meatlovers can feast on rack of lamb or spice-rubbed Angus rib-eye steak. There's an extensive wine list and a lively atmosphere.

LIVERPOOL HOUSE   QUÉBÉCOIS $$
Map p284 (☎514-313-6049; joebeef.ca; ☺dinner Tue-Sat; 2501 Rue Notre-Dame Ouest; mains $18-26; ⓂLionel-Groulx) Run by the same anti-establishment chefs that launched Joe Beef next door, this charming little eatery serves an ever-changing menu of fresh-from-the-market fare.

FURUSATO   JAPANESE $$
Map p288 (☎514-849-3438; 2137 Rue de Bleury; mains $16-30; ☺dinner, Mon-Sat; ⓂPlace-des-Arts) Once known as Osaka, this humble eatery presents some of the most authentic Japanese in town. Ultrafresh sushi, decent sake, shrimp and vegetable tempura, sukiyaki, and grilled horse mackerel *(hokke)* are some of the stars of the menu, along with black sesame ice cream for dessert. Reservations recommended.

BOUSTAN   LEBANESE $
Map p284 (2020 Rue Crescent; mains $5-10; ☺11am-4am; ⓂGuy-Concordia) This friendly little Lebanese joint scores high in popularity on the city's *shwarma* circuit because of its delicious toasted pita sandwiches. Its late hours make it a favorite with pub crawlers in need of sustenance between bars. Can't-go-wrong picks include baba ghanoush, hummus, falafel, stuffed grape leaves with yogurt, and tabbouleh salad with warm pita.

RESTAURANT GLOBE   FRENCH, INTERNATIONAL $$$
Map p278 (☎514-284-3823; www.restaurant globe.com; 3455 Blvd St-Laurent; mains $25-45; ☺dinner; ⓂSt-Laurent, then bus 55) This stylish see-and-be-seen place features an imaginative menu combining high- and lowbrow ingredients to create a decadent kind of comfort food.

LA GARGOTE DES ANTIQUAIRES   FRENCH $$
Map p284 (1708 Rue Notre-Dame Ouest; mains $14-22; ☺11am-8pm Mon-Wed, to 9pm Thu-Sat; ⓂLucien-L'Allier) In the heart of Montréal's antique district, this warm but decidedly unpretentious bistro prepares tasty galettes, chalkboard specials and flavorful desserts (sweet crepes). In addition to the antique-filled dining room, there's a plant-filled outdoor terrace for soaking up this peaceful little stretch of Rue Notre-Dame.

CAFÉ MÉLIÈS   FRENCH $$
Map p288 (☎514-847-9218; www.cafemelies. com; 3536 Blvd St-Laurent; mains $18-27; ☺lunch & dinner daily, brunch Sat & Sun; ⓂSt-Laurent, then bus 55) This chic, modern restaurant and wine bar located in the Excentris cinema and multimedia complex is tailormade for Montréal's flashy showbiz types. The brunch is particularly upscale and popular. At night, movie-goers and politicians rub shoulders over plates of marinated salmon or roasted scallops.

LE TAJ   INDIAN $$
Map p288 (☎514-845-9015; www.restaurantletaj. com; 2077 Rue Stanley; mains $15-22; ☺lunch & dinner Sun-Fri, dinner Sat; ⓂPeel) Proving

that Montréal is more than just a bistro and brasserie kind of town, Le Taj throws down the gauntlet for some excellent Indian dishes. The time to go is at lunch, when downtowners line up for a succulent buffet featuring a bounty of rich flavors from the East – tandoori chicken, vegetable korma, palaak paneer and tender lamb, along with steaming piles of naan bread, custardlike desserts and many other temptations.

BISTRO ISAKAYA
JAPANESE $$

Map p288 (☑514-845-8226; www.bistroisakaya.com; 3469 Ave du Parc; mains $14-23; ☺lunch Tue-Fri, dinner Tue-Sun, 5:30-9pm Sun; ⓂPlacedes-Arts, then bus 80 or 129) This authentic, unpretentious Japanese restaurant has fairly simple decor but the fish is incredibly fresh. The owner, Shige Minagawa, is known for handpicking his seafood and preparing it in classic Japanese fashion. Daily specials such as lobster sashimi, tuna belly or yellowtail are listed on the chalkboard by the kitchen. Reservations are essential.

PHAYATHAI
THAI $$

Map p284 (☑514-933-9949; 1235 Rue Guy; mains $12-18; ☺lunch Tue-Fri, dinner nightly; ⓂGuy-Concordia) Just off the beaten track, this casual little Thai restaurant serves good, fresh-tasting curries, satisfying duck and seafood plates and plenty of other delicacies from the East. The lunchtime and after-work crowds can be thick, so try to avoid arriving at prime time.

MANGO BAY
CARIBBEAN $$

Map p284 (☑514-875-7082; www.mangobay.ca; 1202 Rue Bishop; mains $13-18; ☺11:30am-10pm Sun-Thu, to midnight Fri & Sat; ⓂGuy-Concordia) Situated in a converted Victorian house with pretty stained-glass windows, Mango Bay serves up authentic chicken jerky or stew, curried goat or island chicken fajitas with a terrific side order of plantain. Watch out for the incendiary hot sauces, and be sure to save room for a slice of the signature mango cheesecake or rum cake.

LOLA ROSA
VEGETARIAN $$

Map p288 (545 Rue Milton; mains $12-24; ☺11:30am-9:30pm; ⓂMcGill) On a leafy street near McGill, students, profs and the odd neighborhood regular not associated with the university flock to this charming and low-key vegetarian cafe. A chalkboard menu lists the day's offerings: couscous with fresh vegetables, walnuts and goat cheese, rich tempeh-based stews and bountiful salads with juicy tomatoes and crisp rocket. Fresh juices, desserts and decent coffee complete the picture. Lola Rosa also hosts a popular weekend brunch.

M:BRGR
BURGERS $$

Map p288 (www.mbrgr.com; 2025 Rue Drummond; mains $10-20; ☺11:30am-11pm Mon-Sat, noon-9pm Sun; ⓂPeel) Bringing a gourmet touch to the humble hamburger, this stylish place serves juicy patties that can be dressed with smoked gouda, apple-smoked bacon and other high-end toppings. You can opt for organic, grass-fed beef or even Kobe beef. To complete, add in sweet potato fries and a thick milkshake – or better yet, a cocktail.

REUBEN'S
DELI $

Map p288 (888 Rue Ste-Catherine Ouest; mains $9-18; ☺6:30am-midnight Mon-Wed, to 1:30am Thu & Fri, 8am-1:30am Sat, 8am-midnight Sun; ⓂPeel) Another favorite deli in downtown, Reuben's has squishy booths and a long counter, where patrons line up for towering smoked-meat sandwiches served with big-cut fries. Burgers, smoked pork chops and other old-school favorites round out the menu. Try to avoid the busy lunch rush.

DUNN'S
DELI $

Map p288 (www.dunnsfamous.com; 1249 Rue Metcalfe; mains $6-16; ☺24hr; ⓂMcGill) One of Montréal's oldest smoked-meat institutions, with satisfying sandwiches slapped down on wax paper and served in baskets piled with fries. In addition to classics (like the smoked-meat club sandwich with Swiss cheese and bacon), you'll find burgers, char-grilled steaks, and bagels with lox and cream cheese.

LE FAUBOURG
FOOD COURT

Map p284 (1606 Rue Ste-Catherine Ouest; ☺7:30am-9pm; ⓂGuy-Concordia) Among the smorgasbord of international cuisines in this upstairs food court is the excellent Grumman 78 (tacos $4-7; ☺11:30am-8pm Tue-Sat), the offshoot of a successful food truck that plies festivals in the city. Choose from quirky tacos like the Banh Mi (roasted pork belly with sweet Vietnamese oyster sauce) or Cari d'Agneau (a curry-braised lamb). Drinks come in plastic bags. To find the taco truck, check its Twitter stream: @grumman78.

GUYLAIN DOYLE / GETTY IMAGES ©

1. Marché Atwater (p82)
On the banks of the Canal de Lachine, this market is famed for its fresh produce, plus top-class wine, bread and cheese.

2. Rue Sherbrooke (p82)
Heritage mansions line this prestigious street, along with museums, churches and McGill University.

3. Centre Canadien d'Architecture (p81)
Galleries here focus on remarkable architectural works, with a focus on urban design.

4. Musée des Beaux-Arts de Montréal (p80)
Canada's oldest museum, with works from Old Masters to contemporary artists.

🍸 DRINKING & NIGHTLIFE

DOMINION SQUARE TAVERN TAVERN
Map p288 (www.dominiontavern.com; 1245 Rue Metcalfe; ⊙11:30am-midnight Mon-Fri, 4:30pm-midnight Sat & Sun; ⓂPeel) Once a down-and-out watering hole dating from the 1920s, this beautifully renovated tavern recalls a classic French bistro but with a long bar, English pub-style. Executive chef Éric Dupuis puts his own spin on pub grub, with mussels cooked with bacon and pig's head terrine ploughman's lunch.

BURGUNDY LION PUB
Map p284 (www.burgundylion.com; 2496 Rue de Notre-Dame Ouest; ⊙11:30am-3am Mon-Sat, 9am-3am Sun; ⓂLionel-Groulx) This trendy take on the English pub features British pub fare, beers and whiskies galore, and an attitude-free vibe where everyone (and their parents) feels welcome to drink, eat and be merry. Things get the good kind of crazy late-night weekends. Tip your cap to Queen Elizabeth, whose portrait adorns the bathroom door.

MCKIBBIN'S PUB
Map p284 (www.mckibbinsirishpub.com; 1426 Rue Bishop; ⊙11:30am-3am; ⓂGuy-Concordia) With its garage-sale furniture, McKibbin's cultivates a familiar, down-at-heel pub atmosphere. Its live entertainment varies from Celtic and pop to punk music. The office crowd pops in at lunchtime for burgers, chicken wings and salads.

NYKS PUB
Map p288 (www.nyks.ca; 1250 Rue de Bleury; ⊙11am-3am Mon-Fri, 4pm-3am Sat; ⓂPlace-des-Arts) Its artsy-chic vibe makes this warm bistro pub the preferred lunch and after-work spot of Plateau cool kids who happen to work in downtown offices. Daily happy hours and pub finger-foods are a joy to downtowners seeking an authentic experience. Sometimes it even has live jazz.

PIKOLO ESPRESSO BAR CAFE
Map p288 (3418b Ave du Parc; ⊙7am-7pm Mon-Fri, 9am-7pm Sat & Sun; ⓂPlace-des-Arts; 🛜) Plateau hipsters roll up to this friendly split-level joint nestled in a heritage building at the bottom of Ave du Parc for its yummy baked goods and the signature drink, the Pikolo. It's a *ristretto* shot of espresso that goes down very smoothly indeed.

UPSTAIRS JAZZ
Map p284 (www.upstairsjazz.com; 1254 Rue Mackay; admission $5-30; ⊙5:30pm-2am, music from 8:30pm; ⓂGuy-Concordia) This slick downtown bar hosts quality jazz and blues acts nightly, featuring both local and touring talent. The walled terrace behind the bar is enchanting at sunset, and the dinner menu features inventive salads and meals like the Cajun bacon burger.

BRUTOPIA PUB
Map p284 (www.brutopia.net; 1219 Rue Crescent; ⊙3:30pm-3am Sun-Fri, noon-3am Sat; ⓂGuy-Concordia) This fantastic brewpub has eight varieties of suds on tap, including honey beer, nut brown and the more challenging raspberry blonde. The brick walls and wood paneling are conducive to chats among the relaxed student crowd. Live blues bands play some evenings. It really picks up after the night classes from nearby Concordia get out.

HURLEY'S IRISH PUB PUB
Map p284 (www.hurleysirishpub.com; 1125 Rue Crescent; ⊙11am-3am; ⓂGuy-Concordia) This cozy place features live rock and fiddling Celtic folk on the rear stage and beer-soaked football and soccer matches on big-screen TVs. Standard pub grub – fish 'n' chips, meat pies and burgers – is also served.

PULLMAN BAR
Map p288 (http://pullman-mtl.com; 3424 Ave du Parc; ⊙4:30pm-1am; ⓂPlace-des-Arts) This beautifully designed wine bar is a favorite haunt of the 30-something set. It's primarily a restaurant, but the downstairs bar of this two-level space gets jammed (or *jammé,* as they say in Franglais) after work and becomes quite a pickup spot, so be prepared to engage in some flirting. Sommeliers can help you choose from the sprawling wine list.

LE VIEUX DUBLIN PUB & RESTAURANT PUB
Map p288 (http://dublinpub.ca; 1219a Rue University; ⊙noon-3am Mon-Sat, 5pm-3am Sun; ⓂMcGill) The city's oldest Irish pub has the expected great selection of brews (about $6 per pint) and live Celtic or pop music nightly. Curries rub shoulders with burgers on the menu. Fifty single-malts.

PUB STE-ÉLISABETH PUB
Map p288 (www.ste-elisabeth.com; 1412 Rue Ste-Élisabeth; ⊙3pm-3am; ⓂBerri-UQAM) Tucked off a side street, this awesome little pub is

MONTRÉAL BY BIXI

Montréal is one of the most bike-friendly cities in North America, with hundreds of kilometers of bicycle paths across the city. In 2009 the city unveiled **Bixi** (http://montreal.bixi.com), an extensive network of bike-renting stations around town, with bikes available from April to November. For short jaunts, it's great value (24-hour/72-hour subscription fee is $7/15; bikes are free the first half-hour and $1.75 for the next half-hour). The network includes more than 5000 bikes scattered around 400 stations. Bixi has since inspired bike rental system in other cities, including London and Washington DC.

Checking out a bike from a stand is easy. Just insert a credit card and follow the instructions. The majority of Bixi stands display a network map showing other docking stations across the city. Once you dock the bike, you must wait two minutes before checking out another one. Just reinsert your credit card and go. (Bixi tallies up the charges at the end of a 24-hour period. As long as you always return a bike within 30 minutes, you'll only be charged the one-time fare.) Although the bikes are fine for short hops, the pricing structure discourages longer trips (it costs $1.75 for the second 30 minutes, $3.50 for the next 30 minutes and $7 for every 30 minutes thereafter). If you're planning a long day's outing along the Canal de Lachine, it's better to rent from a bike shop.

frequented by many for its heavenly vine-covered courtyard and drink menu that includes beers galore, whiskies and ports. It has a mind-whirling repertoire of beers on tap, including imports and rarely found microbrewery fare like Boréale Noire and Cidre Mystique.

SIR WINSTON CHURCHILL PUB
Map p284 (www.winniesbar.com; 1459 Rue Crescent; ⊙11:30am-3am; MGuy-Concordia) This Rue Crescent staple is the go-to spot of the block. Winnie's cavernous, split-level pub draws a steady crowd of tourists and students and an older Anglo crowd. In fact, the late, great author Mordecai Richler used to knock back cold ones in the bar upstairs. Among multiple bars, pool tables and pulsating music, meals are served all day and happy-hour drink specials abound.

ZIGGY'S PUB
Map p284 (www.ziggyspub.ca; 1470 Rue Crescent; ⊙1pm-3am; MGuy-Concordia) Walking into this European-style pub and sports bar, you'd never guess it was once the watering hole of some of Montréal's most infamous writers and journalists (for example, the boisterous, late newspaper columnist Nick Auf der Maur practically lived here). These days Ziggy's features imported draft beer, several televisions and celebrity memorabilia, including a hockey jersey autographed by Habs hero Maurice 'The Rocket' Richard.

ELECTRIC AVENUE CLUB
Map p284 (www.clubsmontreal.com; 1469 Rue Crescent; ⊙10pm-3am Thu-Sat; MGuy-Concordia) Duran Duran, INXS, Depeche Mode...the spirit of '80s video pop lives on in this basement club in party-down Rue Crescent. A few mirrors and lamps on satin-covered walls make up the decor, but no matter: from around 11pm on weekends you'll find the dance floor is packed with nostalgic 30-somethings.

☆ ENTERTAINMENT

PLACE DES ARTS PERFORMING ARTS
Map p288 (⊘box office 514-842-2112; www.pdarts.com; 175 Rue Ste-Catherine Ouest; MPlace-des-Arts) Montréal's premier music venue, the storied Place des Arts is at the heart of the growing Quartier des Spectacles. For details, see p81.

L'ASTRAL LIVE MUSIC
Map p288 (⊘514-288-8882; www.sallelastral.com; 305 Rue Ste-Catherine Ouest; MPlace-des-Arts) Recent renovations to the century-old Blumenthal Building have added another venue to Montréal's jazzfest as part of the Quartier des Spectacles. With over 300 seats and standing room for 600, L'Astral nestles in the Maison du Festival Rio Tinto Alcan, which also houses **Le Balmoral**, a jazz club and bistro with a patio on the ground floor.

MONUMENT NATIONAL

PERFORMING ARTS

Map p288 (☎514-871-2224; www.monumentnational.com; 1182 Blvd St-Laurent; Ⓜ St-Laurent) Shows here run the gamut from Oscar Wilde to Sam Shepard, with acting, directing and technical production performed by graduating students of the National Theatre School. There are two halls, one with 800 seats, the other with 150. The smaller theater stages about three original works a year by student playwrights.

THÉÂTRE DU NOUVEAU MONDE

THEATER

Map p288 (☎514-866-8668; www.tnm.qc.ca, in French; 84 Rue Ste-Catherine Ouest; Ⓜ St-Laurent) The New World Theater specializes in classic dramas like Shakespeare's *Hamlet* or Molière's *Les Précieuses Ridicules*. The French-language venue is a 1912 movie house and theater renovated in 1996, now with snappy technical gear. There are matinee and evening performances.

ORCHESTRE SYMPHONIQUE DE MONTRÉAL

CLASSICAL MUSIC

Map p288 (www.osm.ca; Place des Arts, 260 Blvd de Maisonneuve Ouest; Ⓜ Place-des-Arts) This internationally renowned orchestra plays to packed audiences in its Place des Arts base, now home to the new **Maison Symphonique de Montréal**, an acoustically amazing venue inaugurated in 2011. The OSM's Christmas performance of *The Nutcracker* is legendary. Rock-star conductor Kent Nagano, a Californian with a leonine mane and stellar credentials, took over as music director in 2006 and has proven very popular. Check for free concerts at the Basilique Notre-Dame (p52), the Olympic Stadium (p145) and in municipal parks in the Montréal area.

CINÉMA EXCENTRIS

CINEMA

Map p288 (cinemaexcentris.com; 3536 Blvd St-Laurent; tickets $11; Ⓜ St-Laurent) A showcase for independent films from around the world. It's sleek and geared to provide pure movie enjoyment (popcorn and soft drinks are banned, for example, because they distract from the movie-watching experience). Besides several cinemas, this place is full of high-tech film gadgetry you have to see to believe, starting with the box-office cashier whose disembodied head speaks to you through electronic portholes when you buy your tickets.

LE NOUVEAU CINÉMA DU PARC

CINEMA

Map p288 (www.cinemaduparc.com; 3575 Ave du Parc; tickets $11.50; Ⓜ Place-des-Arts, then bus 80) Located in the lower level of La Cité mall complex, Montréal's English-language repertory cinema is a tried-and-true favorite of Plateau cinephiles. It shows cult classics as well as cool new releases and lots of foreign films. Despite the shabby decor, its charm and authenticity add to the cinematic experience.

CINÉMA BANQUE SCOTIA MONTRÉAL

CINEMA

Map p288 (www.paramountmontreal.com; 977 Rue Ste-Catherine Ouest; Ⓜ Peel) This entertainment monstrosity features crowds darting through junk-food kiosks amid a riot of flashing lights and booming sounds to get to the IMAX megascreens. There are also screens showing Hollywood blockbusters in this multilevel cinema.

CLUB SODA

LIVE MUSIC

Map p288 (www.clubsoda.ca; 1225 Blvd St-Laurent; adult/student $5/3; ☺9pm-3am; Ⓜ St-Laurent) This venerable club hosts some of the city's coolest concerts as well as offbeat performances of all musical genres, such as tributes to The Doors and Italian metal bands. Check the website for the concert schedule.

HOUSE OF JAZZ

JAZZ

Map p288 (☎514-842-8656; www.houseofjazz.ca; 2060 Rue Aylmer; ☺6pm-11:30pm Mon, 11:30am-11:30pm Tue-Thu, 11:30am-2am Fri, 6pm-2:30am Sat, 6pm-11:30pm Sun; Ⓜ McGill) Formerly known as Biddle's, this mainstream-but-excellent jazz club and restaurant changed names when owner-bassist Charlie Biddle passed away in 2003. Today, Southern-style cuisine and live jazz are on the menu daily. Prepare to wait if you haven't reserved. Cover is $5 to $10.

METROPOLIS

LIVE MUSIC

Map p288 (www.metropolismontreal.ca; 59 Rue Ste-Catherine Est; Ⓜ St-Laurent) Housed in a former art-deco cinema, this beautiful old space (capacity 2300) has featured everyone from David Bowie to Green Day to local favorite Jean Leloup. It's sometimes used as a party or rave venue with DJs and dancing. Buy tickets at the **box office** (1413 Rue St-Dominique) around the corner.

POLLACK CONCERT HALL
CLASSICAL MUSIC

Map p288 (www.mcgill.ca; 555 Rue Sherbrooke Ouest; MMcGill) McGill University's main music hall features concerts and recitals from its students and faculty, notably the **McGill Chamber Orchestra**. It's in the stately 19th-century building behind the statue of Queen Victoria.

SAT
ARTS CENTER

Map p288 (mixsessions.sat.qc.ca; 1195 Blvd St-Laurent; MSt-Laurent) Officially called La Société des Arts Technologiques, this slick warehouse and new-media space holds the occasional DJ event. DJs and performance artists push the envelope with banks of multimedia installations, while cult brands like NEON throw parties here. Dancing and carousing with the arty, electro-loving glam set.

I MUSICI DE MONTRÉAL
CLASSICAL MUSIC

Map p288 (http://imusici.com; 279 Rue Sherbrooke Ouest; MPlace-des-Arts) Under the leadership of Jean-Marie Zeitouni, this 12-member chamber ensemble has won many awards for its baroque and contemporary performances. Over the past 20 years I Musici, which has its home stage at the Place des Arts, has recorded more than 30 CDs and toured the world.

OPÉRA DE MONTRÉAL
OPERA

Map p288 (www.operademontreal.com; Place des Arts; box office 9am-5pm Mon-Fri; MPlace-des-Arts) Holds lavish stage productions that feature big names from Québec and around the world. The specialty is classics such as *Mefistofele, Aïda* and *Carmen;* translations (French or English) are run on a video screen above the stage. Tickets cost around $40 to $125 during the week and slightly more on Saturday.

ORCHESTRE MÉTROPOLITAIN
CLASSICAL MUSIC

Map p288 (www.orchestremetropolitain.com; 486 Rue Ste-Catherine Ouest; MPlace-des-Arts) This hip 58-member orchestra is made up of young professional musicians from all over Québec, and led by conductor Yannick Nézet-Séguin. The orchestra's mission is to democratize classical music, so besides the swish Place des Arts, you may see it playing Mahler or Haydn in churches or colleges in even the city's poorest neighborhoods for reduced admission.

SALSATHÈQUE
DANCE

Map p288 (www.salsatheque.ca; 1220 Rue Peel; Thu-Sun; MPeel) This bright, busy, dressy place presents large live Latin bands pumping out tropical rhythms. During the breaks slurp a margarita in one of the cinema seats and watch the 25-to-50s crowd gyrate into exhaustion.

SHARX
BILLIARDS

Map p288 (www.sharx.ca; 1606 Rue Ste-Catherine Ouest; 11am-3am; MGuy-Concordia) This underground cavern has no fewer than 20 pool and billiard tables, rows of TV screens beaming sports, golf simulators and a post-apocalyptic feel. The cool bowling alley is bathed in fluorescent light with glowing balls and pins.

COMEDYWORKS
COMEDY

Map p284 (514-398-9661; www.comedyworks montreal.com; 1238 Rue Bishop; 8pm-3am Mon-Sat; MGuy-Concordia) This intimate comedy club has been around forever and is a fun place to catch emerging and established comedy talent. Mondays are open mic, while on Wednesdays noted improv troupe On the Spot Players takes the stage. Reservations required.

FOUFOUNES ELECTRIQUES
PUNK

Map p288 (www.foufounes.qc.ca; 87 Rue Ste-Catherine Est; 3pm-3am; MSt-Laurent) A one-time bastion of the alternafreak, this cavernous quintessential punk venue still stages some neat events (eg a DJ 'starmaker' night or indoor skateboard contest). On weekends the student-grunge crowd plays pool and quaffs brews with electro kids and punk stragglers.

🛍 SHOPPING

HOLT RENFREW
DEPARTMENT STORE

Map p284 (www.holtrenfrew.com; 1300 Rue Sherbrooke Ouest; MPeel) This Montréal institution is a godsend for label-conscious, cashed-up professionals and upscale shoppers. From fragrance to cosmetics, jewelry and men's and women's fashion, 'Holt's' is the go-to spot for prestigious brands like Gucci and Prada. Services include personal shoppers and concierges, and the excellent **Holts Café**.

WORTH A DETOUR

WANDERING IN WESTMOUNT

Though short on traditional sights, the leafy, upper-class neighborhood of Westmount makes for a good afternoon stroll. Here you'll find a mix of sleepy backstreets set with Victorian mansions and manicured parks (parts of the city were named a national historic site in 2012), while the main boulevard, Rue Sherbrooke Ouest, has high-end boutiques, cafes and bistros. Wander about and grab a bite while you're there.

The town's highlight is **Westmount Park & Library** (4575 Rue Sherbrooke Ouest; ⊙10am-9pm Mon-Fri, to 5pm Sat & Sun; MAtwater; ⊗). The lovely Westmount Park encompasses pathways, streams and concealed nooks that recall the whimsical nature of English public gardens. The Westmount Public Library, built in 1899, stands stolid, with its Romanesque brickwork, leaded glass and delightful bas-reliefs dedicated to wisdom. The attached **Westmount Conservatory** is a gorgeous 1927 greenhouse where time stands still among the orchids.

Walking northwest from Westmount Park, you'll pass increasingly large and expensive homes as you climb to **Summit Woods and Summit Lookout**, a 57-acre forest and bird sanctuary atop the hill of Westmount with a belvedere commanding views of the St Lawrence River. Following Summit Circle road and Chemin Belvedere, you can soon walk to Parc du Mont-Royal (p113) and Cimetière Notre-Dame-des-Neiges (p115).

Back down along Rue Sherbrooke Ouest, the faux medieval towers of **Westmount City Hall** (4333 Côte St-Antoine; ⊙8:30am-4:30pm Mon-Fri; ⊙Atwater) come as a surprise after the skyscrapers of downtown. This Tudor gatehouse in rough-hewn stone looks like something from an English period drama. A lawn-bowling green lies in the rear.

For a bite to eat, sidewalk cafes and window-shopping, take a stroll along the pedestrian-friendly **Avenue Greene** to the northeast of Westmount City Hall. **Westmount Square** (Map p284; cnr Ave Greene & Blvd de Maisonneuve Ouest; MAtwater) is a chic 1966 mall by architect Ludwig Mies van der Rohe.

For bagels and sandwiches that can compete with Montréal's best, try nearby **Bagels on Greene** (Map p284; www.bagelsongreene.com; 4160 Rue Ste-Catherine Ouest; ⊙6:30am-7pm Mon-Wed & Sat, to 9pm Thu & Fri, to 6pm Sun; MAtwater). If you prefer something sweeter, there's also **Calories** (Map p284; www.caloriescafe.ca; 4114 Rue Ste-Catherine Ouest; ⊙10am-10pm Mon-Thu, to 11pm Fri, 1pm-12am Sat, to 10pm Sun; MAtwater; ⊗), which has slices of heaven such as carrot caramel cheesecake for $6.

GALERIES D'ART CONTEMPORAIN DU BELGO   ARTS & CRAFTS
Map p288 (www.thebelgoreport.com; 372 Rue Ste-Catherine Ouest; ⊙varies; MPlace-des-Arts) Over a decade ago the Belgo building was a run-down haven for struggling artists. It quickly earned a reputation as one of Montréal's most important exhibition spaces with galleries, dance, yoga and photography studios. Designers, art dealers and architects now make up three-quarters of the tenancy.

LES COURS MONT-ROYAL   MALL
Map p288 (www.lcmr.ca; 1455 Rue Peel; ⊙varies; MPeel) This elegant shopping mall is a reincarnation of the Mount Royal Hotel (1922), at the time the largest hotel in the British Empire. The 1000-room hotel was converted into a snazzy mix of condos and fashion boutiques in 1988. Under the skylight you'll see six birdman sculptures by Inuit artist David Pioukuni. The spectacular chandelier is from Monte Carlo's old casino. You'll find designer names like Armani, Michael Kors, and Versace among the boutiques here.

HUDSON BAY CO   DEPARTMENT STORE
Map p288 (www.thebay.com; 585 Rue Ste-Catherine Ouest; MMcGill) *La Baie*, as it is called in French, found fame three centuries ago for its striped wool blankets used to measure fur skins. The unique blankets are still available, in wool and fleece, on the ground floor. Take the escalators to the clothing boutiques on the 2nd floor, or make a strategic move for the cut-price garments on the 8th floor.

OGILVY
DEPARTMENT STORE

Map p284 (www.ogilvycanada.com; 1307 Rue Ste-Catherine Ouest; MPeel) Founded in 1866 as Canada's first department store, Ogilvy has transformed itself into a collection of high-profile boutiques. When it was remodeled in the late 1920s the owner had a concert hall built on the 5th floor called 'The Tudor' that's still open for viewing; there's an interesting mini-museum outside it. Ogilvy's front window displays mechanical toys that are a Montréal fixture at Christmas. At the time we went to press, renovations were expected to add a condo complex to the building, but it should remain open.

BOUTIQUE EVA B
FASHION, VINTAGE

Map p288 (www.eva-b.ca; 2013 Blvd St-Laurent; 10am-10pm Mon-Sat, noon-8pm Sun; MSt-Laurent) In a space reminiscent of a theater's backstage, this boutique is a riot of recycled women's clothing, retro gear and new streetwear. It's the kind of place where 1950s bowling shoes are proudly arranged beneath a flock of floaty feather boas and yet it all seems very normal.

LUCIE FAVREAU ANTIQUES
ANTIQUES

Map p284 (514-989-5117; www.favreauan tiques.com; 1904 Rue Notre-Dame Ouest; by appointment; MGeorges-Vanier) This colorful, museumlike store is brimming with giggle-inducing housewares, advertising plaques, toys and sports memorabilia like signed baseballs, among other collectibles.

LES ANTIQUITÉS GRAND CENTRAL
ANTIQUES

Map p284 (www.grandcentralinc.ca; 2448 Rue Notre-Dame Ouest; 9am-5:40pm Mon-Sat; MLionel-Groulx) The most elegant store on Rue Notre-Dame's Antique Row is a pleasure to visit for its English and continental furniture, lighting and decorative objects from the 18th and 19th centuries. Get buzzed in to see the Louis XIV chairs, full dining-room suites and chandeliers in Dutch cathedral or French Empire style, with price tags in the thousands.

PARISIAN LAUNDRY
ARTS & CRAFTS

Map p284 (www.parisianlaundry.com; 3550 Rue St-Antoine Ouest; noon-5pm Tue-Sat; MLionel-Groulx) A former industrial laundry turned monster gallery, this space is worth a trip for the old building itself even if you're not a fan of contemporary art. Recent exhibitions have included works by New York conceptual artist Adam Pendleton and Québec sculptor Valérie Blass. The basement bunker gallery is otherworldly.

ROOTS
FASHION

Map p288 (canada.roots.com; 1035 Rue Ste-Catherine Ouest; MPeel) Its reputation is now soooo big worldwide that customers may forget Canada's own Roots started off as a humble shoemaker in the '70s. Now its range includes Roots for kids, Roots athletics, leather and home accessories. Tastes are easily accessible and geared to teens and 20-somethings, fashionable and at times even innovative.

RENAUD BRAY
BOOKS, MUSIC

Map p288 (www.renaud-bray.com; 1 Place Ville-Marie; 8am-6pm Mon-Wed, to 9pm Thu-Fri, 9:30-5pm Sat, 12-5pm Sun; MMcGill) One of 11 branches in greater Montréal, this bright and cheery bookstore specializes in French titles but has token offerings of English novels. A small section of the store is dedicated to music CDs in both languages.

BIRKS JEWELLERS
JEWELRY

Map p288 (www.birks.com; 1240 Square Phillips; MMcGill) For more than a century this upscale vendor of baubles and bangles has been Montréal's answer to Tiffany's of New York. Henry Birks opened his first store in 1879 and expanded throughout Canada. By 1936 the store won the right to supply the British royal family. Just the coffered ceiling in Wedgwood blue warrants a visit to the sales floor.

CENTRE EATON
MALL

Map p288 (www.centreeatondemontreal.com; 705 Rue Ste-Catherine Ouest; MMcGill) This five-story retailing palace on the main shopping drag is home to over 100 restaurants and shops including The Body Shop and Tristan. The **Promenade de la Cathédrale** is an underground passage of the complex that runs beneath the Christ Church Cathedral.

PLACE MONTRÉAL TRUST
MALL

Map p288 (www.placemontrealtrust.com; 1500 Ave McGill College; MPeel) One of downtown's most successful malls, with enough rays from the skylights to keep shoppers on their day clock. Major retailers here include La Senza lingerie, Indigo books, Mexx, Winners and Zara. It has a tremendous water fountain with a spout 30m high, and

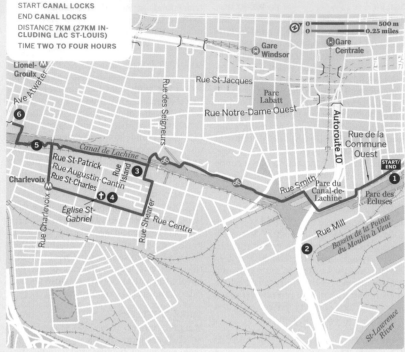

START **CANAL LOCKS**
END **CANAL LOCKS**
DISTANCE **7KM (27KM IN-CLUDING LAC ST-LOUIS)**
TIME **TWO TO FOUR HOURS**

Neighborhood Walk

Cycling the Canal de Lachine

The prettiest cycle path in Montréal stretches along the Canal de Lachine and has easy access from downtown and the Old Port. Warm days draw everyone outdoors: sunbathers flop on the grass, families lunch at picnic tables, while cyclists and in-line skaters glide along the path. For info on bicycle hire and Bixi bikes, see p91.

Start at the **1 Canal locks** at the southwestern end of the Old Port. This area has an industrial feel thanks to the abandoned grain silo just to the southeast of the locks.

Pedaling southwest along Rue de la Commune Ouest, you'll pass under Autoroute 10 and continue along the downtown side of the canal where strips of greenery line both sides. Keep an eye out for the enormous neon sign **2 Farine Five Roses**, which crowns a former flour mill.

The path switches sides at the bridge at Rue des Seigneurs, where you come to a **3 former silk mill** that ran its operations on hydraulic power from the canal. The red-brick factory has been reborn as lofts.

Continue south on Rue Shearer and turn right on Rue Centre, where you'll come to the Romanesque **4 Église St-Charles** on your right. Next push your bike over to the French-style Église St-Gabriel, taking in the charm of this little-visited neighborhood.

Cycle to Rue Charlevoix and turn right and you'll soon meet up with the bike path again. Turn left, and you'll come to **5 H2O Adventures** (p152), a kayak-rental outfit. If you're interested in getting out on the water, this is the place to do it.

Continue on the bike path and turn right at the pedestrian bridge to head to **6 Marché Atwater**, one of the city's best markets. This is a great spot to assemble a picnic, which you can then enjoy by the water, followed by an easy pedal back to the port. If you're keen for more exploring, head west of the market. Another 10km along the path will take you to a sculpture garden at the edge of scenic Lac St-Louis – a favorite spot at sunset. To head back, simply follow the canal path back to the Canal Locks.

during the holidays a Christmas tree illuminates the five-story space.

ADRENALINE
TATTOOS & PIERCING

Map p284 (☑514-938-8884; www.adrenalinetattoos.com; 1541 Rue Sherbrooke Ouest; ☺11am-8pm Mon-Wed, to 9pm Thu-Sat, to 7pm Sun; Ⓜ Guy-Concordia) This friendly, completely non-seedy tattoo parlor is one of the best in the city. For those who aren't ready to make a lifetime commitment to body art, Adrenaline offers red henna 'tattoos,' lasting anywhere from two to eight weeks. Other options include temporary 'airbrushed' tattoos, lasting three to five days.

🏃 SPORTS & ACTIVITIES

CANADIENS DE MONTRÉAL
SPECTATOR SPORT

(http://canadiens.nhl.com; tickets $30 180; ☺season Oct-Apr, playoffs until Jun; Ⓜ Lucien-L'Allier or Bonaventure) The Canadiens of the National Hockey League have won the Stanley Cup 24 times. Although the team has struggled in recent years, Montrealers have a soft spot for the 'Habs' and matches at the **Bell Centre** (Map p284; ☑514-790-2525, 877-668-8269; www.centrebell.ca; 1909 Ave des Canadiens-de-Montréal) sell out routinely. Scalpers hang around the entrance on game days, and you might snag a half-price ticket after the puck drops. Bring your binoculars for the rafter seats. The center also hosts big-name concerts, boxing matches, Disney on Ice and visits by the Dalai Lama.

MONTRÉAL ALOUETTES
SPECTATOR SPORT

(www.montrealalouettes.com; Molson Stadium, 475 Ave des Pins Ouest; tickets $15-165; ☺Jun-Nov; Ⓜ McGill; Ⓟ) The Montréal Alouettes, a star franchise of the Canadian Football League, folded several times before going on to win the league's Grey Cup trophy in 2002, 2009 and 2010. Rules are a bit different from American football: the field is bigger and there are only three downs. Games are held at McGill University's Molson Stadium, and sometimes at the Stade Olympique. The **Alouettes box office** (Map p288; ☑514-790-1245; 2nd fl, 1260 Rue Universi-

ty; ☺9am-5pm Mon-Fri) sells advance tickets. Look for the big red sign.

MY BICYCLETTE
BICYCLE RENTAL

(www.mybicyclette.com; 2985 Rue St-Patrick; bicycle per hr/day $10/30; ☺10am-7pm mid-May–mid-Oct; Ⓜ Charlevoix) Located along the Canal de Lachine (just across the bridge from the Atwater market), this place rents bikes and other gear during the warmer months. It also sponsors city bike tours, and the repair shop next door is a good place to go if your bike conks out on the Lachine Canal path.

ATRIUM LE 1000
SKATING

Map p288 (☑514-395-0555; www.le1000.com; 1000 Rue de la Gauchetière Ouest; adult/child $7/5, skate rental $6.50; ☺11:30am-6pm Mon-Fri, 10:30am-9pm Sat, 10:30am-6pm Sun; Ⓜ Bonaventure; Ⓟ) Enjoy year-round indoor ice skating at this excellent glass-domed rink near Gare Centrale. On weekends, kids and their families have a special session from 10:30am to 11:30am. Special events change regularly – like the summertime 'Bermudas Madness,' a cheesy good time of skating in shorts and T-shirts while DJs spin Hawaiian and summer-inflected beats. Call for operating hours as the schedule changes frequently.

ASHTANGA YOGA STUDIO
YOGA

Map p288 (www.ashtangamontreal.com; ste 118, 372 Rue Ste-Catherine Ouest; 1½hr class $17; Ⓜ Place-des-Arts) Ashtanga, also known as 'power' yoga, is an intense, aerobic form of the exercise. This professional center has big, bright studios, very friendly staff and offers 30-plus classes for all age groups and skill levels. Multiclass discount cards available (five classes $75).

MORETTI STUDIO
PILATES

Map p288 (www.pilates-montreal.com; 1115 Rue Sherbrooke Ouest; private session $65; Ⓜ Peel) This is a relaxed pilates studio providing a practical, down-to-earth approach to getting and staying in shape. Private one-hour instruction is tailored to suit personal needs, with an emphasis on abdominal work, joints and spinal articulation. If you're in town a while, you can also sign up for an eight-week group class.

Quartier Latin & the Village

Neighborhood Top Five

1 Sipping *un café*, beer or whiskey and soaking up the bohemian atmosphere on colorful **Rue St-Denis** (p100).

2 Letting it all hang out while partying until dawn at one of the many bars and clubs in the **Village** (p104).

3 Admiring the elegantly crafted interior of **Église St-Pierre Apôtre** and its unique chapel for AIDS victims (p101).

4 Step back in time to the 1920s at the **Écomusée du Fier Monde** (p101), which highlights contemporary art as well as the history of working-class Montréal.

5 Browsing the books and architecture at the **Bibliotheque et Archives Nationale du Québec** (p101).

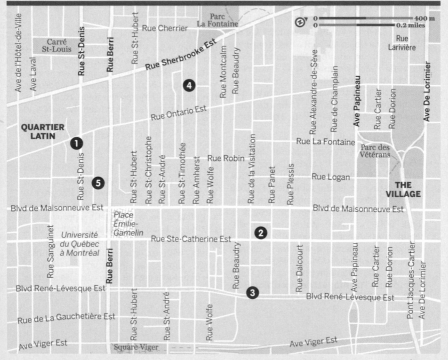

For more detail of this area, see Map p290 ➡

Explore Quartier Latin & the Village

The boisterous district of Quartier Latin and the Village is fairly compact and easy to explore in an afternoon with the option to kick back and party into the night. Start at Rue Sherbrooke and Rue St-Denis and explore the latter to Rue Ste-Catherine. Be sure to pause for a beverage or snack as you go.

St-Denis picks up at night when local watering holes, restaurants, and clubs attract students and other bons vivants who come together over beer and *bouffe* (food). It's best to do a bit of roaming and absorb the free-spirited energy of the quarter. If you want to take a breather during the day, try Carré St-Louis, north of Rue Sherbrooke and off Rue St-Denis, or Place Émile-Gamelin along Rue Ste-Catherine.

One of the hottest gay meccas in North America, the Village is quiet during the day, but starts to pick up around 9pm. Packed with eclectic eateries, shops and nightspots, Rue Ste-Catherine is the main thoroughfare here, so it's easy to navigate. August is the most frenetic time as international visitors gather to celebrate Divers/Cité (p23), the massive annual Gay Pride parade.

Local Life

➡ **Eating out** Even starving artists need fuel. Rue St-Denis has some casual-eating brasseries such as Le Saint-Bock (p104), but the best options, such as Kitchenette (p101), are further afield.

➡ **Nightlife** Start your evening with a drink on Rue St-Denis, then mosey over to the Village for a floorshow in drag at Cabaret Mado (p108) and let the night take its course.

➡ **Festivals** The Montreal World Film Festival (p23) and Gay Pride (p23) make this neighborhood nearly as festive as Downtown on Montréal's celebration circuit.

Getting There & Away

➡ **Metro** The orange and green lines run to Berri-UQAM, with the green line continuing to Beaudry and Papineau.

➡ **Bus** Bus 24 runs along Rue Sherbrooke, the 30 along Rue St-Denis and Rue Berri, and the 15 along Rue Ste-Catherine. The Station Centrale bus terminal (www.stationcentrale.com) is a hub for intercity and international coach services.

➡ **Walking** It's relatively easy to reach the Quartier Latin from either Downtown or Plateau Mont-Royal, and you can also stroll along Rue Ste-Catherine to the Village.

✖ Best Places to Eat

➡ Kitchenette (p101)
➡ Au Petit Extra (p102)
➡ O'Thym (p101)

For reviews, see p101 ➡

🍷 Best Places to Drink

➡ L'Île Noire (p104)
➡ 1000 Grammes (p104)
➡ Le St-Sulpice (p104)
➡ Le Saint-Bock (p104)

For reviews, see p104 ➡

☆ Best Entertainment

➡ Usine C (p108)
➡ Théâtre St-Denis (p108)
➡ Cabaret Mado (p108)

For reviews, see p108 ➡

🔒 Best Places to Shop

➡ Camellia Sinensis (p108)
➡ Zéphyr (p109)
➡ Boutique Spoutnik (p109)

For reviews, see p108 ➡

QUARTIER LATIN & THE VILLAGE

TOP SIGHTS
RUE ST-DENIS

One of the few streets to cross the entire island of Montréal, Rue St-Denis coalesces in four blocks below Rue Sherbrooke that's a carnivalesque collection of restaurants, brasseries, cafes and arts venues. It captures the heart of francophone Montréal, just as St-Laurent was once the preferred hangout of Anglos. This is where you'll find students from nearby Université du Québec à Montréal (UQAM) grabbing a pint after protesting tuition hikes, or big-name U.S. comics doing standup at Théâtre St-Denis. It's a heady mix best enjoyed with a drink in summer.

The terraced cafes and restaurants of the Quartier Latin are great spots to watch the world go by, over coffee, croissants or even a bowl of borscht. Popular with students at UQAM, which number in the tens of thousands, the Quartier Latin is unrivaled when it comes to budget dining, inexpensive bistro fare and meals in a hurry. There are also abundant bars nearby, making for an easy transition from dinner to nighttime amusement.

In the 19th century, the neighborhood was an exclusive residential area for wealthy Francophones. Although many original buildings burned in the great fire of 1852, there are a number of Victorian and art-nouveau gems hidden on the tree-lined streets. Today, the quarter is a hotbed of activity, especially during summer festivals, when energy spills from the streets 24 hours a day.

Rue St-Denis is also an entry of sorts to the Village, one of the largest gay communities in North America. Packed with eclectic eateries, shops and outrageous nightspots, Rue Ste-Catherine is the Village's main thoroughfare, and it closes to traffic periodically in the summer.

DON'T MISS
- People-watching with a drink
- Just for Laughs comedy festival
- Divers/Cité

PRACTICALITIES
- Map p290
- www.quartierlatin.ca/en
- Ⓜ Berri-UQAM

⊙ SIGHTS

BIBLIOTHÈQUE ET ARCHIVES
NATIONALE DU QUÉBEC LIBRARY
Map p290 (www.banq.qc.ca; 475 Blvd de Maisonneuve Est; ⊙10am-10pm Tue-Sun, to 6pm Sat & Sun; ⓂBerri-UQAM) Opened in 2005, this stunning building houses both the library and national archives of Québec. The library itself is 33,000 sq meters, connected to the metro and underground city. Every-thing published in Québec (books, brochures, sound recordings, posters) since 1968 has been deposited here. Bibliophiles can enjoy free guided tours.

ÉGLISE ST-PIERRE-APÔTRE CHURCH
Map p290 (www.stpierreapotre.org; 1201 Rue de la Visitation; ⊙10:15am-4pm Mon-Fri, 12-4pm Sat, 9:15am-4pm Sun; ⓂBeaudry) The Church of St Peter the Apostle belonged to the monastery of the Oblate fathers who settled in Montréal in the mid-19th century. Located in the Village, this neoclassical church has a number of fine decorations – flying buttresses, stained glass, statues in Italian marble – but nowadays the house of worship is more renowned for its gay-friendly Sunday services. It also houses the Chapel of Hope, the first chapel in the world consecrated in 1997 to the memory of victims of AIDS.

ÉCOMUSÉE DU FIER MONDE MUSEUM
Map p290 (www.ecomusee.qc.ca; 2050 Rue Amherst; admission adult/child $6/4; ⊙11am-8pm Wed, 9:30am-4pm Thu & Fri, 10:30am-5pm Sat & Sun; ⓂBerri-UQAM) This magnificent ex-bathhouse explores the history of Centre-Sud, an industrial district in Montréal until the 1950s and now part of the Village. The museum's permanent exhibition, 'Triumphs and Tragedies of a Working-Class Neighborhood,' puts faces on the industrial revolution through a series of excellent photos and multimedia displays. The 1927 building is the former Bain Généreux, an art-deco public bathhouse modeled on one in Paris. Frequent modern-art exhibitions are also held here.

CHAPELLE NOTRE-DAME-
DE-LOURDES CHURCH
Map p290 (www.cndlm.org, in French; 430 Rue Ste-Catherine Est; ⊙11am-6pm Mon-Fri, 10:30am-6:30pm Sat, 9am-6:30pm Sun; ⓂBerri-UQAM) Now hidden among the university buildings, this Romanesque gem was built by the

Sulpicians in 1876 to cement their influence in Montréal. The chapel was designed by Rue St-Denis resident and artist Napoléon Bourassa, whose frescoes dotted about the interior are regarded as his crowning glory.

RUE STE-CATHERINE EST NEIGHBORHOOD
Map p290 Montréal's embrace of the gay community is tightest along the eastern end of Rue Ste-Catherine, a one-time bed of vice and shabby tenements. This strip of restaurants and clubs has been made so presentable that middle-class families mingle with drag queens on the pavements, all part of the neighborhood scenery. One of the anchors of the street is Mado Cabaret, famed for its campy, tongue-in-cheek shows.

UNIVERSITÉ DU QUÉBEC
À MONTRÉAL UNIVERSITY
Map p290 (www.uqam.ca; 405 Rue Ste-Catherine Est; ⓂBerri-UQAM) The modern, rather drab buildings of Montréal's French-language university blend into the cityscape and are linked to the underground city and the Berri-UQAM metro station. The most striking aspect here is the old Gothic steeple of the **Église St-Jacques** (Map p290), which has been integrated into the university's facade.

✕ EATING

KITCHENETTE TEX-MEX $$
Map p290 (☎514-527-1016; www.kitchenetterestaurant.ca; 1353 Blvd René Lévesque Est; mains $20-34; ⊙lunch & dinner Tue-Fri, dinner Sat; ⓂBeaudry) Whether it's blackened catfish with marshmallows or smoked Charlevoix chicken and grits, Texas-born chef Nick Hodges likes experimenting with southern comfort food while keeping it simple, like the airy, elegant decor here, and always delicious. Fridays are given over to mountainous fish 'n' chips. Be sure to reserve.

O'THYM FRENCH $$
Map p290 (☎514-525-3443; www.othym.com; 1112 Blvd de Maisonneuve Est; mains $24-33; ⊙lunch Tue-Fri, dinner daily; ⓂBeaudry) O'Thym buzzes with foodies who flock here from all over town. It features an elegant but understated dining room (exposed brick walls, floodlit windows, oversized mirrors), and beautifully presented plates

THE METRO MUSEUM OF ART

Primarily a mover of the masses, the Montréal metro was also conceived as an enormous art gallery, although not all stations have been decorated. Here are a few highlights from the central zone; many more await your discovery.

Berri-UQAM

A set of murals by artist Robert La Palme representing science, culture and recreation hangs above the main staircase leading to the yellow line. These works were moved here from the 'Man and His World' pavilion of Expo '67 at the request of mayor Jean Drapeau, a buddy of La Palme.

Champ-de-Mars

The station kiosk boasts a set of antique stained-glass windows by Marcelle Ferron, an artist of the Refus global movement. The abstract forms splash light down into the shallow platform, drenching passengers in color as their trains roll through.

Peel

Circles, circles everywhere: in bright single colors on advertising panels, in the marble of one entrance, above the main staircases, as tiles on the floor – even the bulkhead vents are circular. They're the work of Jean-Paul Mousseau of the Québécois art movement Les Automatistes.

Place-des-Arts

The station's east wall has a backlit stained-glass mural entitled *Les Arts Lyriques*, by Québécois artist and Oscar-winning filmmaker Frédéric Back. It depicts the evolution of Montréal's music from the first trumpet fanfare played on the island in 1535 to modern composers and conductors.

of fresh seafood and grilled game. Bring your own wine.

AU PETIT EXTRA   FRENCH $$
Map p290 (☑514-527-5552; www.aupetitextra.com, in French; 1690 Rue Ontario Est; mains $14-28; ☺lunch Mon-Fri, dinner daily; ⓂPapineau) This sweet little place serves traditional bistro fare to a garrulous local crowd. The blackboard menu changes frequently but features simple, flavorful dishes (*steak frites,* foie gras, duck confit, mahimahi), and staff can expertly pair wines with food. Reservations are advised, but you can linger over a glass of wine at the handsome wooden bar if you have to wait.

LE GRAIN DE SEL   BISTRO $$
(☑514-522-5105; www.restolegraindesel.ca; 2375 Rue Ste-Catherine Est; mains $17-29; ☺lunch Tue-Fri, dinner Thu-Sat; ⓂPapineau, then bus 34) This tiny, friendly bistro just beyond the eastern edge of the Village exudes old-world ambience with a small bar and open kitchen. The menu offers bistro fare and other delights such as organic pork shoulder, wild boar mini burgers, and wild mushroom ravioli. The waiters will marry the right wines with your meal. Reservations advised.

LE COMMENSAL   VEGETARIAN $
Map p290 (1720 Rue St-Denis; buffet per kg $17; ☺11am-10:30pm Sun-Thu, 11am-11pm Fri & Sat; ⓂBerri-UQAM) A requisite stop for vegetarian diners in Montréal, this handsomely rustic dining room stocks an impressive variety of high-quality vegetarian cuisine, including baked dishes (lasagna, casseroles, quesadillas), salads, fresh fruits and desserts, sold by weight.

LA PARYSE   DINER $
Map p290 (www.laparyse.com, in French; 302 Rue Ontario Est; mains $8-12; ☺lunch & dinner Tue-Sat; ⓂBerri-UQAM) Often credited with the thickest, juiciest burgers and best fries in town, this smart little retro diner offers an excellent variety of toppings and thick, rich milkshakes. This place is an integral part of the neighborhood and owner Madame Paryse has many fans.

JULIETTE ET CHOCOLAT   CAFE $
Map p290 (www.julietteetchocolat.com; 1615 Rue St-Denis; mains $8-12; ☺11am-11pm Sun-Thu, 11am-12am Fri & Sat; ⓂBerri-UQAM) When the urge to devour something chocolaty arrives, make straight for Juliette et Chocolat, a bustling little cafe where chocolate is served in

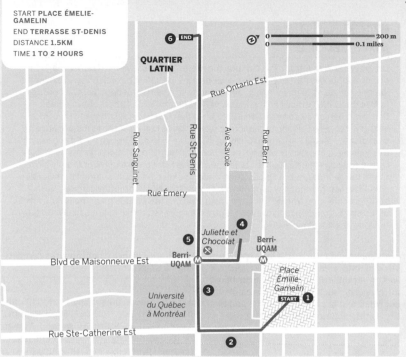

START **PLACE ÉMELIE-GAMELIN**
END **TERRASSE ST-DENIS**
DISTANCE **1.5KM**
TIME **1 TO 2 HOURS**

QUARTIER LATIN & THE VILLAGE NEIGHBORHOOD WALK

Neighborhood Walk
Bohemian Life in the Quartier Latin

Much of the charm of the compact Latin quarter lies not in official sights but in soaking up the laid-back atmosphere; allow yourself to linger, especially along the cafe-filled terraces of Rue St-Denis. Today a nexus of student and alternative life, the neighborhood has French and Roman Catholic roots dating back to the early 19th century.

Begin your walk in the somewhat unkempt ❶ **Place Émilie-Gamelin**, the site of spontaneous concerts, wacky metal sculptures, outdoor chess matches and dozens of punks with their beleaguered pets.

Head southwest along Rue Ste-Catherine, and take a peek inside the ❷ **Chapelle Notre-Dame-de-Lourdes**, commissioned in 1876. This Romanesque gem is filled with imaginative frescoes painted by Napoléon Bourassa.

Back on Rue Ste-Catherine, turn right up Rue St-Denis, where you'll be in the midst

of the – sadly uninspiring – campus of the Université du Québec à Montréal. The most striking building here is the old facade of the ❸ **Église St-Jacques**, with its magnificent Gothic steeple.

Turn right down Blvd de Maisonneuve and continue to the ❹ **Bibliothèque et Archives Nationale du Québec**, a massive library home to an astounding collection of all things Québécois. Head into the main hall and downstairs to a gallery, which often hosts fascinating (and free) exhibitions.

Return to Rue St-Denis and turn right. You'll soon pass two of the neighborhood's cultural mainstays. The ❺ **Théâtre St-Denis** is the city's second-largest theater. Continue up the street, noting the terrace cafes, lively pubs and quirky shops. The little side street, ❻ **Terrasse St-Denis**, used to be a meeting place of Montréal's bohemian set at the turn of the 20th century.

LOCAL KNOWLEDGE

MIXED MEMORIES

On every car in Montréal, you'll notice the motto 'Je me souviens' (I remember). Officially adopted as part of Québec's coat of arms in 1939, it has been the subject of intense debate as to its meaning. Some say it represents Québec's French heritage before the British victory on the Plains of Abraham in 1760. Others believe it has to do with perceived constitutional injustices that Québec has suffered in the 20th century. Actually, Québec bureaucrat Eugene Taché had it carved in the province's coat of arms on the Parliament building in Ottawa in 1883. Though he did not explain its meaning, it appears to originate in a poem he wrote, part of which runs as follows: 'Je me souviens que né sous le lys, je fleuris sous la rose.' (I remember that I was born under the *fleur de lys*, but I blossomed under the rose.) It would suggest that Québec should remember that it was born from France (the lily) but matured under the institutions inherited from Britain (the rose). The motto's cryptic meaning is far from universally agreed upon, however. Montréal's aggressive drivers are usually too busy honking at each other to discuss it.

---

every shape and form – drizzled over crepes, blended into creamy milkshakes and coffees, or straight up in a blood-sugar-boosting chocolate 'shot.' The setting is charming but small and busy. For less hustle and bustle, visit the Laurier location (p132).

🍷 DRINKING & NIGHTLIFE

L'ÎLE NOIRE   PUB
Map p290 (www.ilenoire.com; 1649 Rue St-Denis; ◎3pm-3am; MBerri-UQAM) Roll into this slice of the Scottish Highlands in the heart of the Quartier Latin and sip from their selection of over 140 scotches and whiskeys (from less than $10 to hundreds per glass), as well as 15 varieties of beer on tap and several dozen wine choices. The vibe here is decidedly less bohemian than other watering holes on Rue St-Denis, perfect if you want to take a breather from the surrounding carnival.

SKY PUB & CLUB   GAY
Map p290 (www.complexesky.com; 1474 Rue Ste-Catherine Est; ◎2pm-3am Mon-Fri, noon-3am Sat & Sun; MBeaudry) This is one of those popular Village complexes designed to suck you in for an entire Saturday night of partying. If you're a gorgeous guy or looking for one, start the evening in the 1st-floor pick-up pub before heading up to the dance floors (disco and energized house/hip-hop). The legendary roof terrace is a perfect place to catch L'International des

Feux Loto-Québec (the fireworks competition) in summer.

1000 GRAMMES   CAFE
Map p290 (www.1000grammes.com; 1495 Rue Ste-Catherine Est; ◎11am-11:30pm Sun-Thu, 11am-12:30am Fri & Sat; MPapineau) Known for its decadent desserts such as *tarte aux pacanes* (pecan pie) and ginormous salads and sandwiches, this gay cafe is also a convenient daytime hangout. Grab a table beside the huge windows, sip your coffee and watch life go by. Mille Grammes also has tons of flyers for events nearby. Staff are very friendly and helpful.

LE ST-SULPICE   BAR
Map p290 (www.lesaintsulpice.ca; 1680 Rue St-Denis; ◎noon-3am; MBerri-UQAM) This student evergreen is spread over four levels in an old Victorian stone house – a cafe, several terraces, disco and a sprawling back garden for drinks 'n' chats. The music changes with the DJ's mood, from hip-hop and ambient to mainstream rock and jazz. It uses recyclable glasses and also sells alcohol-free beer.

LE SAINT-BOCK   PUB
Map p290 (www.lesaintbock.com; 1749 Rue St-Denis; ◎11am until late, 1pm until late Sat & Sun; MBerri-UQAM) This convivial, low-lit brasserie has a decent selection of beers on tap and menu offerings that sometimes rise above conventional pub fare. It's a good spot to watch hockey on the screens before getting down to some serious drinking elsewhere.

CIRCUS CLUB

Map p290 (http://circushd.com; 917 Rue Ste-Catherine Est; ☺1:30am-10am Thu-Sat; ⓂBerri-UQAM) Sometimes featuring circus performers and dancers, this hot spot is more glamorous than you might expect from an after-hours joint; in fact, it ranks as the biggest of its kind in all of Canada. More than 200 visiting DJs a year appear behind the decks, to the dancing delight of glo-stick-brandishing ravers and city clubbers who are not yet ready to call it a night. Get there early to avoid the long line; alcohol served before 3am.

LE MAGELLAN BAR BAR

Map p290 (www.pelerinmagellan.com; 330 Rue Ontario Est; ☺11am-midnight; ⓂBerri-UQAM) Once past the mock lighthouse out the front you can enjoy a pleasant evening of eclectic offerings, from jazz to chansons. The interior is sprinkled with maritime doodads (there's an interesting gallery of antique maps upstairs) and the front terrace is great for people-watching, while the back terrace is perfectly verdant in summer. It's joined to Le Pèlerin restaurant.

SALOON GAY

Map p290 (www.lesaloon.ca; 1333 Rue Ste-Catherine Est; ☺11am-10:30pm Mon-Wed, 11:30pm-11pm Thu, 11:30-12am Fri, 10am-12am Sat, 10am-10:30pm Sun; ⓂBeaudry) With nearly 20 years under its belt, this gay bar-bistro has earned a spot in Village hearts for its chilled atmosphere, live DJs, patio seating, cocktails and 'five-continents' menu, including some good vegetarian options. A stylish pre-club pit stop.

APOLLON GAY

Map p290 (www.apollonmtl.com; 1450 Rue Ste-Catherine Est; ⓂBerri-UQAM) Opened in the beautiful Station Postale C, a heritage post office built in 1912 that later hosted Village standby K.O.X., Apollon has a funky open-concept setup where you can look down on the gyrating bodies from balconies above. Saturday nights draw an older crowd, while Friday nights sees a mix of mainstream pop music.

STUD BAR GAY

Map p290 (www.studbar.com; 1812 Rue Ste-Catherine Est; ⓂPapineau) This Village meat market attracts older, heavier men, and its dark, down-at-the-heels design might bring to mind New York gay bars of the 1970s. The upside is that it's not pretentious at all, there's cheap beer and no cover charge, and the upstairs disco can be lots of fun.

CLUB DATE PIANO-BAR PUB

Map p290 (1218 Rue Ste-Catherine Est; ☺8am-3am; ⓂBeaudry) This gay tavern knew exactly what it was doing when it karaokefied the spot. A mixed crowd cheers on aspiring vocalists from all walks of life, from the hilariously awful to the downright star-worthy. Cheap drinks and a weird saloon vibe guarantee you a night to remember – or forget.

QUARTIER LATIN PUB PUB

Map p290 (www.pubquartierlatin.com; 318 Rue Ontario Est; ☺3pm-3am; ⓂBerri-UQAM) This cool bar with 1950s lounge-style decor has a small dance floor and a DJ playing new wave on weekends. A great, reliable hangout any night of the week.

STEREO GAY

Map p290 (www.stereonightclub.net; 858 Rue Ste-Catherine Est; ☺2am-11am Fri & Sat; ⓂBerri-UQAM) Montréal's giant of underground house music has opened and closed for various reasons throughout the years. Still featuring a sound system that's so amazing that regulars gush about out-of-body experiences, Stereo is open for business once again, attracting anyone – gay, straight, students and drag queens – looking to lose sleep in style.

LE DRUGSTORE LESBIAN

Map p290 (www.le-drugstore.com, in French; 1366 Rue Ste-Catherine Est; ☺10am-3am; ⓂBeaudry) This cavernous eight-story complex, capacity 1,800, has six theme bars, billiards, a large delicatessen and a dance club on the fourth floor. It's mostly lesbian but hosts drag queen shows on Friday and Saturday evenings.

UNITY GAY

Map p290 (www.clubunitymontreal.com; 1171 Rue Ste-Catherine Est; ☺10pm-3am Thu-Sun; ⓂBeaudry) Rebuilt after the 2006 World Outgames, this three-floor Village favorite features not only a club and pub but a VIP lounge, pool tables and rooftop terrace. Saturdays are the best nights, while Fridays are given over to a mostly 20-something crowd.

106

1. Rue St-Denis (p100)

A carnivalesque collection of restaurants, brasseries, cafes an d arts venues – sitting alongside some of the city's best historical architecture – Rue St-Denis captures the heart of francophone Montréal.

2. Gay Montréal (p101)

Packed with eclectic eateries, shops and outrageous nightspots, Rue Ste-Catherine is the heart of the city's gay scene.

3. Quartier Latin (p98)

Tens of thousands of university students means Quartier Latin is unrivaled when it comes to budget dining, inexpensive bistro fare and meals in a hurry – not to forget abundant bars.

4. Le St-Sulpice (p104)

This popular student haunt cafe and bar has several terraces, a sprawling back garden and regular DJs.

☆ ENTERTAINMENT

USINE C
PERFORMING ARTS

Map p290 (www.usine-c.com, in French; 1345 Ave Lalonde; MBeaudry) This former jam factory in the Village is home to the award-winning Carbone 14 theatrical dance troupe that performs here regularly. Its two flexible halls (450 and 150 seats) can be rejigged to accommodate circuses or raves, but you're more likely to find interesting international drama collaborations. To bump into its talented performers, head for the cozy basement cafe next to the changing rooms.

THÉÂTRE ST-DENIS
PERFORMING ARTS

Map p290 (www.theatrestdenis.com; 1594 Rue St-Denis; ☺box office noon-9pm; MBerri-UQAM) This Montréal landmark and historic movie house hosts touring Broadway productions, rock concerts and various theatrical and musical performances. Its two halls (933 and 2218 seats) are equipped with the latest sound and lighting gizmos and figure prominently in the Just for Laughs festival.

CINÉMATHÈQUE QUÉBÉCOISE
CINEMA

Map p290 (www.cinematheque.qc.ca; 335 Blvd de Maisonneuve Est; admission $8; ☺10am-9pm Mon-Fri, 4-9pm Sat & Sun; MBerri-UQAM) This is a university-flavored venue noted for showing Canadian, Québécois and international avant-garde films. In the lobby there's a permanent exhibition on the history of filmmaking as well as a TV and new-media section.

CABARET MADO
GAY

Map p290 (www.mado.qc.ca, in French; 1115 Rue Ste-Catherine Est; ☺2pm-3am; MBeaudry) Mado is a flamboyant celebrity who has been featured in *Fugues,* the gay entertainment mag. Her cabaret is a local institution, with drag shows featuring an assortment of hilariously sarcastic performers in eye-popping costumes. Shows take place weekend, Tuesday and Thursday nights; check the website for details.

BISTRO À JOJO
BLUES

Map p290 (www.bistroajojo.com; 1627 Rue St-Denis; ☺1pm-3am; MBerri-UQAM) This brash venue in the Quartier Latin has been going strong for 30 years. It's the nightly place for down 'n' dirty French- and English-language blues and rock groups. Sit close enough to see the band members' sweat.

LE NATIONAL
LIVE MUSIC

Map p290 (http://latulipe.ca; 1220 Rue Ste-Catherine Est; MBeaudry) This 750-capacity concert venue situated in the Village was one of the first professional French theaters in Montréal. In tandem with sister venue **La Tulipe** on Ave Papineau, it hosts a variety of acts from hardcore bands to pop shows. Check the website for listings.

THÉÂTRE STE-CATHERINE
PERFORMING ARTS

Map p290 (http://theatresaintecatherine.com; 264 Rue Ste-Catherine Est; MBerri-UQAM) From film to theater, stand-up comedy to music concerts, this relatively new venue presents a variety of shows: Oscar Wilde one night, burlesque dance the next. Its Sunday Night Improv (sketch and comedy) performances are quite popular with the city's theatrical community; the Montreal Sketch Comedy Festival is in late May.

CINÉMA QUARTIER LATIN
CINEMA

Map p290 (www.cineplex.com; 350 Rue Emery; ☺11:30am-10:15pm; MBerri-UQAM) This large cinema plays French films and French versions of some Hollywood movies, as well as live broadcasts of performances from the Metropolitan Opera in New York on Saturday afternoons. It's also a host theater for the Montreal World Film Festival.

🛍 SHOPPING

TOP CHOICE CAMELLIA SINENSIS
FOOD & DRINK

Map p290 (http://camellia-sinensis.com; 351 Rue Emery; ☺10am-6pm Mon-Wed & Sat-Sun, 10am-9pm Thu-Fri; MBerri-UQAM) Right in front of the Cinéma Quartier Latin, this welcoming tea shop has over 200 varieties of tea from China, Japan, India and elsewhere in Asia, as well as quality teapots, tea accessories, books, and workshops such as pairing tea with chocolate. You can taste many exotic teas, as well as carefully selected desserts, in the salon next door, which features brews from recent staff travels.

AUX QUATRE POINTS CARDINAUX
MAPS

Map p290 (www.aqpc.com; 551 Rue Ontario Est; ☺closed Sun; MBerri-UQAM) The globetrotting folks at AQPC pack a range of goods for the seasoned traveler including atlases, globes, maps, aerial photographs, and travel guides

GREAT MARKETS OF MONTRÉAL

Montréal is famed for its impressive year-round food markets, where you can sample the great bounty of the north. The biggest and best are Marché Jean-Talon in Little Italy and Marché Atwater just west of downtown near the Canal de Lachine. For more visit Marchés Publics de Montréal (www.marchespublics-mtl.com).

➡ **Marché Jean-Talon** (Map p296; 7075 Ave Casgrain; ⊙7am-6pm Mon-Wed, 7am-8pm Thu-Fri, 7am-6pm Sat, 7am-5pm Sun; Ⓜ Jean-Talon) The city's largest market, right in the heart of Little Italy. There are several hundred market stalls on a huge square edged by shops that stock all manner of produce year-round including fruits, vegetables, potted plants, herbs and (of course) maple syrup. Food stalls whip up fresh juices, tender crepes, baguette sandwiches and more. Don't miss the Québécois specialty store Le Marché des Saveurs (p138).

➡ **Marché Atwater** (Map p284; 138 Ave Atwater; ⊙7am-6pm Mon-Wed, 7am-7pm Thu, 7am-8pm Fri, 7am-5pm Sat & Sun; Ⓜ Lionel-Groulx) Located right on the banks of the Canal de Lachine, with scores of vendors outside and high-class delicatessens and specialty food shops inside, in the tiled, vaulted hall under the art-deco clock tower. Try the **Boucherie Claude & Henri** for beautiful racks of lamb, the bakery **Première Moisson** for baguettes or the astounding **Fromagerie du Marché Atwater**, whose hundreds of cheeses reach from runny triple crèmes to hard goudas.

➡ **Marché de Maisonneuve** (4445 Rue Ontario Est; ⊙7am-6pm Mon-Wed, 7am-8pm Thu-Fri, 7am-6pm Sat, 7am-5pm Sun; Ⓜ Pie-IX, then bus 139) About 20 farm stalls, and inside, a dozen vendors of meat, cheese, fresh vegetables, tasty pastries and pastas in a beautiful beaux-arts building (1912–14) in Maisonneuve, girded by pretty gardens.

➡ **Marché St-Jacques** (Map p290; 2035 Rue Amherst; ⊙9am-7pm Mon-Fri, 9am-6pm Sat, 9am-5pm Sun; Ⓜ Beaudry) Traditional food stalls and shops still occupy their 1931 art-deco home in the northern reach of the Village, though some of it is unoccupied.

in English and French, including a good selection of Lonely Planet books.

ZÉPHYR   ART
Map p290 (http://galeriezephyr2112.com; 2112 Rue Amherst; ⊙10am-5pm Mon-Sat; Ⓜ Sherbrooke) One of several interesting shops along this stretch of Amherst, Daniel Roberge's bright gallery focuses on contemporary art from Québec and Canadian artists such as Michel Roy and Danièle DeBlois.

BOUTIQUE SPOUTNIK   ANTIQUES
Map p290 (http://boutiquespoutnik.com; 2120 Rue Amherst; ⊙12-5pm Tue-Wed & Sat-Sun, 12-6pm Thu-Fri; Ⓜ Sherbrooke) Also on Amherst, Spoutnik has enough shiny retro stuff for your home, like vintage wooden desks and globular lighting fixtures, that you'd swear you're back in the shagadelic sixties.

ARCHAMBAULT   BOOKS, MUSIC
Map p290 (www.archambault.ca; 500 Rue Ste-Catherine Est; ⊙9:30am-9pm Mon-Fri, 9am-5pm Sat, 10am-5pm Sun; Ⓜ Berri-UQAM) Behind the art-deco portals you'll find Montréal's oldest and largest book and record shop, an emporium that boasts CDs and books, plus assorted musical supplies such as pianos and sheet music. Some recordings sold here are hard to find outside Québec.

PRIAPE   SEX & FETISH
Map p290 (www.priape.com; 1311 Rue Ste-Catherine Est; ⊙9am-9pm Mon-Sat, 12-9pm Sun; Ⓜ Beaudry) Montréal's biggest gay sex store has been going strong for 15 years. It's plugged into the mainstream erotic wares (videos and DVDs, mags and books) but has branched into high-quality clothing with a titillating edge – shrink-wrapped jeans, but also a vast choice of black leather gear in the basement.

UNDERWORLD   FASHION
Map p290 (www.underworld-shop.com; 251 Rue Ste-Catherine Est; ⊙10am-6pm Mon-Wed & Sat, 10am-9pm Thu & Fri, 11am-6pm Sun; Ⓜ Berri-UQAM) Underworld is a first-class punk refuge and supply house on an appropriately grungy stretch of Rue Ste-Catherine. It's got jeans, shoes, hoodies, hats and a killer selection of skateboards.

QUARTIER LATIN & THE VILLAGE SHOPPING

Plateau Mont-Royal

Neighborhood Top Five

1 Enjoying the fresh air, sweeping vistas and feathered friends of **Parc du Mont-Royal** (p113), the beloved heart of Montréal.

2 Time traveling to a bygone age and feasting on the world's best smoked meat at **Schwartz's** (p116).

3 Exploring the old-world groceries that rub shoulders with chic supper clubs along **Boulevard St-Laurent** (p112).

4 Trolling the quirky shops, from old records to Goth accessories, along bohemian **Avenue du Mont-Royal** (p112).

5 Chilling out in summer and ice-skating in winter in the broad expanse of local favorite **Parc La Fontaine** (p112).

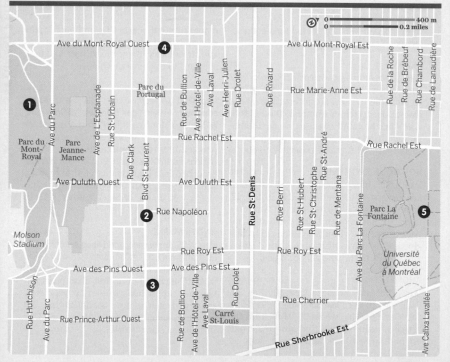

For more detail of this area, see Map p292 ➡

Explore Plateau Mont-Royal

This is a large area, but a good chunk can be explored in a day. Begin at leafy Carré St-Louis, where old slate Victorian mansions and duplexes house bohemian souls and B&Bs. Originally a working-class neighborhood, in the 1960s and '70s the Plateau became the place where writers, singers and all manner of artists lived.

Make your way along Rue Prince-Arthur Ouest to Blvd St-Laurent, the legendary divide between anglophone and francophone Montréal once known as 'the Main.' Today the Main is a mixture of hip cafes and nightspots, old-world delis and grocery stores, and funky hipster shops. The stretch to Ave Duluth, known for its BYOB restos, attracts hordes of 20-somethings on weekend nights. For lunch or a relaxing coffee, take a break at Café Santropol, an old standby on Rue St-Urbain.

Continuing northwest up Blvd St-Laurent, you'll enter Montréal's Portuguese community, passing Parc du Portugal. Another block to the northwest lies Ave du Mont-Royal. It's worth turning right here and wandering down several blocks, lined with eclectic boutiques, record shops and bookstores.

When you're in the mood for fresh air, hop on bus 11 on the northwest side of Ave du Mont-Royal and ride up to 'the Mountain,' the Parc du Mont-Royal. Hop off at the parking lot near Maison Smith, a visitors center where you can buy a map of the park and learn about its history before spending the rest of the day exploring it.

Local Life

➡ **Bar-hopping** Coasting up and down Blvd St-Laurent is the quintessential bar-hopping experience for younger Montrealers (p112).

➡ **Mountainsides** It doesn't get much more Montréal than picnicking, tanning and tobogganing (in winter) on the Mountain (p113).

➡ **Foodie faves** You can't go wrong with a bagel, some smoked meat and *poutine* (p115) in your quest to be an authentic Montrealer.

Getting There & Away

➡ **Metro** Metro access is via the orange line, at the stations of Sherbrooke, Mont-Royal and Laurier.
➡ **Bus** The 55 runs along Blvd St-Laurent; bus 30 coasts along Rue St-Denis; bus 80 travels Ave du Parc; bus 11 climbs up to Parc du Mont-Royal from Ave du Mont-Royal.
➡ **Bike** You can rent a Bixi bike to reach much of Plateau Mont-Royal; pedaling up the mountain itself is a tough slog.

Best Places to Eat
➡ Le Filet (p115)
➡ Au Pied de Cochon (p116)
➡ Schwartz's (p116)
➡ Beauty's (p116)

For reviews, see p115 ➡

Best Places to Drink
➡ Reservoir (p119)
➡ Bily Kun (p119)
➡ Else's (p120)

For reviews, see p119 ➡

Best Entertainment
➡ Casa del Popolo (p124)
➡ Théâtre du Rideau Vert (p124)
➡ La Tulipe (p124)

For reviews, see p124 ➡

PLATEAU MONT-ROYAL

⊙ SIGHTS

BOULEVARD ST-LAURENT   STREET

Map p292 A dividing line between the city's east and west, Blvd St-Laurent ('the Main') has always been a focus of action, a gathering place for people of many languages and backgrounds. In 1996 it was declared a national historic site for its role as ground zero for so many Canadian immigrants and future Montrealers. The label 'the Main' has stuck in the local lingo since the 19th century. Today it's a gateway into the Plateau and a fascinating street to explore.

RUE ST-DENIS   STREET

Map p292 The backbone of Montréal's francophone shopping district, Rue St-Denis is lined with hat and garment shops, uberhip record stores and terrace cafes designed to keep people from getting any work done. Summer crowds flock to the inviting bistros and bars on both sides of the street.

PARC LA FONTAINE   PARK

Map p278 (cnr Rue Sherbrooke Est & Ave du Parc La Fontaine; MSherbrooke) At 34 hectares, this great verdant municipal park is the city's third-largest, after Parc du Mont-Royal and Parc Maisonneuve. In the warmer months weary urbanites flock to leafy La Fontaine to enjoy the walking and bicycle paths, the attractive ponds and the general air of relaxation that pervades the park. The view down the steep banks from Ave du Parc La Fontaine is impressive, especially if the fountains are in play. You can rent paddleboats in summer and go ice-skating in winter. The open-air **Théâtre de Verdure** (☎514-872-4545) draws a laid-back crowd on evenings in July.

ÉGLISE ST-JEAN-BAPTISTE   CHURCH

Map p278 (eglisestjeanbaptiste.com, in French; 309 Rue Rachel Est; ⊙4-6pm Mon-Thu, 4:30-6:30pm Sat, 9:30-11am & 4:30-6:30pm Sun; MMont-Royal) Dedicated to St John the Baptist, the patron saint of French Canadians, this church was the hub of working-class Catholic families in the late 19th and early 20th centuries. The altar is white imported marble, the chancel canopy is pink marble and there are two Casavant organs. The acoustics are splendid and the church plays host to numerous classical-music concerts throughout the year.

AVENUE DU MONT-ROYAL   STREET

Map p292 (MMont-Royal) Old-fashioned five-and-dime stores rub shoulders with a growing collection of trendy restaurants and fashion boutiques on Ave du Mont-Royal. The nightlife here has surged to the point that it rivals Blvd St-Laurent, with bars and nightclubs ranging from the sedate to uproarious. Intimate shops, secondhand stores and ultramodern boutiques offer eye-catching apparel.

CARRÉ ST-LOUIS   SQUARE

Map p292 (cnr Rue St-Denis & Rue Prince-Arthur; MSherbrooke) This lovely green space with a three-tiered fountain is flanked by beautiful rows of Second Empire homes. In the 19th century a reservoir here was filled, and a neighborhood emerged for well-to-do French families. Artists and poets gathered in the area back then, and creative types like filmmakers and fashion designers now occupy houses in the streets nearby. The cafe, which opens in summer, is a good spot for a pick-me-up, with occasional musicians creating the soundtrack for the square.

LOCAL KNOWLEDGE

THE MAIN'S MAIN MAN

Once a 17th-century path between a farm and an estate, and from 1905 the official division between east and west addresses, the Main has a storied history as a boundary between Montréal's anglophone and francophone communities. It has hosted brothels, nightclubs, shooting galleries, tattoo parlors and innumerable bars and restaurants. It has also attracted gangsters, prostitutes, gun-toting madmen and arsonists. One of its most upstanding and hardworking denizens, however, was Fabien Biondi. From 1896 until he retired in 1964, this Italian immigrant shone shoes for nearly 70 years on the Main, counting among his clients judges, lawyers and politicians. Even though he charged only 35 cents per shine, Biondi managed to employ five assistants and raise 18 children. 'Shoe-shining is not one of the most profitable businesses in the world,' he once told a newspaper, 'but one manages to make a living.'

Carré St-Louis feeds west into **Rue Prince-Arthur**, a former slice of 1960s hippie culture that has refashioned itself as a popular restaurant-and-bar strip.

PARC DU PORTUGAL   PARK
Map p292 (cnr Blvd St-Laurent & Rue Marie-Anne)
This quaint little park is dedicated to Portuguese immigrants and their community, founded in Montréal in 1953. At the rear of the park, next to the little summer pavilion, a plaque reads in translation: 'We arrived in this area seeking a new life and ample horizons.' The gates and fountain are covered with colorful glazed tiles.

AVENUE CHÂTEAUBRIAND   STREET
Map p292 This shady little lane is a classic story of Plateau renovation. Until the early 1990s this was one of the Plateau's poorer streets, where residents painted murals on the facades to disguise the deterioration. The murals have long since gone and in their place have emerged colorful homes with trim little gardens and potted plants hanging under the windows.

◉ Parc du Mont-Royal Area

Montrealers are proud of their 'mountain,' so don't call it a hill as Oscar Wilde did when he visited the city in the 1880s. The charming, leafy expanse of Parc du Mont-Royal is charged for a wide range of outdoor activities. The wooded slopes and grassy meadows have stunning views that make it all the more popular for jogging, picnicking, horseback riding, cycling, and throwing Frisbees. Winter brings skating, tobogganing and cross-country skiing. Binoculars are a good idea for the bird feeders that have been set up along some walking trails.

The park was laid out by Frederick Law Olmsted, the architect of New York's Central Park. The idea came from bourgeois residents in the adjacent Golden Square Mile who fretted about vanishing greenery. Note that walking in the park after sunset isn't such a safe idea.

Contrary to what people may try to tell you, this place is *not* an extinct volcano. Rather, Parc du Mont-Royal is a hangover from when magma penetrated the earth's crust millions of years ago. This formed a sort of erosion-proof rock, so while time and the elements were wearing down the ground around it, the 232m-high hunk of

rock, which locals affectionately refer to as 'the Mountain,' stood firm.

On the north side of the park lie two enormous cemeteries; Cimetière Mont-Royal is Protestant and nondenominational, while Cimetière Notre-Dame-des-Neiges is Catholic.

For more info on the park visit www.le montroyal.qc.ca.

BELVÉDÈRE CAMILLIEN-HOUDE   LOOKOUT
(Voie Camillien-Houde; Ⓜ Mont-Royal, then bus 11) This is the most popular lookout on Mont-Royal thanks to its accessibility and large parking lot. Naturally enough, it's a magnet for couples once night falls, making it nearly impossible on summer nights to find a parking space.

You can walk to Chalet du Mont-Royal, about 2km away. To get to this lookout, take the stairs that lead from the parking lot.

CHALET DU MONT-ROYAL   HISTORIC BUILDING
Map p284 (stairs up from Redpath Cres; ☺ seasonal) Constructed in 1932, this grand old white villa, complete with bay windows, contains canvases that depict scenes of Montréal history. You'll also see carved squirrels in the rafters. Big bands strut their stuff on the huge balcony in summer, reminiscent of the 1930s. Most people, however, flock here for the spectacular views of downtown from the **Kondiaronk lookout** nearby. It's about a 1km walk from the park entrance on Ave de Pins.

LAC DES CASTORS   LAKE
Created in a former marsh as part of a work-creation project, Beaver Lake is a center of activity year-round. You can rent paddleboats on the lake or, in winter, ice skates and sleds from **Le Pavillon** (2000 Chemin Remembrance; ☺ 8:30am-9pm Sun-Thu, 8:30am-10pm Fri & Sat). Refreshments and sandwiches are sold at a snack bar; there's also a restaurant with more-elaborate dishes. The slopes above the lake are served by a ski lift when it snows, but most people use them for sledding.

MAISON SMITH   HISTORIC BUILDING
(Voie Camillien-Houde; ☺ 10am-5pm Mon-Sun; 🚌 11) Constructed in 1858 by a merchant who wanted to get away from the pollution and overpopulation of the rest of Montréal, this house was one of 16 private properties on the mountain that were expropriated by the government in 1869 once the land was

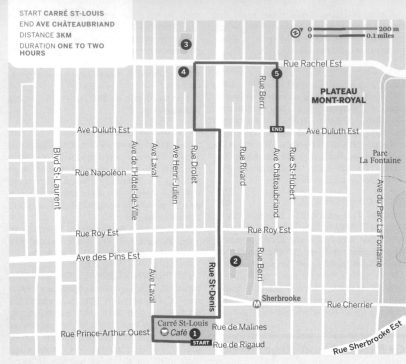

START **CARRÉ ST-LOUIS**
END **AVE CHÂTEAUBRIAND**
DISTANCE **3KM**
DURATION **ONE TO TWO HOURS**

Neighborhood Walk
Strolling the Plateau

➡ The Plateau Mont-Royal area is best known for its eclectic restaurants, colorful bars and cafes, and fashion-forward boutiques, but its leafy residential streets are a great place to stroll. This area epitomizes Montréal's diversity, offering a wide mix of grunge and chic, and it's packed with places of historical interest.

Start at the ❶ **Carré St-Louis** (p112), a pleasant, green, shady oasis with a splashing fountain that's a popular spot for lazing and people-watching. It's surrounded by beautiful old houses that were built for wealthy French residents in the 19th century.

Walk around the park (stopping perhaps for a coffee at the summertime cafe near Ave Laval), then walk up Rue St-Denis. On your right you'll pass the majestic buildings of the former ❷ **Institut des Sourdes-Muettes** (now known as the Institut Raymond-Dewar) – note the little silver cupola.

Turn left onto Ave Duluth and right onto Rue Drolet. At the end of the street, you'll reach the baroque ❸ **Église St-Jean-Baptiste** (p112), its enormous interior decorated with gilded wood and pink marble. The acoustics are excellent, making it a popular venue for concerts.

Exiting the church, look right to see the winged angel on the imposing Sir George-Étienne Cartier monument (p55), way down at the end of the street at the leafy base of Mont-Royal. Directly opposite the church stands ❹ **Les Cours Rachel**, which was once a boarding school but has been converted into condos.

Walk northeast along Rue Rachel Est and turn right onto ❺ **Avenue Châteaubriand**. A run-down street through the 1970s, today this narrow lane has been spruced up with blue, green and turquoise paint and potted plants hanging outside the windows. Here too you'll spot another of this town's signature objects: the external staircase.

officially designated for a park. The building houses a small permanent exhibition on the history of the park, a visitors center and a **cafe** selling soups and sandwiches. There's also a gift shop selling bird-watching paraphernalia, maps of the park and souvenirs.

CROIX DU MONT-ROYAL MONUMENT
About 550m north of Kondiaronk lookout stands the Mont-Royal Cross, one of Montréal's most familiar landmarks. Thirty-one meters tall and made of reinforced steel, the cross was erected in 1924 on the very spot where Maisonneuve placed a wooden cross.

According to legend, when floods threatened the fledgling colony in 1643, Maissonneuve prayed to the Virgin Mary to save the town. When the waters receded, out of gratitude Maisonneuve carried a cross up the steep slopes and planted it there. The white illuminated cross is visible from anywhere downtown.

CIMETIÈRE NOTRE-DAME-
DES-NEIGES CEMETERY
(www.notredamedesneigescemetery.ca; 4601 Chemin de la Côte-des-Neiges; ⊘8am-5pm; ⓂCôte-des-Neiges) More than one million people have found their final resting place here since this Catholic cemetery opened in 1854, making it the largest cemetery in Canada and the third-largest in North America. It was initially inspired by the Père Lachaise Cemetery in Paris.

The catalog of permanent guests includes 20 Montréal mayors, a number of ex-passengers from the *Titanic*, and Calixa Lavallée, the composer of 'O Canada.' The **cemetery office** (⊘8:30am-4:30pm Mon-Fri, 9am-3pm Sat) has brochures for self-guided tours around the tombs but there's also a map posted at the entrance.

CIMETIÈRE MONT-ROYAL CEMETERY
(www.mountroyalcem.com; 1297 Chemin de la Forêt; ⊘10am-6pm; ⓂÉdouard-Montpetit) Celebrating its 160th anniversary in 2012, Cimetière Mont-Royal was founded in 1852 for the last journey of Presbyterians, Anglicans, Unitarians, Baptists and nondenominationals. In 1901 it opened Canada's first crematorium. One famous grave is that of Charles Melville Hayes, the president of the Grand Trunk Railway who went down with the Titanic. The cemetery is laid out like a landscape garden and is perfect for the Goth-

TAM-TAM JAM

Huge crowds of alternative free spirits gather every Sunday afternoon in summer for the legendary 'tam-tam' concerts at the edge of Parc du Mont-Royal, when the pounding rhythms and whirling dancers seem to put everyone in a trance. The action takes place at the **George-Étienne Cartier monument** (off Map p292) opposite Parc Jeanne-Mance, at the corner of Ave du Parc and Ave Duluth. The percussionists are tireless in their dedication, with some riffs going on for an hour or more, and other instruments join in on the odd occasion. Vendors along the grass sell alternative handicrafts (eg dream catchers, crystals and bead jewelry) and sarongs, plus percussion instruments in case you left your tambourine and conga drum at home.

historically interested; it also hosts history walks, open-air plays, and guided tours.

EATING

Plateau Mont-Royal has a fantastic variety of bistros, upscale restaurants and bohemian-style cafes. Rue Prince-Arthur Est is a narrow residential street that has been converted into a dining and entertainment enclave. The restaurant segment runs west from leafy Carré St-Louis (just north of Rue Sherbrooke) to a block west of Blvd St-Laurent. Many of the small, inexpensive and mostly ethnic restaurants here aren't licensed to serve alcohol, so bring your own wine.

TOP CHOICE LE FILET SEAFOOD $$$
Map p292 (✆514-360-6060; www.lefilet.ca; 219 Ave du Mont-Royal Ouest; mains $13-20; ⊘dinner Tue-Sat; ⓂMont-Royal) Claude Pelletier of Club Chasse et Pêche (p62) teams up with Yazu Okasaki in this marvelous new addition to the Plateau dining scene. 'The Net' presents masterfully crafted fish and seafood with Japanese touches in a gorgeously low-lit setting facing Parc Jeanne-Mance.

The grilled octopus with marrow and cherry tomatoes will make you wish there were more than just eight legs. The menu is very market-based and changes often, but other favorites include the Prince Edward Island oysters, Gaspé char, and kurobuta pork. Typical meals run $40 to $60. Be sure to reserve well in advance.

TOP CHOICE SCHWARTZ'S   DELI $

Map p292 (www.schwartzsdeli.com; 3895 Blvd St-Laurent; mains $5-16; ⊘8am-12:30am Sun-Thu, to 1:30am Fri, to 2:30am Sat; MSt-Laurent, then bus 55) Reuben Schwartz, a Romanian Jew, opened the soon-to-be Montréal icon in 1928, and it's been going strong ever since. Schwartz's meat goes through a 14-day regime of curing and smoking on the premises before landing on your plate after a final three-hour steam. It's widely considered to serve the best smoked meat in Montréal, whether it's brisket, duck, chicken or turkey, all piled high on sourdough rye bread. You can order it fat, medium (recommended) or lean. In 2012, Schwartz's was purchased by a consortium including Céline Dion, but they have promised not to allow franchises and to keep the brand authentic. Meanwhile, expect the usual long lines. If you don't feel like waiting, try Lester's (p133) for a somewhat similar experience.

AU PIED DE COCHON   QUÉBÉCOIS $$$

Map p292 (☑514-281-1114; www.restaurantau pieddecochon.ca; 536 Ave Duluth Est; mains $20-51; ⊘dinner Tue-Sun; MSherbrooke) One of Montréal's most respected restaurants (it's so well known that there's no sign) features extravagant pork, duck and steak dishes, along with its signature foie gras plates. Irreverent, award-winning chef Martin Picard takes simple ingredients and transforms them into works of art. The famous and surprisingly magnificent *canard en conserve* ('duck in a can'), for instance, is half a roasted duck *magret* served with foie gras, cabbage, bacon, venison and spices, sealed and cooked in a can – then opened tableside and dumped over celery root puree on toast. Dishes are rich and portions are large, so bring an appetite. Reservations essential.

LES TROIS PETITS BOUCHONS   FRENCH $$

Map p292 (☑514-285-4444; www.lestroispetits bouchons.com, in French; 4669 Rue St-Denis; mains $16-30; ⊘dinner Mon-Sat; MMont-Royal)

In this delightfully convivial minimalist space, chef Audrey Dufresne's motto is '*terroir* products are the basis, and our passion does the rest.' Market-based dishes like chorizo ravioli, veal tartare, Kamouraska lamb and mushroom tartine are some of the gems presented with impeccable service. No wonder some foodies call it the best restaurant in the city. Reservations essential.

L'EXPRESS   FRENCH $$

Map p292 (☑514-845-5333; restaurantlexpress. ca; 3927 Rue St-Denis; mains $11-28; ⊘8am-2am Mon-Fri, 10am-2am Sat, 10am-1am Sun; MSherbrooke) L'Express has all the hallmarks of a Parisian bistro – black-and-white checkered floor, art-deco globe lights, papered tables and mirrored walls. High-end bistro fare completes the picture with excellent seafood dishes (like grilled salmon dressed with sea salt, or almond-crusted sole), and even standards such as *confit de canard* (roast duck) are consistently delicious. The waiters can advise on the extensive wine list. Reservations are essential.

MOISHE'S   STEAKHOUSE $$$

Map p292 (☑514-845-1696; www.moishes.ca; 3961 Blvd St-Laurent; mains $26-54; ⊘dinner; MSt-Laurent, then bus 55) Moishe's feels a bit like a social club, although guests from all backgrounds come to consume its legendary grilled meats and seafood. Closely set tables and old-fashioned hardwood paneling set the backdrop to the feasting. Skip the appetizers and launch straight into a gargantuan rib steak served with tasty fries or a Monte Carlo potato. Reservations are essential.

PINTXO   SPANISH $$

Map p292 (☑514-844-0222; pintxo.ca; 256 Rue Roy Est; mains $20-34, tapas $4-12; ⊘lunch Wed-Sat, dinner daily; MSherbrooke) Tiny plates of tapas rule the day at this petite, artfully decorated Basque restaurant helmed by chef Alonso Ortiz. Start off with poached octopus carpaccio or scallops with olive tapenade before moving onto heartier plates of duck breast risotto and lamb shank with couscous. It's on a peaceful street in the Plateau and gets packed on weekend nights; recommendations are necessary.

BEAUTY'S   DINER $

Map p292 (www.beautys.ca; 93 Ave du Mont-Royal Ouest; breakfasts $10-16; ⊘7am-4pm; MMont-Royal) This sleek, retro '50s diner serves

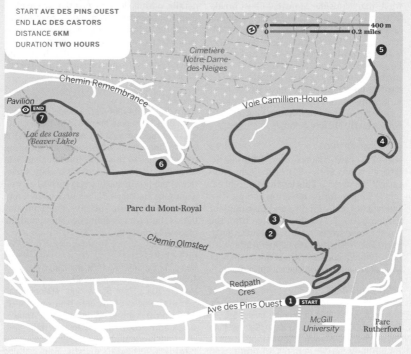

START **AVE DES PINS OUEST**
END **LAC DES CASTORS**
DISTANCE **6KM**
DURATION **TWO HOURS**

Neighborhood Walk
Montréal's Favorite Mountain

Many of Montréal's neighborhoods hug the foot of Parc du Mont-Royal, making everyone feel like they've got a bit of green space in their backyard. 'The Mountain,' as Mont-Royal is affectionately known by locals, is cherished for its winding trails, fresh air and terrific views.

The starting point for this walk is on **1 Avenue de Pins Ouest** at the staircase into the park. It's a fairly brisk 10- to 15-minute climb that alternates between steps and inclined trail.

You cross a large path and continue climbing to the signposted **2 Kondiaronk lookout**. The lookout offers stunning views of the downtown area, best seen in the early evening when the skyscrapers begin to light up. The nearby Chalet du Mont-Royal contains paintings of some key scenes from local history.

From the chalet, walk north along the trail named Chemin Olmsted about 600m to the

3 Croix du Mont-Royal. This is where city founder Maisonneuve allegedly planted a cross in thanksgiving to God for saving the city from flood.

Further along you can descend a set of stairs to reach the scenic lookout of **4 Belvédère Camillien-Houde**, one of the most romantic views in the city.

Returning to the path, head south toward **5 Maison Smith**, an 1858 heritage building that houses a permanent exhibition on the history and ongoing conservation of Mont-Royal. A visitors center doles out information on the park; the on-site cafe is a good spot to grab a bite or a cold drink.

Another 500m further south, the artificial pond **7 Lac des Castors** is a haven of toy-boat captains in summer and ice-skaters in winter. Refreshments are available at the pavilion, and in warm weather the meadows around the pond are full of sunbathers.

what many consider Montréal's best breakfast – all day long. Owner Hymie Sckolnick greets everyone with 'How are you, dahling.' Ask for 'the Special' – a toasted bagel with lox, cream cheese, tomato and onion. From the freshly squeezed juice to the piping-hot eggs, sausages and pancakes, it'll be hard to go anyplace else once you've tried it. Lineups on Saturday and Sunday mornings can run up to 40 minutes long, even in winter (arrive before 10am).

CAFÉ SANTROPOL CAFE $
Map p292 (www.santropol.com; 3990 Rue St-Urbain; mains $7-12; ☺11:30am-10pm; ⓜSt-Laurent, then bus 55) This iconic Montréal eatery is known for its towering and creative sandwiches, colorful digs and lush outdoor garden patio. Its creations range from the sweet root (carrots, raisins, coriander, nuts, mayo and fresh apple) to pepper island with ham (which comes with jalapeño pepper jelly, pesto and cream cheese spread).

ROBIN DES BOIS FRENCH $$
Map p292 (✆514-288-1010; robindesbois.ca, in French; 4653 Blvd St-Laurent; mains $16-26; ☺11:30am-10pm Mon-Fri, 5-10pm Sat; ⓜMont-Royal) Montréal's own Robin Hood, restaurateur Judy Servay donates all profits and tips from this St-Laurent hot spot to local charities. Ever-changing dishes scribbled on the chalkboard could include a succulent venison steak or a creamy wild-mushroom risotto. Reservations are recommended.

JANO PORTUGUESE $
Map p292 (www.restaurantjano.com; 3883 Blvd St-Laurent; mains $14-16; ☺5-11pm Mon-Wed, 11am-11pm Thu-Sun; ⓜSt-Laurent, then bus 55) The scent of charcoal-grilled meats and seafood lingers in the air at this welcoming, family-friendly Portuguese restaurant. The menu features straightforward selections of fresh fish, pork and steak, all grilled to choice tenderness. Warm colors, small tables and a buzzing atmosphere draw in the crowds, particularly on weekends, when waits can be long.

MISTO ITALIAN $$
Map p292 (www.restomisto.com; 929 Ave du Mont-Royal Est; mains $13-24; ☺lunch Wed-Fri, dinner daily; ⓜMont-Royal) Misto was one of the first 'see-and-be-seen' restaurants to open on Ave du Mont-Royal. It's set with exposed-brick walls and polished-wood

details, with a sleek curved bar, while electronic music plays overhead. Like moths to the flame, a fashion-conscious crowd dines here, eyeing one another over organic pastas, thin-crust pizzas, grilled salmon and other tasty but unsurprising fare. There's sidewalk dining in summer.

LA SALA ROSA SPANISH $$
Map p292 (✆514-844-4227; casadelpopolo.com; 4848 Blvd St-Laurent; mains $12-18, tapas $5-10; ☺dinner Tue-Sun; ⓜSt-Laurent, then bus 55) A festive, local and often Spanish-speaking crowd comes to this little Iberian gem. Sala Rosa is best know for its five tasty varieties of paella (including vegetarian) as well as numerous tapas dishes and a changing lineup of Spanish specials. On Thursday nights there's a live flamenco show, and the place gets packed.

AUX VIVRES VEGETARIAN $
Map p292 (✆514-842-3479; www.auxvivres.com; 4631 Blvd St-Laurent; mains $7-14; ☺11am-11pm Mon-Fri, 10am-11pm Sat & Sun; ⓜMont-Royal) Serving some of Montréal's top vegan fare, Aux Vivres whips up tasty fresh salads, soups and sandwiches, a hearty daily special and homemade desserts. The Dragon Bowl is a herbivore's delight. You can also stop in for fresh juices and teas, and dine alfresco in the back garden. Reservations recommended.

EURO DELI ITALIAN $
Map p292 (3619 Blvd St-Laurent; mains $7-10; ☺9am-11pm Sun-Thu, to midnight Fri & Sat; ⓜSt-Laurent, then bus 55) One of the lower Main's gems, for people-watching and its fresh pastas. This bustling eatery is cafeteria-style and food changes daily – just go up and choose your pasta from the counter. If chocolate cake is on offer when you visit, pounce! It's pure decadence.

LA BANQUISE QUÉBÉCOIS $
Map p292 (www.restolabanquise.com; 994 Rue Rachel Est; mains $5-10; ☺24hr; ⓜMont-Royal) A Montréal legend since 1968, La Banquise is probably the best place in town to sample *poutine*. More than two dozen varieties are available, including a veggie *poutine* (peppers, mushrooms, sautéed onions) and straight-up classic *poutine*. There's an outdoor terrace, a full breakfast menu and a selection of microbrews, plus the kitchen never closes.

TALKING FOOD

Menus in Montréal are often – but not always – bilingual. Regardless, if you need help with *le français*, don't be shy to ask (the waiters are used to it). Important note: in French, an *entrée* is an appetizer, not a main course – that's *le plat principal*. Another thing to watch out for is recognizing the difference between *pâte*, which means pasta, and *pâté*, which means that spreadable stuff often made of goose liver (though there are also vegetarian pâtés, such as *pâté aux champignons et tofu* (mushrooms and tofu).

LA BINERIE MONT ROYAL   QUÉBÉCOIS $
Map p292 (www.labineriemontroyal.com; 367 Ave du Mont-Royal Est; mains $6-10; ⊘6am-8pm Mon-Fri, 7:30am-3pm Sat & Sun; ⓂMont-Royal) Authentic Québécois cuisine is served from this dinerlike counter. The menu is crammed full of typical traditional comfort fare including *tourtière* (meat pie) and *pudding chômeur* (a bread pudding with brown sugar syrup), plus hearty egg-and-sausage breakfasts.

ST-VIATEUR BAGEL & CAFÉ   BAGELS $
Map p278 (www.stviateurbagel.com; 1127 Ave du Mont-Royal Est; sandwiches $4-8; ⊘6am-midnight; ⓂMont-Royal) A splendid cafe that serves its signature bagels, grilled or *nature*, with soup or salad. There are about a dozen sandwiches but most popular are the traditional smoked lox with cream cheese, and roast beef with Swiss cheese and tomato. You can also find breakfast bagels with eggs and ham.

MA-AM-M BOLDUC   QUÉBÉCOIS $
Map p292 (maammbolduc.com; 4351 Ave de Lorimier; mains $5-18; ⊘7:30am-10pm Mon-Fri, 8am-10pm Sat, 8:30am-10pm Sun; ⓂPapineau, then bus 10) This neighborhood eatery with piped-in punk and New Age music still serves mainstays of Québécois cuisine: meatball stew, *tourtière*, and more *poutine* than you can shake a trotter at. Long departed, Mme Bolduc's friendly round face still graces the marquee above the terrace tables.

PATATI PATATA   QUÉBÉCOIS $
Map p292 (4177 Blvd St-Laurent; mains $5-8; ⊘8am-11pm Mon-Fri, 11am-11pm Sat & Sun; ⓂSt-Laurent, then bus 55) This matchbox-sized, bohemian-style eatery is known for its *poutine*, borscht and mini burgers. It's a Montréal classic with rocking music and young efficient staff, and there's almost always a line snaking out the front. Grab a seat at the window and watch the city stroll past.

AU FESTIN DE BABETTE   ICE CREAM $
Map p292 (4085 Rue St-Denis; ice creams $3-5; ⊘10am-6pm Sun-Wed, to 10pm Thu-Sat; ⓂMont-Royal) This charming cafe with sidewalk terrace is famed for its homemade ice cream. The supremely satisfying *crème glacée molle à l'ancienne* is chocolate or vanilla ice cream blended on the spot with fresh mango, blueberries, raspberries, lychee, kiwi and other fruits.

🍷 DRINKING & NIGHTLIFE

RESERVOIR   PUB
Map p292 (brasseriereservoir.ca, in French; 9 Ave Duluth Est; ⊘noon-3am Mon, noon-3am Tue-Fri, 10:30am-3am Sat & Sun; ⓂSt-Laurent, then bus 55) We adore this low-key, friendly brasserie. It's nice but not too pricey and the mixed crowd is artsy but unpretentious. If you appreciate good beer, the owners brew their own on the premises. A small kitchen prepares gourmet lunch, after-work snacks and weekend brunch. In summer, the 2nd-floor terrace overlooks this busy corner.

BILY KUN   BAR
Map p292 (bilykun.com, in French; 354 Ave du Mont-Royal Est; ⓂMont-Royal; 🕾) One of the pioneers of 'tavern chic,' Bily Kun is a favorite local hangout for a chilled DJ-spun evening. First-time visitors usually gawk at the ostrich heads that overlook the bar but soon settle into the music groove of DJs and sometimes bands. Upstairs, **O Patro Vys** (⌨514-845-3855) is a performing-arts hall that features anything from electronic installations to poetry slams.

CANDI   BAR
Map p292 (www.gogogroup.ca; 1148 Ave du Mont-Royal Est; ⓂMont-Royal) This trippy bar will takes you back to your childhood – unless you didn't happen to love candy as a kid.

Pony up to the plastic-block bar for Slushie drinks ($11), crank the tabletop candy dispensers for sweets, and park your behind on a leggy barstool. The silliness continues in the bathroom, where guys can pee into mouth-shaped urinals. You'll feel like a kid in a candy store.

ELSE'S
BAR

Map p292 (156 Rue Roy Est; ◷10am-3am; ⓂSher-brooke) This is a warm and welcoming neighborhood bar where, as the saying goes, everyone knows your name. Settle into one of the worn chairs for an order of nachos, a tasty microbrew and a big portion of chat in front of the ceiling-high windows. Late-night jazz is a joy on weekends.

CHEZ JOSÉ
CAFE

Map p292 (173 Ave Duluth Est; ◷7am-7pm Mon-Fri, 9am-7pm Sat, 10am-7pm Sun; ⓂSherbrooke) Jolly owner José often mans the small kitchen of this tiny, colorful cafe. Besides serving some of the 'hood's best and strongest espresso, it's lauded for its breakfasts, seafood soup and Portuguese sausage. A young, bohemian clientele tends to spill onto the sidewalk to chat while eyeing the cast of characters that meanders by.

BARFLY
BAR

Map p292 (www.myspace.com/barflymtl; 4062 Blvd St-Laurent; ⓂSt-Laurent, then bus 55) Cheap, gritty, loud, fun and a little bit out of control – just the way we like our dive bars. Live punk bands and bedraggled hipsters hold court alongside aging rockers at this St-Laurent hole-in-the-wall. A Montréal must.

BAR PLAN B
BAR

Map p292 (www.barplanb.ca; 327 Ave du Mont-Royal Est; ◷3pm-3am; ⓂMont-Royal) Warm decor, elegant snacks and a liquor menu that showcases absinthe make this high-end bar a perfect date and pickup spot. It's also perfect for drinking with friends, and usually not too loud to talk. A sophisticated French-speaking crowd flocks here after work and on weekends. As its name decrees, when there's nowhere else to go, try Plan B.

BAR SALON LA PORTE ROUGE
BAR

(www.barsalonlaporterouge.com; 1834 Ave du Mont-Royal Est; ⓂMont-Royal) This historical old saloon has been fancied up into a trendy hangout. Old-fashioned decor pays tribute to the space's illustrious past, as do drink names like Scarlett O'Hara and Pink Lady.

PLATEAU MONT-ROYAL DRINKING & NIGHTLIFE

POUTINE!
....

Broach the topic of *poutine* with a native Montrealer, and either a look of utter rapture or vomitous disgust will likely cross the face of your interlocutor. One of the world's most humble dishes, *poutine* was invented in rural Québec sometime in the 1950s. According to legend, a restaurateur experienced an epiphany while waiting on a customer who ordered fries while waiting for his cheese curds. The word '*poutine*' itself derives from an Acadian slang term for 'mushy mess' or 'pudding.'

For the uninitiated, *poutine* at first glance looks like the leftovers from a large dinner party all slopped into one giant pile, scraped onto a plate and plunked down on the table. While recipes and imaginations run wild when it comes to *poutine,* the basic building block of the Québécois dish is fries smothered in cheese curds and gravy. Varieties include 'all dress' (sautéed mushrooms and bell peppers), 'richie boy' (ground beef), Italian (beef and spaghetti sauce), barbecue or even smoked meat. In the past, going out for *poutine* had about as much sex appeal as chowing down on boiled hot dogs and tap water; these days, however, even exalted restaurants like Au Pied de Cochon serve the well-known dish.

➜ **La Banquise** (p118) Serving 25 different types of *poutine* round the clock, this is the gold standard for classic *poutine.*

➜ **Au Pied de Cochon** (p116) Elevates the simple dish to respectability with its famous *poutine* foie gras.

➜ **Ma-am-m Bolduc** (p119) Try *poutine* Italian style, with spaghetti sauce or red wine and garlic.

➜ **Patati Patata** (p119) The house special is Patat-ine, with cheese curds served in an edible crispy potato basket.

On Sunday nights, electro DJs draw a trashy-glam fashion crowd, both gay and straight.

BIFTECK

BAR

Map p292 (3702 Blvd St-Laurent; MSt-Laurent, then bus 55; 🛜) Pool, popcorn and indie rockers hold court alongside students and random weirdos at this legendary dive bar that's as much part of the Main's culture as smoked meat and bagels. Drinks are cheap (cash only), the faux country-and-western decor hasn't budged for decades and the rough-around-the-edges staff keep it real. A great place to kick off a night out.

BLIZZARTS

BAR

Map p292 (http://blizzarts.ca; 3956a Blvd St-Laurent; ⊙8pm-3am; MSt-Laurent, then bus 55) Blizz is one of the Plateau's coolest little spots. It's part bar, part pub and part club (at least, when the small dance floor fills up – which is fairly often): local DJs spin house, techno, electro, breaks, jazz, funk, hip-hop, roots and dub to a small crowd both trendy and friendly. The artwork on the walls, exhibited by local artists, changes every month or so.

BLUEDOG MOTEL

BAR

Map p292 (3958 Blvd St-Laurent; MSt-Laurent, then bus 55) Next door to Blizzarts is Blue-dog, painted – you guessed it – blue. With a younger, inebriated crowd of arty urban revelers, music varies from hip-hop to trendy post-electro and dance beats. On Sunday nights there's a free keg on the dance floor!

EDGAR HYPERTAVERNE

BAR

Map p292 (hypertaverne.com, in French; 1562 Ave du Mont-Royal Est; ⊙4pm-1am Mon, 3pm-3am Tue-Sat; MMont-Royal) Once a trashy dive, Edgar's today appeals to the well-educated, cognac-sipping crowd of the Plateau. When they're not air-kissing their groupies, the DJs serve up a discriminating mix of acid jazz and New Age music. The wine list is copious.

GOGO LOUNGE

BAR

Map p292 (www.gogogroup.ca; 3682 Blvd St-Laurent; MSt-Laurent, then bus 55) The retro-kitsch decor here looks like it was copied from an Austin Powers movie: '60s psych-edelics, flower-power motifs, glistening vinyl and teardrop chairs. Friendly, flirty staff shake martinis and dance on the bar, while regulars jump the long lineups for a guaranteed party any night of the week.

L'ESCOGRIFFE

BAR

Map p292 (www.lescobar.com, in French; 4467 Rue St-Denis; MMont-Royal) Though you're apt to see some dubious characters staggering into this small, dungeon-like bar, the 'um, what?' factor is part of L'Esco's enduring punk-rock charm. Over the years many amazing bands have graced its tiny stage, and the bar continues to book acts some nights. On Sundays, resident DJs spin laid-back new wave, indie rock and rockabilly, making this deliciously dark hole-in-the-wall ideal for knocking a few back with friends.

QUAI DES BRUMES

BAR

Map p292 (www.quaidesbrumes.ca, in French; 4481 Rue St-Denis; ⊙3pm-3am; MMont-Royal) This Parisian-style cafe features ornate framed mirrors, curlicue moldings and paneling that's been toasted brown by a million cigarettes. This fine venue for live jazz, rock and blues also has DJ-spun techno in the upstairs disco.

SALON OFFICIEL

BAR

Map p292 (351 Rue Roy Est; ⊙8pm-3am Tue-Sat; MSherbrooke) This small neighborhood bar-meets-club hosts DJ nights with the city's best up-and-comers spinning the platters. Depending on the night, you can get rock, electro, punk or dance stuff. Local club kids are well acquainted with this location in its former incarnation as Roy Bar, a skateboarder scene until 2007. Drinks are still cheap.

LES FOLIES

CAFE

Map p292 (www.restofolies.ca; 701 Ave du Mont-Royal Est; ⊙9am-10:30pm Sun-Thu, to 12:30am Fri & Sat; MMont-Royal) A cross between a bar, cafe and club, the oh-so-chic Folies has a DJ every night spinning trendy music and, much more importantly, the only side-walk terrace on Ave du Mont-Royal. Too-thin models and creative types breeze in to chow down on a quick croque monsieur with mineral water before evaporating into the night.

BIÈRES & COMPAGNIE

PUB

Map p292 (www.bieresetcompagnie.ca, in French; 4350 Rue St-Denis; MMont-Royal) This relaxed pub has a great choice of European and local microbrews alongside excellent pub grub like burgers (bison, caribou or ostrich), beer-breaded onion rings and mussels done several ways.

PLATEAU MONT-ROYAL DRINKING & NIGHTLIFE

DAVID GIRAL / ALAMY ©

1. Plateau Mont-Royal (p110)

Dotted with Victorian mansions, this area boasts a rich blend of parks, boutiques and eateries.

2. Lac des Castors (p113)

'Beaver Lake' in Parc du Mont-Royal is a center for paddleboating in summer and ice-skating in winter.

3. Parc du Mont-Royal (p113)

Montréal's favorite mountain is loved for its winding trails, fresh air and terrific views.

4. Blvd St-Laurent (p112)

'The Main' is a mixture of hip cafes and nightspots, old-world delis and grocery stores, and funky hipster shops.

KOKO
BAR

Map p292 (www.kokomontreal.com; 8 Rue Sherbrooke Ouest; MSt-Laurent) The specialty
cocktails and luxe surroundings of this
loungey restaurant inside the Opus Hotel
attract jet-setters and the city's fashion
crowd. DJs mix house music on weekends
and there's a massive outdoor terrace for a
swanky soiree with hip downtown flair.

SAPHIR
CLUB

Map p292 (www.saphirbar.com; 3699 Blvd St-Laurent; ⊙Wed-Sat; MSherbrooke) Underground
punk, Goth, glam and industrial are in
full effect at this cavernous two-story club.
Cheap drinks, unbridled dance floors and
no attitude make this club experience a
dark and dirty free-for-all.

TOKYO BAR
CLUB

Map p292 (www.tokyobar.com; 3709 Blvd St-
Laurent; MSherbrooke) This successful little
club reels in scenesters and suburbanites in
their 20s and early 30s to dance up a storm.
Weekends are more mainstream, while a
cool crowd hangs out Wednesdays for 'rock
night'. The huge rooftop bar and patio rules
on summer nights! Great staff, too.

☆ ENTERTAINMENT

CASA DEL POPOLO
LIVE MUSIC

Map p292 (☑514-284-3804; casadelpopolo.com;
4873 Blvd St-Laurent; ⊙noon-3am; MSt-Laurent,
then bus 55) One of Montréal's cutest live
venues, the 'House of the People' is also
known for its vegetarian platters and sandwiches, its talented DJs and as an venue for
art-house films and spoken-word performances. Monday and Tuesday DJ nights are
usually free. It's associated with the tapas
bar La Sala Rosa (p118) and its concert venue La Sala Rossa.

THÉÂTRE DU RIDEAU VERT
THEATER

Map p292 (☑514-845-0267; www.rideauvert.
qc.ca, in French; 4664 Rue St-Denis; MMont-Royal)
This quality French-language venue has
an elegant stage that's well suited to classic plays. Its lineup includes both repertory
and contemporary drama with a preference
for timeless works, like a French-language
performance of the Jewish classic *Fiddler
on the Roof*! The theater's stage designs, costumes and lighting have earned accolades.

LA TULIPE
LIVE MUSIC

off Map p292 (☑514-526-4000; www.latulipe.ca;
4530 Ave Papineau; MMont-Royal, then bus 97)
From underground indie bands to musical retrospectives, any of the city's coolest
concerts take place in this beautifully restored and intimate theater. Located in the
French-speaking east area of the Plateau.

AGORA DE LA DANSE
DANCE

Map p292 (www.agoradanse.com; 840 Rue Cherrier; MSherbrooke) Based in the striking old
Palestre National building, this contemporary dance center explores modern and experimental forms. Its student and independent dance companies stage regular performances. Recent artists have included Crystal
Pite, Ghislaine Doté and Deborah Dunn.

LES GRANDS BALLETS CANADIENS
DANCE

Map p292 (www.grandsballets.qc.ca; 4816 Rue
Rivard; MMont-Royal) You can be assured of
a treat if you see Québec's leading ballet
troupe. As well as playing four shows annually in Montréal at various venues, the 34
dancers stage two international tours per
year. Its classical and modern programs are
both innovative and accessible. Check the
website for details.

MAINLINE THEATRE
THEATER

Map p292 (☑514-849-3378; mainlinetheatre.ca;
3997 Blvd St-Laurent; MMont-Royal) Located on
the Main (hence the name), this intimate
indie theater presents mostly new plays. It
also serves as headquarters for the annual
Montréal Fringe theater festival.

THÉÂTRE DE QUAT' SOUS
THEATER

Map p292 (☑514-845-7277; www.quatsous.com,
in French; 100 Ave des Pins Est; MSherbrooke) In
a former synagogue, this cozy theater is a
launchpad for the careers of young singers,
directors and playwrights. Its forte is intellectual and experimental drama.

LE DIVAN ORANGE
LIVE MUSIC

Map p292 (divanorange.org; 4234 Blvd St-Laurent; ⊙4pm-3am Tue-Sat; MSt-Laurent, then bus
55) This fantastic space was launched as a
kind of restaurant-entertainment venue co-
op. There's a terrific artistic vibe here. On
any given night there may be a DJ, world
music performer or record launch.

THÉÂTRE LA CHAPELLE
THEATER

Map p278 (lachapelle.org, in French; 3700 Rue St-
Dominique; MSherbrooke) This little mecca of

OUR LADY OF THE SNOWS

The Cimetière Notre-Dame-des-Neiges has several interesting mausoleums. The Pietà Mausoleum contains a full-scale marble replica of Michelangelo's famous sculpture in Saint Peter's Basilica in Rome. Other mausoleums in the cemetery emit solemn music, including that of Marguerite Bourgeoys, a nun and teacher who was beatified in 1982 (see Chapelle Notre-Dame-de-Bonsecours, p54). Built in 2007, the Esther Blondin Mausoleum is a modern facility housing 6000 crypts and niches, reflecting the increasing popularity of communal memorial spaces.

contemporary works presents cutting-edge theater and dance. It's also a studio space for artistic creation, aiming to mentor young, cutting-edge artists while contributing new energy to the city's cultural life.

🛍 SHOPPING

LIBRAIRIE MICHEL FORTIN BOOKS
Map p292 (www.librairiemichelfortin.com; 3714 Rue St-Denis; MSherbrooke) A mecca for every foreign-language student and linguist freak in town. You can find books, cassettes or novels on just about every language in the world from Thai to Basque to Georgian.

ORIGINAL BOUTIK FASHION
Map p292 (www.originalboutik.com, in French; 4897 Blvd St-Laurent; ☺11am-6pm Mon-Wed, to 8pm Thu & Fri; MMont-Royal) Print your photo, logo or personal creed on customizable T-shirts, caps and bags at this funky minimalist space. You can choose from a variety of cool designs, and you'll get a discount for printing in bulk.

LOLA & EMILY FASHION
Map p292 (www.lolaandemily.com; 3475 Blvd St-Laurent;☺11am-6pm Mon-Wed, to 9pm Thu & Fri, to 5pm Sat, 12-5pm Sun; MSherbrooke) Less is more at this whimsically girlie shop designed like your dream vintage apartment. Carefully selected clothes by brands like Swedish designer Filippa K, Denmark's Designers Remix, Belgium's Essential and Canada's Ça Va de Soi are displayed in antique Indian furniture, which is also for sale.

SCANDALE FASHION
Map p292 (scandale.com; 3639 Blvd St-Laurent; ☺11am-6pm Mon-Wed & Sat, to 7pm Thu, to 9pm Fri, 12pm-5p Sun; MSt-Laurent, then bus 55) The magnificent Marie-Josée Gagnon has been running this boutique since 1977, bringing in exotic Parisian imports and more recently showing off the creations of Georges Lévesque, one of Québec's most exciting designers, known for cutting-and-pasting shapes and fabrics.

U&I FASHION
Map p292 (www.boutiqueuandi.com; 3650 Blvd St-Laurent; MSherbrooke) Local designers like Denis Gagnon are featured at this award-winning boutique peppered with offerings from Paris and other fashion capitals. Brands include Moncler, Canada Goose, Levi's and Comme des Garcons accessories.

DUO FASHION
Map p292 (www.boutiqueduo.com; 30 Rue Prince-Arthur Ouest; MSherbrooke) If you're a suave fellow looking to dress sharp, head to this well-stocked little shop, staffed (it would appear) by models with a penchant for men's fashion. Duo carries hot brands like Swedish suitmaker J.Lindeberg and Canada's own DSquared, as well as designer sneakers and accessories. Fedora, anyone?

KANUK FASHION, OUTERWEAR
Map p292 (www.kanuk.com; 485 Rue Rachel Est; MMont-Royal) When people in Québec say 'Kanuk' they mean the winter coats that last a lifetime, and stay toasty in temperatures dipping to -30°C. Although they're found throughout the province, this flagship store has the best selection (plus seasonal sales), along with raincoats, swimsuits, backpacks and hiking gear.

COFFRE AUX TRÉSORS
DU CHAINON FASHION, VINTAGE
Map p292 (www.lechainon.org; 4375 Blvd St-Laurent;☺closed Mon; MSt-Laurent, then bus 55) There are several *friperies* (used clothing stores) in this area, where Chainon takes the cake for its vintage hipster accoutrements. Browse through endless racks for five-dollar gold pumps and monogrammed bowling shirts, tea sets, horn-rimmed glasses, houndstooth ties and other treasures.

BIRD-WATCHING ON 'THE MOUNTAIN'

Parc du Mont-Royal has some fantastic bird-watching opportunities, particularly in spring. A great number of migrators use the area as a passage on their way to breeding grounds. In both the park and in nearby Cimetière Mont-Royal, look out for screech owls, red-shouldered hawks, northern orioles, rose-breasted grosbeaks, bluebirds, olive-sided flycatchers, indigo buntings and many more species. In winter hardy bird-lovers come out for walks along the bird-feeder circuit that goes around the Summit Loop (the park places feeders out from November to April). Guided walks with a member of the park's conservation staff are held on Saturdays from January to mid-March. Contact **Les Amis de la Montagne** (www.lemontroyal.qc.ca), located at Maison Smith (p113), for more information.

FRIPERIE ST-LAURENT   FASHION, VINTAGE
Map p292 (3976 Blvd St-Laurent; MSherbrooke) This is another favorite *friperie* because of its small but extremely well-chosen selection. Famous 1940s ties, cowboy and motorcycle boots and Gothic-flavored blouses adorn fresh and colorful window displays.

CRUELLA   GOTH & FETISH
Map p292 (www.cruella.ca; 263 Ave du Mont-Royal Est; MMont-Royal) With a coffin centerpiece and one of the biggest arrays of Goth and fetish clothing in Montréal, Cruella is the biggest apparition in the Plateau grave-digger's scene. Slip into a chain-link miniskirt, dominatrix leggings or a Victorian shroud to give your party that something extra, or pick up vampire fangs and bondage icons.

ZONE   HOMEWARES
Map p292 (www.zonemaison.com; 4246 Rue St-Denis; ☺10am-7pm Mon-Wed, to 9pm Thu & Fri, to 5:30pm Sat, to 5pm Sun; MSherbrooke) Affordably chic housewares and home accents is the name of the game at this chain of shops. The simple and pretty kitchen accessories, picture frames, linens, lamps, lighting and bathroom stuff make terrific gifts for yourself or someone else.

🏃 SPORTS & ACTIVITIES

LE GRAND CYCLE   BICYCLE RENTAL
Map p292 (www.legrandcycle.com; 901 Rue Cherrier Est; bicycle per 4 hr/day $25/35; ☺9am-7pm Mon-Fri, 10am-5pm Sat & Sun; MSherbrooke) Le Grand Cycle is a fine place to get you rolling, with good eight-speed city bikes for rent plus all the extras. The dinerlike counter is a nice touch: you can grab a sandwich,

cold drink or espresso and get the latest on Montréal's rapidly changing bike scene.

LA MAISON DES CYCLISTES   BICYCLE RENTAL
Map p292 (www.velo.qc.ca; 1251 Rue Rachel Est; bicycle per day $30; ☺9am-6pm; MMont-Royal) Described as the nerve center of Québec's biking culture, this three-story house in the Plateau is an essential stop for avid cyclists in the city. You'll find a shop with cycling books, maps and guides; the Velo Québec association (involved in developing one of the largest bicycling networks in North America); a travel agency for planning biking trips; info on upcoming events; and a cozy cafe. It's right along the bike path that runs above Parc La Fontaine.

STUDIO BLISS   SPA
Map p292 (☎514-286-0007; www.studiobliss.ca; 3841 Blvd St-Laurent; 1hr class $17; MSherbrooke) Equal parts spa and yoga studio, Studio Bliss aims to rejuvenate the body by a variety of passive and kinetic means. Yoga classes run throughout the week, along with prenatal yoga and meditation workshops. You can also opt for vitality wraps, therapeutic baths and various massages.

AVEDA MONTRÉAL LIFESTYLE SALON SPA & ACADEMY   SPA
Map p292 (☎514-499-9494; www.avedamontreal-lifestyle.com; 3613 Blvd St-Laurent; ☺9am-5pm Mon, to 8pm Tue & Wed, 10am-9pm Thu & Fri; MSt-Laurent, then bus 55) This renovated 930-sq-meter spa and salon offers a wide range of treatments and pampering packages. A favorite is the Rejuvenating Experience ($175), featuring a rosemary-mint body wrap, a 30-minute massage and a manicure and pedicure. You can also opt for facials, various massages (chakra balancing massage, stone massage), waxing, peels and haircuts.

Little Italy, Mile End & Outremont

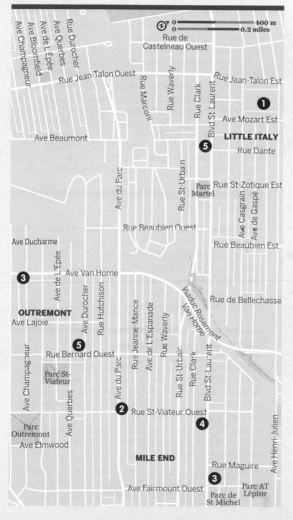

Neighborhood Top Five

1 Exploring the fresh produce, hawker stalls, and delightful seafood, sandwiches and desserts at the colorful **Marché Jean-Talon** (p129).

2 Snacking on the best bagels in the world – bar none – at **St-Viateur Bagel** (p131).

3 Spoil yourself with some of Montréal's best dining options at charmers such as **Van Horne** (p129) and **Lawrence** (p131).

4 Trolling quirky neighborhood shops such as **Monastiraki** (p137) for retro junk – or treasures, depending on your taste.

5 Old-world pleasures: Nursing an espresso at **Caffè Italia** (p132) and munching on a smoked meat on rye at **Lester's** (p133).

For more detail of this area, see Map p296 ➡

Best Places to Eat

➡ Van Horne (p129)
➡ Kitchen Galerie (p131)
➡ Lawrence (p131)
➡ Jun I (p131)
➡ Dépanneur Le Pick Up (p131)
➡ Lester's (p133)

For reviews, see p129 ➡

Best Places to Drink

➡ La Buvette Chez Simone (p136)
➡ Whiskey Café (p136)
➡ Chez Serge (p136)
➡ La Croissanterie Figaro (p137)
➡ Caffè Italia (p132)
➡ L'Assomoir (p136)

For reviews, see p136 ➡

Best Places to Shop

➡ Monastiraki (p137)
➡ Les Touilleurs (p138)
➡ Galerie CO (p139)

For reviews, see p137 ➡

Explore Little Italy, Mile End & Outremont

These three neighborhoods are a foodie's nirvana, distilled from a potent mish-mash of Italian, Portuguese, Jewish, and Québécois roots. The good thing is there's plenty of walking to be done to burn off those extra calories. Most of the area can be explored in a day, though you might want to return once or twice in the evening for dinner.

Start your day at the flavor cornucopia that is Marché Jean-Talon, grabbing fresh fruit or a crepe for breakfast before diving deeper into Little Italy, taking in the 1930s ceiling fresco of Mussolini at the Église Madonna Della Difesa. Stroll down Blvd St-Laurent, where the green-white-red flag is proudly displayed, pausing for an espresso at Caffè Italia and some fine contemporary art at three galleries near Rue Beaubien.

A bus along the boulevard can bring you back downtown if you're tired out, or drop you near Ave Fairmount. This area is a good spot to explore Mile End, a multi-ethnic neighborhood with great dining along Ave Laurier, fantastic bagels, and increasingly trendy hangouts at its epicenter: Rue St-Viateur and Blvd St-Laurent.

Further west, Outremont is largely a residence for wealthy Francophones. Fabulous old mansions lie on leafy streets northwest of Rue Bernard. There is also a significant Hassidic community in Outremont.

Local Life

➡ **Eating out** This area has some of Montréal's best up-and-coming restaurants including Lawrence (p131).
➡ **Catch the game** Take in soccer with locals at Café Olimpico (p137) or hockey at Chez Serge (p136).
➡ **For the kitchen** Cruise the high-end cooking boutiques like L'Émouleur (p138) along Ave Laurier or try a cooking course at Les Touilleurs (p138).

Getting There & Away

➡ **Metro** Though not ideally located, Laurier on the orange line gives you access to Ave Laurier, while Jean-Talon (on the orange and blue lines) puts you within easy reach of Marché Jean-Talon. Outremont has its own station on the blue line.

➡ **Bus** Bus 55 runs along Blvd St-Laurent; bus 46 runs on part of Rue Bernard and Ave Laurier; bus 80 runs along Ave du Parc.

➡ **Walking** This is a large area to walk, but strolling along Laurier, Bernard or Saint-Viateur, as well as parts of Blvd St-Laurent, makes for enjoyable exploring.

◉ SIGHTS

MARCHÉ JEAN-TALON
MARKET

Map p296 (www.marchespublics-mtl.com; 7070 Ave Henri-Julien; ⊙7am-6pm Mon-Wed & Sat, 7am-8pm Thu & Fri, 7am-5pm Sun; ⓂJean-Talon) The pride of Little Italy, this huge covered market is Montréal's most diverse. Many chefs buy ingredients for their menus here or in the specialty food shops nearby. Three long covered aisles are packed with merchants selling fruit, vegetables and flowers as well as baked goods. The market is flanked by delis and cafe-restaurants with tiny patios. Even in winter the market is open under big tents.

Be sure to stop by the Marché des Saveurs du Québec (p137), one of the few large stores in town devoted entirely to Québec specialties such wine and cider, fresh cheeses, smoked meats, preserves and a huge number of tasteful gifts.

ÉGLISE ST-MICHEL ET ST-ANTOINE
CHURCH

Map p296 (http://swmichalmontreal.com; 5580 Rue St-Urbain; ⊙9am-10am Mon-Fri, 9:30am-12:30pm Sun; ⓂRosemont) This Byzantine-style church dominates the corner of Rue St-Urbain and Rue St-Viateur. Its dome and soaring turret make it one of the more unusual examples of church architecture in Montréal.

Completed in 1915, St Michel served a mostly Irish community up through the 1960s. Intriguing elements include the massive dome with a depiction of St Michael vanquishing the seven-headed serpent (representing the seven deadly sins), figures of descending angels (representing the fallen angels cast into hell) painted on the pendentives, and the shamrocks hidden in the design elements. Today, the church serves a largely Polish community, the latest wave of immigrants to the area.

ÉGLISE MADONNA DELLA DIFESA
CHURCH

Map p296 (http://difesa.ca; 6800 Ave Henri-Julien; ⊙2-6pm Tue-Thu, Sat & Sun; ⓂJean-Talon) Our Lady of Protection Church was built in 1919 according to the drawings of Florence-born Guido Nincheri (1885–1973), who spent the next two decades working on the Roman-Byzantine structure. The artist painted the church's remarkable **frescoes**, including one of Mussolini on horseback with a bevy of generals in the background. The work honored the formal recognition by Rome of the pope's sover-eignty over Vatican Ci... unveiled a few years l... to power. During WW... ers who had worked... interned by the Cana... fresco can be viewed... altar.

ÉGLISE ST-VIATEUR

Map p296 (www.saintviateu... 1175 Ave Laurier Ouest; ⊙4pm-5:30pm Mon... Thu, 10:30am-noon & 4:30-6pm Sun; ⓂLaurier, then bus 51) If you are already on Ave Laurier for the shopping and food, poke your head into this church, which opened in 1913. The interior is pure Gothic Revival with ornate paintings, stained glass, hand-crafted cabinets and sculptures by renowned Montréal artists; the impressive ceiling vaults depict the life of St Viateur. It's also home to a magnificent, century-old Casavant organ.

PARC OUTREMONT
PARK

Map p296 (cnr Ave Outremont & Ave St-Viateur; ⓂRosemont) One of Montréal's best-kept secrets, this small leafy green space is a great place for a bit of quiet time after exploring the neighborhood. Lovely Victorian homes ring the park, and benches provide a nice vantage point for viewing the small pond with fountain. This is a good spot to go, ice cream in hand, after a visit to Le Bilboquet (p133) two blocks northwest.

✗ EATING

Little Italy is a neighborhood full of old-fashioned trattorias and lively little cafes, where the heavenly aroma of freshly brewed espresso hangs in the air. Stylish new eateries, including some of the best in Montréal, have also established a strong presence here.

Mile End and Outremont are duly blessed in the dining department. Strewn with an impressive variety of Parisian-style bistros, high-end ethnic eateries and low-key cafes, these neighborhoods also boast two oven-baked stars of the city's culinary history: the famous Montréal bagel shops.

TOP CHOICE VAN HORNE
FRENCH $$

Map p296 (☑514-508-0828; http://vanhorneres taurant.com; 1268 Ave Van Horne; mains $20-28; ⊙dinner Tue-Sat; ⓂOutremont) Sophisticated,

GIBI CAFÉ
ST-VIATEUR
LE 2KM
1 TO 2 HOURS

OUTREMONT

LE ITALY, MILE END & OUTREMONT NEIGHBORHOOD WALK

Neighborhood Walk
Exploring Mile End & Outremont

Multicultural Mile End and Outremont are home to Hassidic Jews, Portuguese, Greeks and Italians, among others. You'll also find eclectic cafes, eye-catching boutiques, vegetarian restaurants, lively bars, leafy parks and great bagels.

Start at one of Mile End's great little spots, **1** **Le Cagibi Café**. Grab a coffee for fuel, or return at night for film screenings, live bands, book launches and other eclectic fare.

Turn right along **2** **Blvd St-Laurent** and take in some of the galleries and curio shops such as the prestigious Galerie Simon Blais.

Continue along Blvd St-Laurent and turn right onto Ave Fairmount. Near the corner is **3** **Au Papier Japonais**, a sweet little store specializing in gorgeous handmade paper plus Japanese-style blinds and more.

Made famous in a Mordecai Richler novel, **4** **Wilensky's Light Lunch** hasn't changed much since opening in 1937. For grilled salami and bologna sandwiches, Wilensky's is your place.

Continue the walk along Ave Fairmount, stopping for a bagel taste-test at the famous **5** **Fairmount Bagel**, archrival of St-Viateur Bagel.

Continuing on Fairmount, turn left on Ave de l'Épee and right on Ave Laurier. The magnificent church on the corner is **6** **Église St-Viateur**, an icon of the neighborhood.

Exiting the church, turn right up Ave Bloomfield and in two blocks you'll reach **7** **Parc Outremont**, a beautiful park with a tiny lake and a playground. Lovely Victorian homes surround it.

Exit the park onto Ave Outremont and continue up this street until reaching Rue Bernard. Go left to reach **8** **Le Bilboquet**, one of the best ice-cream shops in Montréal.

Zigzag over to **9** **Parc St-Viateur**, another peaceful green space in the neighborhood, and enjoy your ice cream!

market-sourced works of art are beautifully presented in this intimate spot that pays tribute to American businessman and gourmet William Van Horne. Chef Eloi Dion has a limited but rotating menu, featuring delectable choices like rabbit loin rolled in bacon and striped bass with ratatouille and coriander. Even the desserts are artful: watch out for the raspberry and lemon dome shaped like a breast.

TOP CHOICE ST-VIATEUR BAGEL BAKERY $

Map p296 (www.stviateurbagel.com; 263 Ave St-Viateur Ouest; bagels $0.75; ⊘24hr; ⓂPlace-des-Arts, then bus 80) Currently the bagel favorite of Montréal, St-Viateur Bagel was set up in 1957 (see p133) and has a reputation stretching across Canada and beyond for its perfectly crusty, chewy and slightly sweet creations – check out the newspaper articles from around the world by the entrance before you approach the inner sanctum to these baked rings. The secret to their perfection seems to be boiling in honey water followed by baking in the wood-fired oven. Whether you go with sesame seed, poppy, plain, or one of the other flavors, you'll be biting into a circle of dough made in heaven.

LAWRENCE EUROPEAN $$

Map p296 (☑514-503-1070; http://lawrencerestaurant.com; 5201 Blvd St-Laurent; mains $11-29; ⓦlunch Wed-Fri, dinner Wed-Sat, brunch Sat & Sun; ⓂLaurier) This gorgeously designed, high-style hipster eatery helmed by British chef Marc Cohen of The Sparrow offers a braised kid on toast that's to die for. With high windows looking out over the Main and an airy vibe, it's a perfect spot to sink your teeth into mussels steamed in wine or grilled ox heart and potatoes. Just don't expect anything too conventional.

MILOS GREEK $$$

Map p296 (☑514-272-3522; http://milos.ca; 5357 Ave du Parc; mains $29-47; ⊘noon-3pm Mon-Fri, 5:30-11pm daily; ⓂPlace-des-Arts, then bus 80) Rock stars, socialites and business leaders flock to this fashionable restaurant with Mediterranean stucco, big urns filled with dried flowers and refrigerated counters of mouthwatering fish and fruits. Dinner for two – e.g. a range of Greek appetizers, grilled loup de mer (seabass), fried veggies with tzatziki and fried cheese – could set you back $150 with wine. Reservations are essential.

KITCHEN GALERIE FRENCH $$$

Map p296 (☑514-315-8994; http://kitchengalerie.com, in French; 60 Rue Jean-Talon Est; mains $30-50; ⊘dinner Tue-Sat; ⓂJean-Talon) Jovial chefs Mathieu Cloutier and Jean-Philippe St-Denis are well situated by the Marché Jean-Talon for their succulently fresh market offerings, which change daily. Expect carnivore-oriented choices like bavette saignant (flank steak) with mashed potatoes, or foie gras in various incarnations. Be sure to call and reserve. If you can't get a table here, you can try their seafood-centric outpost on Rue Notre-Dame Ouest in Old Montréal, Kitchen Galerie Poisson (aka KGP).

DÉPANNEUR LE PICK UP DINER $

Map p296 (☑514-271-8011; http://depanneurlepickup.com; 7032 Rue Waverly; mains $4-7; ⊘7am-7pm Mon-Fri, 9am-7pm Sat, 10am-6pm Sun; ⓂDe Castelnau) Another hipster favorite, unpretentious Le Pick Up began as an authentic 1950s dépanneur (convenience store) and snack bar before the current owners took it over and added zines (homemade magazines) to the daily necessities on the shelves and 80s synth-pop to the stereo. Nosh on yummy veggie burgers, or grilled haloumi and pulled pork sandwiches at the grill counter; you can also soak up some rays at the picnic tables outside.

JUN I JAPANESE $$

Map p296 (☑514-276-5864; http://juni.ca; 156 Ave Laurier Ouest; mains $13-36; ⊘lunch Tue-Fri, dinner Mon-Sat; ⓂLaurier) Montréal has few authentic Japanese eateries, and fewer sushi specialists, but chef Junichi Ikematsu presents a menu you might find in Tokyo's posh Ginza shopping district. That isn't to say he doesn't deviate from Tokyo-style Edomae sushi with the the B-52, a toothsome delight of red tuna, crispy rice, spicy mayo and avocado. For landlubbers, there's also a delish roasted Nagano pork loin and pan-seared turkey terrine, along with a decent sake menu.

LEMÉAC FRENCH $$$

Map p296 (☑514-270-0999; http://restaurantlemeac.com; 1045 Ave Laurier Ouest; mains $20-36; ⊘noon-midnight Mon-Fri, 10am-midnight Sat & Sun; ⓂLaurier) A well-respected name among the well-heeled Laurier crowd, Leméac has a light and airy setting with huge windows overlooking the street, a lively ambience and beautifully turned-out plates. It's a popular brunch spot on weekends, and at night – the after-10pm three-course prix-fixe menu is an excellent value at $25.

CHEZ LÉVÊQUE
FRENCH $$

Map p296 (⏱514-279-7355; www.chezleveque. ca, in French; 1030 Ave Laurier Ouest; mains $19-26; ◔10am-11pm Sun-Tue, 10:30am-midnight Wed-Sat; Ⓜ️Place-des-Arts, then bus 80) This classic bistro attracts the beautiful people of Mile End and Outremont to chat about fashion, movies and business under irreverent religious art. Paris-born owner Pierre Lévêque presents a superb choice of traditional French cuisine with grilled meats (rack of lamb or caribou) and fresh seafood (red snapper, Atlantic salmon or bouillabaisse). Many of the fine wines are sold by the glass.

LA KHAÏMA
AFRICAN $$

Map p296 (⏱514-948-9993; http://lakhaima. net; 142 Fairmount Ouest; mains $14-18; ◔6pm-midnight Tue-Sun; Ⓜ️Laurier) For a taste of West Africa, head to this warm and welcoming Mauritanian spot. The friendly owner, in traditional dress, cooks up tasty slow-cooked recipes like spiced lentil soup and lamb or vegetables in peanut sauce over couscous. His 'nomad cusine' menu changes regularly and features only a few dishes per day, with emphasis on mezze-style offerings. There are regular live music performances too. Call to reserve.

LE PETIT ALEP
MIDDLE EASTERN $$

Map p296 (⏱514-270-9361; 191 Rue Jean-Talon Est; mains $12-28; ◔bistro 11am-11pm Tue-Sat, restaurant 5-10pm Tue & Wed, 5-11pm Thu-Sat; Ⓜ️Jean-Talon) The complex flavors of Syrian-Armenian cuisine draw diners from all over Montréal. A big menu includes hummus, salads and *muhammara* (spread made of walnuts, garlic, breadcrumbs, pomegranate syrup and cumin), plus beef kababs smothered in tahini, spices and nuts. Dine in the bright restaurant (the front wall opens up onto the street during nice weather) or, in the evening, the slightly swish dining room next door.

CAFFÈ ITALIA
CAFE $

Map p296 (⏱514-495-0059; 6840 Blvd St-Laurent; sandwiches $7 coffees $2-3; ◔6am-11pm; Ⓜ️Jean-Talon) This old-time Italian cafe has a loyal neighborhood following for its unpretentious charm. Plain Formica counters and faded Italian soccer posters

set the stage for lingering over excellent espresso and unfussy sandwiches. Depending on how things are going (with AC Milan football club), staff can be grumpy and terse or enthusiastically welcoming.

JULIETTE ET CHOCOLAT
CAFE $

Map p296 (http://julietteetchocolat.com; 377 Ave Laurier Ouest; mains $8-12; ◔11am-11pm Mon-Thu, 11am-midnight Fri, 10am-midnight Sat, 10am-11pm Sun; Ⓜ️Laurier) Montréal's chocolate lovers unite at this sweet two-level cafe on Laurier. The menu is built around chocolate, from decadent piping-hot crepes to milkshakes, smoothies and chocolate 'shots,' not to mention cups of creamy hot chocolate. The varieties (rated by bitterness, country of origin, percentage of cocoa etc) are endless. Black-and-white tile floors and an inviting ambience seduce lingerers. There's another location in the Quartier Latin (p102).

LA PANTHÈRE VERTE
VEGETARIAN $

Map p296 (www.lapanthereverte.com; 66 Rue St-Viateur Ouest; mains $7-11; ◔11am-9pm Mon-Sat, 11am-7pm Sun; Ⓜ️Rosemont) Green in every sense of the word, La Panthère Verte is a small casual vegetarian spot, where you can stop in for delicious falafel sandwiches, energy-charging juices and smoothies ,and fresh salad specials that change daily. Hanging plants, a zippy green paint job and curious colander lamps help to set set the scene.

PHAYATHAI
THAI $$

Map p296 (http://www.phayathailaurier.com; 107 Ave Laurier Ouest; mains $10-18; ◔noon-2:30pm & 5:30-10:30pm; Ⓜ️Laurier) Although the jury is out on who serves the city's best Thai food, this elegant little restaurant on Laurier is a strong contender. It's hard to go wrong with anything on the menu, with delicious and flavorful seafood soup, tender roasted duck and whole red snapper basted in red chili.

PIZZERIA NAPOLETANA
ITALIAN $

Map p296 (www.napoletana.com; 189 Rue Dante; mains $9-17; ◔11am-11pm Mon-Wed, 11am-midnight Thu-Sat, noon-10:30pm Sun; Ⓜ️De Castelnau) Homemade pasta sauces and thick-sauced pizzas (over 30 different types of each) draw Italian-loving crowds here all year long. The pizza crust – nice and crunchy – is the secret to Napoletana's success. The dining room is simple with neat

THE GREAT BAGEL DEBATE

The Montréal bagel has a long and venerable history. It all started in 1915 when Isadore and Fanny Shlafman, Jews from Ukraine, opened a tiny bakery on Rue Roy in the Plateau. They made the yeast bread rings according to a recipe they'd brought from the bakery where Shlafman's father worked. By 1919 they started the Montréal Bagel Bakery in a wooden shack just off Blvd St-Laurent, a few doors down from Schwartz's deli.

After WWII many Holocaust survivors emigrated to Montréal and the bagel market boomed. Isadore Shlafman decided to build a bakery in the living room of his house at 74 Ave Fairmount, where he opened Fairmount Bagel (p131) in 1950. Meanwhile Myer Lewkowicz, a Polish Jew who had survived Auschwitz, went on to establish St-Viateur Bakery (p131) in 1957. A legendary rivalry was born and scores of other bagel bakeries sprang up in their wake.

Ask any Montrealer whose bagel is best and passions will flare. Year-in and year-out tireless critics tour the main bagel bakeries to chat, chew and cogitate. In recent years St-Viateur has edged out Fairmount for the number-one slot. But locals do agree on one thing: they believe that Montréal's bagels are superior to their New York cousins. The Montréal bagel is lighter, sweeter and crustier, and chewy but not dense thanks to an enriched eggy dough that looks almost like batter. The dough hardly rises and the tender rings are formed by hand and boiled in a honey-and-water solution before baking in a wood-burning oven.

wood tables and chairs. Lines can be long, particularly in summer, so avoid peak hours. Bring your own wine. They only accept cash.

LE CAGIBI CAFÉ
VEGETARIAN $

Map p296 (www.lecagibi.ca; 5490 Blvd St-Laurent; mains $7-10; ☉6pm-midnight Mon, 9am-1am Tue-Fri, 10:30am-1am Sat, 10:30am-midnight Sun; Ⓜ Rosemont) Music-lovers and Plateau eccentrics hold court at this plant- and antique-filled vegetarian restaurant by day, bar by night. The menu features tasty soups, salads and baked goods. There's a good entertainment lineup by night: DJs, live bands, film screenings, book readings, slide shows and other eclectic fare.

LESTER'S
DINER $

Map p296 (www.lestersdeli.com; 1057 Rue Bernard Ouest; mains $6-14; ☉9am-9pm Mon-Fri, 9am-8pm Sat; Ⓜ Outremont) Serving some of the city's best smoked meat since 1951, this delicatessen is as much a part of Montréal folklore as the three-hour lunch. With its art-deco meets 1950s diner-style decor and period knickknacks adorning the walls, the restaurant attracts a fiercely loyal following of locals looking for the perfect smoked-meat sandwich (the old-fashioned is formidable), but there's also smoked salmon or salads and *karnatzel* (dried sausage).

LE BILBOQUET
ICE CREAM $

Map p296 (www.bilboquet.ca; 1311 Rue Bernard Ouest; cones $2-5; ☉11am-midnight in summer, until 8pm otherwise; Ⓜ Laurier) A legendary institution in Montréal, Le Bilboquet whips up highly addictive homemade ice cream and refreshing sorbets. On warm summer nights (and even on chilly evenings), long lines snake out the door. Although there's no seating inside, there are a couple of sidewalk tables, and some lovely little parks nearby.

WILENSKY'S LIGHT LUNCH
DINER $

Map p296 (34 Ave Fairmount Ouest; sandwiches $3-5; ☉9am-4pm Mon-Fri, 10am-4pm Sat; Ⓜ Laurier) Celebrating its 80th anniversary in 2012, Wilensky's feels like walking onto a 1950s Hollywood movie set. Rickety wooden stools line the counter and photographs from the 1930s festoon the walls. But this is no place for reminiscing or small talk: with little ceremony, the somewhat grumpy staff will hand-pump your soda and crank out the Wilensky's Special – a double-grilled salami and bologna sandwich that's pressed flat (delicious, no doubt, but it's a long way from a 'light lunch'). Immortalized in Mordecai Richler's novel *The Apprenticeship of Duddy Kravitz* and the subsequent film, Wilensky's remains a unique part of the city's culinary culture.

MEGAPRESS / ALAMY ©

GUYLAIN DOYLE / GETTY IMAGES ©

1. Parc Outremont (p130)
Set amid Victorian-era houses, this beautiful park features a tiny lake and a playground.

2. Little Italy eateries (p129)
Head here for a blend of traditional trattorias and cutting-edge restaurants.

3. Marché Jean-Talon (p109)
See hundreds of vendors hawking fresh produce, seafood, bakery items and gourmet goods.

4. St-Viateur Bagel (p131)
A classic cream cheese and smoked salmon combo from this Montréal institution.

MARTIN THOMAS PHOTOGRAPHY / ALAMY ©

ALATI-CASERTA
BAKERY $

Map p296 (http://alaticaserta.com; 277 Rue Dante; dessert $3-5; ⊙10am-5pm Mon, 8am-6pm Tue & Wed, 8am-7pm Thu & Fri, 9am-5pm Sat & Sun; MJean-Talon) For more than four decades, this marvelous family-owned pastry shop in Little Italy has wowed Montrealers with its deliciously decadent cannoli, almond cake, tiramisu and *sfogliatelle* (pastries stuffed with orange and ricotta cheese). Master baker Ernesto Bellinfante prepares many types of pastries and cakes each day, but arrive early for the best selection.

FAIRMOUNT BAGEL
BAKERY $

Map p296 (www.fairmountbagel.com; 74 Ave Fairmount Ouest; bagels from $0.75; ⊙24hr; MLaurier) One of Montréal's famed bagel places – people flood in here around the clock to scoop them up the minute they come out of the oven. Bagels are one thing Montrealers don't get too creative with. They stick to classic sesame or poppy seed varieties, though you can pick up anything from cinnamon to all-dressed here too.

MARCHÉ MILANO
SUPERMARKET

Map p290 (☑514-273-8558; 6862 Blvd St-Laurent; ⊙8am-6pm Mon-Fri, 8am-5pm Sat & Sun; MDe Castelnau) This local food store has a mouthwatering selection of fresh pasta, antipasti and olive oil. The fun here is seeing the old-timers do the rounds. Stop, watch, listen, stalk (but do so politely) and buy what they buy. You'll be on your way to an authentic Italian meal.

🍷 DRINKING & NIGHTLIFE

TOP CHOICE LA BUVETTE CHEZ SIMONE
WINE BAR

Map p296 (4869 Ave du Parc; MLaurier) An artsy-chic crowd of (mostly) francophone bons vivants and professionals loves this cozy wine bar. The staff know their vino, and the extensive list is complemented by a gourmet tapas menu. Weekends, the place is jammed from *5-à-7* into the wee hours. Alone, you can comfortably park it on a barstool, though you probably won't be solo for long.

TOP CHOICE BALDWIN BARMACIE
LOUNGE

Map p296 (http://baldwinbarmacie.com; 115 Ave Laurier Ouest; MLaurier) Loud music, live DJs and beautiful 20- and 30-somethings rule this small, apothecary-themed lounge and club. Showy staff mix specialty cocktails while poppy 1960s-inspired design fills your party prescription for flirting. Don't let its location in a quiet residential location fool you, this joint goes off.

WHISKEY CAFÉ
LOUNGE

Map p296 (www.whiskeycafe.com; 5800 Blvd St-Laurent; MSt-Laurent, then bus 55) Cuban cigars and fine whiskies are partners in crime at this classy 1930s-styled joint, hidden near the industrial sector of the Mile End. The well-ventilated cigar lounge is separated from the main bar, which stocks 150 Scotch whiskies, plus wines, ports and tasting trios. Snacks range from foie gras to Belgian chocolates. Music is as sexy-smooth as the leather chairs.

DIEU DU CIEL
BREWERY

Map p296 (www.dieuduciel.com; 29 Ave Laurier Ouest; ⊙3pm-3am Mon-Fri, 1pm-3am Sat & Sun; MLaurier) Packed every night with a young, francophone crowd of students, this unpretentious bar serves a phenomenal rotating menu of microbrew beers, running from classic ales to homemade stouts like the Mean Aphrodite with cocoa and smoked hot pepper.

NOTRE DAME DES QUILLES
BAR

Map p296 (www.facebook.com/notredamedes quilles; 32 Rue Beaubien Est; ⊙3pm-1am Sun-Wed, until 3am Thu-Sat; MBeaubien) Does drinking improve your bowling game? That seems to be the eternal question at this hipster outpost near Little Italy, where two free lanes have been set up with pint-sized pins. There's a good mix of Anglophones and Francophones here, as well as fish sandwiches like the Grease Truck.

L'ASSOMMOIR
PUB

Map p296 (www.assommoir.ca; 112 Rue Bernard Ouest; ⊙11am-11pm Sun-Thu, 11am-3am Fri & Sat; MLaurier) The science and art of bartending is the inspiration behind this bustling local resto. Professional staff know their drinks, mixing more than 250 cocktail choices. World cuisine features ceviches and tartares. DJs and regular live jazz bands (Sunday to Tuesday) complete the recipe.

CHEZ SERGE
SPORTS BAR

Map p296 (5301 Blvd St-Laurent; MSt-Laurent, then bus 55) How can you go wrong with a bra-adorned moose head on the wall? Hockey games, unbridled kitsch and a mechanical bull reel in neighborhood kids. With cold beer, flashing lights and staff who love dancing (sometimes on the bar), this homey spot gets out of control during hockey and soccer seasons.

CAFÉ OLIMPICO   CAFE
Map p296 (124 Rue St-Viateur Ouest; ⊙7am-11:30pm; ⓂLaurier) Its espresso is among the city's best, yet this no-frills Italian cafe is all about atmosphere, as hipsters and unassuming local rock stars rub elbows with elderly gentlemen and quirky regulars. It's big on sports, so there are large TVs inside. In spring and summer, the benches of the sunny outdoor terrace, a people-watching paradise, are jammed.

LA CROISSANTERIE FIGARO   CAFE
Map p296 (www.lacroissanteriefigaro.com; 5200 Rue Hutchison; ⊙7am-1am; ⓂLaurier) A charming Parisian bistro popular with well-heeled locals. Located in a converted old house in a beautiful residential neighborhood, its terrace is among the city's prettiest. Although it can be a bit of a scene, La Croissanterie is a lovely spot to nurse a coffee or cocktail all afternoon or evening. It also serves homemade croissants, salads and other goodies.

LE CAGIBI CAFÉ   CAFE
Map p296 (www.lecagibi.ca; 5490 Blvd St-Laurent; ⊙6pm-midnight Mon, 9am-1am Tue-Fri, 10:30am-1am Sat, 10:30am-midnight Sun; ⓂLaurier) Music-loving bohemians and Plateau eccentrics hold court at this vegetarian restaurant by day, bar by night. The large space is filled with a hodgepodge of plants and antique furnishings reminiscent of your grandmother's living room gone wild. Some nights, live bands play in the back room, while thrift-store-clad DJs spin on others.

BU   WINE BAR
Map p296 (www.bu-mtl.com; 5245 Blvd St-Laurent; ⓂLaurier) This elegant, Italy-inspired wine bar is where Montréal's real wine aficionados go to drink. The 500-strong list features approximately 25 wines by the glass, and the excellent service is worth the steep price. The kitchen whips up fine Italian antipasto dishes.

LE CLUB SOCIAL   CAFE
Map p296 (180 Rue St-Viateur Ouest; ⊙8am-2am; ⓂLaurier) Another character-filled magnet

literally a block away from Café Olimpico. Its terrace is equally sun-kissed, its coffee as flavorful, its ambience as lively. Most patrons split their time between these two legendary establishments.

TOI, MOI & CAFÉ   CAFE
Map p296 (www.toimoicafe.com; 244 Ave Laurier Ouest; ⊙7am-11pm Mon-Fri, 8am-11:30pm Sat & Sun; ⓂLaurier) It's best known for breakfasts, but this chic Laurier cafe embodies Montréal's European flair from morning to night. As you sip your café au lait on the outdoor terrace (alongside sophisticates of all ages) you'll feel as if you've crossed the pond yourself. It also serves tasty lunch and dinner, and its specialty coffee, roasted onsite, is sold around town.

☆ ENTERTAINMENT

THÉÂTRE OUTREMONT   THEATER
Map p296 (☑514-495-9944; www.theatreoutremont.ca; 1248 Rue Bernard Ouest; ⊙box office 4-8pm Mon, 12-6pm Tue-Fri, 12-5pm Sat; ⓂOutremont) Built in 1929, this theater was both a repertory cinema and a major concert hall until it was shuttered in the late 1980s. The municipality of Outremont later brought it back to life and the theater was reopened in 2001. Now, everything from pop concerts and dance performances to Monday-evening film screenings take place here.

🛍 SHOPPING

TOP CHOICE MONASTIRAKI   VINTAGE
Map p296 (http://monastiraki.blogspot.ca; 5478 Blvd St-Laurent; ⊙noon-6pm Wed, until 8pm Thu & Fri, until 5pm Sat & Sun; ⓂLaurier) This unclassifiable store named after a flea-market neighborhood in Athens calls itself a 'hybrid curiosity shop/art space', but that doesn't do justice to what illustrator Billy Mavreas sells: 1960s comic books, contemporary zines (homemade magazines), silkscreen posters, and myriad antique and collectible knickknacks, as well as recent works mainly by local graphic artists. It's a must-visit for artsy hipster types, but nearly everyone can find something in this carefully selected, fascinating jumble.

NECTAR OF THE GODS

Québec produces about three-quarters of the world's maple syrup, which is perhaps why it enjoys such pride of place, appearing on everything from meat and desserts to foie gras, blended with smoothies and of course in maple beer. French settlers began producing it regularly in the 1800s after learning from Canadian Aboriginies how to make it from maple tree sap. Sap is usually extracted in spring after enzymes convert starch into sugars over the winter. Once the weather warms and the sap starts flowing, Quebecers head to *cabanes à sucre* (sugar shacks; see p202) out in the countryside. There they sample the first amber riches of the season and do the taffy pull, where steaming maple syrup is poured into the snow and then scooped up on a popsicle stick once it's cooled.

LE MARCHÉ DES SAVEURS
DU QUÉBEC
FOOD & DRINK

Map p296 (www.lemarchedessaveurs.com; 280 Pl du Marché du Nord; ⊙9am-6pm daily, until 8pm Thu & Fri; ⓂJean-Talon) Everything here is Québécois, from the food to the handmade soaps to one of the best collections of artisanal local beer, maple products and cheeses in the city. The store was established so local producers could gain wider exposure for their regional products, and it's a joy to browse.

GALERIE SIMON BLAIS
ART

Map p296 (www.galeriesimonblais.com; 5420 Blvd St-Laurent; ⊙10am-6pm Tue, Wed, Fri, until 8pm Thu, until 5pm Sat; ⓂLaurier) One of the most prestigious galleries in Canada, Simon Blais carries works by well known international and domestic artists such as Lucien Freud and Jean-Paul Riopelle as well as emerging contemporary artists from Montréal and Quebec. There's always an interesting exhibition on here, and staff are eager to explain what's on.

DRAWN & QUARTERLY
BOOKS

Map p296 (http://211blog.drawnandquarterly. com; 211 Rue Bernard Ouest; ⊙Mon-Wed 11am-7pm, until 9pm Thu & Fri, 10am-7pm Sat & Sun; ⓂOutremont) The flagship store of this cult independent comic-book and graphic-novel publisher has become something of a local literary haven. Cool book launches take place here, and the quaint little shop sells all sorts of reading matter including children's books, vintage Tintin comics and art books.

AU PAPIER JAPONAIS
ORIGAMI

Map p296 (www.aupapierjaponais.com; 24 Ave Fairmount Ouest; ⓂLaurier) You might never guess how many guises Japanese paper can come in until you visit this gorgeous little shop, which has some 800 varieties. The lamps and kites make great gifts and you can fold them for easy transport; origami kits and books are good choices too. This store has also become an arts and crafts hub and offers workshops and seminars.

STYLE LABO
VINTAGE

Map p296 (www.stylelabo-deco.com; 5765 Blvd St-Laurent; ⊙10:30am-6pm Tue & Wed, until 7pm Thu & Fri, until 5pm Sat, 11:30am-5pm Sun; ⓂRosemont) Owners Anne Defay and Romain Castelli mix industrial remnants with quirky antique signage, farmers' furniture and even vintage dentistry equipment in this emporium of tools and gear from yesteryear. They also have accessories ranging from designer clock radios to old flags. An essential stop for feathering your loft.

LES TOUILLEURS
HOMEWARES

Map p296 (www.lestouilleurs.com; 152 Ave Laurier Ouest; ⓂLaurier) Beautifully designed Les Touilleurs celebrates Mile End's love affair with good food, presenting gorgeous highend cookware and cookbooks by local and international chefs. There's a very popular teaching kitchen at the back of the shop, but workshops sell out well in advance. Courses are held in French but attendees can usually ask questions in English.

L'ÉMOULEUR
HOMEWARES

Map p296 (www.emouleur.com; 1081 Ave Laurier Ouest; ⊙noon-7pm Wed-Fri, 10am-5pm Sat, 12-5pm Sun; ⓂLaurier) Don't be surprised to find these incredibly sharp and durable handcrafted Japanese kitchen knives here. It's proof that Mile End and Montréal chefs take their food very seriously indeed. Most blades will cut your wallet down by several hundred dollars, and some are as pricey as $3000.

QUINCAILLERIE DANTE
HOMEWARES

Map p296 (6851 Rue St-Dominique; MDe Castelnau) This quirky little Italian-owned hardware and cooking supply store is a household name, selling everything from first-class pots and pans to espresso makers, fishing rods and hunting gear.

PHONOPOLIS
MUSIC

Map p296 (http://phonopolis.ca; 207 Rue Bernard Ouest; ☺11am-7pm Mon-Wed & Sat, until 9pm Thu & Fri, until 6pm Sun; MOutremont) Indie rock, jazz, blues and classical sounds – and hybrids thereof – are the raison d'être of this little record shop, which buys and sells CDs and LPs.

UN AMOUR DES THÉS
FOOD & DRINK

Map p296 (www.amourdesthes.com; 1224 Rue Bernard Ouest; ☺10am-6pm Mon-Fri, 9am-5pm Sat, 11am-5pm Sun; MOutremont) Over 260 types of loose tea sit in canisters behind the counter of this charming shop. It stocks leaf varieties and flavors you've likely not only never heard of, but never imagined (tea with maple syrup, tea with chocolate oils, cream of Earl Grey). Regular tea workshops (in French) are also held.

JET-SETTER
TRAVEL GOODS

Map p296 (www.jet-setter.ca; 66 Ave Laurier Ouest; MLaurier) An orgy of state-of-the-art luggage and every travel gadget known to man, it's got luggage alarms, pocket-sized T-shirts, 'dry-in-an-instant' underwear and towels, mini-irons and hairdryers. You can also shop online.

GALERIE CO
HOMEWARES

Map p296 (www.galerie-co.com; 5235 Blvd St-Laurent; ☺10am-6pm Tue-Thu, until 7pm Fri, 10am-6pm Sat, noon-5pm Sun; MLaurier) Selling all manner of beautiful objects, from cushions adorned with massive fruits to funky wooden flashlights to cutting boards shaped like dead rats (okay, not everything is beautiful), Galerie CO (from 'economy, ecology and community') supports products that benefit the environment and sustainable development.

🏃 SPORTS & ACTIVITIES

OVARIUM
SPA

Map p296 (☎514-271-7515; 877-356-8837; www.ovarium.com; 400 Rue Beaubien Est; ☺8:30am-10pm; MBeaubien) The excellent staff and the Ovarium weightlessness experience have garnered a loyal following at this day spa. Packages are available, such as the half-day 'Essential,' a flotation bath followed by a massage ($125). Ovarium's flotation tanks are egg-shaped tubs filled with water and 2000 cups of Epsom salts, making you gravity-free.

Southwest & Outer Montréal

SOUTHWEST MONTRÉAL | CÔTE-DES-NEIGES | NOTRE-DAME-DE-GRÂCE | OLYMPIC PARK & AROUND | OUTER DISTRICTS

Neighborhood Top Five

1 Witnessing the soaring architecture of the **Oratoire St-Joseph** (p142), one of North America's grandest churches.

2 Working off those calories from munching *poutine* on the **Canal de Lachine** (p143) and its 14km of bike paths.

3 Bringing out your green side at one of the world's largest gardens, the **Jardin Botanique** (p144) and its Insectarium.

4 Chilling out with the penguins and many other fish and fowl at the **Biodôme** (p145), which takes you through four ecosystems.

5 Learning about the history of Canadian railroads at the excellent, kid-friendly **Musée Ferroviaire Canadien** (p147).

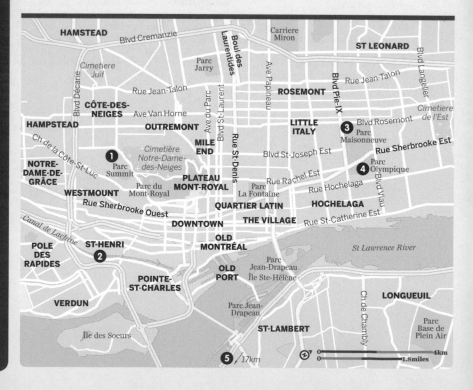

Explore Southwest & Outer Montréal

This chapter takes in several outlying residential neighborhoods of Montréal, allowing you to get a deeper experience of life on the island. A good chunk of them lie to the south and west of downtown (remember that Montréal's 'east–west' streets actually run northeast–southwest). Since they're far-flung, it's best to explore them over several days, though it's possible to combine contiguous areas like Côte-des-Neiges and Notre-Dame-de-Grâce.

A must-experience is the Canal de Lachine, Montréal's best biking course. In downtown or Old Montréal, find your way to a Bixi bike-rental stand and roll down to the Old Port. From there, get on the bike path that winds along the canal and out to Lachine, where several museums and a breezy riverside park await.

It will take at least an hour, but if you don't want to go that far, stop at the Marché Atwater, walk to Lionel-Groulx metro station and go to Côte-des-Neiges, which lies off the western slope of Parc du Mont-Royal. The magnificent Oratoire St-Joseph and the buzzing campus of the prestigious Université de Montréal are the main draws here. Notre-Dame-de-Grâce (or simply NDG) is a sleepy residential district, livened up by the cafes and restaurants along Ave Monkland.

Also easily accessible by metro is the Olympic Park, which nestles in the heart of the blue-collar Hochelaga-Maisonneuve district. The big draw here is the massive Olympic Stadium, built for the 1976 Olympic Games, the kid-friendly Biodôme and the verdant Jardin Botanique.

Best Places to Eat

➡ Tuck Shop (p150)
➡ Su (p150)
➡ Mangan (p150)

For reviews, see p150 ➡

Best Activities

➡ Strøm Nordic Spa (p151)
➡ Skyventure (p151)
➡ Croisiére Patrimoniale du Canal (p151)
➡ Parc de La Rivière-des-Mille-Îles (p152)

For reviews, see p151 ➡

Local Life

➡ **Sunning** Rent a Bixi bike, scoot along the Canal de Lachine and pause along its banks to soak up some rays (p143).
➡ **Ahoy there!** Montréal is surrounded by rivers, so why not rent a canoe or kayak (p151) and go with the flow?
➡ **Over the hill** For a good workout, hike from downtown over Mont-Royal to Côte-des-Neiges (p144), following the street of the same name.

Getting There & Away

➡ **Metro** Metro access to the area is via Villa-Maria station for NDG, while the Côte-des-Neiges station is for the neighborhood of the same name. To get to the east side of town, take the green metro line to either Pie-IX or Viau.
➡ **Bike** You can rent a Bixi bike to reach NDG, Petite-Bourgogne, St-Henri and Pointe-St-Charles, and to roll along the Canal de Lachine. Bikes are best avoided in hilly Côte-des-Neiges.

SOUTHWEST & OUTER MONTRÉAL

AFLO CO LTD / ALAMY ©

TOP SIGHTS
ORATOIRE ST-JOSEPH

This stunning church built on the flanks of Mont-Royal commands grand views of the the Côte-des-Neiges area and northwest Montréal. The majestic basilica is a tribute to mid-20th-century design as well as an intimate shrine to Brother André, a local saint said to have healed countless people.

The largest shrine ever built in honor of Jesus' father, this Renaissance-style building was completed in 1960 and commands fine views of the northern slope of Mont-Royal. The oratory dome is visible from anywhere in this part of town.

The oratory is also a tribute to the work of Brother André (1845–1937), the determined monk who first built a little **chapel** here in 1904. Brother André was said to have healing powers – as word spread, a larger shrine was needed, so the church began gathering funds to build one. Rows of discarded crutches and walking sticks in the basement **Votive Chapel** testify to this belief and the shrine is warmed by hundreds of candles. When Brother André died at age 91, a million devotees filed past his coffin over the course of six days. His black granite **tomb** in the Votive Chapel was donated by Québec premier Maurice Duplessis. Brother André was beatified in 1982 and finally canonized in 2010. His **heart** is on display too, in an upstairs museum dedicated to him (for more on this reliquary, see p152).

Religious pilgrims might climb the 300 wooden steps to the oratory on their knees, praying at every step; other visitors take the stone stairs or one of the free shuttle buses from the base parking lot.

DON'T MISS

→ Brother André's room and 1904 chapel
→ Brother André's tomb and heart
→ The Votive Chapel
→ The Grand Organ

PRACTICALITIES

→ www.saint-joseph .org
→ 3800 Chemin Queen-Mary
→ admission free
→ ⊙church & votive chapel 6:30am-9:30pm, museum 7am-5pm
→ Ⓜ Côte-des-Neiges

 **SIGHTS**

Southwest Montréal

CANAL DE LACHINE CANAL

The Lachine Canal was built in 1825 as a means of bypassing the treacherous Lachine Rapids on the St Lawrence River. It was closed to shipping in 1970, but the area has been transformed into a 14km-long cycling and pedestrian pathway, with picnic areas and green spaces. Since the canal was reopened for navigation in 2002, flotillas of pleasure and sightseeing boats glide along its calm waters (see p151). Old warehouses converted into luxury condos line the canal near Atwater market.

It's well worth hiring a bike or in-line skates and heading out along the canal path, but try to avoid summer weekends, when it's particularly crowded. For bike rental, see p71; for kayak rental, see p152.

FUR TRADE AT LACHINE NATIONAL HISTORIC SITE MUSEUM

(www.pc.gc.ca/lhn-nhs/qc/lachine/index.aspx; 1255 Blvd St-Joseph; adult/child $4/2; ☺9:30am-12:30pm & 1-5pm, check website for seasonal closings; Ⓜ Lionel-Groulx, then ➌496, Mon-Fri) This 1803 stone depot in Lachine is now an engaging little museum telling the story of the fur trade in Canada. The Hudson Bay Company made Lachine the hub of its fur-trading operations because the rapids made further navigation impossible. Visitors can view the furs and old trappers' gear, and costumed interpreters show how the bales and canoes were schlepped by native trappers.

A little office display near the Fur Trade site relates the history of the Canal de Lachine, and guided tours are conducted along the canal on request.

MAISON ST-GABRIEL MUSEUM

(www.maisonsaint-gabriel.qc.ca; 2146 Pl Dublin; adult/child/student $10/3/5; ☺1-5pm Tue-Sun early Jan–mid-Jun & early Sep–mid-Dec, 11am-6pm mid-Jun–Sep; Ⓜ Charlevoix, bus 57 est) This magnificent farmhouse in Pointe St-Charles is one of the finest examples of traditional Québec architecture. The house was bought in 1668 by Marguerite Bourgeoys to house a religious order. Young women, called the Filles du Roy, who were sent from Paris to Montréal to find husbands also stayed here. The 17th-century roof of the two-story building is of particular interest for its intricate beam work, one of the few of its kind in North America. The museum has an excellent collection of artifacts going back to the 17th and 18th centuries, with unusual items including sinks made from black stone and a sophisticated water-disposal system.

FREE **MUSÉE DE LACHINE** MUSEUM

(http://ville.Montréal.qc.ca; 1 Chemin du Musée; ☺noon-5pm Tue-Sun, closed late Nov–late Mar; Ⓜ Angrignon, then ➌110) Practically right on the Canal de Lachine, it's a great bike ride to this museum, also one of the oldest houses (1669) in the Montréal region, with shooting holes inserted for defense. Back then Lachine was the last frontier for trappers heading west and the final stop for fur shipments. You can see and smell the old fur-storage building from the original trading days. Adjacent to the museum is a huge waterfront sculpture garden that you can visit anytime from dawn to dusk.

PARC DES RAPIDES PARK

(http://ville.Montréal.qc.ca; cnr Blvd LaSalle & 7e Ave; Ⓜ De l'Église, then ➌58) This space on the St Lawrence is the spot to view the Lachine Rapids (and the jet boats that ride them). The park attracts hikers and anglers, and cyclists who pedal the riverside trail. It's also a renowned bird sanctuary – located on a small peninsula, with what's said to be Québec's largest heron colony. The 30-hectare sanctuary is an important site for migratory birds, with some 225 species passing through each year. Some information displays relate the history of the rapids and of the old hydroelectric plant on the grounds.

You can rent kayaks and sign up for classes where you'll learn to surf or kayak the Lachine Rapids – scaredy-cats need not apply. An adrenaline-rushing experience can be had with Rafting Montréal (p152), a jet-boating and rafting outfit located 2km west of the Parc des Rapides.

FREE **MOULIN FLEMING** MUSEUM

(http://ville.Montréal.qc.ca; 9675 Blvd LaSalle, LaSalle; ☺1-5pm Sat & Sun May-Aug; Ⓜ Angrignon, then ➌110) This restored five-story windmill was built for a Scottish merchant in 1816, and a multimedia exhibit inside covers its two centuries of history. It's a nice diversion if you're out here visiting the other Lachine sites, and a great photo op.

⊙ Côte-des-Neiges & Notre-Dame-de-Grâce

ORATOIRE ST-JOSEPH   CHURCH
See p142.

HOLOCAUST MEMORIAL CENTRE   MUSEUM
(www.mhmc.ca; 5151 Chemin de la Côte-Ste-Catherine; adult/child $8/5; ◷10am-5pm Mon, Tue & Thu, to 9pm Wed, to 4pm Fri & Sun; ⊠Côte-Ste-Catherine) The Montréal Holocaust Memorial Centre provides a record of Jewish history and culture from pre-WWII Europe and holds seminars, exhibitions and other events. The museum has many powerful exhibits, including testimonies by Holocaust survivors for groups of 10 or more. The museum is closed on Jewish holidays; see the website to confirm Friday hours between November and March.

AVE MONKLAND   STREET
Over the past decade or so Ave Monkland in NDG has been transformed, with coffee bars, restaurants and condominiums springing up like mushrooms after a warm rain. It certainly has a village character as many people walk to the shops from their homes. Access is via the Villa-Maria metro station, from where you can walk down Monkland.

UNIVERSITÉ DE MONTRÉAL   UNIVERSITY
(2900 Blvd Édouard-Montpetit; ⊠Université-de-Montréal) This is the second-largest French-language university in the world, after the Sorbonne in Paris. Located on the north side of Mont-Royal, its most recognizable building is an art-deco tower and pale-yellow brick structure. The university was founded in 1920.

⊙ Olympic Park & Around

JARDIN BOTANIQUE   GARDENS
(www.ville.Montréal.qc.ca/jardin; 4101 Rue Sherbrooke Est; adult/child $17.75/9, incl Biodôme $31.50/16; ◷9am-6pm mid-May–early Sep, to 9pm early Sep-Oct, to 5pm Tue-Sun rest of year; ⊠Pie-IX) Montréal's Jardin Botanique is the third-largest botanical garden in the world, after London's Kew Gardens and Berlin's Botanischer Garten. Since its 1931 opening, the 75-hectare garden has grown to include tens of thousands of species in about 30 thematic gardens, and its wealth of flowering plants is carefully managed to bloom in stages. The rose beds in particular are a sight to behold in summertime. Climate-controlled greenhouses house cacti, banana trees and 1500 species of orchid. Bird-watchers should bring their binoculars.

A popular drawcard is the landscaped Japanese Garden with traditional pavilions, tearoom and art gallery; the bonsai 'forest' is the largest outside Asia. The twinning of Montréal with Shanghai gave impetus to plant a Chinese Garden. The ornamental *penjing* trees from Hong Kong are up to 100 years old. A Ming-dynasty garden is the feature around Lac de Rêve (Dream Lake). In the northern part of the Jardin Botanique you'll find the Maison de l'Arbre (Tree House), a permanent exhibit on life in the 40-hectare arboretum. Displays include the yellow birch, part of Québec's official emblem. The First Nations Garden reveals the bonds between 11 Amerindian and Inuit nations and indigenous plants such as silver birches, maples, Labrador and even tea. The Orchidée Gift Shop in the main building has a wonderful selection, including handmade

---

MONTRÉAL'S GARBAGE-POWERED CIRCUS CITY

Take a jaunt to Montréal's circus mecca in its working-class St-Michel district and be prepared to be wowed. This innovative complex, named **TOHU** (☑514-376-8648; www.tohu.ca; 2345 Rue Jarry Est & Rue d'Iberville; admission $6-7; ◷9am-5pm Mon-Fri) – which comes from the French expression *tohu-bohu,* for hustle and bustle – was built on the site of North America's second-largest waste dump and the whole complex is now powered completely by methane gas from the landfill garbage beneath. It includes an arena designed only with the circus arts in mind, Cirque du Soleil's international headquarters and artists' residence and the National Circus School.

You can visit its complex on your own (via guided audio tour), or on a guided 90-minute tour. Get there by taking the blue metro line to D'Iberville station and then hopping onto bus 94 north (or walking 1km northwest up Rue d'Iberville).

HARVARD DE MONTRÉAL

For all the Francophiles among you, the **Université de Montréal** is kind of like the French-speaking Harvard in Canada. The second-largest French-speaking university in the world, it has more than 55,000 students. Maybe because it's on the mountain far from downtown and feels removed from the rest of the city, you'll find an array of cultural events and happenings that remain virtually unknown to those outside the area.

Nearby Chemin de la Côte-des-Neiges is a lively street for strolling, with cafes, bookstores and a green market, the **Marché Côtes-des-Neiges** (cnr Chemin de la Côte-des-Neiges & Rue Jean- Brillant), open 24 hours a day in summer. A splendid place to while away a few hours is the indie bookstore **Librairie Olivieri** (5219 Chemin de la Côte-des-Neiges), which also has an excellent bistro serving poached salmon, *magret de canard* (duck breast) and changing daily specials.

From here you're also within walking distance of the Oratoire St-Joseph, a great spot to visit at sunset. Two handy metro stations – Côte-des-Neiges and Université de Montréal – provide easy access to the area.

jewelry and crafts, stuffed animals and beautifully illustrated books.

In fall (mid-September to early November) the Chinese garden dons its most exquisite garb for the popular Magic of Lanterns, when hundreds of handmade silk lanterns sparkle at dusk. Montrealers are devoted to this event and it can feel like it's standing-room only even though it's held in a huge garden.

Creepy-crawlies get top billing at the bug-shaped Insectarium. Most of the 144,000 specimens are mounted but live displays include bees and tarantulas.

The admission ticket includes the gardens, greenhouses and the Insectarium.

BIODÔME   ZOO

(www2.ville.Montréal.qc.ca/biodome; 4777 Ave Pierre-de-Coubertin; adult/child $17.75/9, incl Jardin Botanique & Insectarium $31.50/16; ⊗generally 9am-6pm late Jun-Aug, to 5pm Sep-late Jun; M Viau) At this captivating, kid-friendly exhibit you can amble through a rainforest, explore Antarctic islands, view rolling woodlands or wander along the raw Atlantic oceanfront – all without ever leaving the building. Be sure to dress in layers for the temperature swings.

The four ecosystems house many thousands of animal and plant species; follow the self-guided circuit and you will see everything. Penguins frolic in the pools a few feet away from groups of goggle-eyed children; the tropical chamber is a cross-section of Amazonia with mischievous little monkeys teasing alligators in the murky waters below. The Gulf of St Lawrence has an underwater observatory where you can watch cod feeding alongside lobsters and sea urchins in the tidal pools. The appearance of the Laurentian Forest varies widely with the seasons, with special habitats for lynx, otters and around 350 bats.

The Biodôme is wildly popular, so try to visit during the week, avoiding the middle of the day if possible. Plan two hours to do it justice. You can bring a packed lunch for the picnic tables or dine in the cafeteria. In summer there are educational day camps for kids.

OLYMPIC STADIUM   STADIUM

(www.parcolympique.qc.ca; 4141 Ave Pierre-de-Coubertin; tower adult/child $16/8; ⊗9am-10pm mid-Jun–early Sep, to 5pm Sun-Thu rest of year; M Viau) The Stade Olympique seats 56,000 and remains an architectural marvel, though these days it hosts mostly concerts and trade shows and only rarely hosts sports events.

The best thing to do is take the bilevel cable car up the Montréal Tower (Tour de Montréal, also called the Olympic Tower) that lords over the stadium. It's the world's tallest inclined structure (165m at a 45-degree angle). The glassed-in observation deck (with bar and rest area) definitely isn't for the faint of heart but it does afford a bird's-eye view of the city. In the distance you'll see the pointy modern towers of the Olympic Village, where athletes stayed in 1976.

The Centre Aquatique (p153) is the Olympic swimming complex, with six pools, diving towers and a 20m-deep scuba pool.

THE BIG OWE

Built for the 1976 Olympic Games, Montréal's Olympic Stadium was plagued with difficulties right from the start. A strike by construction workers meant the inclined tower wasn't finished on time – in fact it took another 11 years to complete. The stadium's affectionate nickname, the 'Big O' (in reference to the huge oval stadium), was redubbed the 'Big Owe' by irate Montrealers.

The 65-ton stadium roof took another two years to complete but never worked properly. Made of Kevlar, the material used in bulletproof vests, the striking orange dome worked like a huge retractable umbrella that opened and closed by the tower cables. It was a sight to behold (if you were so lucky), but winds ripped the 'bulletproof' Kevlar and mechanical glitches led to its permanent closure. Even when the roof was functioning, there were problems. For instance, the roof could not be moved when winds gusted greater than 40km/h. This resulted in the occasional rain delay during baseball season – an irritating event for fans who were waiting for the roof to simply be closed.

In 1998 the umbrella was folded up for good and replaced with a set model (costing $37 million) that didn't open – though this roof too malfunctioned, collapsing one year later, dumping snow and ice on workers setting up for the Montréal Auto Show (the roof installers were later sued by the stadium). Another unfortunate event over the years was the collapse of a 55-ton support beam in 1991, though luckily no one was injured.

Provincial officials calculated that the total price tag of the stadium (including construction, repairs etc) when it was finally paid off in late 2006 amounted to $1.6 billion (or $1000 per person, if every man, woman and child in the city of Montréal had to pay up).

The irony of the Big O is that now that it's paid off and the roof is no longer broken, no one seems remotely interested in using the stadium. The city's baseball team, the Montréal Expos, played its last game in the stadium in 2004 before it was packed off to Washington DC and rechristened the Capitals. Today the stadium is often empty save for the odd trade show, big-name concert, soccer match and the occasional visitor (maybe you) who finds themself staring up at the empty seats, wondering how such a place could ever be so cursed.

The Tourist Hall is a three-story information center with a ticket office, restaurant and souvenir shop, as well as the cable-car boarding station. There are regular English-language stadium tours (adult/child $9/4.50) from 10am in spring and summer, and five tours a day starting at 11am in fall and winter.

CHÂTEAU DUFRESNE   HISTORIC BUILDING
(www.chateaudufresne.qc.ca; 2929 Ave Jeanne-d'Arc; adult/child $9/5, incl Olympic Stadium $14/7; ◎10am-5pm Wed-Sun; Ⓜ Pie-IX) In 1916 brothers Oscar and Marius Dufresne commissioned this beautiful beaux-arts mansion, along the lines of the Versailles Palace in France. Ultimately they moved in with their families – Oscar on one side and Marius on the other.

The interiors are stunning – tiled marble floors, coffered ceilings in Italian Renaissance style, stained-glass windows – and are open for the public to explore. Italian artist Guido Nincheri was in charge of interior decoration and painted many murals, including one of dainty nymphs in the Petit Salon.

Marius' side of the building is furnished in a more masculine style, with a smoking room fitted to look like a Turkish lounge with hookah pipes. The furniture, art and other objects reflect the tastes of Montréal's bourgeoisie of the period, and the building has been declared a national monument.

The frequent temporary exhibits explore all aspects of early-20th-century culture, from art to lifestyle.

◉ Outer Districts

MUSÉE FERROVIAIRE CANADIEN   MUSEUM
(www.exporail.org; 110 Rue St-Pierre/rte 209,
St-Constant; adult/child $16.50/8; ☺generally
10am-5pm, see website for details) The Canadian Railway Museum contains more than
150 historic vehicles, ranging from locomotives, steam engines, Old Montréal street-
cars and passenger cars to snow plows.
It's widely acknowledged as one of North
America's most outstanding collections.
Not particularly well known by Montrealers, this museum gets raves from those
who make the trek, especially families, and
many claim it's the best museum in the
Montréal area.

The aerodynamic steam engine *Dominion of Canada* broke the world speed record
in 1939 by clocking over 200km/h. A special
sight is Montréal's famous *Golden Chariot*,
an open-air streetcar with tiers of ornate
seats and gilt ironwork. Another good exhibit is the school car, a Canadian invention
that served the railway towns of northern
Ontario: two cars of each teaching train
had a kitchen, living area and classroom
with 15 desks.

There always seems to be something
special going on here, whether it's the miniature railway or streetcar rides, weather
permitting.

By car, take the Pont Champlain from
Montréal to Autoroute 15, then Hwy 132
at the Châteauguay cutoff to rte 209. It's a
20-minute drive.

COSMODÔME   MUSEUM
(www.cosmodome.org; 2150 Autoroute des Laurentides; adult/under 7yr/student/family $15/
free/12/40; ☺9am-5pm late Jun-early Sep, 10am-
5pm Tue-Sun & holidays rest of year; ⓂMontmor-
ency, then ⓠ61 or 70) You (or your kids) can
experience the thrill of space flight in this
interactive museum of space and new technologies. Virtual missions include a moon
landing and Mars exploration, while exhibits focus on the solar system, satellite com-
munications and space travel, and there
are mock-ups of rockets, the space shuttle
Endeavor and planets. The center also runs
space camps for one to five days for kids
aged five to eight in a sort of mini-NASA
training.

MORGAN ARBORETUM   GARDENS
(www.morganarboretum.org; 150 Chemin des
Pins, Ste-Anne-de-Bellevue; adult/child $5/2;
☺9am-4pm) This arboretum holds the
country's largest grouping of native trees:
fragrant junipers, cedars and yews but also
exotic species like ginkgo, cork and yellow-
wood. There's a wonderful trail map and
the area is perfect for a long hike in the
woods, strolling through magnolia blos-
soms or having a family picnic. Spring and
fall offer the best colors.

The grounds of the arboretum serve as
an educational facility for McGill's Mac-
Donald agricultural school. There are several species of wildlife and reptile, and it's
also a stop for 170 species of wintering or
migratory birds, making it a thrill for bird-
watchers.

In winter, this is a beautiful location for
cross-country skiing.

Located about 15km west of Montréal on
the western tip of the island, the arboretum
can be reached most easily from Autoroute
40. Take exit 41 and follow signs for Chemin
Ste-Marie; at the stop sign at the top of the
hill, turn left onto Chemin des Pins for the
registration office.

PARC NATURE DU CAP-ST-JACQUES   PARK
(20099 Blvd Gouin Ouest, Pierrefonds; ☺10am-
6pm Jun-Aug, otherwise generally 10am-5pm;
ⓂHenri-Bourassa, then ⓠ69; Ⓟ) Arguably the
most diverse of Montréal's nature parks,
Cap-St-Jacques has a huge beach, over 40km
of trails for hiking and skiing, a farm and
even a summer camp. The maple and mixed
deciduous forest in the interior is a great
patch for a ramble, and in spring a horse-
drawn carriage brings visitors to a sugar
shack to watch the maple sap boil. On the
north shore there's the Eco-Farm, a working
farm with two barns and horses, pigs and
chickens, as well as a large greenhouse for
viewing. Picnic tables abound and a restaurant serves the farm's produce. The **beach**
(adult/child $4.50/3) is a comfortably wide
stretch of fine white sand, and the shallow
water is wonderful for splashing with kids,
but bear in mind it gets as popular as Cape
Cod on summer weekends. You can also rent
canoes, kayaks and pedal boats.

By car, take Autoroute 40 west from
Montréal to exit 49 (Rue Ste-Marie Ouest),
turn north on Rue l'Anse-à-l'Orme and continue on to Blvd Gouin Ouest.

2

3

1. Biodôme (p145)
Four ecosystems house thousands of animal and plant species at this kid-friendly zoo, including penguins, monkeys, lynx, otters and bats.

2. Jardin Botanique (p144)
One of the world's largest (at 75 hectares), this botanic garden has dozens of thematic sections, including Chinese and Japanese exhibits.

3. Canal de Lachine (p143)
Once an industrial canal, today it's a popular sailing and kayaking spot that also boasts a 14km-long cycling and pedestrian pathway.

EATING

TOP CHOICE TUCK SHOP   QUÉBECOIS **$$**

(☎514-439-7432; http://tuckshop.ca; 4662 Rue Notre-Dame Ouest; mains $23-32; ☺dinner Tue-Sat; MPlace Saint-Henri) Set in the heart of working-class St-Henri, Tuck Shop could have been plucked from London or New York if it weren't for its distinctly local menu, a delightful blend of market and *terroir* offerings such as Kamouraska lamb shank, Arctic char and a Québec cheese plate, all prepared by able chef Theo Lerikos. The lively atmosphere, warm service and excellent dishes are pitch-perfect, so it's no wonder this place fills up fast. Be sure to reserve.

SU   TURKISH **$$**

(☎514-362-1818; www.restaurantsu.com; 5145 Rue Wellington; mains $18-34; ☺lunch & dinner Tue-Fri, dinner Sat; MVerdun) Chef Fisun Ercan takes her home-style but inventive Turkish cuisine beyond your expectations of kabobs, yogurt and coffee. She prepares feather-light fried calamari, *karniyarik* (eggplant stuffed with Kamouraska lamb), and delicious *lokum* (Turkish delight). It's worth the trip to Verdun; be sure to reserve.

MAGNAN   TAVERN **$$**

(www.magnanresto.com; 2602 Rue St-Patrick; mains $12-20; ☺11am-11pm; MCharlevoix) Founded in the 1930s as a blue-collar diner, Taverne Magnan has long since raised meat and potatoes to an art form. Its reputation is fantastic roast beef – long-marinating, speckled with peppercorns and served in its own juice. This is the place to refuel after a day's cycling along the Canal de Lachine (just around the corner). There's open-air seating (next to a parking lot) in back.

LA LOUISIANE   CAJUN **$$**

(☎514-369-3073; www.lalouisiane.ca; 5850 Rue Sherbrooke Ouest; mains $15-31; ☺dinner Tue-Sat; MVendôme, then ☐105) Montréal meets the Deep South in this casual Cajun eatery, with amazing results. The menu bears the hearty, delicious flavors of jambalaya, shrimp Creole or chicken *étouffée*, all armed with mysterious peppers and spices. The rich 'voodoo pasta' has spicy Cajun sausage and tomatoes in white wine and cream. While you're here, be sure to check out paintings of street scenes by New Orleans native James Michelopoulos. Reserve ahead.

GIBEAU ORANGE JULEP   FAST FOOD **$**

(7700 Blvd Décarie; mains $4-6; ☺8am-3am; MNamur) Shaped like a giant orange, this vintage snack bar along the busy Décarie Expressway is a nostalgic soft spot for generations of Montrealers. While the roller-skating waitresses are long gone, you can still nosh on greasy French fries and hot dogs in your car outside, washing them down with the signature Orange Julep drink that was created by Hermas Gibeau in the 1920s.

🍷 DRINKING & NIGHTLIFE

TYPHOON LOUNGE   LOUNGE

(www.typhoon.ca; 5752 Ave Monkland; ☺4pm-3am Mon-Sat, noon-3am Sun; MVendôme, then ☐105) Young yuppies, anglo- and franco-phone, slip in to this Côte-des-Neiges watering hole for a beer and chicken legs on the way home, or camp out for jazz, blues and world beats. It's hard to shake the office-worker ambience but on summer nights it's a good pit stop while cruising Ave Monkland.

☆ ENTERTAINMENT

MONTRÉAL IMPACT   SPECTATOR SPORT

(www.Montréalimpact.com; Saputo Stadium, 4750 Rue Sherbrooke Est; tickets $20-85; ☺Apr-Sep; MViau) Although Canadians aren't known for doling out the soccer love, the Montréal Impact has played its heart out to earn a local following. Saputo Stadium is a 14,000-seat venue built in 2008 for the club and the second-largest soccer stadium in Canada. The Impact's big rivals are Toronto FC, whom they sometimes play at the nearby Olympic Stadium because the games draw over 20,000 fans.

SEAGAL CENTRE   PERFORMING ARTS

(☎514-739-7944; www.segalcentre.org; 5170 Chemin de la Côte-Ste-Catherine; MCôte-Ste-Catherine) Montréal's Jewish theater stages dramatic performances in English, Yiddish and Hebrew – although as one of the city's most prominent professional theater venues, plays presented are by no means exclusively Jewish. Recent productions have

LOCAL VOICES: DINING À LA QUÉBÉCOISE

Frédéric Morin, one of the chef-owners of Joe Beef (p85), has garnered much attention for his innovative Québécois fare. He's at the forefront of a movement to bring attention to the great *produits du terroir* (foods sources from local markets and farms).

What keeps you in Montréal? It's cool to be in such a culturally rich place – growing up, your best friends are Italian and Lebanese, there's a Jewish neighborhood up the street, and you're the only Québécois kid on your block. You move between French and English – not just linguistically, but culturally. I like that quote by the prime minister during the independence drive: 'We're all ethnics here; it just depends on your date of arrival.'

What are your favorite dishes? I really love beef – a braised meat in winter, a thick steak in the summer. Sometimes I crave oysters and get the urge for greens. And I love Dover sole.

So what's the story behind the new garden you've created behind your restaurant? I get some things for the restaurant in there, but most of my greens come from the Atwater market (see boxed text, p109). I do the garden for me. I love working in there. It's my happy place.

What's your take on the restaurant scene here? I love Paris and New York, but it's competitive. Cooks in restaurants here are friends. People rarely come to work pissed off. Maybe it's this laid-back city – the Canal de Lachine, the parks...

included *Billy Bishop Goes to War, Inherit the Wind* and *Lies My Father Told Me.*

WHEEL CLUB DANCE
(☎514-489-3322; thewheelclub.wordpress.com; 3373 Blvd Cavendish; ◉noon-9pm, to later Mon, live band nights; ⒨Vendôme, then ⊡105) This venerable country-and-western bar is famous for its Hillbilly Night on Mondays, featuring bluegrass, cowboy and fiddle music. House band Vintage Wine, which plays late 1960s and '70s covers, can also get your heels hopping. Otherwise, there are dartboards, a pool table and a full bar. Call ahead for live-music schedules.

🏃 SPORTS & ACTIVITIES

TOP CHOICE STRØM NORDIC SPA SPA
(☎514-761-2772; www.stromspa.com; 1001 Blvd de la Forêt; ◉10am-10pm; ⒨Square-Victoria, then ⊡168) For a get-away-from-it-all experience, it's hard to top this beautifully set-up spa located on the Île des Soeurs, a few kilometers south of downtown. The trim Nordic-style buildings overlook a watery and tree-lined expanse, with grassy lawns and outdoor pools with tiny waterfalls from which to enjoy the pretty scenery. A range of treatments and packages

is available, and there's also a good bistro on hand. Hour-long Swedish massages are $84, and you can add in the 'thermal experience' from $29 – featuring use of outdoor Jacuzzis, thermal and Nordic baths, Finnish sauna and eucalyptus steam bath.

TOP CHOICE SKYVENTURE SKYDIVING
(☎514-524-4000; www.skyventureMontréal.com; 2700 Ave du Cosmodôme, Laval; flight packages from $62; ◉flights 2-10pm Mon-Thu, 9am-11pm Fri & Sat, 9am-10pm Sun; ⒨Montmorency, then ⊡61 or 70) Canada's only skydiving simulator lets you stretch your wings inside a massive vertical wind tunnel that keeps you aloft with gusts of 110mph. You'll get a brief training session with an instructor, a flightsuit, helmet and goggles; kids aged four years and over can try it too. It's no easy feat maneuvering in the wind tunnel during the one-minute flights, and you may find yourself bumping into the transparent walls in a very ungainly fashion. Helpful instructors fly with you, though, and part of the fun is watching them perform gravity-defying skydiving acrobatics. Be sure to stretch before and after!

CROISIÉRE PATRIMONIALE DU CANAL CRUISE
Map p284 (☎514-283-6054; www.pc.gc.ca/lachinecanal; Marché Atwater; 2hr tour adult/child $18/11; ◉10:30am & 2pm daily late Jun-early

LOCAL KNOWLEDGE

THE GREAT HEART HEIST

How much is a holy man's heart worth? Fifty-thousand dollars, according to thieves who broke into a locked room in the Oratoire St-Joseph in March 1973. They made off with Brother André's heart sealed in a vial and demanded the sum in a ransom note that scandalized Montréal. The purloined organ was the subject of tabloid articles, musical compositions and even an art exhibition. Church officials reportedly refused the ransom demand, and nothing more was seen of the heart until December 1974 when Montréal lawyer to the underworld Frank Shoofey received a mysterious phone call asking him if he wanted to know its whereabouts. Shoofey was directed to an apartment building storage locker that contained a box, and inside was the vial housing Brother André's heart. The thieves were never found, and today the heart is secure in the Oratoire behind a metal grille and a sturdy transparent display case. But some believe the Church actually did pay the ransom to get it back. Was Shoofey, who was shot to death in 1985 in a still-unsolved murder, a go-between? Whatever the case, Montréal's great heart heist has continued to inspire artists long after the saint himself died.

Sep, weekends & holidays only May-Oct; MLionel-Groulx) Operated by the Parks Canada service, this sightseeing cruise offers a good overview of one of North America's most dramatic urban-renewal projects. A Parks Canada interpreter brings to life the canal's industrial and commercial history and you visit an archaeological site. The two-hour round-trip begins at the canal dock near the pedestrian footbridge just south of Atwater market and goes all the way to the Old Port locks.

PARC DE LA
RIVIÈRE-DES-MILLE-ÎLES   WATER SPORTS
(www.parc-mille-iles.qc.ca, in French; 345 Blvd Ste-Rose; kayak/canoe per hr $11/12, per day $37/40; ☉9am-6pm, to 8pm Fri & Sat mid-Jun–mid-Aug; MCartier, then ☒73) This is one of the most beautiful spots for canoeing and kayaking. This park on the Rivière des Mille-Îles near Laval has 10 islands where you can disembark on self-guided water tours, and about 10km of the river (including calm inner channels) are open for paddling. You can rent a wide range of watercraft, including 10-seat *rabaska* – canoes like those used by fur trappers.

ACTION 500   GO-KARTING
(www.action500.com; 5592 Rue Hochelaga; ☉6pm-midnight Mon-Thu, noon-midnight Fri, 9am-midnight Sat & Sun; ML'Assomption, then ☒85) Canada's largest indoor go-kart center provides plenty of amusement for gearheads. Sharpen your skills in 10-minute races on a large indoor karting track. The racers blaze around the circuit at speeds of up to 75km/h. Uniforms and safety helmets are provided; it's $22 to $25 per race.

You can also let off steam in a round of paintball on four terrains strewn with obstacles, bunkers, pyramids and catacombs. The games pit security agents against thieves in a dozen splattering scenarios. Paintball packages (from $30) include mask, paint gun and paintballs.

H2O ADVENTURES   WATER SPORTS
(☎514-842-1306; www.aventuresh2o.com; 2985B Rue St-Patrick; pedal boat/kayak/electric per hr $10/15/40; ☉9am-9pm May-Sep; MCharlevoix) Located across from the Atwater market on the banks of the Canal de Lachine, H2O rents out kayaks and pedal boats for a gentle glide along the water. There is a variety of courses on offer – white-water, rolling clinic, introductory two-hour classes ($39 to $45).

RAFTING MONTRÉAL   RAFTING
(www.raftingMontréal.com; 8912 Blvd LaSalle; jet boat per adult/child/teen $53/33/43, rafting $43/26/37; ☉9am-6pm May-Sep; MAngrignon, then ☒110; P) Located near the Lachine Rapids in LaSalle, this outfit offers the same brand of adrenaline-charged white water as Saute Moutons (p71).

L'ÉCOLE DE VOILE DE LACHINE   SAILING
(☎514-634-4326; www.voilelachine.com, in French; 3045 Blvd St-Joseph, Lachine; boat rental per hr $20-35, per 3hr $35-80; ☉10am-6pm Mon-Thu, 9am-8pm Sat & Sun May-Sep; MLionel-Groulx,

then (⊡173; P) Located on the edge of Lac St-Louis, the Lachine Sailing School organizes regattas on the St Lawrence River, gives free boat tours in late June and early July and rents light craft (windsurfing boards, small sailboats and catamarans). Qualified instructors give windsurfing and sailing courses in summer. One-week sailing courses cost $160.

CENTRE D'ESCALADE
HORIZON ROC   ROCK CLIMBING

(www.horizonroc.com; 2350 Rue Dickson; admission from $15; ⊘5-11pm Mon-Fri, 9am-6pm Sat, 9am-5pm Sun; Ⓜ L'Assomption, then ⊡85) This enormous 2600-sq-meter climbing gym features 12m walls and hundreds of lead and top-rope routes; it's one of the world's largest indoor climbing facilities. You can sign up for lessons, and all the gear (rope, harness, climbing shoes etc) is on hand for hire. There's also a cafe on-site.

CENTRE AQUATIQUE   SWIMMING

(⊘514-252-4622; www.parcolympique.qc.ca; 4141 Ave Pierre-de-Courbertin; per adult/child $7/5; ⊘6:30am-9pm Mon-Fri, 9am-4pm Sat & Sun; Ⓜ Viau; P) The competition pools at the Olympic Stadium are great for laps – they're among the fastest in the world thanks to a system that reduces water movement. The six indoor pools include a wading pool for tots, a water slide and a diving basin. Call or check online for the current schedule, which can change owing to events and competitions.

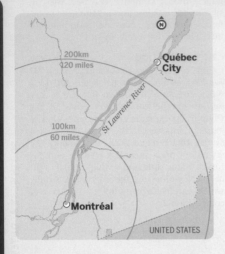

Québec City

Québec City Top Five

❶ Racing down the hair-raising toboggan run in winter, watching street performers strut their stuff in summer, or taking in the dramatic views of the St Lawrence River any time of year on the **Terrasse Dufferin** (p158).

❷ Strolling, shopping and admiring the murals, museums and historic buildings in the 17th-century **Quartier Petit-Champlain** (p163).

❸ Photographing the imposing **Château Frontenac** (p156) from every possible angle.

❹ Visualizing the legendary rivalry between French and English on a tour of **La Citadelle** (p155).

❺ Sipping ice cider from a frosty glass and praying that the chandelier won't fall on your head at the **Ice Hotel** (p196).

TOP SIGHTS
LA CITADELLE

Towering above the St Lawrence River, this massive, star-shaped fort is a living museum that offers something for all ages. The exhibits on military life from colonial times to today will appeal to anyone interested in Québécois history, while children will be enthralled in summertime by the daily changing of the guard and the weekend beating of the retreat, which features soldiers banging on their drums at shift's end.

French forces started building a defensive structure here in the late 1750s, but the Citadelle we know today was built in the early to mid-1800s by the British, who feared two things: an American invasion of the colony and a possible revolt by the French-speaking population (that's why the cannons point not only at the river, but at Québec City itself).

By the time the Citadelle was completed, things were calming down. In 1871, the Treaty of Washington between the United States and the newly minted Dominion of Canada ended the threat of American invasion.

The Citadelle now houses about 200 members of the Royal 22e Régiment. The Vandoos, a nickname taken from the French for 22 (*vingt-deux*), is the only entirely French-speaking battalion in the Canadian Forces. The second official residence of the Governor-General (the Queen of England's Canadian representative) has also been located here since 1872.

Hour-long guided tours of the Citadelle are excellent and will give you the lowdown on the spectacular architecture.

DON'T MISS

➡ The summer-only changing of the guard (10am daily) and beating of the retreat (Friday and Saturday at 6pm)

➡ The spectacular panoramas from the northeastern ramparts

PRACTICALITIES

➡ Map p160

➡ ✆418-694-2815

➡ www.lacitadelle .qc.ca

➡ 1 Côte de la Citadelle

➡ adult/child/student $10/5.50/9

➡ ⊗9am-5pm May-Sep, 10am-4pm Apr, 10am-3pm Oct, guided visit 1:30pm daily Nov-Mar

TOP SIGHTS
CHÂTEAU FRONTENAC

STEVEN MIRIC / GETTY IMAGES ©

This audaciously elegant structure is not only Québec City's most luxurious hotel, but also its most iconic tourist site. Its fabulous turrets, winding hallways and imposing wings graciously complement its dramatic location atop Cap Diamant, a cliff that swoops down into the St Lawrence River. Over the years, it's lured a never-ending line-up of luminaries, including Alfred Hitchcock, who chose this setting for the opening scene of his 1953 mystery *I Confess*.

It's probably one of the rare hotels where most people in the lobby aren't even guests but rather tourists visiting to get close to the history and architecture (this is the world's most photographed hotel, after all).

Designed by New Yorker Bruce Price (father of manners maven Emily Post), the Château was named after the mercurial Count of Frontenac, Louis de Buade, who governed New France in the late 1600s. Completed in 1893, it was one of the Canadian Pacific Railway's series of luxury hotels built across Canada.

During WWII, the Québec Conferences involving British prime minister Winston Churchill, US president Franklin Roosevelt and Canadian prime minister William Lyon Mackenzie King were all held here. Other illustrious guests have included King George VI, Chiang Kai-shek and Princess Grace of Monaco.

Sadly, guided tours of the building were discontinued in 2011, but nonguests can still wander through the reception area and stop in for a drink or a bite at the hotel's restaurant or bar.

DON'T MISS

➡ A drink in the hotel's panoramic St-Laurent Bar
➡ Arriving here by calèche (horse-drawn carriage)
➡ Views of the château illuminated at night

PRACTICALITIES

➡ Map p160
➡ ☑418-692-3861, 866-540-4460
➡ www.fairmont.com/frontenac
➡ 1 Rue des Carrières
➡ admission free to lobby, bar and restaurant

Explore

The crown jewel of French Canada, Québec City is one of North America's oldest and most magnificent settlements. Its picturesque Old Town is a Unesco World Heritage site, a living museum of narrow cobblestone streets, 17th- and 18th-century houses and soaring church spires, with the splendid Château Frontenac towering above it all. There's more than a glimmer of Old Europe in its classic bistros, sidewalk cafes and manicured squares.

You can get a taste of the city in a single day, but linger at least a weekend if you can. The city's compact size makes it ideal for walking, and it shines brightest when you slow down.

The main focus of your visit should be the Old Town, split between the Haute Ville (Upper Town), perched above the St Lawrence River on the Cap Diamant cliffs, and the Basse Ville (Lower Town), where Samuel de Champlain established the first French foothold in 1608. The Old Town is packed with museums, mansard-roofed houses and cobblestone streets just begging to be explored.

Outside the walls, through the historic town gates of Porte St-Louis and Porte St-Jean, four additional neighborhoods are easily accessible: St-Jean Baptiste, Colline Parlementaire, Montcalm and St-Roch, each boasting wonderful restaurants, shopping and nightlife. Also noteworthy here are the vast Plains of Abraham, where the British defeated the French in 1759; nowadays enshrined as a national park, this area offers superb recreational opportunities.

Québec City goes to great lengths to entertain visitors. All summer long, musicians, acrobats and actors in period costume take to the streets, while fantastic festivals fill the air with fireworks and song. In the coldest months of January and February, Québec's Winter Carnival is arguably the biggest and most colorful winter festival around. Fall and spring bring beautiful foliage, dramatically reduced prices and thinner crowds.

Best Places to Eat

➡ Le Saint-Amour (p172)

➡ Panache (p174)

➡ Le Café du Clocher Penché (p178)

For reviews see p171 ➡

Best Places to Drink

➡ Le Moine Échanson (p180)

➡ La Barberie (p182)

➡ Ice Hotel (p196)

For reviews see p180 ➡

Best Places to Stay

➡ Auberge St-Antoine (p195)

➡ La Marquise de Bassano (p193)

➡ Auberge JA Moisan (p196)

For reviews see p192 ➡

Top Tip

Make lunch your main meal. Most restaurants, including some of Québec City's finest, offer a bargain-priced midday table d'hôte (fixed-price menu), often costing about half the price of a comparable dinner.

Getting There and Away

Train Via Rail (www.viarail.ca) runs four trains daily from Montréal's Gare Centrale to Québec's Gare du Palais (three to 3½ hours, one way/return $63/126).

Bus Greyhound (www.greyhound.com) and Orléans Express (www.orleans express.com) offer frequent bus service from Montréal (three to 3½ hours, one way/return $57/91).

Car Driving from Montréal to Québec City takes just over three hours, via Hwy 40 (north of the St Lawrence River) or Hwy 20 (south of the river).

Air Air Canada operates regular flights (45 minutes) from Montréal to Québec City's newly renovated Jean Lesage Airport. There are also some direct flights from the United States and Europe.

Getting Around

Bus RTC (Réseau de Transport de la Capitale; ☎418-627-2511; www.rtcquebec.ca) offers efficient service all around town. To get around the Old Town, your best bet is the nifty new Ecolobus, which runs on electric power and charges only $1 per ride. Single rides on other RTC buses cost $3; alternatively, purchase a day pass for $7, or a two-day pass for $11.50. The most convenient hub for catching multiple buses is on Place d'Youville, just outside

QUÉBEC CITY

the Old Town walls; to get here from the Gare du Palais train station or the long-distance bus station, take bus 21 or 800.

....

Need to Know

➡ **Area Code** ☎418
➡ **Location** 260km northeast of Montréal
➡ **Tourist Office** (Centre Infotouriste; Map p160; ☎877-266-5687; www.bonjourquebec.com; 12 Rue Ste-Anne; ⊙8:30am-7pm late Jun-Aug, 9am-5pm rest of year)

◉ SIGHTS

Most of Québec City's sights are found within the compact cluster of old town walls, or just outside them, making this a dream destination for pedestrians.

◉ Old Upper Town

The heart of Québec City, the Old Town is where you will be spending most of your time because it's packed with the city's blockbuster sights and numerous museums on everything from history and the military to religious life in New France. The narrow, winding roads are lined with extraordinary old architecture, with some buildings dating from the 1600s. The grandest military structures, churches and buildings are concentrated in the Old Upper Town.

CHÂTEAU FRONTENAC　　HISTORIC BUILDING
See p156.

LA CITADELLE　　FORTRESS
See p155.

TERRASSE DUFFERIN　　VIEWPOINT
(Map p160) Outside the Château Frontenac, along the riverfront, this 425m-long promenade is a marvelous setting for a stroll, with dramatic views over the river from its cliff-top perch, 60m above the water. In the summer it's peppered with street performers, and you can stop at a well-placed snack stand for ice cream or a cold drink. Near the statue of Samuel de Champlain, stairways descend below the boardwalk to the recent excavations of Champlain's second fort, which stood here from 1620 to 1635. Nearby, you can take the **funicular** (Map

p160, $2 one way; ⊙7:30am-10:45pm Sep–mid-Jun, to 11:45pm mid-Jun-Aug) to the Old Lower Town. Just above the Terrasse Dufferin is the leafy **Jardin des Gouverneurs**, a peaceful refuge from the holidaying masses.

FORTIFICATIONS OF QUÉBEC　　HISTORIC SITE
Map p160 (www.pc.gc.ca/eng/lhn-nhs/qc/fortifi cations; Rue d'Auteuil, near Rue St-Louis; ⊙10am-6pm late May-Aug, 10am-5pm Sep-early Oct; ☐3, 11) These largely restored old walls are a national historic site. You can walk the complete 4.6km circuit on top of it all around the Old Town for free. From this vantage point, much of the city's history is within easy view. In summer 90-minute **guided walks** (adult/ child $10/5; ⊙2pm Jun-early Oct, plus 10am Jul & Aug) are also available, beginning at the Frontenac kiosk (the historic site's information center on Terrasse Dufferin) and ending at Artillery Park.

ARTILLERY PARK　　HISTORIC SITE
Map p160 (www.pc.gc.ca/eng/lhn-nhs/qc/for tifications/natcul/natcul2.aspx; 2 Rue d'Auteuil; adult/child $4/2; ⊙10am-6pm mid-May-Aug, to 5pm Sep–mid-Oct; ☐3, 7, 11, 28) The French chose this location for their army barracks because of its strategic view of the plateau west of the city and the St Charles River, both of which could feed enemy soldiers into Québec City. English soldiers moved in after the British conquest of New France. The English soldiers left in 1871 and it was changed into an ammunition factory for the Canadian army. The factory operated until 1964 and thousands of Canadians worked there during the World Wars. Now you can visit the **Officers' Quarters** and the **Dauphine Redoubt** where guides greet you in character (ie the garrison's cook) and give you the scoop on life in the barracks. There's also a huge 19th-century model of Québec City in the old **Arsenal Foundry**.

FREE **ST-LOUIS FORTS & CHÂTEAUX NATIONAL HISTORIC SITE**　　ARCHAEOLOGICAL SITE
Map p160 (www.pc.gc.ca/eng/lhn-nhs/qc/saint louisforts/index.aspx; ⊙10am-6pm mid-May-early Oct) Hidden underneath Terrasse Dufferin are the ruins of four forts and two chateaus constructed by Samuel de Champlain and other early Québec residents between 1620 and 1694. These structures, excavated between 2005 and 2007, served as residences for the French and English governors of Québec for over 200 years before falling

victim to bombardment, fire and neglect. In warm weather, Parks Canada offers free hourly tours of the archaeological site and the artifacts unearthed there.

MUSÉE DE L'AMÉRIQUE FRANÇAISE
MUSEUM

Map p160 (www.mcq.org/en/maf; 2 Côte de la Fabrique; adult/child/student $8/2/5.50, free Tue Nov-May; ☉9:30am-5pm daily late Jun-early Sep, 10am-5pm Tue-Sun early Sep-late Jun; ☐3, 7, 11) On the grounds of the **Séminaire de Québec** (the Québec Seminary), this excellent museum is purported to be Canada's oldest. (The Musée Scientifique du Séminaire de Québec opened here in 1806.) The museum that stands here today has brilliantly atmospheric exhibits on life in the seminary during the colonial era as well as religious artifacts and temporary exhibitions on subjects like endangered species. The priests from the Québec Seminary were avid travelers and collectors and there are some magnificent displays of the scientific objects they brought back with them from Europe, such as old Italian astronomical equipment. The exhibits are capped off by a wonderful short film on New World history from a Quebecer's perspective.

FREE BASILIQUE-CATHÉDRALE NOTRE-DAME-DE-QUÉBEC
CHURCH

Map p160 (☎418-692-2533; www.nddq.org; 20 Rue de Buade; guided tours $5; ☉7am-4pm; ☐3, 7, 11) This basilica got its start as a small church in 1647. In the ensuing years, the churches built here suffered everything from frequent fires to battle damage, especially during fighting between British and French armies in 1759. But no matter what, the church was rebuilt and repaired. Each replacement was bigger than the last until it reached the size you see today – a structure completed in 1925. The interior is appropriately grandiose, though most of the basilica's treasures didn't survive the 1922 fire that left behind only the walls and foundations. To have a look at the crypt, you'll have to sign on to a guided tour; call ahead or check inside the church for tour schedules. Everyone from governors of New France to archbishops and cardinals has been laid to rest here.

CATHEDRAL OF THE HOLY TRINITY
CHURCH

Map p160 (www.cathedral.ca; 31 Rue des Jardins; ☉10am-5pm late May–mid-Oct; ☐3, 7, 11) Built from 1800 to 1804, this cathedral was designed by two officers from the British army's military engineering corps and modeled on St Martin-in-the-Fields Church in London, England. This elegantly handsome Anglican cathedral was the first ever built outside the British Isles, with oak imported from Windsor Castle's Royal Forest just to make the pews. Upon its completion, King George III sent the cathedral a treasure trove of objects, including candlesticks, chalices and silver trays. The elaborateness of the gifts heading toward the New World sent London's chattering classes atwitter. The royal box for the reigning monarch or her representative is located in the upper left balcony if you are facing the altar. (Look for the royal coat of arms.) The cathedral's bell tower, an impressive 47m high, competes for attention with the Basilique Notre-Dame located nearby. You will find that a guide is usually around in the summer months and conducts free 10-minute tours of the cathedral.

MUSÉE DES URSULINES
MUSEUM

Map p160 (www.ursulines-uc.com/musees.php; 12 Rue Donnacona; adult/youth/student $8/4/6; ☉10am-5pm Tue-Sun May-Sep, 1-5pm Tue-Sun Oct-Apr; ☐3, 7, 11) The fascinating story of the Ursuline nuns' lives and their influence in the 17th and 18th centuries is told in this thoughtful, well laid-out museum, which was fully renovated in 2011 to accommodate visitors with limited mobility. The sisters established the first girls' school on the continent in 1641, educating both aboriginal and French girls. Marie de l'Incarnation, the founder, was one of the most intriguing figures from the order. Leaving a young son in France after she was widowed, she joined the Ursulines and moved to New France, where she lived well into old age. She taught herself Aboriginal languages and her frequent and eloquent letters to her son back in France are held by historians to be some of the richest and most valuable material available to scholars studying life in the French colony. The Ursulines were also expert embroiderers and many examples of their work are on display. There's a lovely chapel at the same address. It dates from 1902 but retains some interiors from 1723.

MUSÉE DU FORT
MUSEUM

Map p160 (www.museedufort.com; 10 Rue Ste-Anne; adult/student $8/6; ☉10am-5pm Apr-Oct, 11am-4pm Thu-Sun Nov-Mar, closed 2wk in Jan; ☐3, 7, 11) Not really a museum at all, the

Québec City Old Town

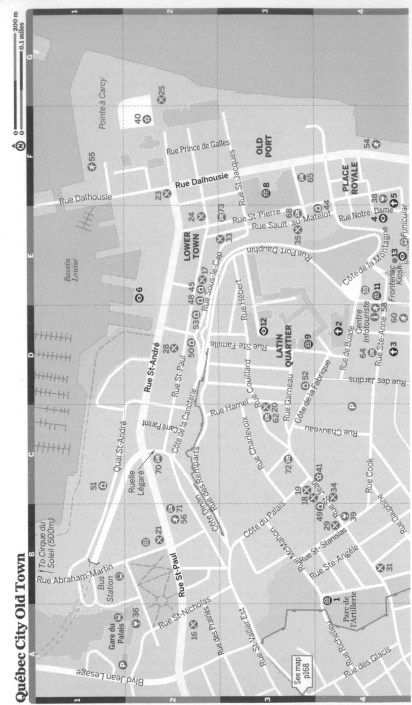

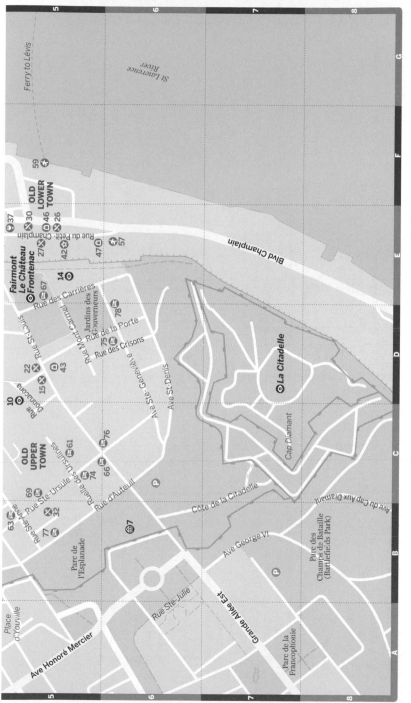

St Lawrence River

Ferry to Lévis

OLD LOWER TOWN

59

37
30
27
42
46
26
47
57
Rue du Petit-Champlain

Fairmont Le Château Frontenac

14
67
Rue des Carrières

Rue Ste-Ursule

Rue Mont-Carmel
Jardins des Gouverneurs
Rue de la Porte
Rue des Crisons

22
15
43
10
Rue Donnacona

Ave Ste-Geneviève
Ave St-Denis

78
75

Blvd Champlain

La Citadelle

Cap Diamant

OLD UPPER TOWN

69
61
74
66
76
Ruelle des Ursulines
Rue d'Auteuil

63
77
32
Rue Ste-Ursule

7

Côte de la Citadelle

Ave du Cap Aux Diamant

Ave George VI

Parc de l'Esplanade

Place d'Youville

Ave Honoré Mercier

Rue Ste-Julie

Grande Allée Est

Parc des Champs de Bataille (Battlefields Park)

Parc de la Francophonie

Québec City Old Town

Musée du Fort houses a 30-minute multimedia show on the many attempts over the centuries to take Québec City. It's all played out on a model/diorama that lights up in the middle of a mini-theater. The breathless narration and anemic smoke-puffs that pass for special effects are a bit hokey, but it does give a quick, enjoyable, easy-to-grasp audiovisual survey of local battles, providing a good introduction to the city's history. English-language shows are held on the hour (French-language versions on the half-hour).

Old Lower Town

Sandwiched between the Upper Town and the waterfront, this area has the city's most intriguing museums, plus numerous plaques and statues and plenty of outdoor cafes and restaurants along its pedestrian-friendly streets. Street performers in period costume help recapture life in distant centuries.

Teeming Rue du Petit-Champlain is said to be, along with Rue Sous-le-Cap, the narrowest street in North America, and it forms the heart of Quartier Petit-Champlain, the continent's oldest commercial district. Look for the incredible wall paintings that feature on the 17th- and 18th-century buildings.

Place-Royale, the principal square of Québec City's Lower Town, has 400 years of history behind it. When Samuel de Champlain founded Québec, it was this bit of shoreline that was first settled. In 1690 cannons placed here held off the attacks of the English naval commander Phipps and his men. Today the name 'Place-Royale' often generally refers to the district.

Built around the old harbor in the Old Lower Town northeast of Place-Royale, the Vieux-Port (Old Port) is being redeveloped as a multipurpose waterfront area.

From the Upper Town, you can reach the Lower Town in several ways. Walk down Côte de la Canoterie from Rue des Remparts to the Old Port or edge down the charming and steep Rue Côte de la Montagne. About halfway down on the right there is a shortcut, the Escalier Casse-Cou (Break-Neck Stairs), which leads down to Rue du Petit-Champlain. You can also take the funicular (p158).

MUSÉE DE LA CIVILISATION MUSEUM

Map p160 (www.mcq.org/en/mcq; 85 Rue Dalhousie; adult/child/student $14/4/9, free Tue Nov-May; ⊙9:30am-6:30pm late Jun-early Sep, 10am-5pm Tue-Sun early Sep-late Jun) The Museum of Civilization wows you even before you've clapped your eyes on the exhibitions. It is a fascinating mix of modern design that incorporates pre-existing buildings with contemporary architecture. The permanent exhibits, such as the one on the cultures of Québec's Aboriginals and the one titled 'People of Québec: Then and Now,' are unique and well worth seeing, and many include clever interactive elements. At any given moment there's an outstanding variety of rotating shows on topics as diverse as Oceania, ancient Rome, the history of Radio Canada or the work of Québécois writer Michel Tremblay. This is really the only museum in town that regularly focuses on contemporary issues and culture. It's a big place with lots to see, so focus on only one or two exhibitions if you're not planning to make a full day of it.

CENTRE D'INTERPRÉTATION DE PLACE-ROYALE MUSEUM

Map p160 (www.mcq.org/en/cipr; 27 Rue Notre-Dame; adult/child/student $7/2/5; ⊙9:30am-5pm late Jun-early Sep, 10am-5pm Tue-Sun early Sep-late Jun; 🚇1) This interpretive center touts the Place-Royale neighborhood as the cradle of French history. The exhibits focus on the individual people, houses and challenges of setting up on the shores of the St Lawrence River. It goes a bit heavy on random artifacts, but it still includes some worthwhile displays that help illuminate what local life was like from the 1600s to the 20th century. Children will have lots of fun dressing up in historical costumes in the downstairs play area, and tours of the Lower Town are offered by guides in period garb during summer.

ÉGLISE NOTRE-DAME-DES-VICTOIRES CHURCH

Map p160 (www.nddq.org; Place-Royale; ⊙10am-5pm May-Oct, open for Mass & concerts only rest of year; 🚇1) Dating from 1688, Our Lady of Victories Church is the oldest stone church in North America. It stands on the spot where Champlain set up his 'Habitation,' a small stockade, 80 years prior to the church's arrival. Inside are copies of works ℹ️

TRIPLE YOUR ENJOYMENT OF QUÉBEC CITY'S MUSEUMS

Serious museum-goers can save money by purchasing Québec's three-museum pass, which grants entry into Musée de l'Amérique Française, Musée de la Civilisation and Centre d'Interprétation de Place-Royale. The cost is $21 for adults, $19 for seniors, $6 for children 12 to 16, or $14.50 for students; children under 12 are free; check it out online at www.mcq.org/en/maf/renseignements.html.

by Rubens and Van Dyck. Hanging from the ceiling is a replica of a wooden ship, the *Brézé,* thought to be a good-luck charm for ocean crossings and battles with the Iroquois. The church earned its name after British ships were unable to take Québec City in 1690 and again in 1711.

ESPACE 400 GALLERY
Map p160 (http://espace400bell.com; 100 Quai St-André; 🖥️1) Unveiled in 2008 for the city's 400th birthday celebrations, this sparkling new pavilion on the Old Port waterfront features a new exhibit every summer, with themes ranging from ice hockey to the wreck of the *Titanic* to immigration along the St Lawrence River.

👁️ St-Jean Baptiste

The heart of this area is Rue St-Jean, which extends from the Old Town west through Porte St-Jean. It's one of Québec's best streets for strolling, with an excellent assortment of colorful shops and restaurants, hip little cafes and bars. Near the corner of Rue St-Augustin is also where you'll find the epicenter of the city's tiny, unofficial gay 'village'. From Rue St-Jean, take any side street and walk downhill (northwest) to the narrow residential streets like Rue d'Aiguillon, Rue Richelieu or Rue St-Olivier. Note the smattering of outside staircases and row-style houses, some with very nice entrances, typical of Québec City's residential landscape.

ÉGLISE ST-JEAN-BAPTISTE CHURCH
Map p168 (www.saintjeanbaptiste.org/eglise-saint-jean-baptiste; 400 Rue St-Jean; 👁️2-

5:30pm Mon-Fri) This colossus completely dominates its area on the southwest end of Rue St-Jean. The first church was built in 1842 but was destroyed by fire in 1881. It was completely rebuilt by architect Joseph-Ferdinand Peachy and open again for business by 1884. Peachy drew on well-known French churches for inspiration: Notre-Dame-de-Paris for the pillars, Église St-Sulpice for the vaults and Église de la Trinité for the facade. In summer the church presents modest but well-researched exhibitions on church or neighborhood history.

👁️ Montcalm & Colline Parlementaire

A stroll west of the Old Town through Porte St-Louis leads to the Montcalm neighborhood, home to several impressive sites, including the historic Battlefields Park, the Québécois parliament building and one of the province's best fine-arts museums. About 10 blocks west of the gate, Rue Cartier is the heart of the upscale Montcalm district, lined with gourmet bistros, cafes, shops and a popular market.

PARC DES CHAMPS DE BATAILLE (BATTLEFIELDS PARK) HISTORIC SITE
(Map p168) One of Québec City's must-sees, this verdant, cliff-top park contains the **Plains of Abraham** (www.ccbn-nbc.gc.ca), the stage for the infamous 1759 battle between British General James Wolfe and French General Montcalm that determined the fate of the North American continent. The park, named for Abraham Martin, a Frenchman who was one of the first farmers to settle in the area, is packed with old cannons, monuments and commemorative plaques. The park is a big draw for locals, who come for outdoor activities such as running, in-line skating, cross-country skiing and snowshoeing, as well as the frequent open-air concerts in summertime at the Kiosque Edwin-Bélanger (p183). On warm days, the tree-lined 'plains' also make a good spot for picnics.

The area became an official park in 1908 and has been the site of many modern historical events as well: 'O Canada', the Canadian national anthem, written by Sir Adolphe Routhier with music by Calixa

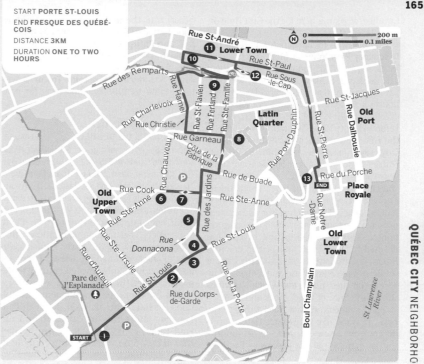

START **PORTE ST-LOUIS**

END **FRESQUE DES QUÉBÉ-
COIS**

DISTANCE **3KM**

DURATION **ONE TO TWO
HOURS**

QUÉBEC CITY NEIGHBORHOOD WALK

Neighborhood Walk
Historic Stroll Through the Old Town

This historical walking tour encompasses a mix of well-known and lesser-known Vieux-Québec attractions. Set off early, before tour buses fill the streets.

Begin at **1** **Porte St-Louis**, an impressive gate first erected in 1693 (though this version dates from 1878). Follow Rue St-Louis to the corner of Rue du Corps-de-Garde, where a **2** **cannonball** sits embedded in a tree (allegedly since 1759). Nearby, **3** **47 Rue St-Louis** is where French General Montcalm died, a day after being shot by the British during the destiny-changing Plains of Abraham Battle in September 1759.

At 34 Rue St-Louis, a 1676 home houses the Québécois restaurant **4** **Aux Anciens Canadiens**. Its steeply slanted roof was typical of 17th-century French architecture. Follow Rue des Jardins to the **5** **Ursuline Convent**, where generations of nuns educated both French and Aboriginal girls starting in 1639.

Left down Rue Cook is **6** **Edifice Price**, one of Canada's first skyscrapers, built in 1929 for $1 million. Next door, admire the art-deco lobby of Québec City's oldest hotel, the elegant 1870 **7** **Hotel Clarendon**.

Follow Rue des Jardins to the **8** **Québec Seminary**, founded in 1663; American officers were imprisoned here after their unsuccessful siege of Québec in 1775–76. Detour down pretty Rue Garneau, then descend to **9** **Rue des Remparts** for fine views over Québec City's waterfront factory district.

Descend **10** **Côte de la Canoterie**, a longtime link between the Lower and Upper Towns. Hope Gate stood atop the *côte* until 1873 to keep the riffraff from entering the Upper Town. Turn right onto **11** **Rue St-Paul**, the heart of Québec's antique district, then take a peek at 12 Rue Sous-le-Cap, a former red-light district.

Turn right and follow Rue Sault-au-Matelot to the 420-sq-meter trompe-l'oeil **12** **Fresque des Québécois**, where you can pose for the requisite tourist pic alongside historical figures like Jacques Cartier and Samuel de Champlain.

Lavallée, was sung here for the first time on June 24, 1880.

The gateway to Battlefields Park is the **Discovery Pavilion** (Map p168; www.ccbn-nbc.gc.ca; 835 Ave Wilfrid-Laurier; ☺8:30am-5:30pm daily Jul & Aug, 8:30am-5pm Mon-Fri, 9am-5pm Sat, 10am-5pm Sun Sep-Jun; ▣11), which houses a museum as well as a branch of the excellent Québec City tourist office, Centre Infotouriste (p158). The main draw here is the fine multimedia history show entitled **Odyssey** (adult/teenager/child $10/8/free; ☺10am-5:30pm Jul & Aug, to 5pm Sep-Jun). This year-round, permanent exhibition leads you through a series of three small theaters, where the history of the Plains of Abraham is depicted through clever audiovisual presentations and generous doses of good humor. There's a fine exhibit at the end devoted to the French and British colonial military, with displays depicting the lives of soldiers in the New World and a nicely done section on their uniforms, which describes the significance of the designs and colors.

There's no charge to wander through the park. If you'd like to explore the grounds on your own, you can pick up a bilingual tourist map ($4) at the Discovery Pavilion. However, if you want to get the whole experience – and are visiting in summer with four hours to spare – consider purchasing a **day pass** (adult/teenager/child $14/10/4) at the information desk on the lower level of the Discovery Pavilion. This three-for-one pass includes admission to the Odyssey show, the 40-minute **Abraham's Bus Tour** (☺6 departures daily Jul & Aug), in which an actor in period costume points out historical sites of interest with some colorful asides, and a visit to **Martello Tower 1** (Map p168; Battlefields Park; ☺10am-5pm Jul-early Sep), the only one of several British-built defensive towers that's still regularly open to the public. Despite its small appearance, the tower is jam-packed with fascinating exhibits that delve into the engineering history of the structures and describe living conditions for the soldiers based here.

History buffs can seek out a couple more British defensive towers in the surrounding area. Inside the park, **Martello Tower 2** (Map p168; cnr Aves Taché & Wilfrid-Laurier, Battlefields Park) opens to the public only during staged events, which operate primarily in summer and vary year to year. For info about current offerings, inquire at the Discovery Pavilion. **Martello Tower 4** (Rue Lav-

igueur) is in the St-Jean-Baptiste neighborhood between Rue Félix-Gabriel-Marchand and Rue Philippe-Dorion. It's closed to the public but worth a quick look from the outside if you're passing by. (Oh, and in case you're wondering, **Martello Tower 3** was torn down in 1905 to make way for construction.)

MUSÉE NATIONAL DES BEAUX-ARTS DU QUÉBEC   ART GALLERY

Map p168 (www.mnba.qc.ca; Battlefields Park; adult/child/student $15/4/7; ☺10am-6pm Thu-Tue, 10am-9pm Wed Jun-Aug, 10am-5pm Tue & Thu-Sun, 10am-9pm Wed Sep-May; ▣11) Anyone curious about Québécois art needs to carve out at least half a day for a visit to this museum, one of the best in the province. There are expert permanent exhibitions that range from art in the early French colonies to Québec's abstract artists. There are also individual halls devoted entirely to the province's artistic giants of the last century.

The do-not-miss permanent exhibitions include one devoted to Jean-Paul Lemieux (1904–90) and another to Jean-Paul Riopelle (1923–2002), which includes *L'hommage à Rosa Luxemburg* (Tribute to Rosa Luxemburg; 1986), his largest work.

The Brousseau Inuit Art Collection of 2639 pieces spanning 50 years was a personal collection of Inuit art acquired by the museum in 2005.

There are also frequent exhibitions from abroad and elsewhere in Canada. The museum is spread out through three halls including the Pavilion Charles-Baillairgé, Québec City's former prison. Audioguides are available for the permanent collections and often for temporary exhibitions as well. Other events include film screenings (often documentaries on prominent international artists), drawing and painting classes open to the public, and a concert series.

If all this cultural activity is wearing you out, you can grab a snack or the daily lunch special at the on-site **cafe**, or visit the museum's **restaurant**, which enjoys superb views of Battlefields Park from its bay windows and outdoor terrace.

FREE HÔTEL DU PARLEMENT   HISTORIC BUILDING

Map p168 (☎418-643-7239; www.assnat.qc.ca/en/visiteurs; cnr Ave Honoré-Mercier & Grande Allée Est; ☺9am-4:30pm Mon-Fri year-round, plus 10am-4:30pm Sat & Sun late Jun-early Sep; ▣3, 11,

GUIDED WALKING TOURS

Several companies offer guided walking tours of the city; look for them on the left side as you enter the tourist office opposite Château Frontenac. Here are a few themed itineraries to get you started:

➡ **Podcast Tour of Old Lower Town** (www.mcq.org/place-royale) Visitors to the Old Lower Town can download the free Place-Royale from Today to Yesterday podcast, produced by the Musée de la Civilisation. This historic walking tour of the neighborhood is divided into five distinct zones surrounding the main square. For further info, visit the **Centre d'Interprétation de Place-Royale** (27 Rue Notre-Dame).

➡ **Historic Tour of Old Lower Town** (☑418-646-3167; www.mcq.org/en/cipr; 27 Rue Notre-Dame; tours free; ◷tours 11:30am, 1:30pm & 3pm daily Jun 24-Labor Day) Guided tours of the Old Lower Town are offered free of charge all summer long by guides from the Centre d'Interprétation de la Place-Royale. Tours are in French or English, depending on who shows up first.

➡ **Ghost Tours of Québec** (☑418-694-2412, 866-694-2412; www.ghosttoursofquebec.com; 98 Rue du Petit-Champlain; adult/student/child under 11 $19/16/free; ◷tours 8pm daily May-Oct, plus 9pm daily Jul & Aug) This lantern-lit, 90-minute walking tour of the Old Town, led by a guide in period costume, recounts a series of ghost stories and tales of murders and hauntings, providing a spooky perspective on Québec's historic streets.

➡ **Gourmet Food Tour** (☑418-694-2001; www.toursvoirquebec.com; 12 Rue Ste-Anne; adult $38; ◷tours 2:30pm Tue-Sat) Winding through the St-Jean Baptiste neighborhood, this 2½-hour culinary tour offers tastings of wines, cheeses, crepes, chocolate, maple products and other Québécois specialties at a variety of shops and restaurants. It's one of several city tours offered by Tours Voir Québec.

QUÉBEC CITY SIGHTS

800, 801) Home to the Provincial Legislature, the National Assembly building is a Second Empire structure completed in 1886. Free tours are given in English and French year-round; call for the schedule. The 30-minute visits get you into the **National Assembly Chamber**, the **Legislative Council Chamber** and the **Speakers' Gallery**. The facade is decorated with 23 bronze statues of significant provincial historical figures, including explorer Samuel de Champlain (1570–1635), early New France governor Louis de Buade Frontenac (1622–98) and battle heroes such as James Wolfe (1727–59) and Louis-Joseph Montcalm (1712–59), the English and French generals who met, fought and received mortal wounds on the nearby Plains of Abraham. On the grounds are more recent figures in Québec's tumultuous history, including Maurice Duplessis (1890–1959), who kept a stranglehold on the province during his 20-year-long premiership. The grounds are also used for staging events during Winter Carnival. Note the flower-trimmed fountain facing the grounds, installed in 2008 to celebrate Québec City's 400th anniversary. It's a fine vantage point for photographing the building.

LA MAISON HENRY-STUART HISTORIC BUILDING
Map p168 (☑418-647-4347; www.cmsq.qc.ca/mhs; 82 Grande Allée Ouest; adult/child $8/3; ◷1-5pm Wed-Sun late Jun-early Sep) This handsomely preserved cottage, built in 1849, once belonged to an upper-middle-class Anglophone family, and contains period furnishings from the early 1900s. Guided tours help elucidate what life was like in those days, and tea and lemon cake makes it seem all the sweeter. A small but verdant garden surrounds the cottage. Visits are by guided tour, which take place every hour on the hour between 1pm and 4pm. Call for the latest schedule.

OBSERVATOIRE DE LA CAPITALE VIEWPOINT
Map p168 (www.observatoire-capitale.com; 1037 Rue de la Chevrotière, Édifice Marie-Guyart; adult/student $10/8; ◷10am-5pm daily Feb–mid-Oct, 10am-5pm Tue-Sun mid-Oct–Jan; ◳11, 25, 28) Head 221m up to the 31st floor for great views of the Old Town, the St Lawrence River and (if it's clear enough) even the Laurentians. It all helps to get your bearings, while the information panels along the way will get you up to speed on some of the local history.

Québec City Outside the Walls

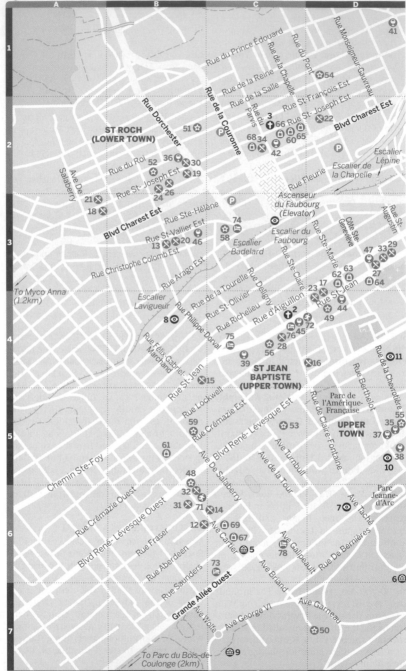

FREE NUNAVIK

INFORMATION CENTRE CULTURAL BUILDING

Map p168 (www.nunavik.ca; 1204 Cours du Général-de-Montcalm; ⊙11am-1pm & 2-7pm Jul-Sep, 9am-noon & 1-5pm Mon-Fri Oct-Jun; ⊡11, 25, 28) Far in Québec's north, Nunavik (not to be confused with Canada's third territory, Nunavut) is almost completely inhabited by Inuit. With no trains or roads into Nunavik, even most Quebecers know little about the Inuit culture or this fascinating region. This modest center was opened mainly to promote tourism to the area's 14 villages, but it's an interesting place for a short stop just to look at the wall pictures or the small craft displays. It's an incredibly friendly place and the employees are more than willing to shoot the breeze for the genuinely curious, answering questions on anything from the Inuit language to Inuit culture.

◉ St-Roch

St-Roch, to the northwest of the Old Town, is an up-and-coming neighborhood sprinkled with stylish nightspots, eclectic eateries, boutiques and vintage shops. In recent years this neighborhood has gone from a working-class district for factory and naval workers to an abandoned urban wasteland to an emerging nightlife district (see boxed text, p171). It's a great area for a bit of urban exploring, though not as established as the neighborhood of St-Jean-Baptiste to the south – some would say that's exactly the charm of St-Roch.

Thanks to the **Ascenseur du Faubourg** (lower entrance cnr Rues St-Vallier & La Couronne, upper entrance cnr Rues St-Réal & Ste-Claire; ⊙7am-7pm Mon-Wed, 7am-10pm Thu & Fri, 10am-10pm Sat, 10am-7pm Sun), a free elevator that eliminates much of the climb, pedestrians can get from Rue St-Joseph (St-Roch's main thoroughfare) to Rue St-Jean in 15 minutes or less.

ÉGLISE ST-ROCH CHURCH

Map p168 (www.saint-roch.qc.ca; 590 Rue St-Joseph; ⊙9am-5pm) There are giants and then there is this, the biggest church in Québec City. Measuring over 80m long, 34m wide and 46m high including the steeples, it was built between 1914 and 1923. When the original architects died, the neo-Gothic, neo-Roman structure was finished off by Louis-Napoléon Audet, the

Québec City Outside The Walls

same man who worked on the monumental Ste-Anne-de-Beaupré Basilica 35km to the east. The marble inside the church is from Saskatchewan. See if you can find faint fossil imprints in it.

In mid-August the church hosts its annual **Bénédiction des Chiens** (Benediction of the Dogs), an event unparalleled elsewhere in Canada; this is followed in September by the **Festival International des Musiques Sacrées de Québec** (Festival of Sacred Music; p28). Both are wonderful times to see the church at its best.

◎ Ste-Foy-Sillery

Ste-Foy and Sillery were actually two separate neighborhoods before municipal mergers joined them together. Both are about 5km west of downtown Québec City, although each still retains its own distinct character. Ste-Foy, roughly north of Blvd Laurier, has a stranglehold on the city's malls but is enlivened by the student population at Laval University. Sillery, which is roughly south of Blvd Laurier, has leafy streets lined with affluent homes; places like Ave Maguire are lined with charming cafes. Aside from the aquarium, there isn't much here in the way of sights, but if you're in the neighborhood you should make sure to drop by the Pointe à Puiseaux down at the foot of Rue d'Église. Here you can take in a gorgeous view of the St Lawrence River.

AQUARIUM DU QUÉBEC   AQUARIUM
(www.sepaq.com/paq/en; 1675 Ave des Hôtels; adult/child $15.50/7.75; ☉10am-5pm Jun-Aug, to 4pm Sep-May; ☐13, 25) Spread across 40 hectares, Québec's aquarium contains some 10,000 aquatic creatures, in the form of freshwater and saltwater fish, amphibians, reptiles, invertebrates and marine mammals. The park is divided into several habitats, including a wetlands region and an arctic sector (with an underwater observation window of the polar bears). There's also a food court with a terrace overlooking the river. You can catch daily events like walrus and polar bear feedings and a trained harbor seal show; times vary throughout the year; see aquarium website for details. It's located about 11km west of the city center, near the Pont Pierre Laporte bridge.

REBIRTH OF ST-ROCH

Once a gritty area better left unexplored, the neighborhood of St-Roch has gone through a remarkable rebirth in the past two decades. Under an ambitious urban renewal plan, the city created a public garden, restored a shuttered theater and hired artists to paint frescoes in the neighborhood. Artists and entrepreneurs began moving back into the area, bringing cafes and shops on their heels. Today, 'le nouveau' St-Roch has become one of Québec City's trendiest neighborhoods. Rue St-Joseph has everything from art galleries and glitzy boutiques to junk shops and fine dining – all drawing a similarly eclectic mix of locals – as well as some excellent nightlife options. For a dynamic slice of contemporary Québec City, take a stroll, heading 1km west, outside the old quarter.

PARC DU BOIS-DE-COULONGE   PARK
Map p168 (1215 Grande-Allée Ouest; ☉dawn-dusk; ☐11, 800; P) Not far west of the Plains of Abraham lie the colorful gardens of this park, a paean to the plant world and a welcome respite from downtown. Now open to the public, this wonderful woodland with extensive horticultural displays used to be the private property of a succession of Québec's and Canada's religious and political elite.

✕ EATING

Québec City's restaurant scene has never been better. These days interesting budget eateries share the foodie landscape with some of the most acclaimed restaurants in Canada. While the capital has always excelled at classic French food, in recent years a number of new arrivals have put a trendy modern spin on the bistro experience. Many of the better places can get a bit pricey, but don't write them off. Do what the locals do; a carefully chosen table d'hôte at lunchtime will give you exactly the same food for a more manageable price.

QUÉBEC CITY DINING TIPS

Opening Hours & Meal Times

Most restaurants in Québec City are open for lunch and dinner in the off-season and from about 11am to whenever the last customer leaves in peak summer season or during Winter Carnival. Standard lunch hours are noon to 2:30pm, with dinner from 6pm to 10pm. Places really tend to fill up from 8pm onwards in the francophone tradition. Note that outside of Winter Carnival, many restaurants in winter may be closed Sunday and Monday or both. Breakfast cafes open around 7am (later on weekends).

How Much?

Midrange places in Québec City will, on average, charge $15 to $25 for a main course. Top-end restaurants run upwards of $30 for a main; a culinary temple of some renown might charge $60 to $100 or more for a four-course gourmet dinner, including wine. Count on $6 to $10 for a glass of drinkable red and $25 to $35 (and up) for a bottle from the house cellar. Taxes amounting to nearly 15% apply at all restaurants. Most do not include the taxes in their menu prices, but check the fine print.

Booking Tables

If you're in Québec City between May and October, or during Winter Carnival, definitely book ahead to dine in one of the finer restaurants. During this peak season, popular places can fill up quickly, even at odd times like Monday nights.

Tipping

A tip of 15% of the pretax bill is customary in restaurants. Most credit card machines in Québec will calculate the tip for you based on whatever percentage you specify, or allow you to tip a dollar amount of your own choosing. Some waiters may add a service charge for large parties; in these cases, no tip should be added unless the service was extraordinary. If tipping in cash, leave the tip on the table or hand it directly to staff.

✖ Old Upper Town

If you are not eating at the places we've listed below, be choosy about where you spend your money in the Old Town. Though many restaurants have gorgeous settings, and may be great places for coffee, tea or a beer, food can often be disappointing.

LE SAINT-AMOUR FRENCH, QUÉBÉCOIS $$$
Map p160 (☑418-694-0667; www.saint-amour .com; 48 Rue Ste-Ursule; mains $38-50, fixed-price menus $63-115; ☺lunch Mon-Fri, dinner daily) One of the top-end darlings of the capital, Le Saint-Amour has earned a loyal following over the years for its beautifully prepared grills and seafood. Perhaps more impressive than the food is the excellent wine selection, with over 10,000 bottles in the cellar. The setting is warm and inviting beneath the glass-domed ceiling trimmed with hanging plants. The midday table d'hôte here (available Monday through Friday) offers that rarest of Upper Town experiences – a world-class meal at an extremely reasonable price.

CONTI CAFFE ITALIAN $$
Map p160 (☑418-692-4191; www.conticaffe.com; 32 Rue St-Louis; mains $17-32; ☺11:30am-10:30pm) Set on busy Rue St-Louis, the handsome Conti Caffe features an impressive selection of flavorful Italian classics. Start off with prosciutto-wrapped shrimp or tomato bruschetta, before moving on to penne with gorgonzola, apples and walnuts or lobster risotto with steamed green asparagus. The dining room is a warmly lit retreat, with exposed brick walls trimmed with art and big windows overlooking the street. The lunchtime table d'hôte ($11 to $18 for soup or juice, main dish, coffee and dessert) is one of the Old Town's best deals.

PAILLARD CAFÉ-BOULANGERIE BAKERY, SANDWICHES $
Map p160 (www.paillard.ca; 1097 Rue St-Jean; sandwiches $7-9; ☺7:30am-7pm Sun-Thu, to 9pm Fri & Sat) This bright and buzzy space

has high ceilings, huge windows looking onto the street and long wooden tables down the middle where diners tuck into tasty gourmet sandwiches (ham with green apples and brie; hot roast beef with blue cheese, caramelized onions and horseradish), satisfying soups and fresh salads. The attached bakery with its alluring display cases is almost impossible to resist – try the tentation, a delicious sweet pastry loaded with berries, or indulge in a savory olive fougasse. It's a bit of a madhouse at lunchtime.

AUX ANCIENS CANADIENS
QUÉBÉCOIS $$

Map p160 (☑418-692-1627; www.auxanciens canadiens.qc.ca; 34 Rue St-Louis; mains $23-36; ☺4:30-9pm Mon-Thu, noon-9pm Fri-Sun) Housed in the historic Jacquet House, which dates from 1676, this place is a well-worn tourist destination, specializing in robust country cooking and typical Québécois specialties. Here, waitstaff in historic garb serve dishes like caribou in blueberry wine sauce, duckling in maple-syrup sauce or Lac St-Jean meat pie served with pheasant and buffalo casserole. Lunch is served noon to 5:45pm and is by far the best deal (from $23 for three courses, including a glass of wine or beer and coffee or tea). The restaurant gets its name from the novel *Les Anciens Canadiens* by Philippe-Aubert de Gaspé, who lived in the house from 1815 to 1824. The original rooms have been left intact, resulting in several small, intimate dining areas.

LE PAIN BÉNI
QUÉBÉCOIS $$

Map p160 (☑418-694-9485; www.auberge placedarmes.com; 24 Rue Ste-Anne; mains $25-34; ☺11:30am-10:30pm daily May-Oct, lunch Mon-Fri & dinner daily Nov-Apr) Another great gourmet outing can be had at this small, unpretentious dining room inside the Auberge Place d'Armes. Le Pain Béni serves an excellent assortment of dishes with Québec highlights. Recent favorites include red deer with blackcurrant and juniper sauce, grapefruit-poached wild salmon and almonds, and house-made black pudding. Delectable desserts are the coup de grâce.

LE PATRIARCHE
QUÉBÉCOIS $$$

Map p160 (☑418-692-5488; www.lepatriarche .com; 17 Rue St-Stanislas; mains $30-47; ☺dinner Tue-Sun Sep-Jun, daily Jul & Aug) The nouvelle cuisine echoes the contemporary art hanging on the 180-year-old stone walls in this top-class restaurant. Imaginative culinary creations seem almost too lovely to eat, but the feeling soon passes when you read the restaurant's roll call of local suppliers. Start off with coconut and lemongrass poached scallops before moving on to roasted rack of lamb, caribou steak or a garden-vegetable mushroom risotto.

LE PETIT COIN LATIN
BREAKFAST $

Map p160 (8½ Rue Ste-Ursule; mains $9-20; ☺8am-11pm) For omelets, croissants, bowls of café au lait and other French-style breakfast items, this cheerful cafe just up from Rue St-Jean is a good choice, especially in summer when you can lounge on its sunny back patio. The menu also includes salads, soups and specialty items such as raclette (a Swiss dish of melted cheese, potatoes, ham, and pickles) and *tourtière* (a Québécois caribou meat pie served with berries, mashed potatoes and salad).

CASSE-CRÊPE BRETON
CREPERIE $

Map p160 (http://cassecrepebreton.com; 1136 Rue St-Jean; mains $5-9; ☺7am-10:30pm) Tiny and unassuming, this perennial favorite specializes in hot, fresh crepes of every kind starting as low as $4.50. Some diners like to sit at the counter and watch the chef at work.

CHEZ TEMPOREL
CAFE $

Map p160 (25 Rue Couillard; mains $6-10; ☺8am-10pm Mon-Fri, 9am-10pm Sat & Sun) Hidden away on a side street just off the beaten path, this charming little cafe serves tasty sandwiches, homemade soups and quiches, plus prodigious salads, fresh-baked goods and excellent coffees. It attracts a curious mix of locals and travelers.

CHEZ ASHTON
FAST FOOD $

Map p160 (www.chezashton.ca; 54 Côte du Palais; mains $5-10; ☺11am-11:30pm Sun-Wed, to 4am Thu-Sat) For a break from fine dining, head to Chez Ashton, a Québec City fast-food institution with dozens of restaurants across town. Some locals swear it's *the* best *poutine* (fries smothered in cheese curds and gravy) in the province (Montrealers, of course, would dismiss the idea). Though *poutine* is the draw, Ashton also whips up roast beef sandwiches and decent burgers.

QUÉBEC CITY EATING

✗ Old Lower Town

Rue St-Paul and Rue Sault-au-Matelot are lined with restaurants. In warm weather, they fling their windows open and set up outdoor seating on the streets. With the revelry overflowing outdoors there's a terrific atmosphere – there's not a single terrace that doesn't seem warm and inviting. In winter the streets outside may be deserted, but the revelry packs indoors, and windows positively glow with the warmth and good cheer inside. Many of the best bistros in town are located on this strip.

TOP CHOICE PANACHE   FRENCH, QUÉBÉCOIS $$$

Map p160 (☑418-692-1022; www.saint-antoine .com/en/dining; 10 Rue St-Antoine; lunch mains $22-27, dinner mains $31-49; ☺lunch Mon-Fri, dinner daily) This celebrated restaurant at the Auberge St-Antoine receives high marks for its delectable, imaginatively prepared Québécois cuisine and top-notch service. The feast, which can easily last three or four hours, might feature the likes of maple-glazed halibut, Appalachian red deer with wild berry sauce, spit-roasted duck or caramelized giant scallops. It's set in a stone-walled 19th-century maritime warehouse, with rustic wood beams nicely complementing the elegant place settings. The price tag for all this, not surprisingly, is high.

TOP CHOICE L'ÉCHAUDÉ   BISTRO $$

Map p160 (☑418-692-1299; www.echaude.com; 73 Rue Sault-au-Matelot; mains $18-38; ☺lunch & dinner) This classic little bistro has a refreshingly relaxed and nonstuffy waitstaff. All of the classics are on offer here – including duck confit, *steak frites*, fresh fish of the day and braised lamb shank – along with more daring options like Cornish hen with braised shrimp, and pan-fried foie gras with grilled mushrooms. All come beautifully plated to the table and bursting with flavor, which is why L'Échaudé is one of the rare places in the Old Town where locals regularly outnumber tourists. The terrific wine list favors bottles from France. After 9pm (21 hours on the Québécois clock), the fabulous '21-at-21' special lets you choose any three dishes for $21 (smaller appetites can enjoy a single main for only $8).

TOAST!   BISTRO $$$

Map p160 (☑418-692-1334; www.restauranttoast. com; 17 Rue Sault-au-Matelot; dishes from $15, 3-/4-course meal from $45/60; ☺dinner) Inside Le Priori Hotel, Toast! is another contender for best restaurant in the city. The trim, attractive dining room with fireplace and fiery red decor is the setting for an eclectic array of dishes, from foie gras appetizers (one of the house specialties) to mains like poached lobster risotto or teriyaki-glazed scallops with crispy pork belly, to maple-pear clafoutis for dessert. Most items on the menu cost around $15; from these you can build as simple or as complex a meal as you like. You'll find excellent wine selections, and generally good service. In the summer, you can dine alfresco in the vine-covered courtyard out back.

LE LAPIN SAUTÉ   FRENCH $$

Map p160 (☑418-692-5325; www.lapinsaute.com; 52 Rue du Petit-Champlain; mains $20-26; ☺11am-10pm Mon-Fri, 9am-10pm Sat & Sun) This cozy, rustically set restaurant brings a breath of the French countryside into the Old Town. Naturally *lapin* (rabbit) plays a starring role on the menu, in dishes like rabbit cassoulet and rabbit pie, but you can also opt for marinated salmon cooked on cedar, filet mignon, or lighter fare like French onion soup or a pear, cranberry and artisanal cheese turnover. For romantics there's also the 'picnic for two', a smorgasbord of rabbit pâté, smoked salmon, apple-beet salad, roasted garlic, herbed focaccia, crostini with tapenade and local cheese, and carrot-onion confit. In good weather, you can sit on the flowery patio overlooking tiny Félix Leclerc park.

LAURIE RAPHAËL   FRENCH, QUÉBÉCOIS $$$

Map p160 (☑418-692-4555; www.laurieraphael .com; 117 Rue Dalhousie; lunch table d'hôte $26, 3-course dinner menu $60, dinner mains $36-52; ☺lunch Tue-Fri, dinner Tue-Sat) This highly respected restaurant features a blend of *produits du terroir* (local Québec produce), along with international accents. Delectable favorites include giant scallops with coconut milk and exotic fruits, and lamb with mint and anise. Chef Daniel Vézina keeps menu descriptions to a minimum, saying he wants to 'leave room for imagination and discovery'. There's also a spontaneous chef's menu ($60) 'for those that like to be surprised'.

THE QUÉBÉCOIS TABLE

French food is king in Québec City. The lack of a significant immigrant population means that there is not the kind of massive ethnic smorgasbord that you'll find in Montréal; even so, the quality of restaurants here is outstanding. While for years Québec City locals were known to drive to Montréal for fine dining, these days Montrealers are making their way to Québec City to dine in top-of-the-line restaurants such as Le Saint-Amour (p172) and Panache (opposite).

Québec City also boasts at least one drink that you won't find in Montréal. Caribou is an alcoholic beverage that resembles a very powerful and sweet red wine, almost like a marriage of port and sherry, and warms the body – if not the soul. It's available for purchase on streets around Québec City during Winter Carnival.

BUFFET DE L'ANTIQUAIRE　　　　DINER $

Map p160 (95 Rue St-Paul; breakfast $4-9, mains $11-16; ☺6am-9pm) Tucked in among the bistros and the galleries is this convivial little diner with an old-school vibe. Locals and tourists alike crowd in for hearty breakfasts, steaming plates of *poutine*, savory meat pies and other tasty comfort fare. Grab a booth, a seat at the narrow counter, or a table on the small balcony upstairs and prepare to be amazed at the friendly efficiency of the lone, peripatetic waitress; in warm weather, there are also sidewalk tables out front.

LE 48 SAINT-PAUL　　　　BISTRO $$

Map p160 (☎418-694-4448; www.le48.ca; 48 Rue St-Paul; 3-course lunch menu $13-20, mains $14-23; ☺8am-midnight) This stylish spot leans toward theatricality with its sleek black tables and chairs and Cirque du Soleil footage playing in the background. The menu features tasty global bistro fare (Asian noodle soups, gourmet burgers, salads, pizzas) and there's an outdoor patio. Because it's open straight through from early morning to midnight, it's a great choice for a snack outside of standard meal times. Service is hit-or-miss.

LE MISTRAL GAGNANT　　　　FRENCH $$

Map p160 (☎418-692-4260; www.mistralgagnant .ca; 160 Rue St-Paul; mains $16-32, menus $25-39; ☺lunch & dinner Tue-Sat) The sunny flavors of Provence prevail at this eatery tucked in among the antique shops on Rue St-Paul. Specialties include bouillabaisse, lamb chops with thyme and basil, and duck breast in peach sauce. Happy yellow tablecloths festooned with olive branches set a festive mood.

SO-CHO　　　　FAST FOOD $

Map p160 (www.so-cho.com; Marché du Vieux-Port, 160 Quai St-André; sandwiches $5.25;

☺9am-6pm Mon-Fri, to 5pm Sat & Sun) Locals flock to this humble stand inside Marché du Vieux-Port to indulge in an ever-changing array of delectable homemade sausages. A dozen flavors are on offer each day, from fines herbes to lamb with mint and garlic, either packed up to cook at home or served on a roll to enjoy on the spot with sauerkraut and mustard.

BRYND　　　　DELI $

Map p160 (☎418-692-4693; www.brynd.com; 369 Rue St-Paul; mains $7-13; ☺11am-9pm Sun & Mon, to 10pm Tue-Thu, to 11pm Fri & Sat) Smoked meat sandwiches (somewhat akin to pastrami in the United States) are very popular throughout Québec, and this place opposite the train station is a long-standing local favorite. Bagel sandwiches and salads also appear on the menu, but most of the dedicated carnivores who eat here will tolerate nothing greener than the giant pickle that accompanies each sandwich (brought out on a little cutting board for customers to slice up as they please)!

LE CAFÉ DU MONDE　　　　BISTRO $$

Map p160 (☎418-692-4455; www.lecafedumonde .com; 84 Rue Dalhousie; 3-course lunch menu $14-19, mains $22-39; ☺11:30am-11pm Mon-Fri, 9am-11pm Sat & Sun) This Paris-style bistro is the only restaurant in town directly on the St Lawrence River, although actually getting a table with a view can sometimes be a challenge. Bright, airy and casually elegant, it swears by bistro classics like *steak frites* and *saucisse de Toulouse,* but there's also a great choice of other dishes like roasted pork rack with honey and lobster ravioli. The accent is on local Québec produce.

LE COCHON DINGUE　　　　BISTRO $$

Map p160 (☎418-692-2013; www.cochondingue .com; 46 Blvd Champlain; 3-course lunch menu

$14-20, mains $14-28; ⊘7am-midnight Mon-Fri, 8am-midnight Sat & Sun) Since 1979 this ever-popular choice has been serving visitors and locals straight-ahead French stand-bys, from *café au lait en bôl* to *croque monsieur*, sandwiches, *steak frites*, sal-ads, mussels or quiche. It's all good day-to-day food and a kid-friendly place to boot. There's outside seating in warm weather for crowd-watching.

LE PETIT COCHON DINGUE CAFE $

Map p160 (24 Blvd Champlain; mains $7-12; ⊘7:30am-10pm) Just down the street from Le Cochon Dingue, this dapper if touristy cafe and patisserie is a convenient destina-tion for coffee, desserts, salads, baguette sandwiches or grilled panini. The helpful staff keep the crowds moving.

✕ St-Jean Baptiste

St-Jean outside the walls is Québec City's most popular local thoroughfare, with restaurants for every taste and budget interspersed with some of the town's best groceries and bakeries.

CICCIO CAFÉ ITALIAN $$

Map p168 (⊘418-525-6161; 875 Rue de Claire-Fontaine; mains $12-23; ⊘lunch Mon-Fri, dinner daily) Tucked up a steep hill between Rue St-Jean and the Grand Théâtre de Québec, this hidden gem serves excellent Italian fare in a charming but low-key setting. Reliable old-world favorites such as linguini with clams share the menu with more adventurous of-ferings including rib steak with Roquefort or tortellini with gorgonzola and sun-dried tomato pesto.

CHEZ VICTOR BURGERS $

Map p160 (⊘418-529-7702; www.chezvictor burger.com; 145 Rue St-Jean; burgers from $12; ⊘11:30am-9:30pm Sun-Wed, to 10pm Thu-Sat) One of the best-loved little neighborhood eateries in the city, Chez Victor specializes in juicy burgers, served with more than a dash of creativity. Choose from ostrich, deer, elk, wild boar, straight-up beef or veg-etarian, which you can then dress a number of ways (brie, smoked bacon, cream cheese etc). The sides are also nice, including fresh coleslaw and fries, which you can get with a variety of sauces (including the recom-mended curry sauce). Dine on the tiny out-door patio or in the cozy, exposed-brick din-ing room. You'll find several other branches around town, including one down by the **Vieux-Port** (300 Rue St-Paul).

ÉPICERIE EUROPÉENNE DELI $

Map p168 (http://v1.epicerie-europeenne.com; 560 Rue St-Jean; sandwiches $6; ⊘9am-6pm Mon-Wed, to 9pm Thu & Fri, to 5pm Sat) This gourmet grocery, in business since 1959, stocks a delectable mix of meats, cheeses, olive oils, vinegars, teas and coffees. It's a good place to buy culinary-themed gifts or picnic supplies; at noon the deli case is well-stocked with delicious pre-made panini such as the Fiorentino (Italian-style roast pork, garlic-marinated spinach, mascar-pone and black pepper) and the Lyonnais (duck pâté, Dijon mustard, cornichons and onion confit).

LE HOBBIT BISTRO $$

Map p168 (⊘418-647-2677; www.hobbitbistro .com; 700 Rue St-Jean; 3-course lunch menu $15-17, mains $14-27; ⊘8am-10:30pm Mon-Fri, 9am-10:30pm Sat & Sun) This popular and inviting bistro on Rue St-Jean has outdoor seating, a casual atmosphere and good-value lunch and dinner specials (check out the chalk-board). The classics are all nicely done, in-cluding French onion soup, juicy duck confit and *steak frites* – plus Québécois specialties such as elk with sautéed apples and leeks. There's a small but fairly priced wine list. Various fresh pasta dishes and salads round out the menu.

LE COMMENSAL VEGETARIAN $$

Map p168 (www.commensal.com; 860 Rue St-Jean; per kg $22; ⊘11am-9pm Sun-Wed, to 10pm Thu-Sat; ⊘) An endless choice of strictly veg-etarian food dishes, including vegan and organic options, lines the buffet counters in this huge and bright self-serve restau-rant. The menu changes daily, but typically features lasagna, savory veggie pies, stews, curries, wraps, ratatouille, veggie pâté, soups, salads, fresh fruits and berries, plus a large dessert counter (the maple sugar pie is tops, as is the raspberry cheesecake). You can bring your own wine.

LE BILLIG CREPERIE $

Map p168 (526 Rue St-Jean; crepes $5-20; ⊘lunch & dinner Mon-Sat, lunch Sun) This Breton-owned eatery excels at crispy gal-ettes (buckwheat-flour crepes) with tra-ditional fillings such as ham and cheese, along with specialty crepes like the Orientale (*merguez* sausage, goat cheese and grilled vegetables) or the Gwened (smoked salmon, walnuts, lemon juice and olive oil). The orange-hued, checkerboard-floored dining room provides a relaxed setting, and the service is unfailingly friendly and efficient. There are several beers and ciders on tap, as well as a delicious *moût de pommes et canneberges* (sweet apple-cranberry cider). Finish with a flaming dessert crepe, featuring fillings ranging from maple syrup to poached pears, dark chocolate and vanilla ice cream.

TUTTO GELATO
ICE CREAM $

Map p168 (www.tuttogelato.ca; 716 Rue St-Jean; 1/2 scoops $2/3.25; ⊘9:30am-10pm Sun-Thu, to 11pm Fri & Sat) There's a reason people line up halfway out the door at all hours for Tutto Gelato. The creamy, rich, homemade ice cream here is simply too good to pass up. Over two dozen varieties of the Italian-style gelato and nine different sorbets (plus four soy-based varieties for the vegan crowd) vie for attention behind the glass counters. Top picks include *fraise des champs* (wild strawberries), passion fruit, pistachio, Bacio (milk chocolate and hazelnut) and green tea. Young, efficient staff move things along quickly.

✖ Montcalm & Colline Parlementaire

Here you'll find two small but terrific main eating districts: Ave Cartier between Grande Allée and Blvd René-Lévesque is packed with upscale delis, bistros and markets, while Grande Allée a few blocks west of Porte St-Louis is home to a popular and lively strip of more than a dozen alfresco, economic, visitor-oriented restaurants complete with touts.

TOP CHOICE MORENA
BISTRO $$

Map p168 (☑418 529-3668; www.morena-food.com; 1038 Ave Cartier; mains $14-17; ⊘8am-6pm Sat & Sun, to 7pm Mon-Wed, to 8pm Thu & Fri) Tucked into a gourmet grocery and deli on Rue Cartier, this Italian-themed neighborhood bistro makes a lively but low-key lunch stop. Daily specials, scrawled on a four-sided columnar chalkboard, range from osso buco to spinach gnocchi to skewers of shrimp, scallops and salmon. Everything's beautifully presented, with fresh veggies on the side and a soup or salad appetizer. After 3pm there's an à la carte snack menu. Dine solo at the counter or enjoy a tête-à-tête with your traveling companion at one of the

QUÉBEC CITY EATING

QUEBEC CITY'S BEST BAKERIES

Like any self-respecting cradle of French culture, Québec is swarming with fabulous bakeries and patisseries – no matter where you are in the city, there's one near you!

Two perennial favorites are Le Croquembouche (p179) and Paillard Café-Boulangerie (p172). Here are a few others worth trying, if you want to do a little taste-testing as you stroll:

➡ **La Boîte à Pain** (Map p168; http://boiteapain.com; 289 Rue St-Joseph Est; ⊘6:30am-8pm Mon-Sat, to 5:30pm Sun) Watch through the window as the bakers roll out their dough, then pop in next door and sample the finished product. Among the many treats worth tasting are the gigantic *brioches à la cannelle* (cinnamon rolls). It's down in St-Roch, on the same block as Le Croquembouche.

➡ **Éric Borderon** (Map p168; www.artisanborderon.com; 1191 Ave Cartier; ⊘8am-7pm Mon-Wed, to 9pm Thu & Fri, to 6pm Sat & Sun) Look for this renowned baguette master's stand just inside the front entrance of the Halles du Petit Quartier market, in Montcalm.

➡ **Le Paingruel** (Map p168; 375 Rue St-Jean; ⊘6:30am-6:30pm Tue-Fri, to 5pm Sat) In the heart of St-Jean Baptiste, this place bakes up an ever-changing lineup of hearty breads, from classic baguettes to loaves laced with walnuts, hazelnuts, chocolate and cranberries.

➡ **Le Panetier Baluchon** (Map p168; www.panetier-baluchon.com; 764 Rue St-Jean; ⊘7:30am-7:30pm) In business for over 30 years, this bakery a few blocks west of Porte St-Jean uses organic grains grown on its own farm in Beauce, 55km outside the city.

little tables for two. After your meal it's also a fun place to browse for food-related gifts.

TOP CHOICE BISTRO B
BISTRO $$

Map p168 (☑418-614-5444; www.bistrob.ca; 1144 Ave Cartier; mains $17-28; ☺lunch Mon-Fri, dinner daily) The brainchild of chef François Blais, formerly of Panache (p174), this is one of the toniest new restaurants to open in Québec City in recent years. A well-heeled crowd comes in for business lunches, when reasonably priced specials are chalked up on the giant board above the large open kitchen. New menus are improvised daily based on whatever ingredients are freshest at the Halles du Petit Quartier market down the street.

CAFÉ KRIEGHOFF
CAFE $

Map p168 (☑418-522-3711; www.cafekrieghoff .qc.ca; 1091 Ave Cartier; breakfast $6-13, lunch or dinner $10-19; ☺7am-9pm Mon-Fri, 8am-9pm Sat & Sun) This brilliant little resto is a city classic, with a varied bistro menu, extensive breakfast choices and some of the best coffee in town. If it's warm, you can watch the comings and goings on Ave Cartier from a table on the massive front porch, or head to the laid-back terrace out back. Inside, the dining room is decorated with reproductions from the cafe's namesake artist, Cornelius Krieghoff (1815–72), one of Québec's master painters of the 20th century, who lived just down the street from here on Grande Allée.

PICARDIE
DELI $

Map p168 (www.picardiedelices.com; 1029 Ave Cartier; deli items from $7; ☺8am-6pm Mon-Wed, to 7pm Thu & Fri, to 5pm Sat & Sun) Featuring a tantalizing array of sweet and savory snacks, this neighborhood traiteur (deli) is a browser's delight. The display case up front is devoted to croissants, chocolatines and other baked goodies, while the longer case beyond is filled to capacity with quiches, salmon pies, gourmet sandwiches, tomato and camembert tarts, and *tartiflette* (an Alpine dish of potatoes, cheese, cream and bacon). If you've got access to a kitchen, you might even consider the gourmet frozen meals to go, in the freezer opposite the main deli counter.

VOODOO SUPPERCLUB
INTERNATIONAL $$

Map p168 (☑418-647-2000; www.voodoogrill .com; 575 Grande Allée Est; lunch mains $12-22, dinner mains $17-40; ☺11:30am-11pm Mon-Fri, 5-11pm Sat) Attractive young servers, thumping electronica and wildly eclectic decor set the stage for this buzzing fusion restaurant. African and Asian statues peer down at the tables and the dining room is done up in dark, rich tones. Specialties here include tartare of steak, salmon or tuna, filet mignon with Ciel de Charlevoix blue cheese, pasta dishes, salads and savory Asian soups. After a big meal, diners can burn off the calories at the Chez Maurice (p181) nightclub upstairs.

GRAFFITI
QUÉBÉCOIS $$

Map p168 (☑418-529-4949; www.restaurantgraf fiti.com; 1191 Ave Cartier; mains $19-35; ☺lunch & dinner) This classy eatery focuses on classic Québécois ingredients such as deer, duck, salmon and shellfish served with exquisite sauces and fresh vegetables from the adjacent Halles du Petit Quartier market. At $30 to $44 for four courses, the table d'hôte here is pricier than at many other restaurants, but the quality is top-notch and the dishes are beautifully conceived, from fish stew with fennel and saffron, to lobster ravioli with tarragon butter, to duck breast with maple-blueberry sauce.

✗ St-Roch

The rejuvenation of St-Roch means everything from shopping to entertainment has become more exciting – and the eating scene is no exception. What's refreshing here is that, despite the number of stylish and trendy eateries, not a trace of snobbery has entered into the mix. There are some terrific eating experiences to be had and new places are opening all the time.

TOP CHOICE LE CAFÉ DU CLOCHER PENCHÉ
BISTRO $$

Map p168 (☑418-640-0597; www.clocherpenche .ca; 203 Rue St-Joseph Est; brunch around $16, mains $23-30; ☺8am-11pm Mon-Fri, 11am-11pm Sat & Sun) This splendid cafe serves classy, classic bistro fare and proudly shows off local products such as Québécois *fromages* (cheeses). What sets it apart are the one-of-a-kind weekend brunches. Brioche comes with caramelized pears, homemade crème fraîche, caramel sauce and almonds. An English muffin is served with veggie pâté, poached eggs, cheddar cheese, pesto vinaigrette, roasted potatoes and vegetarian chili. Reservations recommended.

⬧TOP CHOICE⬧ LE CROQUEMBOUCHE BAKERY $

Map p168 (http://lecroquembouche.com; 225 Rue St-Joseph Est; pastries from $2; ⊙7am-6:30pm Tue-Sat, to 5pm Sun) Quite possibly Québec City's finest bakery, this place draws long lines of devoted locals from dawn to dusk. Among the delicacies in the gorgeous display case are countless varieties of *danoises* (Danish pastries), including orange and anise, cranberry, pistachio and chocolate, and lemon, ginger and poppy seed. You'll also find fluffy-as-a-cloud croissants, brioches brimming with fresh raspberries, shelves full of tantalizing cakes and éclairs, and sandwiches made on the bakery's own fresh bread.

L'AFFAIRE EST KETCHUP BISTRO $$

Map p168 (☑418 529-9020; http://laffaireestketchup.net; 46 Rue St-Joseph Est; mains $17-24; ⊙lunch Tue-Fri, dinner Tue-Sat) Since opening in late 2010, this homey little place with only eight tables has taken St-Roch by storm. Dressed in T-shirts and baseball caps, bantering relaxedly with one another as they whip up fine cuisine on a pair of electric stoves, founders François and Olivier are clearly enthusiastic about food. The ever-changing menu ranges from classics like duck breast with lentils, or stewed pork with mashed potatoes, to the unexpected – octopus salad with crunchy vegetables, or lime gelatin with apple, cucumber and mint mousse. A good selection of wines and mixed drinks is available from the well-stocked bar. Book ahead – it fills up fast.

LARGO RESTO-CLUB BISTRO $$

Map p168 (☑418-529-3111; www.largorestoclub.ca; 643 Rue St-Joseph Est; mains $16-26; ⊙lunch & dinner daily, brunch from 10:30am Sat & Sun) Rich wood tones, exposed brick and a gigantic wall-length red couch create a welcoming ambience at this restaurant and jazz club in the heart of St-Roch. The menu is small, featuring simple ingredients, but the preparation is excellent, making for a rewarding dining experience. *Tartelette de canard* (savory duck pie), seafood linguini and grilled squid with vegetables and polenta are popular selections. Also popular are the weekend brunches (mains $12 to $15) and live jazz sessions Wednesday through Saturday nights (see p186). The club also does gallery duty, showing off the work of local painters and sculptors.

LA CUISINE DINER $

Map p168 (☑418-523-3387; 205 Rue St-Vallier Est; mains $10; ⊙11am-1am Mon-Wed, 11am-3am Thu & Fri, 2pm-3am Sat, 2pm-1am Sun) Retro decor and comfort food served till the wee hours are the hallmarks of this trendy eatery midway between St-Jean Baptiste and St-Roch. Formica tables, mismatched china and silverware, light fixtures made from colanders and a vintage Wurlitzer jukebox give the place a fun, relaxed feel, while the menu features five no-nonsense mains each day, from chile con carne to grilled cheese sandwiches to chicken salad; if you're still hungry, you can add soup of the day for $3, or coffee and dessert for $4.

CAFÉ BABYLONE INTERNATIONAL $

Map p168 (☑418-523-0700; www.cafebabylone.com; 181 Rue St-Vallier Est; mains $9-15; ⊙9am-11pm Tue-Sun; ✐) This eatery on the upper fringes of St-Roch is popular with locals day and night for its brunches, reasonably priced lunch specials and dinner concerts featuring an eclectic mix of international music. The vegetarian-friendly menu includes creative sandwiches and main dishes from a dozen countries, including Iran, Mali and Peru. There's also a reasonably priced kids' menu.

YUZU JAPANESE $$

Map p168 (☑418-521-7253; www.yuzu.ca; 438 Rue du Parvis; mains $14-25; ⊙lunch Mon-Fri, dinner daily) This stylish, warmly lit restaurant (lightboxes, bonsai trees) spreads a tempting array of sushi and creative dishes (think tempura soft-shell crab), plus a multicourse tasting menu with foie gras thrown in for good measure. A young, hip crowd stops in before hitting the nearby bars.

HOSAKA-YA RAMEN JAPANESE $

Map p168 (☑418-780-1903; www.hosaka-ya.com; 75 Rue St-Joseph Est; mains from $12; ⊙lunch Tue-Fri, dinner Tue-Sat) Catering to a young, informal clientele, this straight-ahead noodle house has quickly earned a loyal following for its delicious soups filled with ramen and every conceivable complement: pork, fish, tofu and loads of veggies. It's a cozy place for a sit-down meal, but also a great take-out option if you'd rather hunker down in the hotel for a night.

LE POSTINO ITALIAN $$

Map p168 (☑418-647-0000; www.lepostino.com; 296 Rue St-Joseph Est; mains $13-22;

⊙11:30am-9pm Mon-Wed, 11:30am-10pm Thu & Fri, 5-10pm Sat) Prime people-watching coupled with friendly, unpretentious waitstaff make this place a popular low-key option in St-Roch. There are plenty of classic pasta dishes on the menu, as well as a fantastic choice of risottos with genius combinations such as rabbit confit, roasted parsnips, caramelized shallots and wild mushrooms.

🍷 DRINKING & NIGHTLIFE

Let's be honest. Québec City isn't exactly considered a party town. That said, what the city does offer after dark is quite special, fun and refreshingly attitude-free. What the swankier supper clubs and restaurants may lack in urban edge, they more than make up for in friendly ambience and top-notch service; simply put, you get the feeling that everyone is welcome.

For club, bar and other entertainment listings, pick up the weekly *Voir Québec* newspaper (published every Thursday). Other useful free publications include *Scope*, a glossy monthly that focuses on music and cultural events, *Fugues*, a free monthly gay and lesbian entertainment guide and *Le Clap*, a bimonthly guide to cinema. Have fun!

🍷 Old Upper Town

PUB ST-ALEXANDRE BAR
Map p160 (www.pubstalexandre.com; 1087 Rue St-Jean; ⊙11am-3am) High ceilings and dark wood house a regular mix of tourists and loyal locals. The pub grub is fine, though generally unremarkable. It's the atmosphere and the near encyclopedic range of suds (250 sorts!) and over three dozen types of single malt that will keep you coming back. There's occasional live music (Celtic, blues, jazz and more) on Thursday, Friday and Saturday.

🍷 Old Lower Town

LE PAPE-GEORGES BAR
Map p160 (8 Rue de Cul-de-Sac; ⊙11:30am-3am daily May-Sep, 4pm-3am Mon-Wed & noon-3am Thu-Sun Oct-Apr) With live music at least three nights a week (more in the summer)

from 10pm, this charming bar located in a 300-year-old house also serves cheeses, meats and baguettes with a healthy dollop of Québécois culture.

L'ONCLE ANTOINE BAR
Map p160 (29 Rue St-Pierre; ⊙11am-3am) Set clandestinely in the stone cave-cellar of one of the city's oldest surviving houses (dating from 1754), this great tavern pours out excellent Québec microbrews (try the Barberie Noir stout or the strong Belgian-style Fin du Monde), several drafts *(en fût)* and various European beers.

AVIATIC CLUB WINE BAR
Map p160 (http://aviatic.ca; 450 Ave de la Gare-du-Palais; ⊙11:30am-9pm Mon & Tue, 11:30am-10pm Wed-Fri, 5-10pm Sat & Sun) This elegant wine bar and restaurant is nestled in the historic Gare du Palais train station and attracts a professional crowd. A rotating list of 50 wines is served by the glass, and a vibrant terrace, featuring live DJs, is open during summer.

🍷 St-Jean Baptiste

TOP CHOICE LE MOINE ÉCHANSON WINE BAR
Map p168 (☎418-524-7832; www.lemoineechanson.com; 585 Rue St-Jean; ⊙5-11pm Thu-Sat, to 10pm Sun, Tue & Wed) New darling of the city's wine connoisseurs, this convivial brick-walled bistro pours an enticing and ever-changing array of wines from all over the Mediterranean, by the glass and by the bottle, accompanied by hearty and homespun snacks ($6-10) and main dishes ($21 to $23) such as blood sausage, sauerkraut, or lentil soup with ginger and mint. Each season brings a new theme, with emphasis placed on a single French region or department (Ardèche, Jura etc) or Mediterranean country. Crowds pour into after work, quickly filling the two rooms to capacity, starting with aperitifs and lingering on through dinner; reservations are a must. During business hours it also doubles as a wine merchant, selling hard-to-find bottles to take away.

TOP CHOICE LE SACRILÈGE BAR
Map p168 (www.lesacrilege.net; 447 Rue St-Jean) To find this popular bar, keep an eye out for the sign with a laughing, dancing monk saucily showing off his knickers. It's been around for over 15 years, but it's still the

GAY & LESBIAN VENUES

The city's gay and lesbian club scene is tiny, with pretty much everything centered around Le Drague (p181). Another address of interest is **Galerie DomaHom** (www .domahom.com; 221 Rue St-Jean; ☺10am-3pm Thu-Sat), a cafe-art gallery that features the work of local gay and lesbian artists by day, then morphs after dark into the all-male **Club ForHom** (www.forhom.ca; ☺5pm-1am Tue-Sun), with nightly drink specials, gay film nights and more. Plenty of other bars and clubs are gay-friendly, including Chez Maurice (below), Chez Dagobert (below) and Le Sacrilège (opposite).

In late August or early September, the city's GLBT (gay, lesbian, bisexual and transgender) community comes out in full force for the annual **Fête Arc-en-Ciel** (Rainbow Festival; www.glbtquebec.org/fete_aec.html). For info on parties and other gay events, *Fugues* (www.fugues.com) is the free gay and lesbian entertainment guide with listings for the entire province of Québec.

watering hole of choice for most night owls, who start or end their weekend revelry here. Even on Monday night, it's standing-room only. There's a popular terrace out back; get to it through the bar or the tiny brick alley next door.

LE DRAGUE   GAY
Map p168 (www.ledrague.com; 815 Rue St-Augustin) The star player on the city's tiny gay scene, Le Drague comprises a front outdoor terrace, a two-level disco where drag shows are held, a slightly more laid-back tavern – and then there's Base 3. The men-only Base 3 is...well...let's just say it turns the capital's conservative reputation on its head and has even seen-it-all Montrealers saying 'I didn't know they had that in Québec City.'

NELLIGAN'S IRISH PUB   PUB
Map p168 (http://pubnelligans.ca; 789 Côte Ste-Geneviève) Tucked into a pair of brick-walled upstairs rooms just downhill from Rue St-Jean, this Irish pub makes a cozy spot to sip an Irish whisky on a cold winter's night or down a few pints on a midsummer's evening. There's also occasional live Irish music and pub grub ranging from Harp-battered fish and chips to rosemary-scented duck *poutine*.

🍷 Montcalm & Colline Parlementaire

INOX   BREWERY
Map p168 (www.inox.qc.ca; 655 Grande Allée Est) Twenty-five years old and counting, this is one of Québec's most venerated micro-breweries. The current brewpub only opened its doors in 2009, but it's already a

well-established stop on the Grande Allée party circuit. Grab a table in the spacious high-ceilinged main room or sidle up to the metallic bar in the center. Popular choices here include the coriander-infused Trouble-Fête (available year-round) and seasonal brews such as Viking, a concoction of barley, wheat, honey and cranberries inspired by old Norse recipes (February only).

CHEZ MAURICE   CLUB
Map p168 (www.mauricenightclub.com; 575 Grande Allée Est; ☺Wed-Sat) Set up in a gutted, châteaulike mansion and cheekily named after hard-ass former Québec premier Maurice Duplessis, this entertainment complex has three separate partying spaces, including the Maurice nightclub, the **Charlotte Ultra Lounge** (www.voodoogrill.com/fr/charlotte) bar, and the **Société Cigare** (www.voodoo grill.com/fr/societe-cigare), with 200 sorts of cigars to choose from.

AUX VIEUX CANONS   BAR
Map p168 (http://auxvieuxcanons.com; 650 Grande Allée Est; ☺11:30am-10pm) Set with a spacious front terrace on restaurant-lined Grande Allée, this place serves fairly mainstream bistro fare – roast chicken, spaghetti bolognaise, *steak au poivre* (pepper steak), grilled meats, French onion soup. The real draw here is the beer; it's poured in yard-long glasses and served with a wooden brace. A fine place to refresh after a day exploring the city.

CHEZ DAGOBERT   CLUB
Map p168 (http://dagobert.ca; 600 Grande Allée Est; ☺Wed-Sun) Multifloors, multibars, multiscreens – the capital's classic disco behemoth has everything from live rock to

CITY OF HISTORICAL SUPERLATIVES

As befits a place that played such a crucial role in the history of the New World, Québec City is awash in historical superlatives. Among other things, the city is home to the continent's first parish church, first Anglican cathedral and first French-speaking university. When you flip through the *Quebec Chronicle-Telegraph*, you're reading North America's oldest newspaper, and if you have to pay a visit to L'Hôtel Dieu de Québec, console yourself with the thought that it's the continent's oldest hospital!

naughty DJs. The music may change; the young, randy crowd stays the same.

🍷 St-Roch

TOP CHOICE ▷ LA BARBERIE BREWERY
Map p168 (http://labarberie.com; 310 Rue Saint-Roch; ⊘noon-1am) This cooperative microbrewery in St-Roch is beloved for its spacious tree-shaded outdoor deck and its ever-evolving selection of eight home brews, from classic pale ales to more inventive options such as orange stout or blonde ale with lime and ginger. Choose whatever flavor grabs your fancy, or sample all the current offerings in the popular eight-beer carousel. The brewery's other claim to fame is its unusual BYO policy: it doesn't serve food, but customers are welcome to bring their own snacks or meals from outside.

LES SALONS D'EDGAR BAR
Map p168 (http://lessalonsdedgar.com; 263 Rue St-Vallier Est; ⊘Wed-Sun) The unofficial 'official' hangout for the city's theater community. The eavesdropping here is as much fun as the drinking – you'll be privy to conversations on roles lost and roles gained.

BRASSERIE LA KORRIGANE BREWERY
Map p168 (www.korrigane.ca; 380 Rue Dorchester; ⊘Tue-Sun) St-Roch's newest microbrewery features a full rainbow of flavors, including specialty brews such as Emily Carter blueberry beer and the maple-laced Croquemitaine, all served up with pub grub from artisanal producers. You'll also find Sunday improv nights and swing dancing on Wednesday evenings.

LE BOUDOIR LOUNGE
Map p168 (www.boudoirlounge.com; 441 Rue du Parvis; ⊘11am-midnight Mon-Wed, 11am-3am Thu & Fri, 4pm-3am Sat & Sun) Part restaurant, part nightclub, all scene, this posh but low-key lounge in the hip St-Roch district is pretty much the place for well-heeled locals to party. On weekends two DJs let you choose between downtempo and dancing, while games include billiards, Wii and Pac-Man!

☆ ENTERTAINMENT

The performing arts are in fine form in Québec City. The city boasts a symphony orchestra, L'Orchestre Symphonique de Québec (p186), and an opera company, Opéra de Québec (p183). Homegrown Québécois bands perform regularly, as do touring bands from across Canada, the US and Europe, especially during the Festival d'Été in July. Live performance venues abound, from concert halls to open-air amphitheaters to little jazz and rock clubs to exuberant *boîtes à chanson* (Québec folk-music clubs), where generations of locals dance and sing with uncensored glee. French-language theater is also an interesting scene here, with tons of small companies producing a variety of shows.

☆ Old Upper Town

LES GROS BECS THEATER
Map p160 (www.lesgrosbecs.qc.ca; 1143 Rue St-Jean; ⊘shows Sep-May) Devoted to children and young people, this brilliantly creative theater company mounts over a dozen shows annually. Its colorful catalog specifies suggested age ranges – from one to 17 – for every production.

☆ Old Lower Town

TOP CHOICE ▷ IMAGE MILL MULTIMEDIA PROJECTION
Map p160 (http://lacaserne.net; Vieux-Port de Québec; ⊘Tue-Sat late Jun-early Sep) The brainchild of Québécois visionary Robert Lepage, this colossal multimedia projec-

tion, beamed onto a long row of oversized grain silos along the Vieux-Port waterfront, is one of Québec City's most unique events. Starting just past sundown six days a week in summer, a mix of silent film and still images explores the region's history, accompanied by music. Initiated as part of Québec City's 400th anniversary celebrations, the projections were enhanced with 3D in 2011 and have been extended until at least summer 2013. They're large enough to be viewed for free from many points in town, but if you want a front-row seat, $15 will get you a reserved spot behind the Espace 400 pavilion.

CIRQUE DU SOLEIL CIRCUS
(☑800-450-1480; www.cirquedusoleil.com; 271 Rue de l'Estuaire) The province's world-renowned circus troupe performs every summer in Québec City. For several years they've been offering free shows at Îlot Fleurie, under the highway overpass near the Vieux-Port, as well as regular paying shows. As this book goes to press, free shows are again scheduled, although there's periodic talk of discontinuing them in future years. Check with the tourist office opposite Château Frontenac or directly with Cirque du Soleil for up-to-the-minute information.

THÉÂTRE PETIT-CHAMPLAIN THEATER
Map p160 (www.theatrepetitchamplain.com; 68 Rue du Petit-Champlain) Various theater productions take place here in the summer. During the rest of the year this is a great place to see Québec's most popular singing stars.

AGORA LIVE MUSIC
Map p160 (www.agoraportdequebec.ca; 120 Rue Dalhousie, Vieux-Port) Fantastic open-air rock shows are held here all summer.

☆ St-Jean Baptiste

PALAIS MONTCALM LIVE MUSIC
Map p168 (www.palaismontcalm.ca; 995 Pl d'Youville) Just outside the Upper Town's walls, this recently renovated theater hosts a stellar lineup of concerts year-round, featuring everthing from opera to chamber music to jazz to rock. The main performance space, the Salle Raoul-Jobin, is renowned for its superb acoustics.

LE THÉÂTRE CAPITOLE LIVE MUSIC
Map p168 (www.lecapitole.com; 972 Rue St-Jean) A terrific, historic old theater that now stages everything from musicals to concerts. Check out the sumptuous attached hotel (p196). This is where Hitchcock held his *I Confess* premiere.

FOU-BAR LIVE MUSIC
Map p168 (www.foubar.ca; 525 Rue St-Jean; ☺2:30pm-3am Mon-Fri, noon-3am Sat & Sun) Laid-back and with an eclectic mix of bands, this bar is one of the town's classics for good live music. It's also popular for its reasonably priced food menu and its free appetizers on Thursday and Friday evenings.

L'ESPACE CONTEMPORAIN GALLERY
Map p168 (www.lespacecontemporain.com; 313 Rue St-Jean) This dynamic little art gallery displays an ever-rotating showcase of beautiful contemporary works, and hosts many vernissages for solo and thematic group shows.

☆ Montcalm & Colline Parlementaire

LE GRAND THÉÂTRE DE QUÉBEC PERFORMING ARTS
Map p168 (☑418-643-8131, tollfree in Québec 877-643-8131; www.grandtheatre.qc.ca; 269 Blvd René-Lévesque Est) Le Grand Théâtre is the city's main performing-arts center with a steady diet of top-quality classical concerts, dance and theater. **Opéra de Québec** (Map p160; www.operadequebec.qc.ca) performs here under the artistic direction of Grégoire Legendre. This world-class company presents classics like *Aida*, *Pagliacci*, *Madame Butterfly*, *La Traviata*, *Carmen* and more.

KIOSQUE EDWIN-BÉLANGER LIVE MUSIC
Map p168 (☑418-648-4050; www.ccbn-nbc. gc.ca/_en/edwinbelanger.php; Battlefields Park 418) Each summer dozens of free concerts are staged in the middle of Battlefields Park. Music covers everything from pop, jazz and world music to blues.

THÉÂTRE PÉRISCOPE THEATER
Map p168 (☑418-529-2183, 418-648-9989; www.theatreperiscope.qc.ca; 2 Rue Crémazie Est) A terrific place to see creative and cutting-edge contemporary productions.

Québec City Top Five

Québec City's historic architecture, dramatic setting and French-Canadian flair make it one of North America's most irresistible cities. Here are five things not to miss during your visit.

Château Frontenac

1 The crowning jewel in Québec City's harmonious collection of architectural treasures, this 19th-century hotel (p156) is magnetically attractive inside and out. Admire it from the Terrasse Dufferin boardwalk below, or grab a seat inside the hotel bar for sweeping river views.

Quartier Petit-Champlain

2 Centerpiece of Québec City's 17th-century Old Lower Town (p163), narrow Rue du Petit-Champlain is especially picturesque when seen from the steep heights of Escalier Casse-Cou (Break-Neck Stairs) or from Québec's cliff-hugging funicular.

Winter Fun

3 You haven't really seen Québec City until you've toured the ice sculptures and fur-lined beds at the Ice Hotel or paraded through the streets with Bonhomme de Carnaval, the friendly snowman and official mascot of Québec's Winter Carnival (p248).

La Citadelle

4 Straddling the Plains of Abraham, where France's New World fortunes took a dramatic downhill turn, this star-shaped fort (p155) provides stunning Old Town views and a perfect backdrop for understanding Québécois history.

Summer Festivals

5 Summertime in Québec City is a never-ending street party, with ambulatory performers, parks that double as open-air concert venues and comedians keeping the town in stitches (p27).

....

Clockwise from top left
1 Château Frontenac **2** Québec City's Historical Lower Town **3** An ice sculpture from the annual Winter Carnival

LE THÉÂTRE DU TRIDENT
THEATER

Map p160 (☑418-643-5873; www.letrident.com; 269 Blvd René-Lévesque Est) Another terrific company that stages an exciting mix of modern and classical works.

L'ORCHESTRE SYMPHONIQUE DE QUÉBEC
CLASSICAL MUSIC

Map p160 (www.osq.org; 401 Grande Allée Est) For more than a century, this internationally recognized symphony orchestra has performed for more than 100,000 people a year. Concerts are usually broadcast on the radio by public broadcaster Radio Canada. Led by new music director Fabien Gabel, the orchestra is also active in the community.

LES VOÛTES DE NAPOLÉON
LIVE MUSIC

Map p168 (☑418-640-9388; www.voutesdenapoleon.com; 680A Grande Allée Est; ⊙8:30pm-3am) At this jubilant *boîte à chanson* (Québécois folk cabaret) it will likely be just you and the locals. There's lively Québécois music nightly, usually of the 'singer-with-guitar' variety, with lesser-known, up-and-coming acts featuring prominently.

CINÉMA CARTIER
CINEMA

Map p168 (www.cinemacartier.com; 1019 Ave Cartier; ⊙1pm-late) This huge building really was a former movie theater until it was sliced up with a store on the bottom and retail space up top. The 2nd floor houses an independent video shop with a little movie theater in the back showing independent films. It's deliciously old-world, completely pitch-black except for the screen, and set up with big comfy chairs. Subtitles in French only.

☆ St-Roch

TOP CHOICE LE CERCLE
LIVE MUSIC

Map p168 (☑418-948-8648; www.le-cercle.ca; 226½ Rue St-Joseph Est; ⊙11:30am-3am Mon-Fri, 10am-3am Sat & Sun) Restaurant, art gallery and show venue, this very cool joint draws a hip crowd for its international DJs and underground bands, ranging from indie rock to electronica, blues to cajun. It also hosts a wide range of other events, including film, fashion and comic strip festivals, book- and album-release parties, wine tastings and more. Affordable tapas, weekend brunches and an atmospheric bar

space with 20-foot ceilings sweeten the deal even more.

LARGO RESTO-CLUB
JAZZ

Map p168 (☑418-529-3111; www.largorestoclub.ca; 643 Rue St-Joseph Est; ⊙jazz shows 8pm) Wednesday through Saturday, the music-mad Largo owner lets the jazz-club side of this resto shine, bringing in local bands, singers and musicians from as far away as Los Angeles. Upscale, ultrarelaxed, slightly swish vibe.

LA ROTONDE
DANCE

Map p168 (☑418-649-5013; www.larotonde.qc.ca; 336 Rue du Roi) This contemporary dance center presents shows from touring companies and dancers from the world as well as local dancers, including experimental and cutting-edge works. It also offers workshops and classes, and is pivotal in keeping dance alive in Québec.

LE LIEU
GALLERY

Map p168 (www.inter-lelieu.org; 345 Rue du Pont) With art installations, sound art, video art and other multidiscliplinary exhibitions, this St-Roch artist center is more than a gallery. Visitors are welcome to browse and experience this local community arts hub, which aims to share Québec art with the world.

SCANNER
LIVE MUSIC

Map p168 (www.scannerbistro.com; 291 Rue St-Vallier Est; ⊙3pm-3am Sat-Thu, 11:30am-3am Fri) Ask any local between the ages of 18 and 35 to suggest a cool place for a drink and this is where they might send you. Live bands perform Thursday through Saturday nights, playing everything from hard rock to punk to rockabilly. There's a terrace outside in summer, plus foosball and pool inside year-round.

☆ Elsewhere Outside the Walls

LE CLAP
CINEMA

(www.clap.qc.ca; 2360 Chemin Ste-Foy; ⊙screenings from noon) Located in the Ste-Foy-Sillery borough, Le Clap's mandate is to show off the best of what's going on in the film world. On any given afternoon, you'll find an eclectic mix of films that could include the latest British hit, an old indie French film and probably one American blockbuster. Non-French-language films are almost always dubbed in French instead of subtitled but call ahead to double-check.

COLISÉE PEPSI　　　LIVE MUSIC, HOCKEY

(☑418-691-7211, 418-525-1212; Parc de l'ExpoCité, 250 Blvd Wilfrid Hamel) Nowadays this 15,000-person arena gets the likes of Iron Maiden and Metallica, and hosts games of the Remparts, from the Québec Major Junior Hockey League. Many local hockey fans still consider it hallowed ground, as it was once home to the late, great Québec Nordiques (see p191).

🛍 SHOPPING

While it may not have as many big international stores and high-end designer boutiques as some larger cities, Québec is a shopper's paradise in its own special way. Small, unique and authentic little boutiques are this touristy town's claim to retail fame, and the city's small size makes it ideal for strolling around and browsing for surprises. Local clothing, eyewear and jewelry designers, purveyors of specialty foods and homemade chocolate, and the antique dealers down on Rue St-Paul all are representative of the city's small-scale, classy approach to commerce.

You'll find that many stores within the Old Town walls cater primarily (if not exclusively) to tourists, whereas those in the outlying neighborhoods draw a much more local crowd. Unless indicated otherwise, following listings observe the standard business hours specified in the bookwide Directory (p255). As a general rule, stores in Québec City keep later hours on Thursday and Friday nights.

🛍 Old Upper Town

SIMONS　　　DEPARTMENT STORE

Map p160 (www.simons.ca; 20 Côte de la Fabrique) One of the city's business success stories, Simons was started by the son of a Scottish immigrant who set up a dry-goods store in Québec City. By 1952 his descendants had turned the business into a successful clothing store. It's popular all over Québec for stocking items more cutting-edge than those at competing department stores. There's been a Simons at this location since 1870.

GALERIE ART INUIT　　　ARTS & CRAFTS

Map p160 (www.artinuit.ca; 35 Rue St-Louis; ⏱9:30am-5:30pm) Devoted to Inuit carvings from artists all over arctic Canada, this place is gorgeously set up and elaborately lit, with well-trained staff who knowledgeably answer questions. Carvings range from the small to the large and intricate. Be prepared for both steep prices and fantastic quality. It ships internationally.

LES 3 TOURS　　　CLOTHING

Map p160 (1124 Rue St-Jean) Devoted to all things medieval, this Québec company sells clothes, jewelry and accessories, many of them the work of Québécois designers. This is one of many such stores around the province.

🛍 Old Lower Town

TOP
CHOICE **MARCHÉ DU VIEUX-PORT**　　FOOD & DRINK

Map p160 (www.marchevieuxport.com; 160 Quai St-André; ⏱9am-6pm Mon-Fri, to 5pm Sat & Sun) At this heaving local food market, you can buy fresh fruits and vegetables as well as dozens of local specialties, from Île d'Orléans blackcurrant wine to ciders, honeys, cheeses, sausages, chocolates, herbal hand creams and, of course, maple-syrup products. Weekends are huge crowds and more wine tastings than can be considered sensible.

LA FROMAGÈRE　　　FOOD & DRINK

Map p160 (Marché du Vieux-Port; ⏱9am-6pm Mon-Fri, to 5pm Sat & Sun) This shop near the entrance of the Vieux-Port market sells an awe-inspiring selection of Québécois cheeses. For a notion of the tremendous variety available here, check out the Québec dairy association website, www.ourcheeses.com.

LES BRANCHÉS LUNETTERIE　　FASHION

Map p160 (www.lesbrancheslunetterie.com; 155 Rue St-Paul) Displaying a fanciful, wildly colorful mix of designer eyewear from Québec, France and Spain, this is a fun place to browse, even if you're not necessarily in the market for new glasses frames. The centerpiece of the collection is the room dedicated to frames from **Montures Faniel** (www.monturesfaniel.com), a Québécois business founded by opera-singer-turned-designer Anne-Marie Faniel; her music also graces the store.

GALERIE D'ART BEAUCHAMP ARTS & CRAFTS
Map p160 (www.galeriebeauchamp.com; 69 Rue St-Pierre; ☺9:30am-6pm) With seven galleries and counting, this important contemporary art company features the work of Québécois, Canadian and international artists. It also hosts special events like virtual exhibitions and operate a nonprofit organization that works to bring art to underprivileged children in Québec City. Artists also come to paint on-site in the Artist in Gallery program. Visit the website for other gallery locations.

GÉRARD BOURGUET ANTIQUAIRE ANTIQUES
Map p160 (www.gerardbourguet.com; 97 Rue St-Paul; ☺10am-noon & 1:30-5pm) This specialist in Québécois antique furniture has a wide range of lovely pieces, including painted chests, cupboards and tables, as well as a nice selection of ceramics and folk art wood carvings. The owner makes frequent buying trips, so call ahead to make sure he's open.

LE RENDEZ-VOUS DU COLLECTIONNEUR ANTIQUES
Map p160 (123 Rue St-Paul; ☺10am-5pm) Antique lamps and silverware from Château Frontenac are among the many items crowding the shelves at this well-established shop on the Lower Town's antiques row.

VÊTEMENTS 90 DEGRÉS CLOTHING
Map p160 (141 Rue St-Paul; ☺usually 11am-6pm) Set up by Québec City artist Denis Tremblay, who decided to slap simple, strong images and cheeky French text onto T-shirts and tank tops, this store is now going gangbusters. Even non-French speakers are taken with the shirts.

JOAILLERIE JULES PERRIER JEWELRY
Map p160 (www.jewelryjulesperrier.com; 39 Rue du Petit-Champlain) Passion is the inspiration behind this well-known jeweler's stunning designs, unique earrings, brooches, pendants and more. It's full of precious stones, making browsing in this elegant locale – still a family business – feel like perusing art. The shop also carries brands such as Movado.

LA PETITE CABANE À SUCRE DU QUÉBEC FOOD & DRINK
Map p160 (www.petitecabaneasucre.com; 94 Rue du Petit-Champlain) Maple syrup is a massive industry in Québec, and this touristy little shop sells it in every shape and form: candies, delicacies, ice cream, snacks, syrup-related accessories and, of course, the sweet stuff itself.

🏠 St-Jean Baptiste

CHOCO-MUSÉE ÉRICO FOOD & DRINK
Map p168 (www.chocomusee.com; 634 Rue St-Jean) The exotic smells and flavors here will send a chocolate lover into conniptions of joy. The ever-evolving offerings include strawberry-basil truffles, chocolate-chip cookies packed with semisweet chocolate chunks, dates and black tea, and seasonal offerings ranging from chocolate bunnies, and chickens at Easter time to ice cream in summer, with exotic flavors like orange pekoe tea and beet-and-raspberry. There's a little museum in the back and a window where you can watch the chocolatiers work.

JA MOISAN ÉPICIER FOOD & DRINK
Map p168 (www.jamoisan.com; 699 Rue St-Jean; ☺8:30am-9pm) Established in 1871, this is considered the oldest grocery store in North America. The store is beautifully set up and fun just to browse – ever seen black-and-white, zebra-striped bow pasta? The products do generally fall on the 'You've got to be kidding!' side of expensive but there will be items here you've never seen before along with heaps of local goods.

CHLÖE & JUSTIN CHILDREN'S
Map p168 (586B Rue St-Jean) Named after the owner's son and daughter, this newly opened store features a variety of children's clothing and toys from Québécois and European designers.

🏠 Montcalm & Colline Parlementaire

BOUTIQUE KETTÖ CERAMICS, JEWELRY
Map p168 (www.kettodesign.com; 951 Ave Cartier) Illustrator Julie St-Onge-Drouin started up Kettö after her illustrative designs kept finding their way onto ceramic surfaces. Now at this big, bright and beautifully set-

THE INSIDE INFO

➡ **Shopping Streets** Stroll Rue St-Jean outside the walls in St-Jean Baptiste, Rue St-Joseph in St-Roch, Ave Cartier in Montcalm, or Rue Maguire in Sillery.

➡ **Markets** For the freshest cheeses, meats and produce, locals head for Les Halles du Petit Quartier (below) in Montcalm and the Marché du Vieux-Port (p187) down by the waterfront.

➡ **Hangouts** Graze the gorgeous display cases full of baked goods at Le Croquem-bouche (p179) on a Sunday morning, or while away a summer evening drinking beer with laid-back locals on the shady outdoor terrace of La Barberie (p182).

up boutique, they're on everything from plates and mugs to ceramic jewelry and necklaces. Great gifts, her designs are sold in small boutiques throughout Québec, but here you'll find the best selection.

SILLONS MUSIC
Map p168 (www.sillons.com; 1149 Ave Cartier) This independent record store has been around for almost 20 years and specializes in jazz, world music and performers from Québec and France. It's a great place to build up your library of Québécois music and learn what's new on the regional scene.

LES HALLES DU PETIT QUARTIER FOOD & DRINK
Map p168 (http://hallesdupetitquartier.com; 1191 Ave Cartier; ⏰7:30am-7pm Sat-Wed, to 9pm Thu & Fri) Montcalm's very popular local food market features individual stalls for bakers, butchers, fruit, vegetable, cheese and fish vendors, plus a cluster of restaurants.

🔒 St-Roch

MYCO ANNA CLOTHING
Off Map p168 (www.mycoanna.com; 615 Rue St-Vallier Ouest) Old meets new at this bright and daring women's fashion line's signature shop. Launched in 1996, Myco Anna is known for bright, patchworky, flirty and sexy dresses – all made from at least some recycled material.

BENJO TOYS
Map p168 (www.benjo.ca; 543 Rue St-Joseph Est) This toy shop gives a glimpse into what the world would be like if kids ran the show. Even the front door is pint-sized (the adult-sized door for grown-ups is off to the side). There's a train that goes around the store on weekends, and arts and crafts for little ones during the week (around $10 to $15).

JOHN FLUEVOG SHOES
Map p168 (www.fluevog.com; 539 Rue St-Joseph Est) Canada's 2012 'Shoe Person of the Year' (yes, there really is such an award!), Vancouver-based John Fluevog has been designing outlandishly colorful and stylish shoes for over four decades. His first store in Québec City, opened in 2011, fits in perfectly with the trendy St-Roch neighborhood.

MOUNTAIN EQUIPMENT CO-OP OUTDOOR EQUIPMENT
Map p168 (www.mec.ca; 405 Rue St-Joseph Est) The mountain man (or woman) in all of us needs his fix, especially if you're planning to conquer the great Québec wilderness. Enter this sprawling shop, the largest from the renowned Canadian brand, complete with an outdoor resource center to help you plan your adventure.

JB LALIBERTÉ CLOTHING
Map p168 (www.lalibertemode.com; 595 Rue St-Joseph Est) Founded in 1867, this furrier has grown into one of Canada's major players. So it's not everyone's cup of tea, but you'll find fancy collections of furs, coats, accessories and more, quite reasonably priced.

🏃 SPORTS & ACTIVITIES

Whether it's summer or deepest, darkest winter, you can expect to find Québec City locals enjoying life outdoors. Aside from strolling the cobblestone streets of the Old Town, there's a whole range of activities on offer in and around town.

Inside the city limits there are picturesque parks and paths ideal for an early-morning jog or bike ride, as well as a host of winter sports – skating, cross-country skiing and tobogganing – when the weather

CALÈCHE

For a scenic, old-fashioned journey about town, climb aboard a calèche (horse-drawn carriage). While rides are not cheap – about $80 for 45 minutes – drivers can give you an earful of history as they take you to historic points around the city. Find them by the entrance to the Porte St-Louis.

turns cold. Just outside of town, you can also go rafting along the Jacques Cartier River or downhill skiing at Mont Ste-Anne.

There's a large network of bike paths feeding from the Vieux-Port out into the surrounding countryside. Ask for the free bike route map at the tourism offices. Île d'Orléans can also be a fantastic setting for a bike outing, but because there are no bike paths and heaps of traffic in summer, this route is not recommended for children.

If you prefer a more sedentary approach, check out the Massif de Charlevoix's new train tour along the St Lawrence River, or the cluster of boat-tour operators moored near Place-Royale; these cross the St Lawrence to Lévis or go downriver towards Montmorency Falls and Île d'Orléans.

GLISSADE DE LA TERRASSE
TOP CHOICE   SNOW SPORTS

Map p160 (Terrasse Dufferin; per person $2.50; ⊙11am-11pm end Oct–mid-Mar; ᷿3, 11) Outside the Château Frontenac, the scenic Terrasse Dufferin on the riverfront stages this invigoratingly fast toboggan slide all winter long. Toboggans accommodating up to four people are available for rent at the bottom.

CORRIDOR DU LITTORAL/ PROMENADE SAMUEL-DE-CHAMPLAIN
TOP CHOICE   RECREATION PATH

This beautiful pair of recreation paths follows the St Lawrence River for 8.5km west of the Old Lower Town. The westernmost section, constructed for Québec's 400th anniversary celebrations, is lined with sculptures, sports fields and green space, with a cafe and a 25m observation tower at Quai des Cageux, its western terminus. It's popular with cyclists, walkers and inline skaters.

CYCLO SERVICES
CYCLING

Map p160 (☑418-692-4052; www.cycloservices .net; 289 Rue St-Paul; hybrid bike per day $35) This

outfit rents bikes and organizes excellent cycling tours of the city and outskirts to places like Wendake or Parc de la Chute Montmorency (both p196). The knowledgeable and fun guides frequently give tours in English.

LÉVIS FERRY
FERRY

Map p160 (www.traversiers.gouv.qc.ca; 10 Rue des Traversiers; adult/child round-trip $6/4) For city views, you can't beat the 10-minute ferry ride to Lévis; boats depart daily, every 30 to 60 minutes from 6am to at least midnight. If you purchase a round-trip ticket, you can remain on the boat for the return journey; there's usually a 20-minute layover in Lévis.

AML CRUISES
CRUISE

Map p160 (☑866-856-6668; www.croisieresaml .com; Quai Chouinard, 10 Rue Dalhousie, Vieux-Port) Get a new perspective of the city aboard AML's small vessels on a dining or sightseeing cruise, including a popular trip along the St Lawrence (adult/child $34/19) and a brunch cruise (adult/child $49/29), each 90 minutes in length.

CROISIÈRES LE COUDRIER
CRUISE

Map p160 (☑418-692-0107, 888-600-5554; www .croisierescoudrier.qc.ca; 180 Rue Dalhousie, Bassin Louise, Quai 19, Vieux-Port) This company's sightseeing cruises (1½ hours) run all the way to Île d'Orléans (adult/child $34/19). Other offerings include five-course dinner cruises (adult $82) and special three-hour cruises during Les Grands Feux Loto-Québec (p27).

PLACE D'YOUVILLE
SKATING

Map p160 (just outside Porte St-Jean; ⊙end Oct–mid-Mar) In the shadow of the old town walls, this improvised outdoor rink is one of the most scenic and popular places for ice-skating once winter rolls around. It's a great place to mingle with locals, and you can also rent skates here.

VÉLOS ROY-O
BICYCLE RENTAL

Map p168 (www.velosroyo.com; 463 Rue St-Jean; bike rental per day $25; ⊙8am-6pm Mon-Wed, 8am-8pm Thu & Fri, 9am-5pm Sat & Sun) Located in the St-Jean-Baptiste neighborhood, this place rents and repairs all sorts of bikes. It also has lots of high-quality Canadian-made bike accessories for sale.

BATTLEFIELDS PARK
TOP CHOICE   OUTDOORS

Map p168 Conveniently close to the Old Town, this vast park (p164) is a great spot for outdoor activity. You can walk or run along the network of trails, or pound the pavement of a terrific jogging track based on a former horse-racing course. The park is also great for in-line skating. In winter people come here for Québec's well-known winter activities like snowshoeing, cross-country skiing or a romantic moonlight sleigh ride.

RUNNING ROOM   RUNNING
Map p168 (www.runningroom.com; 1049 Ave Cartier; ⊙9:30am-9pm Mon-Fri, 9:30am-6pm Sat, 8:30am-5pm Sun) This Alberta-based chain sells running shoes and accessories but also has free employee-led group runs on Wednesdays at 6pm and Sundays at 8:30am. Just meet at the store. Its website also offers fantastic downloadable route maps.

PARC NATIONAL DE LA
JACQUES-CARTIER   OUTDOORS
(www.sepaq.com/pq/jac) The mountain and river scenery is picture-perfect at this national park straddling a glacial valley about 40km north of Québec City via Rte 175. There's a range of snowshoeing and cross-country skiing circuits here, from easy to difficult, and in summer there's excellent hiking, mountain biking and boating.

VÉLOPISTE JACQUES-CARTIER/
PORTNEUF   CYCLING
(http://velopistejcp.com) Formerly a railway line linking St-Gabriel-de-Valcartier and Rivière-à-Pierre, this 68km cycling trail winds its way through verdant country scenery. It's linked to downtown Québec City by another rails-to-trails project, the 22km Corridor des Cheminots. (Incidentally, cyclists can also reach this trail by train from Montréal; VIA Rail offers thrice-weekly service from Montréal to Rivière-à-Pierre, the trail's western terminus.)

VILLAGE VACANCES VALCARTIER   RAFTING
(⊘418-844-2200, 888-384-5245; www.rafting valcartier.com; 1860 Blvd Valcartier, St-Gabriel-de-Valcartier; 3hr trip $50; ⊙May–mid-Sep) For an adrenaline rush, head off on a white-water rafting trip down the Jacques Cartier River. This outfit also has guided trips for families, suitable for both beginners and experienced rafters. For the biggest thrills, come from May to June when the water is at its highest. You must reserve at least three days in advance. It's a 20-minute drive from Québec City along Hwy 73 north (exit St-Émile/La Faune).

MONT-STE-ANNE   SKIING
(www.mont-sainte-anne.com; 2000 Blvd Beau-Pré, Beaupré; ⊙mid-Nov-Apr) A hugely popular ski resort with 66 ski trails, 17 of which are set aside for night skiing (from 4pm to 9pm). You'll find all sorts of other winter activities here, including snowshoeing, skating and even dogsledding. You can rent skis and snowboards too.

LE MASSIF DE CHARLEVOIX   SKIING
(www.lemassif.com; 1350 Rue Principale, Petite-Rivière-St-François; ⊙mid-Nov–Apr) Serious skiers should consider making the trek 160km

QUÉBEC CITY SPORTS & ACTIVITIES

THE LOSS OF (HOCKEY) IDENTITY

Until 1995 Québec's National Hockey League (NHL) team, the Nordiques, was the sports sensation in town and the city laughed with the team's every success and cried at its every defeat. When rumors began to circulate that the team would be moved, protests were launched and gallons of ink spilled, but the franchise left town anyway. Pretty much any Quebecer you talk to will say that the loss of the city's hockey team was their saddest day in sport. But there was also province-wide outrage, as the move put an end to one of the most infamous sports rivalries – between the Nordiques and the Montréal Canadiens. It was especially wrenching as pretty much every hockey fan felt the Nordiques' time had come and that they were on their way to Stanley Cup glory. And win they did. Exactly a year after they moved, the ex-Nordiques, now Colorado Avalanche, took home the 1996 trophy.

These days fans content themselves with supporting the **Québec Remparts** (www.remparts.qc.ca/eng), who play in the Québec Major Junior Hockey League, coached by NHL Hall-of-Famer Patrick Roy. They play regularly at the Colisée Pepsi (p187). You can keep track of the team on its website. Meanwhile, Quebec City's big-league dreams live on. As this book goes to press, a new $400 million, 18,000-seat arena is slated for construction by 2015, in hopes of luring an NHL franchise back this way.

east of Québec City to this well-regarded ski resort, which has eastern Canada's highest vertical drop and routinely gets more snow than other slopes in the region. In addition to standard skiing and snowboarding, the resort also features a rip-roaring 7.5km groomed luge run, which takes you down the mountain at speeds approaching 50km per hour.

LE TRAIN DE CHARLEVOIX   TRAIN TOUR
(www.lemassif.com/en/train; tours $119-275) Launched in fall 2011, this tourist train makes periodic runs along a scenic stretch of the St Lawrence River, starting at Parc de la Chute Montmorency (just east of Québec City) and ending at La Malbaie, 140km to the northeast. A variety of tours is available, including ski packages in winter and dinner tours in summer, some allowing stops at intermediate destinations such as the Massif de Charlevoix ski resort or the town of Baie St-Paul.

STATION TOURISTIQUE STONEHAM   SKIING
(www.ski-stoneham.com; 600 Chemin du Hibou, Stoneham-et-Tewkesbury; ☺late Nov–mid-Mar) Smaller than Mont-Ste-Anne and only about 20 minutes from Québec City, this ski area has 32 slopes for downhill skiing and snowboarding, including night skiing runs. Take Hwy 73 north until the Stoneham exit.

🛌 SLEEPING

From old-fashioned B&Bs to stylish boutique hotels, Québec City has some fantastic overnight options. The best choices are the numerous small European-style hotels and Victorian B&Bs scattered around the Old Town. As you'd expect in such a popular city, the top choices are often full, so make reservations well in advance, especially for weekends. It's unwise to show up in the city on a Saturday morning in summer or during holidays and expect to find a room for the same night.

Prices rise in the high-season summer months and during Winter Carnival. At other times of year, you can usually save 30% or so off the high-season prices listed here.

Budget accommodations also fill up quickly during high season – with student groups block-booking entire hostels. If you're in a bind, student dorms are available to travelers during the summer at

Université Laval (☎418-656-5632; www.resi dences.ulaval.ca; Local 1618, Pavillon Alphonse-Marie Parent; s/d $46/62; ☺May-Aug). Located in the borough of Ste-Foy-Sillery, about a 15- to 20-minute bus ride away from the Old Town, rooms are clean but very plain and have shared bathrooms.

Outlying motels are concentrated primarily in three areas. The first, Beauport, is just a 12-minute drive northeast of the city. To get there, go north along Ave Dufferin, then take Hwy 440 until the exit for Blvd Ste-Anne/Rte 138. The motels are on a stretch between the 500 and 1200 blocks. A second area is located west of the center on Blvd Wilfrid-Hamel (Rte 138) – head west on Hwy 440 to the Henri IV exit. The third area is Blvd Laurier in the borough of Ste-Foy-Sillery. To get there, follow Grande Allée west until it turns into Blvd Laurier.

City buses run to these areas, so whether you have a car or not, they may be the answer if you find everything booked up downtown. The further out you go, the more the prices drop. However, prices are still generally higher than usual for motels, averaging upwards of $100 in high season.

A couple more caveats: first, many guesthouses in the Old Town simply do not have elevators; be sure to inquire on the room location if you're packing a lot of luggage and not keen on walking up a few flights of stairs. Secondly, a minimum stay (usually of two nights) may be required at some places in the height of summer. This is particularly true if arriving on the weekend.

🛌 Old Upper Town

This area has the widest choice of accommodations in town, from hostels and family-run B&Bs to cheap little hotels, intimate, luxurious inns and the granddaddy of them all – the Château Frontenac.

🔺TOP CHOICE LA MARQUISE DE BASSANO   B&B $$
Map p160 (☎418-692-0316, 877-692-0316; www .marquisedebassano.com; 15 Rue des Grisons; r $99-175; P ☞) The young, gregarious owners have done a beautiful job with this late 19th-century Victorian home, outfitting its five rooms with thoughtful touches, whether it's a canopy bed or a claw-foot bathtub. Despite being just minutes from the important sights, this house is located on a low-traffic street surrounded by period homes.

Only two rooms have private bathrooms; the other three share a bathroom. Breakfast includes fresh croissants and pastries, meats, hard-boiled eggs, cheese and fruit. Parking nearby costs $14 per night.

MANOIR SUR LE CAP   B&B $$

Map p160 (☎418-694-1987, 866-694-1987; www
.manoir-sur-le-cap.com; 9 Ave Ste-Geneviève; r $95-160, ste $195; P❋🛜) Manoir sur le Cap is a lovely guesthouse with 14 rooms, some overlooking the Jardin des Gouverneurs, the Château or the river. It's in a wonderful, quiet location, well away from the tourist throngs on Rue St-Louis. Some rooms are on the small side with slightly dated furnishings. The best have tiny balconies and attractive stone or brick walls. There's also one suite (the Condominium) with fireplace and full kitchen. Limited parking is available on-site for $15; otherwise you can park at nearby garages ($15 to $22).

FAIRMONT LE CHÂTEAU FRONTENAC   HOTEL $$$

Map p160 (☎418-692-3861, 866-540-4460; www.fairmont.com/frontenac; 1 Rue des Carrières; r from $309; P❋@🛜⚐) More than just a hotel, the iconic Château Frontenac is one of the enduring symbols of Québec City. It's also one of the busiest places in town, with over 600 rooms and busloads of guests and nonguests alike filling its halls. Rooms are elegantly decorated and come in all shapes and sizes with a number of views to choose from. Service is professional and generally staff are adept at handling the big crowds. While some guests enjoy connecting with a little slice of Québec City history, others say the grand dame doesn't quite live up to its storied reputation.

MANOIR D'AUTEUIL   B&B $$

Map p160 (☎418-694-1173; www.manoirdauteuil.com; 49 Rue d'Auteuil; r $119-199, ste $249-299; P❋@🛜) This hotel fills two 19th-century manor houses across from the Old Town walls. Rooms range widely in size and amenities; the nicest offer high ceilings, stone walls, fireplaces and canopy beds, or – in the case of the Edith Piaf suite – an ultra-spacious blue-tiled bathroom. At the time of writing, construction was underway on nine new rooms, plus a pair of pretty high-ceilinged breakfast rooms and an outdoor terrace. American expatriate owners Dan and Linda are friendly and knowledgeable about the local area.

AUBERGE PLACE D'ARMES   INN $$$

Map p160 (☎418-694-9485, 866-333-9485; www.aubergeplacedarmes.com; 24 Rue Ste-Anne; r $159-219, ste $259-324; @🛜⚐) Recently overhauled from top to bottom, this place now has some of the most dapper rooms in town. Everything from the halls to the guest rooms is done up in rich crimsons, navy blues and golds, and many rooms have exposed red-brick walls. The inn is located across from the Church of the Holy Trinity and is only a short stroll from the funicular to Lower Town. It's also pet-friendly – for $25 extra per night, Fido can sleep right beside you!

LE CLOS SAINT-LOUIS   HOTEL $$$

Map p160 (☎418-694-1311, 800-461-1311; www.clossaintlouis.com; 69 Rue St-Louis; r $199-250; P❋🛜) It's hard to tell which trait is more evident here: the obvious care of the owners or the building's natural 1844 Victorian charm. The 18 spacious, lavishly decorated rooms each has a jacuzzi in a beautifully tiled bathroom. The suites are like Victorian apartments, apart from the TV in the mini drawing room. Parking is $17 to $20 extra.

CHEZ HUBERT   GUESTHOUSE $$

Map p160 (☎418-692-0958; www.chezhubert.com; 66 Rue Ste Ursule; r without bathroom $115-125; P🛜) This dependable family-run choice is in a Victorian townhouse with chandeliers, fireplace mantels, stained-glass windows, a lovely curved staircase and oriental rugs. The three tasteful, warm-hued rooms, two with a view of the Château, all share a pair of bathrooms and come with a large buffet breakfast and free parking.

LA MAISON DEMERS   GUESTHOUSE $$

Map p160 (☎418-692-2487, 800-692-2487; hotel lamaisondemers@gmail.com; 68 Rue Ste-Ursule; r with bathroom $100-125, s/d without bathroom from $60/75, P❋🛜) Run by a friendly couple, La Maison Demers has a handful of old-fashioned rooms that are great value for the area. Most are carpeted with homey touches – as if junior had gone away to college and you're renting his room. Several rooms have tiny balconies, just large enough to step out and watch the sunset. Room 1, on the ground floor, can be noisy; the other rooms (on the 2nd and 3rd floors) are quieter. Free parking is included in the price.

HÔTEL ACADIA   HOTEL $$

Map p160 (☎418-694-0280, 800-463-0280; www.hotelsvieuxquebec.com/en/hotel/hotel-acadia;

43 Rue Ste-Ursule; r $109-219; (P)(@)(⌘) This hotel, which is part of a small chain, is spread over three adjacent historical houses along a quiet, convenient side street. Rooms run the gamut from small with shared bathrooms to quite luxurious with fireplaces or jacuzzis. Common areas include a nice sitting room, a spa and a deck overlooking a peaceful garden and the Ursuline convent. Breakfast is served at the Feu Sacré restaurant around the corner, and parking costs $18 extra.

AU PETIT HÔTEL   HOTEL $$

Map p160 (⌂418-694-0965; www.aupetithotel .com; 3 Ruelle des Ursulines; r $70-135; (P)(✱)(⌘)) Sitting on a tranquil dead-end lane, this former rooming house has a range of clean, simply furnished rooms, each with a private bathroom. Some of the options are small and rather drab, while others are airy and borderline charming. Only a couple of rooms have air conditioning. Overall, it's good value for the Old Town, and parking right next door costs only $8 to $12.

HÔTEL DU VIEUX-QUÉBEC   HOTEL $$$

Map p160 (⌂418-692-1850; www.hvq.com; 1190 Rue St-Jean; r $198-278; (P)(✱)(@)(⌘)) Considering its prime location, this hotel is disappointingly short on historical character, but its environmental credentials are impressive. Thanks to its use of Forest Stewardship Council–certified wood, recycled furniture, and rooftop beehives and gardens (that keep things cool in summer while producing veggies, herbs and honey for guests), it won the 2010 Energy and Environment Award from the Hotel Association of Canada, along with top marks from the Green Key eco-rating program. Corner rooms have nice views up Rue St-Jean, while others come with kitchenettes or fireplaces. Look online for deals.

AUBERGE DE LA PAIX   HOSTEL $

Map p160 (⌂418-694-0735; www.aubergedela paix.com; 31 Rue Couillard; dm/d/tr $26/72/85, all incl breakfast; (@)(⌘)) On a quiet street, this funky old-school hostel has relaxed, welcoming staff and 60 brightly colored rooms with comfy wooden furniture. With the cheerfully painted halls and guests lounging in the tree-filled garden out back, it feels less institutional than the official HI hostel nearby. Most accommodation is in four- to eight-bed dorms; there are also four coveted private rooms (with shared bath) that must be booked well in advance. A continental breakfast is served each morning and bedding is provided for $5 per stay.

AUBERGE INTERNATIONALE
DE QUÉBEC   HOSTEL $

Map p160 (⌂418-694-0755, 866-694-0950; www.aubergeinternationaledequebec.com; 19 Rue Ste-Ursule; dm $24-36, r with/without bathroom $102/76; (@)(⌘)) Floors are creaky and the frustrating labyrinth of corridors goes on forever, but this lively place heaves with energy and bustle year-round. It attracts a wide mix of independent travelers, fami-

---

QUÉBEC'S COOLEST HOTEL

Visiting the **Ice Hotel** (⌂418-623-2888, 877-505-0423; www.hoteldeglace-canada.com; 9530 Rue de la Faune; d from $318; ⊙tours noon-5:30pm) is like stepping into a wintry fairy tale. Nearly everything here is made of ice: the reception desk, the sink in your room, your bed – all ice.

Some 500 tons of ice and 15,000 tons of snow go into the five-week construction of this perishable hotel. First impressions are overwhelming – in the entrance hall, tall, sculpted columns of ice support a ceiling where a crystal chandelier hangs. To either side, carved sculptures, tables and chairs fill the labyrinth of corridors and guest rooms. Children will love the long curving ice slide just beyond the reception area, while grown-ups gravitate to the ice bar, where stiff drinks are served in cocktail glasses made of ice (there's hot chocolate for the kids too).

The Ice Hotel usually opens from January to March and offers packages starting at $318 per double. Overnight guests say the beds are not as frigid as they sound, courtesy of thick sleeping bags laid on plush deer pelts.

If you're not staying, buy a **day pass** (adult day/evening $17.50/13.50, child under 13 half-price), which grants access to the hotel's bar and other public spaces. The hotel is about 15 minutes north of Québec City, via Hwy 175 and Hwy 73. Take exit 154 (Rue de la Faune) off Hwy 73 and follow the signs.

PARKING

Compact Old Québec lends itself better to exploration on foot than by car. If you're driving up here, plan to park your vehicle for as much of your stay as possible.

Parking garages in and around the Old Town typically charge a day rate of $14 to $17.50 Monday to Friday, and $6 to $10 on weekends. The most central garage, and one of the cheapest, is underneath the Hôtel de Ville, just a couple of blocks from the Château Frontenac. Metered street parking is also widely available, but expensive ($2 per hour). Many guesthouses provide discount vouchers for nearby parking garages. In winter, nighttime snow removal is scheduled on many streets between 11pm and 6:30am. Don't park during these hours on any street with a '*déneigement*' (snow removal) sign and a flashing red light, or you'll wake up to a towed vehicle and a hefty fine!

lies with small children and groups. Staff are friendly but often harried just trying to keep up with all the comings and goings. It's usually full in summer, despite having almost 300 beds, so book ahead if you can.

Old Lower Town

A cluster of the most tantalizing boutique hotels in the city is found in this area, along with a handful of hip, small inns.

TOP CHOICE AUBERGE ST-ANTOINE
LUXURY HOTEL $$$

Map p160 (☑418-692-2211, 888-692-2211; www.saint-antoine.com; 8 Rue St-Antoine; r from $299; P ❄ @ ☎ 🐾) The Auberge St-Antoine is one of the finest hotels in Canada. With phenomenal service, plush rooms and endless amenities, this hotel delivers near-perfect execution. The spacious rooms are elegantly set with high-end mattresses, goose-down duvets, luxury linens and atmospheric lighting. Walking the halls is like strolling through a gallery – when the neighboring parking lot was dug up to expand the hotel, thousands of historical relics from the French colony were discovered and put on display. Panache (p174) restaurant, the darling of Québec's fine-dining scene, is located just off the hotel's lobby.

TOP CHOICE HÔTEL LE GERMAIN-DOMINION
LUXURY HOTEL $$$

Map p160 (☑418-692-2224, 888-833-5253; www.germaindominion.com; 126 Rue St-Pierre; r from $235; ❄ @ ☎ 🐾) The flagship hotel of a classy Québécois chain, the Dominion is another outstanding Lower Town option combining understated luxury with great service. It occupies two adjacent historic buildings, one a former bank, one a former

fruit-and-vegetable market. Rooms are quiet, cozy and tastefully designed, with high-end fittings (sumptuous mattresses, Egyptian cotton bedding, good lighting, big windows) and a few quirks (bathroom sinks that glow in the dark). Dogs get first-class treatment too; $35 per night gets you a doggie bed, plus food and water bowls.

HÔTEL DES COUTELLIER
HOTEL $$$

Map p160 (☑418-692-9696, 888-523-9696; www.hoteldescoutellier.com; 253 Rue St-Paul; r from $175; ❄ @ ☎) Convenient to the train station and the Marché du Vieux-Port, this handsome small hotel offers style, comfort and friendly service. Refreshingly unpretentious rooms are bright and spacious with modern furnishings (flat-screen TVs, iPod docks and high-end coffeemakers). A tasty continental breakfast is packed up in a wicker basket for you every morning and hung outside your door.

HÔTEL 71
HOTEL $$$

Map p160 (☑418-692-1171, 888-692-1171; www.hotel71.ca; 71 Rue St-Pierre; r from $275; ❄ @ ☎) Set in an imposing greystone building that dates to the 1800s, Hôtel 71 provides the boutique experience par excellence. Rooms are sleek, with a minimalist design, while not stinting on comfort (fantastic mattresses, plush down comforters, oversized TVs, dramatically lit bathrooms). The top floor corner suite commands some of the most astounding views in Québec City, with big windows on all sides providing a sweeping perspective on Place-Royale, the St Lawrence River and the Château Frontenac.

HÔTEL BELLEY
HOTEL $$

Map p160 (☑418-692-1694, 888-692-1694; www.hotelbelley.com; 249 Rue St-Paul; r $110-160; ❄ ☎) A great place for the young and hip who still like their creature comforts,

THE WONDROUS BACKYARD OF QUÉBEC CITY

Québec City is surrounded by stunning countryside with attractions for every interest. The sights below, except for Wendake, can be reached via Rte 138 northeast of town.

Île d'Orléans

This stunning place can be visited on a day trip but is easily worth two days or more. Cut off from the rest of Québec for centuries (the Taschereau Bridge was only built in 1935), there is plenty to see, from gorgeous scenery to 300-year-old stone homes. **Maison Drouin** (www.fondationfrancoislamy.org; 4700 Chemin Royal; admission $4; ☉10am-6pm daily mid-Jun–late Aug, 11am-5pm Sat & Sun late Aug-early Oct), a 1730 house, is fascinating as it was never modernized (ie no electricity or running water) even though it was inhabited until 1984. Guides in period dress run tours in summer. At **Parc Maritime de St-Laurent** (www.parcmaritime.ca; 120 Chemin de la Chalouperie, St-Laurent; adult/child under 13 $5/free; ☉10am-5pm early Jun-early Oct) you can learn about the parish's ship-building history. There's a **tourist office** (☑418-828-9411, 866-941-9411; www.iledorleans.com; 490 Côte du Pont, St-Pierre; ☉8:30am-7:30pm mid-Jun–early Sep, 9am-5pm Mon-Fri & 11am-3pm Sat & Sun early Sep–mid-Jun) on the island just after you cross the bridge. Île d'Orléans is about a 15-minute drive from Québec City.

Parc de la Chute Montmorency

This 83m-high waterfall is right by the Taschereau Bridge on the way to Île d'Orléans. While it tops Niagara Falls by about 30m, it's not nearly as wide, but what's cool is walking over the falls on the suspension bridge, with the water thundering below. The **park** (www.sepaq.com/chutemontmorency; 2490 Ave Royale, Beauport; admission free, parking per car $5, cable car adult/child $10/5; ☉8:30am-7:30pm summer, reduced hours rest of year, closed Nov-Christmas) is about 12km from Québec City.

Wendake

The major attraction at this Huron Aboriginal reserve is the **Onhoúa Chetek8e** (www.huron-wendat.qc.ca; 575 Rue Chef Stanislas Koska; adult/child $12.50/7.50; ☉9am-5pm May-Oct, 10am-4pm Nov-Apr, last tour 1hr before closing; ▣72), a reconstructed Huron village. Excellent guides explain Huron history, culture and daily life. By car, take Hwy 73 (exit 154) about 20 minutes west of Québec City.

Ste-Anne-de-Beaupré

About 35km from Québec City, this village is known for its Goliath-sized **Basilique Ste-Anne-de-Beaupré** (www.sanctuairesainteanne.org; 10018 Ave Royale) and its role as a shrine. Try to visit on July 26, Ste-Anne's feast day, when the place goes berserk. The church fills to capacity, the nearby camping grounds are swamped with pilgrims, hotels are booked full and the whole village starts feeling like a kind of religious Woodstock.

this personable eight-room hotel offers spacious, uniquely designed rooms with features including brick walls or wood paneling; some have original details such as beamed ceilings. You might also find French doors to the bathroom, a claw-foot tub – or, on the downside, a very tiny bathroom. Many rooms include microwave ovens or small refrigerators.

▣ St-Jean Baptiste

Accommodations here mean you'll be rubbing elbows with locals more than you would in the Old Town.

TOP CHOICE **L'HÔTEL DU CAPITOLE** HISTORIC HOTEL **$$$**

Map p160 (☑418-694-4040, 800-363-4040; www.lecapitole.com; 972 Rue St-Jean; r from $275; ▣❄⚛) Right on top of the stately Théâtre Capitole (p183), this hotel is one of the city's gems. Rooms vary, but may feature floor-to-ceiling windows, exposed brick walls and velvety red furniture with a touch of old-fashioned theatricality. Some rooms are quite small, while others have balconies overlooking the old city walls. Staff generally earn high marks for service. Valet parking costs $20 per night, or you can park at the public garage just across the street.

TOP CHOICE AUBERGE JA MOISAN GUESTHOUSE $$

Map p168 (☑418-529-9764; www.jamoisan.com/
auberge; 695 Rue St-Jean; r $120-160; P@令)
This lovely top-floor B&B sits directly
above the famous JA Moisan grocery store.
Bedrooms are small and tucked under the
eaves, while the floor below holds a cluster of common areas, including a parlor,
tea room, solarium, terrace and computer
room. Host Clément St-Laurent is a delightful conversationalist and goes out of his
way to make guests feel at home. Rates include a three-course breakfast and parking.

CHÂTEAU DES TOURELLES B&B $$

Map p168 (☑418-647-9136, 866-346-9136; www
.chateaudestourelles.qc.ca; 212 Rue St-Jean; r incl
brekfast $164-184; 令) On a great little strip of
Rue St-Jean, lined with interesting stores
and eateries, this B&B's soaring turret will
get your attention long before you reach the
door. The lovely owners have done a stunning job with this old house; it's cozy and
rustic without straying into kitsch. Rooms
are beautifully decorated, while a rooftop
terrace has a 360-degree view of just about
everything of note in town. In the off-season,
rates drop substantially.

LE CHÂTEAU DU FAUBOURG B&B $$

Map p168 (☑418-524-2902; www.lechateaudu
faubourg.com; 429 Rue St-Jean; r $119-159;
P✱令) Built by the massively rich Imperial Tobacco family in the 1800s, this is one
of the city's most atmospheric B&Bs. The
interior is pure British-Lord-of-the-Manor
meets French-Marquis style, replete with
old oil paintings, antique furnishings
and shimmering chandeliers. While some
rooms are packed with old-world details,
others seem a little cramped (notably the
Boudoir du Josephine in the attic).

🛌 Montcalm & Colline Parlementaire

AUBERGE CAFÉ KRIEGHOFF B&B $$

Map p168 (☑418-522-3711; www.cafekrieghoff
.qc.ca; 1089 Ave Cartier; s/d incl breakfast
$135/160; P令) Hidden in the house above
Café Krieghoff (p178) is a cluster of spacious,
simply decorated rooms with offbeat touches like antique hat boxes. All rooms have
modern bathrooms and flat-screen TVs but
no phones. A common area has a phone, um-
brellas to borrow and a computer with inter-

net, all free for guests. Another bonus is the
breakfast voucher for the cafe each morning.
Parking is available for $14 per day.

AUBERGE DU QUARTIER HOTEL $$

Map p168 (☑418-525-9726, 800-782-9441; www
.aubergeduquartier.com; 170 Grande Allée Ouest; r
$120-225; P✱@令) Around the corner from
restaurant-lined Ave Cartier, this friendly
(and gay-friendly) hotel offers sleek modern rooms and professional service. Rooms
range in size from small and modestly
furnished to spacious numbers with nice
extras such as a fireplace. They're done up
in masculine tones with rich burgundies,
exposed steel beams or original brickwork
adding to the atmosphere.

RELAIS CHARLES-ALEXANDRE HOTEL $$

Map p168 (☑418-523-1220; www.relaischarles
alexandre.com; 91 Grande Allée Est; r $134-144;
P✱令) This is a small, cozy hotel with a
great location near both the Musée National
des Beaux-Arts du Québec and Battlefields
Park. Rooms are all different and are
best described as low-key and comfortable
with modern furnishings. Standard rooms
are bright and comfortably set, but with a
view onto the parking lot. Some of the superior rooms have big bay windows and fireplaces (plus plasma-screen TVs). Parking
just behind the hotel costs $8 extra.

🛌 St-Roch

Steeply downhill about 1km from the walled
city, St-Roch is a less convenient base than
some neighborhoods, although the *ascenseur* eliminates part of the climb.

AUBERGE LE VINCENT BOUTIQUE HOTEL $$$

Map p168 (☑418-523-5000; www.aubergelevin
cent.com; 295 Rue St-Vallier Est; r $199-279;
P✱@令) This hotel's nondescript brick facade looks unpromising indeed, but things
improve dramatically once you step inside.
The lobby and adjacent stone-walled breakfast area, with their comfy furniture and
pleasant fireside reading nook, are instantly
inviting, while the rooms upstairs, especially corner suites No 4 and 8, are stylishly
comfortable, with brick walls, tall windows,
mod couches and sleek bathtubs. Quintuple-
paned windows keep out the street noise.
All rooms have plasma TVs with DVD players, ideal for taking advantage of the sizable
video library at the front desk.

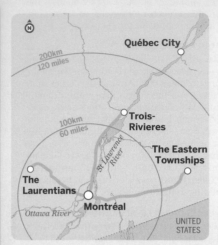

Day Trips from Montréal

Trois-Rivières p199

Midway between Montréal and Québec City, this historic town makes a pleasant stopover, with its attractive riverfront backed by a small cluster of museums and historic buildings.

The Laurentians p201

Montréal's backyard mountain playground, the Laurentians offer countless recreational opportunities, including hiking, downhill and cross-country skiing, and cycling on a 230km converted railway bed.

The Eastern Townships p204

Québec meets New England in this pretty landscape of rolling hills, sparkling lakes, picturesque villages and farms specializing in cider, wine, cheese and maple syrup.

Trois-Rivières

Explore

The pleasant town of Trois-Rivières boasts a history dating back to 1634, making it North America's second-oldest city north of Mexico. Although much of the historic center burned down in 1908, a compact cluster of old buildings remains, creating a harmonious ensemble with the town's picturesque tree-lined streets and scenic location along the St Lawrence River's north shore.

The name Trois-Rivières is a bit of a misnomer. Don't bother looking – there aren't three rivers. The name refers to the way the St Maurice River divides as it approaches the St Lawrence.

Events like the two-week **Festival International de la Poésie** (International Poetry Festival; www.fiptr.com) in October, or the three-day Italian-themed **Ferragosto** (www.ferragosto.ca) in August are great times to visit.

The Best...

➡ **Sight** Musée Québécois de Culture Populaire (right)

➡ **Place to Eat** Le Poivre Noir (p200)

➡ **Place to Drink** Gambrinus (p201)

Top Tip

If you read French, don't miss the interesting interpretive plaques sprinkled around Trois-Rivières' riverfront district, enlivened by vintage photos and engravings tracing four centuries of local history.

Getting There & Away

Bus Orléans Express (⌨514-842-2281; www.orleansexpress.com) runs six to seven buses daily from Montréal to Trois-Rivières ($35, two hours). Buses arrive at Trois-Rivières' Gare d'Autocars (⌨819-374-2944; 275 Rue St-Georges), within a 10-minute walk of the historic riverfront district.

Car Autoroute 40

Need to Know

➡ **Area Code** ⌨819

➡ **Location** 139km northeast of Montréal

➡ **Tourist Office** (⌨819-375-1122; www.tourismetroisrivieres.com; 1457 Rue Notre-Dame; ◷9am-8pm mid-Jun–Aug, 9am-5pm Mon-Fri & 10am-4pm Sat & Sun mid-May–mid-Jun & Sep–mid-Oct, 9am-5pm Mon-Fri mid-Oct–mid-May)

⊙ SIGHTS

MUSÉE QUÉBÉCOIS DE CULTURE POPULAIRE MUSEUM

(⌨819-372-0406; www.culturepop.qc.ca; 200 Rue Laviolette; adult/child/student $10/6/8, incl En Prison $16/9/11.50; ◷10am-6pm daily late Jun Aug, to 6pm Tuo Sun Sep-late Jun) The most interesting stop in town, this museum's changing exhibits run the gamut from folk art to pop culture, delving into the social and cultural life of the Québécois. Recent exhibits have focused on subjects as diverse as rooster carvings, the criminal

DAY TRIPS FROM MONTRÉAL TROIS-RIVIÈRES

SLEEPING IN TROIS-RIVIÈRES

Le Gîte Loiselle (⌨819-375-2121; www.giteloiselle.com; 836 Rue des Ursulines, Trois-Rivières; r from $89; ❀⧉) Smack in the middle of Trois-Rivières' historic district, within easy walking distance of the St Lawrence River and the museums, this immaculate and cyclist-friendly B&B makes a cozy spot to spend the night. Attractions include plush beds, tasty breakfasts, 19th-century architectural details and an inviting fireplace in the parlor downstairs.

Le Fleurvil (⌨819-372-5195; www.fleurvil.qc.ca; 635 Rue des Ursulines, Trois-Rivières; r from $89; @⧉⊠) Operated by a gregarious Harley aficionado with a knack for decorating, this inn near the riverfront is backed by a lush garden with pool. Most of the five rooms have private facilities.

Auberge Internationale de Trois-Rivières (⌨819-378-8010, 877-378-8010; www.hihostels.ca; 497 Rue Radisson, Trois-Rivières; dm/d $28/60; @⧉) This wonderfully clean and friendly youth hostel is set in a two-story brick Georgian home.

history of Québec and the making of the popular Québécois soap opera *Le Temps d'une Paix*.

EN PRISON
HISTORIC SITE

(📞819-372-0406; www.enprison.com; 200 Rue Laviolette; adult/child/student $10/6/8, incl Musée Québécois de Culture Populaire $16/9/11.50; ◷hourly tours 10:30am-4:30pm late Jun–Aug, tours based on demand & guide availability 10am-5pm Tue-Sun rest of year) Adjacent to the Musée Québécois de Culture Populaire is Trois-Rivières' former prison; it was Canada's oldest continually in-use jail when it closed in 1986. Highly recommended 75-minute tours of the facility are led by former convicts – perhaps the only job in Canada where a criminal record is a prerequisite. The tours cover not only the history of this particular prison but life in Canada's prisons in general. It's fascinating but at times rather disturbing stuff; guides try to lighten things up by throwing in the occasional joke. Only a few guides speak English, so call ahead for availability.

URSULINE MUSEUM
MUSEUM

(www.musee-ursulines.qc.ca; 734 Rue des Ursulines; adult/child/student $4/free/3; ◷10am-5pm Tue-Sun May-Nov, 1-5pm Wed-Sun Mar & Apr) Founded by Ursuline nuns in 1639, this museum has a fine collection of textiles, ceramics, books and prints related to Catholicism. Frescoes adorn the adjacent chapel. Nearby, Rue des Ursulines is a pleasant place to stroll, with its picturesque homes (some of which are now B&Bs) and its unseen history, much of which is described on informational plaques throughout the neighborhood.

CATHÉDRALE DE L'ASSOMPTION
CHURCH

(362 Rue Bonaventure; ◷7am-noon & 2-5pm) Church admirers should pay a visit to the this colossal cathedral in the heart of town, a soaring neo-Gothic confection with exquisite sculpture and intricate Florentine stained-glass windows.

MS JACQUES-CARTIER
BOAT TOUR

(📞819-375-3000, 800-567-3737; www.croisieres.qc.ca; 1515 Rue du Fleuve; 90min Discovery Cruise adult/child $33/free) Cruises along the St Lawrence River are available from the dock in Parc Portuaire, at the foot of Blvd des Forges in the center of the old town.

✗ EATING & DRINKING

LE POIVRE NOIR
FUSION $$$

(📞819 378-5772; www.poivrenoir.com; 1300 Rue du Fleuve; mains $29-34; ◷lunch Wed-Fri, dinner Tue-Sat) Since opening in 2008, this upmarket place down by the riverfront has become one of Trois-Rivières' favorite eateries. Chef José Pierre Durand's inspired, often daring blend of traditional French and Québécois cuisine (interspersed with Asian and other international influences) creates a memorable dining experience. Appetizers such as asparagus and blood orange salad, or warm goat-cheese 'snowballs' with tomatoes and pistachios, are followed by main dishes like Québécois deer with pine nut–squash risotto and cranberry chutney, while the truly adventurous can finish their meal with pan-fried foie gras with dark chocolate and Jack Daniels–infused caramel sauce! Reservations are suggested.

WORTH A DETOUR

A DELIGHTFUL SUMMER RETREAT

If you're continuing east from Trois-Rivières toward Québec City, don't miss **La Domaine Joly de Lotbinière** (📞418-926-2462; www.domainejoly.com; Rte de Pointe-Platon, Hwy 132, Ste-Croix; adult/student $14/8; ◷10am-5pm mid-May–mid-Oct). This stately museum on a riverside point along the south bank of the St Lawrence River was built for former Québec premier Henri-Gustave Joly de Lotbinière (1849–1908). It's one of the most impressive manors built during the seigneurial period of Québec and has been preserved in its late-19th-century state. The outbuildings and huge cultivated garden are a treat, and the cafe serves lunch and afternoon teas. There's also a farm stand that sells vegetables from mid-June to early September.

LE GRILL
STEAKHOUSE $$

(www.restolegrill.com; 350 Rue des Forges; mains $12-19; ⊙lunch & dinner) A couple of blocks from the cathedral and the prison museum, this steakhouse does it all: gourmet burgers; meal-sized salads topped with grilled salmon, sesame chicken, or apples and walnuts; every kind of grilled meat imaginable; and, of course, *poutine* (fries smothered in cheese curds and gravy).

GAMBRINUS
BREWERY

(www.gambrinus.qc.ca; 3160 Blvd des Forges; ⊙11am-1am Mon-Fri, 3pm-1am Sat) About 3km north of the riverfront, this decade-old brewery serves over a dozen varieties of beer, including seasonal cranberry, raspberry and apple ales, an excellent IPA, and an unconventional hemp-and-honey blend called Miel d'Ange.

The Laurentians

Explore

Named for their location along the northern side of the St Lawrence River, the Laurentians (Les Laurentides) are one of Québec's great outdoor playgrounds. In winter outdoor enthusiasts and nature-lovers take to the clear lakes and forest-covered peaks for downhill and cross-country skiing, snowshoeing and snowmobiling. When the weather warms, hikers, cyclists, kayakers and campers come to soak up the natural beauty. People also visit in fall to take in the changing leaves, with hues of ocher, gold and vermilion dramatically coloring the landscape.

While it's possible to come up on a long day trip, some prefer to linger in the region's alpine-style villages, overnighting in cozy chalets, spa retreats and atmospheric B&Bs. Expect higher prices and heavy crowds during high season, which includes the summer months and Christmas holidays.

The Best...

➡ **Sight** Parc National du Mont-Tremblant (right)

➡ **Place to Eat** Le Creux du Vent (p203)
➡ **Place to Drink** Microbrasserie La Diable (p203)

Top Tip

Even without your own bicycle, you can cycle Canada's longest rails-to-trails route, the 230km P'tit Train du Nord; Autobus Le Petit Train du Nord will rent you a bike and provide transportation to and from the start and end points of your choice; see p203.

Getting There & Away

Bus Bus Galland (☑514-333-9555, 514-842-2281; www.galland-bus.com) runs buses from Montréal's main bus station to the Laurentians three times daily. Towns serviced include St-Sauveur-des-Monts ($22, 1¾ hours), St-Agathe-des-Monts ($27, 2½ hours) and Mont-Tremblant ($35, three hours).

Car Autoroute 15 (Autoroute des Laurentides) and provincial Hwy 117

Need to Know

➡ **Area Code** ☑450, 819
➡ **Location** 80km to 150km northwest of Montréal
➡ **Laurentians Tourist Association** (Association Touristique des Laurentides; ☑450-224-7007, 800-561-6673; www.laurentides.com; La Porte du Nord, exit 51, Autoroute 15, St-Jérôme; ⊙8:30am-8pm late Jun-late Aug, 8:30am-5pm rest of year)

◉ SIGHTS

TOP CHOICE PARC NATIONAL DU MONT-TREMBLANT
PARK

(☑819-688-2281,800-665-6527;www.sepaq.com /pq/mot; 4456 Chemin du Lac-Supérieur, Lac-Supérieur; adult/child $5.50/2.50; ⊙7am-10pm summer, call for winter hours) Established over a century ago, the wild, wooded Parc National du Mont-Tremblant covers more than 1500 sq km of gorgeous Laurentian lakes, rivers, hills and woods. The most developed of the park's sectors is Le Diable, close to Mont-Tremblant and north of pretty Lac Supérieur. The information center here has details about the region's fantastic campsites, canoe routes and hiking and mountain-biking trails; it also offers kayak, pedal-boat and canoe rentals. The three-hour Méandres de la Diable canoe excursion from Lac Chat to Mont de la Vache Noire (guided tour $57.50) is especially popular.

MONT-TREMBLANT   VILLAGE
The village of Mont-Tremblant (Secteur Village), some 4km southwest of the Mont-Tremblant ski resort, is spread along the shores of pretty Lac Mercier. You'll find shops, cafes, B&Bs, restaurants and a walking path around the lake. You can also take a cruise out on the water.

STE-AGATHE-DES-MONTS   VILLAGE
This mountain village has a prime location on Lac des Sables. By the beginning of the 1900s, it was a well-known spa town. Later, famous guests included Queen Elizabeth (who took refuge here during WWII) and Jackie Kennedy. **Bateaux Alouette** (☑819-326-3656; www.croisierealouette.com; adult/child $16/6) offers 50-minute cruises on the lake.

VAL-DAVID   VILLAGE
Tiny Val-David was a major hippie mecca in the '60s, a hangover still apparent today. The village has two artisanal bakeries, jazz music in its cafes on summer weekends and more than its share of arts and crafts people.

ST-SAUVEUR-DES-MONTS   VILLAGE
St-Sauveur-des-Monts is a small resort town with four nearby ski hills. Its main drag is often clogged on weekends when day-trippers shuffle through the cafes, restaurants and shops.

SUGAR SHACKS

Québec is the undisputed world champion of maple sugar production, and there's a long-standing tradition of early-spring visits to *cabanes à sucre* (maple sugar shacks); English-speaking Quebeckers refer to such trips as 'sugaring off'. With a roaring fire boiling the sap down into syrup, these cozy places can be found all over the province in March and April, including the Laurentians and the Eastern Townships.

For a list of over 100 sugar shacks open to the public, see www.bonjourquebec .com/qc-en/attractions-directory/sugar-shack/. Below are a few popular shacks within easy driving distance of Montréal to get you started:

Cabane à Sucre Bouvrette (☑450-438-4659; www.bouvrette.ca; 1000 Rue Nobel, St-Jérôme; ☉Tue-Sun Mar & Apr) This big retro shack only 45 minutes from Montréal is a great choice, with a dining room, dance hall, fireplace, petting zoo, and 15-minute rides through the woods on a horse-drawn sleigh or an old-fashioned locomotive. The set menu ($15 to $20) includes ham, bacon, maple sausages, *oreilles de crisse* (deep-fried pork jowls), fried potatoes, oven-baked 48-egg omelets, pea soup, baked beans, beet juice and homemade pickles, all slathered in maple syrup. For dessert don't miss the classic *tire d'érable*, maple taffy made by pouring hot, concentrated maple syrup over snow, then rolling the congealed syrup onto wooden sticks.

Cabane à Sucre Millette (☑819-688-2101, 877-688-2101; www.tremblant-sugar-shack .com; 1357 Rue St-Faustin, St-Faustin; ☉11:30am-1:30pm & 5:30-7:30pm Tue-Fri, 11:30am-8pm Sat, 10am-7pm Sun Mar & Apr, by reservation rest of year) Run by the same family for five generations, this sugar shack only 15 minutes from Mont-Tremblant is famous for its multicourse menu of traditional country food, with maple pies, buckwheat crepes and maple taffy for dessert. Tour the farm on foot or on snowshoes and see how the sap is tapped into giant barrels, then carried away on horse-drawn sleds.

Cabane à Sucre Au Pied de Cochon (☑450-258-1732; http://cabaneasucreaupied decochon.com; 11382 Rang de la Fresnière, St-Benoît de Mirabel; ☉by reservation) This high-end version of the sugar-shack experience is brought to you by renowned Montréal chef Martin Picard. Book well in advance for his gourmet menu of maple-based delights (adult/child $57/20).

STE-ADÉLE VILLAGE

If you're traveling in summer, stop by Ste-Adéle for a meal. There are several interesting eateries across the street from Lac Rond.

MUSÉE D'ART CONTEMPORAIN DES LAURENTIDES MUSEUM

(www.museelaurentides.ca; 101 Pl du Curé-Labelle, St-Jérôme; adult/child $4/free; ⊙noon-5pm Tue-Sun) Less than an hour from Montréal, this contemporary-art museum has small but fine exhibitions of regional artists' works.

🍴 EATING & DRINKING

LE CREUX DU VENT QUÉBÉCOIS $$

(⌂819-322-2280; www.lecreuxduvent.com; 1430 Rue de l'Académie, Val-David; lunch/dinner menus from $15/28) Tucked into a quiet part of town by the rushing Rivière du Nord, this attractive restaurant has a seasonal menu inspired by what's available at the local markets. Bask on the delightful outdoor terrace while enjoying multicourse menus of Québécois classics. The lunchtime table d'hôte (fixed-price menu) is especially good value.

ORANGE & PAMPLEMOUSSE FUSION $$

(⌂450-227-4330; www.orangepamplemousse.com; 120 Rue Principale, St-Sauveur-des-Monts; mains $10-30; ⊙8am-3pm daily, 5-9pm Wed-Sun) In a tranquil setting complete with bamboo fountain, this popular place serves complex pasta dishes and extraordinary grilled fish. Breakfasts are also recommended.

LA PETITE CACHÉE MEDITERRANEAN $$

(⌂819-425-2654; www.petitecachee.com; 2681 Chemin du Village, Mont-Tremblant; mains $19-35) In a charming chalet en route to the ski slopes, this place offers tasty choices such as shrimp and fennel fettuccine, grilled rainbow trout with roasted pepper sauce, or *merguez* sausage pizza with apples, feta and mint.

LA FORGE BAR & GRILL BURGERS, STEAKHOUSE $$$

(www.laforgetremblant.com; Pl St-Bernard, Station Mont-Tremblant; mains bistro $14-33, restaurant $32-50) La Forge offers a laid-back bistro on the lower level with tasty burgers, pastas and salads; the upstairs restaurant has delicious grilled meats cooked over a maple-wood fire, along with excellent views.

MICROBRASSERIE LA DIABLE BREWERY $$

(www.microladiable.com; 117 Chemin Kandahar, Station Mont-Tremblant; mains $12-25) This hugely popular place brews seven beers on-site and serves satisfying comfort food (the sausages are famous).

🏃 SPORTS & ACTIVITIES

TOP CHOICE P'TIT TRAIN DU NORD CYCLING, SKIING

(www.laurentides.com/parclineaire) One of the region's essential experiences, this 230km path follows the old Laurentian train line between Mont-Laurier and Bois-des-Filion. Cyclists hit the path when the weather warms; in winter it's open to cross-country skiers and snowshoers (parts are also open to snowmobiles). B&Bs and bike shops are easily found along the route, and many old train stations now house mini-museums, cafes and tourist info offices. For bike rentals and shuttle services along the route, contact **Autobus Le Petit Train du Nord** (⌂450-569-5596, 888-893-8356; www.autobuslepetittraindunord.com; shuttle ticket $24-52, rental bike per day/week $25/126; ⊙mid-May–mid-Oct).

MONT-TREMBLANT SKI RESORT SKIING

(⌂888-738-1777; www.tremblant.ca; 1000 Chemin des Voyageurs, Mont Tremblant Village; lift ticket adult/youth/child $75/54/44; ⊙8:30am-3pm late Nov–mid-Apr) This ski center has the area's highest peak (968m) and more than 60 runs. Its state-of-the-art facilities include golf courses, water sports, cycling and tennis courts. Bikes and skates can be rented at the ski center for the 10km skating/cycling path that runs up to the mountain's edge.

MONT ST-SAUVEUR SKIING

(⌂450-227-4671; www.mssi.ca; 350 Ave St-Denis, St-Sauveur-des-Monts; ⊙9am-10pm Sun-Thu, to 10:30pm Fri & Sat mid-Nov–Apr) Mont St-Sauveur is one of the Laurentians' main ski centers. The hills are a bit tame but there's night skiing, a huge variety of runs and guaranteed 100% snow coverage in season, thanks to snow blowers built right into the slopes.

SLEEPING IN THE LAURENTIANS

La Maison de Bavière (☎819-322-3528, 866-322-3528; www.maisondebaviere.com; 1470 Chemin de la Rivière, Val-David; r $90-150; 🐾) Done up like a Bavarian lodge, this *gîte* (B&B) has a stunning location on the Rivière du Nord, across the street from the P'tit Train du Nord recreation path. Breakfasts are prepared with hungry cyclists and cross-country skiers in mind.

Auberge de St-Venant (☎819-326-7937; www.st-venant.com; 234 St-Venant, Ste-Agathe-des-Monts; r $110-155; 🐾) This B&B has nine bright, colorful rooms, enthusiastic owners and plenty of nooks and crannies where you can perch in a deck chair and take in the sparkling view of Lac des Sables.

Mont-Tremblant International Hostel (☎819-425-6008; www.hostellingtremblant.com; 2213 Chemin du Village, Mont-Tremblant Village; dm/r $29/74; @🐾) A cozy hostel with clean rooms and great staff, located just outside Mont-Tremblant village.

ACRO-NATURE   OUTDOORS

(☎450-227-2020; www.acronature.com; 231 Rue Bennett, Morin Heights; adult/youth/child $34/25/21; ☉10am-4pm late May-Oct, longer hours in summer) One hour northwest of Montréal, this place features a two- to three-hour obstacle course for adults, where you can sail from tree to tree on two dozen zip lines; there's also a mini-course for kids.

The Eastern Townships

Explore

Rolling wooded hills, clear blue lakes, quaint villages, covered bridges and round barns set the scene for a delightful ramble through the picturesque Eastern Townships (Cantons de l'Est or l'Estrie in French). Once the homeland of Abenaki Indians, this region just north of the Vermont and New Hampshire borders became a refuge for Loyalists fleeing the USA after the revolution of 1776; even today it remains one of Québec's most perfectly bilingual regions.

Spring is the season for tapping, boiling and preparing maple syrup. Summer brings fishing and swimming in the numerous lakes; in fall the foliage dazzles with gorgeous colors, and fresh-pressed apple cider is served in local pubs. Skiing is a major winter activity, with centers at Mont Orford and Sutton. The district also boasts several up-and-coming vineyards.

The Best...

➡ **Sight** Parc de la Gorge de Coaticook (opposite)

➡ **Place to Eat** Le Tire-Bouchon (boxed text, p206)

➡ **Place to Drink** Pilsen (p206)

Top Tip

During the busy summer and fall foliage seasons, travel midweek to avoid the crowds and the two-night weekend minimum imposed by many B&Bs.

Getting There & Away

Bus Transdev Limocar (☎514-842-2281; www.transdev.ca) has services from Montréal's main bus station to Magog ($34, 1¾ hours) and Sherbrooke ($38, 2¼ hours) up to 12 times daily, with less frequent service to Granby ($24, two hours). Veolia Transport (☎877-348-5599; www.veoliatransport.qc.ca) operates daily services between Montréal and Sutton ($21, two hours) and Knowlton ($22, 2¼ hours).

Car Autoroutes 10 Est (East) and 55 Sud (South)

Need to Know

➡ **Area Code** ☎450, 819

➡ **Location** 80km to 165km east and southeast of Montréal

➡ **Tourist Office** (☎450-375-8774, 866-472-6292; www.easterntownships.org; Hwy 10, exit 68, 100 Rue du Tourisme, St-Alphonse-de-Granby; ☉9am-5pm Oct-May, 8am-7pm Jun-Sep)

 **SIGHTS**

PARC DE LA GORGE DE COATICOOK PARK
(☎819-849-2331; www.gorgedecoaticook.qc.ca; 135 Rue Michaud, Coaticook; adult/child $8/5; ☺10am-5pm May–mid-Jun & Sep-Oct, 9am-7pm mid-Jun–Aug, call for winter hours) Straddling a lovely forested gorge just outside the town of Coaticook, this scenic park is famous for having the world's longest suspension bridge. Visitors come year-round for hiking, mountain biking and horseback riding in the summer, and snow-tubing and snowshoeing in winter. You can also camp or stay in one of the park's cabins. The surrounding area boasts some of the Eastern Townships' prettiest scenery, not to mention some wonderful cheese makers (get the cheese-route brochure from the Coaticook tourist office).

NORTH HATLEY VILLAGE
Beautifully sited at the north end of Lac Massawippi, this picturesque village was a popular second home for wealthy US citizens who enjoyed the scenery – and the absence of Prohibition – during the 1920s. Many historic residences have been converted into inns and B&Bs, and there's a choice of antique and craft shops, restaurants, and galleries such as **Galerie Jeannine Blais** (☎819-842-2784; www.galeriejeannineblais.com; 102 Rue Main), devoted entirely to art naïf. In summer English-language dramas, concerts and comedy acts play at **Piggery Theatre** (☎819-842-2431; www.piggery.com; 215 Chemin Simard). Aside from this, the most popular activities are swimming, boating and taking in the natural beauty along the lakeshore.

PARC NATIONAL DU MONT-ORFORD PARK
(☎819-843-9855; www.sepaq.com/pq/mor; 3321 Chemin du Parc, Canton d'Orford; adult/child $5.50/2.50; ☺year-round, call for hours) Just outside the town of Magog, Mont Orford (792m) dominates the lush Parc National du Mont-Orford. In winter, the park is a cross-country and downhill skiing center, with summer bringing hiking (on 80km of trails), camping, lake swimming and canoe/kayak rental.

ORFORD ARTS CENTRE ARTS CENTRE
(www.arts-orford.org) Each summer this renowned music academy, dating back to 1951, hosts the **Orford Festival**, a celebration of music and art that features over 60 concerts by international musicians, including performances by guest artists as well as the academy's own advanced students.

ABBAYE ST-BENOÎT-DU-LAC MONASTERY
(☎819-843-4080; www.st-benoit-du-lac.com; ☺church 5am-8:30pm, gift shop 9-10:45am & 11:45am-4:30pm Mon-Sat year-round, 12:15-4:30pm Sun late Jun–mid-Oct) Famous throughout Québec, this lovely century-old monastery sits on the western shores of Lac Memphrémagog, the largest lake in the Eastern Townships. People descend on the abbey's shop to buy the monks' homemade cider, cheeses, jams, sweets, jellies and chocolate-covered blueberries. Visitors can also attend services and join the monks in Gregorian chanting at 7:30am, 11am and 5pm. Overnight accommodation ($60 per person, including three meals) is available for men at the monastery and for women next door at the **Hôtellerie des Dames** (☎819-843-2340; www.st-benoit-du-lac.com/villa/villa.html).

CHARTING YOUR COURSE THROUGH THE TOWNSHIPS

There are a number of interesting and well signposted driving and cycling routes through the Eastern Townships.

The **Chemin des Cantons** (www.chemindescantons.qc.ca) is a 415km circuit that takes in most of the Townships' prettiest villages and scenery. Coming from Montréal, pick up the route in Granby, Knowlton or Sutton, then simply follow the signs as far as you like.

The **Route des Vins** (www.laroutedesvins.ca) threads its way past 18 wineries on a 120km ramble through the rolling country between Granby and the Vermont border. The route is well signposted from exits 48, 68 and 90 off Hwy 10. Variants of the route focus on gastronomy, outdoor activities and the arts; see the website for details.

For 365km of local **cycling routes** (www.easterntownships.org/cycling), visit the Eastern Townships tourism website, or pick up its excellent printed map describing over a dozen cycling itineraries.

SUTTON VILLAGE

One of southern Québec's most attractive villages, Sutton is popular with artsy types and skiers, who come to appreciate the scenic beauty of the surrounding landscape, dominated by the northern Green Mountains. The downtown strip is filled with cafes, restaurants, inns and B&Bs, along with a very helpful tourist office. Family-operated **Mont Sutton** (☏450-538-2545; www.montsutton.com), the ski area 5km east of town, offers 60 downhill runs for all abilities and is especially well known for its glade skiing.

LAC BROME VILLAGE

South of Autoroute 10, on Hwy 243, is the township of Lac Brome, made up of seven former English Loyalist villages. The main village of Knowlton is one of the most interesting and picturesque: the main street is lined with restored Victorian buildings, including many craft and gift shops. A favorite meal in this area is Lac Brome duck, which shows up frequently on the better menus and is celebrated with the town's annual **Duck Festival** in fall.

FRELIGHSBURG VILLAGE

A few miles from the Vermont border, this village makes a pleasant stop along the Eastern Townships Route des Vins (Wine Route). A cluster of stone and wood homes straddles the banks of the brook that runs through town, and there are a few eateries specializing in local smoked fish and maple products; if you have a sweet tooth, don't miss the famous maple tarts at the old general store-cafe in the center of town.

GRANBY ZOO ZOO

(☏450-372-9113, 877-472-6299; www.zoodegranby.com; 525 Rue St-Hubert, Granby; adult/child $34.50/22.50; ⊙10am-5pm late May-late Jun, 10am-7pm late Jun–Aug, 10am-5pm Sat & Sun Sep & Oct) This popular zoo features 1000-plus animals, including reptiles, gorillas and kangaroos. Don't miss the Hippopotamus Pool, where you can watch hippos lumber from the ground before they swim past viewing windows.

SHERBROOKE CITY

Sherbrooke is the Eastern Townships' commercial center, with a wide selection of restaurants and a pleasant central core lying between two rivers. The downtown area is an good place to wander, with 11 large outdoor wall murals (pick up a map at the tourist office). The 18km walking and cycling path along the Magog River, known as **Réseau Riverain**, also makes for an agreeable stroll, starting at Blanchard Park west of downtown. The city's small but beautifully conceived **Musée des Beaux-Arts** (☏819-821-2115; www.mbas.qc.ca; 241 Rue Dufferin; adult/child $7.50/5; ⊙noon-5pm Tue-Sun) has works by Québécois and Canadian artists.

EATING & DRINKING

PILSEN PUB $$

(www.pilsen.ca; 55 Rue Main, North Hatley; mains $12-35; ⊙restaurant 11:30am-9pm, pub 11:30am-midnight) The liveliest restaurant in North Hatley is famous for its salmon, both grilled and smoked, along with upmarket pub fare

---

ICE WINE

Ice wine was discovered in Germany by accident, when growers found that pressing wine grapes after they froze on the vine left a sweet, highly concentrated juice. Ice wine results when this juice is left on the vine to ferment, creating one of the most coveted dessert wines on the market; it's so expensive because of the amount of grapes that need to be pressed for enough juice to be extracted. If you're following the Eastern Townships Route des Vins, you'll come across many local varieties. In Dunham, **Vignoble l'Orpailleur** (☏450-295-2763; www.orpailleur.ca; 1086 Rte 202, Dunham; ⊙9am-5pm May-Dec, 10am-5pm Jan-Apr) is arguably the province's best-known wine producer. It has a terrific little display on the history of alcohol in Québec, as well as captions in the vineyards explaining the grape varieties and how they grow. Tours of the vineyards ($7 to $12 including tasting) are offered three times daily from June through October. The on-site restaurant, **Le Tire-Bouchon** (☏450-295-3335; www.tire-bouchon-orpailleur.ca; mains $18-24; ⊙11:30am-4pm late Jun-early Oct), serves delicious high-end bistro fare, with seating on a pleasant outdoor terrace.

SLEEPING IN THE EASTERN TOWNSHIPS

Manoir Hovey (☑819-842-2421, 800-661-2421; www.manoirhovey.com; 575 Chemin Hovey, North Hatley; d from $390; 🛜🐕) This world-class resort offers handsomely set rooms in a picturesque lakeside setting. You'll find expansive gardens, a heated pool, an ice rink (in winter) and numerous outdoor activities, including windsurfing, lake cruises and golfing. The award-winning restaurant is among the best in the Eastern Townships, with three-course meals featuring refined Québécois fare.

Le Bocage (☑819-835-5653; www.lebocage.qc.ca; 200 Chemin de Moe's River, Compton; r $110, ste $185-240; 🛜🐕) From the welcome to the antiques, this Victorian gem of a B&B in the countryside between Coaticook and Sherbrooke is hard to fault. A multi-course meal (three/four/five/six courses $41/46/53/64) is served nightly and can feature dishes like guinea fowl stuffed with mushrooms, wild boar, red deer medallions or other wild game. Reservations essential.

Auberge du Centre d'Arts Orford (☑819-843-3981, 800-567-6155; www.arts-orford .org/auberge; 3165 Chemin du Parc, Orford; r $68; ✱🛜) This no-frills lodging offers 89 rooms without TV or telephone, on 222 acres at the edge of Parc National du Mont-Orford. It's affiliated with the Orford Arts Centre (p205), which means that rooms are unavailable during the summer music festival. However, come fall, winter or spring, it makes a lovely retreat where you can enjoy trails and mountain scenery right outside your door. A two-night minimum stay is required

such as duck drumsticks with honey and lemon, mussels with French fries, or its famous duo of sausages (duck-blueberry and wild boar-apricot) served with sauerkraut. Steaks, burgers, fish and pasta round out the menu. There are two nice terraces – one facing the river, another facing the lake – plus a cozy fireplace in the pub downstairs for those frigid winter nights.

LE CAFETIER
CAFE $

(9 Rue Principale N, Sutton; mains $7-13; ☺7am-7pm; 🛜) This bustling, cheery cafe at the heart of downtown Sutton is a true community hub. Locals flock here for coffee, croissants, smoothies, homemade muesli and other breakfast treats in the morning, then return again in the afternoon for big salads, vegetarian chili, panini and *croque monsieurs*, or glasses of beer and wine. Grab one of the comfy tables, or sit at the raised counter in the center of the restaurant. Free wi-fi, decks of playing cards and toys for the kids encourage people of all ages to linger.

LES SUCRERIES DE L'ÉRABLE
BAKERY, CAFE $

(www.lessucreriesdelerable.com; 16 Rue Principale, Frelighsburg; mains $8-12; ☺9am-5pm Thu-Mon) Best known for its scrumptious maple pies, this bakery in an attractive old brick-walled general store does double duty as a simple restaurant, serving breakfast and lunch five days a week. Breakfast treats include waffles with blueberries, bananas,

crème fraîche and maple sugar, while lunch revolves around salads and sandwiches; try a bagel topped with local maple-smoked salmon, accompanied by a glass of apple cider made right here in town. Save room for fresh maple ice cream or – of course – maple pie. In summer, it's delightful to sit on the outdoor deck near the river out back.

LE RELAIS
QUÉBÉCOIS $$

(www.aubergeknowlton.ca/relais; 286 Chemin Knowlton, Knowlton; mains $11-26; ☺11am-3pm & 4:30-10pm Mon-Fri, 8am-10pm Sat) Set in a landmark 1849 inn, this place features juicy Lac Brome duck served many ways, such as duck ravioli in mushroom sauce, duck confit in orange sauce and duck livers with blackened butter. There are many other options, including pork tenderloin with calvados, veal piccata and garlic scampi, along with burgers, salads, soups and pasta. There's terrace seating in summer.

LION D'OR
PUB

(www.lionlennoxville.com; 2 Rue College, Lennoxville) Québec's first microbrewery, the Golden Lion operates a lively pub with nightly meal specials in the college town of Lennoxville. Thanks to a large population of students from Bishop's, the local English university, this is one of those rare places in rural Québec where you're still more likely to be greeted in English than in French. For tours of the brewery, call ahead.

🛏 Sleeping

Montréal's accommodation scene is blessed with a tremendous variety of rooms and styles. Though rates aren't particularly cheap, they are reasonable by international standards – or even compared with Canadian cities such as Toronto or Vancouver. French- and Victorian-style inns and independent hotels cater to a variety of budgets.

Hotels

The reopening in 2012 of the Ritz-Carlton Montréal underlined the city's love of luxury hotels, but they have a surprising number of rooms that fall into the midrange category. This is true even if you book at the last minute but especially in low season. Keep an eye out for cut-rate weekend and internet specials.

Small Hotels & B&Bs

Small, European-style hotels are a Montréal specialty. Located downtown and in the Quartier Latin, they occupy Victorian-era homes that are plain and functional or comfy and charming. Prices are graded by facilities (eg with sink, toilet and/or full bathroom), but note that not all places have air-con.

B&Bs are a wonderful alternative. Many of them are set in attractive, 19th-century stone houses close to the Plateau's bar-and-restaurant strips of Blvd St-Laurent and Rue St-Denis, or near Rue Ste-Catherine Est in the Village. The many B&Bs offer heaps of character – the precious commodity that can make all the difference – and their owners are often invaluable sources of travel advice. There are many comfortable but bland chain hotels in town, which may be useful in peak season, when the B&Bs and guesthouses are booked solid.

Budget Sleeps

Montréal has an abundance of good budget accommodations. Apart from the usual dorm beds, hostels may offer basic single and double rooms – though these are often booked out months in advance. In addition, the universities throw open their residence halls to nonstudents in summer and prices are competitive.

Planning in advance is key to finding accommodations during big events. The summertime festival season, from late June to the end of August, is the peak period, and conventions can crimp availability in late summer.

Lonely Planet's Top Choices

Ritz-Carlton Montréal
(p213) Newly renovated with a $200 million overhaul, the Ritz sparkles with elegant decor and detailed service.

Hôtel Le St-James (p210) Refined opulence in a 19th-century building in Old Montreal.

La Maison Pierre du Calvet (p210) The baroque rooms in this centuries-old gem are absolutely over the top.

Hôtel Nelligan (p210) With one of the best rooftop patios in the city, the Nelligan wins with its old-world setting and great staff.

University Bed & Breakfast Apartments (p213) These tidy rooms in the heart of the city are great value.

Best by Budget

$
Le Jazz Hostel St-Denis (p217)
Hostel Montréal Central (p218)
HI Auberge de Montréal (p216)
HI Montréal St-Antoine (p216)

$$
Les Bons Matins (p214)
Armor Manoir Sherbrooke (p215)
Les Bons Matins (p214)
Zero 1 (p216)

$$$
Ritz-Carlton Montréal (p213)
Hôtel Le St-James (p210)
Hôtel Nelligan (p210)
La Maison Pierre du Calvet (p210)
Fairmont Le Reine Elizabeth (p213)

Best B&Bs
Gingerbread Manor B&B (p219)
Bob & Mariko's Bed & Breakfast (p219)
Alexandre Logan (p217)
Aux Portes de la Nuit (p219)
Les Bons Matins (p214)

Best Heritage Stays
La Maison Pierre du Calvet (p210)
Auberge du Vieux-Port (p212)
Alexandre Logan (p217)
Hôtel Nelligan (p210)

Best Funky Stays
Le Petit Hôtel (p211)
Au Piano Blanc (p220)
Zero 1 (p216)
Au Gît'ann (p218)

NEED TO KNOW

Price Range
In our listings we've used the following price codes to represent the cost of a double room in high season:

$	under $80
$$	$80 to $180
$$$	over $180

Room Rates
In Montréal, the average room rate is around $150, with some seasonal fluctuations (in January to March, rates fall by about 30%). Prices listed in this book are for high-season travel (June to September) and do not include taxes, which add another 17% or so (5% GST, 9.5% provincial sales tax plus a 'hospitality tax' of 3.5%).
Note that hotels charge a premium during week of the Grand Prix (late May and early June). Check websites for details.

Discounts
Rack rates are quoted here, but prices can vary drastically. Most business and high-end hotels offer discounts, often significant ones, for reservations made in advance via phone or internet.

Reservations
Book your hotel well in advance. For more accommodation reviews and recommendations, check out our online booking service at hotels.lonelyplanet.com.

Tourisme Montréal
(☑888-234-5504; www.tourisme-montreal.org/Accommodations)

Hostelworld (www.hostelworld.com)

SLEEPING

Where to Stay

Neighborhood	For	Against
Old Montréal	ultraconvenient for many sights, old-world charm, access to Old Port	crowded with tourists at peak times, few inexpensive rooms, hard to find parking
Downtown	convenient for public transport and sights throughout the city	can be congested, with few inexpensive options compared with other districts
Quartier Latin & the Village	semiresidential area with bohemian charm, restaurants and cafes	somewhat remote from central sights; has been the center of student protests
Plateau Mont-Royal	home to the city's most charming B&Bs; atmospheric neighborhood with many parks	removed from central Downtown and Old Montréal; few key sights

SLEEPING OLD MONTRÉAL

🛏 Old Montréal

Old Montréal has the city's most atmospheric – and highest priced – hotel rooms. Over the last decade or so, many of the area's old buildings have been converted into impeccable boutique hotels with unique ambience and careful, confident service. The proliferation of such distinctive hotels has also inflated the area's B&B and inn rates.

TOP CHOICE HÔTEL LE ST-JAMES   BOUTIQUE HOTEL $$$
Map p280 (☑514-841-3111; www.hotellest
james.com; 355 Rue St-Jacques; d from $400;
P✳@; MSquare-Victoria) Housed in the former Merchants Bank, the Hôtel Le St-James is a world-class establishment. Lavish guest rooms are decorated in a heritage style complete with antique furnishings and oil paintings adorning the walls – covering five continents throughout the hotel. There's a candlelit spa, a library and high-tea service. The concierge and staff are particularly kind and helpful. The ornately decorated restaurant has lovely ambience but surprisingly unimpressive dishes – chefs tend to go a bit heavy on the complexity.

TOP CHOICE LA MAISON
PIERRE DU CALVET   HISTORIC INN $$$
Map p280 (☑514-282-1725, 866-544-1725; www
.pierreducalvet.ca; 405 Rue Bonsecours; r from
$195; P✳; MChamp-de-Mars) The heritage hotel experience par excellence! This historic landmark in Old Montréal was built right into the city defense walls in 1725, and staying here is like stepping back in time: massive stone fireplaces with original carvings, gilded picture frames and four-poster beds surrounded by carefully preserved antiques. Benjamin Franklin stayed here in 1775 while trying to garner support for the American Revolution. The salon, library, wine cellar and dining rooms all drip the moneyed elegance of the period. There's also a Victorian greenhouse and pretty vine-covered terrace.

TOP CHOICE HÔTEL NELLIGAN   BOUTIQUE HOTEL $$$
Map p280 (☑514-788-2040; www.hotelnelligan
.com; 106 Rue St-Paul Ouest; d from $229;
P✳@🛜; MPlace-d'Armes) Housed in two restored buildings and named in honor of Québec's most famous and tragic poet, Émile Nelligan (see the boxed text, p63), m woods, original details (like exposed brick or stone in some rooms) and luxurious fittings (down comforters, wi-fi, high-quality bath products, Jacuzzis in some rooms).

Verses, a plush bar and restaurant, is next door, with a magnificent roof patio, Terrasse Nelligan.

HÔTEL GAULT BOUTIQUE HOTEL **$$$**

Map p280 (☎514-904-1616; www.hotelgault.com; 449 Rue Ste-Hélène; d from $289; P ❄ @; M Square-Victoria) The Gault delivers both beauty and comfort in its 30 spacious rooms. The lovely heritage building figures in some rooms, with exposed-stone walls, though for the most part the Gault boasts a fashion-forward, contemporary design. Rooms have extremely comfortable beds, ergonomic chairs, high ceilings, huge windows and spotless bathrooms (though most lack bathtubs) with heated tile floors.

HÔTEL ST-PAUL BOUTIQUE HOTEL **$$$**

Map p280 (☎514-380-2222; www.hotelstpaul.com; 355 Rue McGill; d from $229; P ❄ @; M Square-Victoria) The lobby here greets you with a fireplace flickering inside a wall of glowing alabaster – which is a fine introduction to this swanky beaux-arts hotel. The 120 rooms and 24 suites feature dark-wood furnishings, nice lighting, hardwood floors and large windows (in most but not all rooms). Excellent amenities also are available – from free high-speed internet and CD players to a fitness center and a high-end restaurant that becomes a popular nightspot on weekends (take note, light sleepers near the bar).

INTERCONTINENTAL MONTRÉAL LUXURY HOTEL **$$**

Map p280 (☎514-987-9900; www.montreal.intercontinental.com; 360 Rue St-Antoine Ouest; d from $168; P ❄ @; M Square-Victoria) This enormous InterContinental has a unique location between a new high-rise and a restored annex of the 19th-century Nordheimer building. Photography and paintings by local artists adorn all 357 rooms; the turret suites are particularly attractive, with superb views to Mont-Royal. There are extensive facilities, including a piano bar and restaurant.

LE PETIT HÔTEL BOUTIQUE HOTEL **$$$**

Map p280 (☎514-940-0360; www.petithotelmontreal.com; 168 Rue St-Paul Ouest; d incl breakfast from $219; P ❄ @ ᯤ; M Place-d'Armes) This small, 24-room boutique hotel dispenses with the inflated talk of 'superiors' and 'deluxes'. Instead, Le Petit Hôtel uses small, medium, large and extra large to describe its four room classes – which are indeed identical save for the size. Like the Hôtel Place-d'Armes (which is owned by the same group), rooms here boast a sleek, contemporary design (polished wood floors, atmospheric lighting, dark woods and fluffy white duvets), while showcasing the old stone walls in some rooms. You'll also find iPod docking stations, wi-fi access and dashes of color – orange! – that give a creative tint to the overall look. There's a small spa here and an enticing little cafe, with down-tempo beats, on the ground floor.

LONGER-TERM RENTALS

The universities offer good deals from May to August, though you should not expect much more than dormitory amenities.

For a taste of life in the 'real' Montréal, away from the hotel circuit, seek out the clean, trim **Studios du Quartier Latin** (Map p290; ☎514-845-0916; www.studiosquartierlatin.com; 2022 Rue St-Hubert; apt per day/week/month from $80/420/960; ❄ ᯤ; M Berri-UQAM) in the Quartier Latin, the Plateau and Little Italy. All studios generally have fully equipped kitchenette, TV, private telephone and bed linen, plus wireless access.

The modern high-rise **Trylon Apartments** (Map p288; ☎514-843-3971, 877-843-3971; www.trylon.qc.ca; 3463 Rue Ste-Famille; apt per day/week/month from $95/525/1500; P ❄ ᯤ; M Place-des-Arts) are a plush alternative to top-end hotels at a fraction of the price. The small studios (36 sq meter) and one-bedroom apartments (51 sq meter) all have contemporary furnishings with kitchenettes, and guests can enjoy the indoor swimming pool, sauna, exercise room and rooftop terrace. Some rooms have balconies.

AUBERGE BONSECOURS INN $$$
Map p280 (📞514-396-2662; www.aubergebon
secours.com; 353 Rue St-Paul Est; s/d from $180;
P ❄ 🛜; M Champ-de-Mars) The unusual ambi-
ence of these renovated stables lends this
secluded hotel particular appeal. All seven
rooms have bare brick walls, designer light-
ing and floral linen piled high, but each
room is cut differently. The front-facing
room with the pine floors and sloping ceil-
ing is especially popular, and all quarters
are set around an inner courtyard, remain-
ing blissfully quiet at night.

HÔTEL PLACE-D'ARMES BOUTIQUE HOTEL $$$
Map p280 (📞514-842-1887; www.hotelplaced
armes.com; 55 Rue St-Jacques Ouest; d from
$189; P ❄ @ 🛜; M Place-d'Armes) Spread
among three regal buildings on the edge of
Place d'Armes, this luxury hotel has earned
many admirers for its stylish rooms, excellent service and historic location in Old
Montréal. Rooms are set with first-class
fittings – antique moldings, brick or stone
walls, black granite and white marble in
the bathrooms, and an entertainment system in every room. Even small quarters feel
spacious thanks to the views of Mont-Royal
or the Basilique Notre-Dame. There's a full-
service spa, fitness center, restaurant and
bar, but the crowning touch is the splendid rooftop patio, Terrasse Place d'Armes,
which on a summertime night is a magnet
for the beautiful crowd.

AUBERGE DU VIEUX-PORT BOUTIQUE HOTEL $$$
Map p280 (📞514-876-0081; www.aubergedu
vieuxport.com; 97 Rue de la Commune Est; d
from $219; P ❄ 🛜; M Champ-de-Mars) Set in
a stolid 1882 warehouse, the Auberge du
Vieux-Port is a stylish boutique hotel with
exposed brick or stone walls, wooden
beams, wrought-iron beds, high-quality
furnishings (including antiques here and
there) and big windows overlooking the
waterfront. For more space and seclusion
(a kitchen, multiple rooms), you can book
one of its minimalist **lofts** (www.loftsdu
vieuxport.com; $239) in a separate building
round the corner.

**AUBERGE BONAPARTE
INN & RESTAURANT** BOUTIQUE HOTEL $$
Map p280 (📞514-844-1448; www.bonaparte.com;
447 Rue St-François-Xavier; d from $189, ste
$355, all incl breakfast; P ❄ @; M Place-d'Armes)
Wrought-iron beds and Louis Philippe furnishings lend a suitably Napoleonic touch to
this historic 30-room inn, a former judge's
residence built in 1886. The best rooms
are warmly decorated and boast high ceilings, dormer windows and bronze lamps.
Low-end rooms can seem a little dark and
dowdy. Those at the rear overlook a pretty
garden with views of the Basilique Notre-
Dame. Breakfast is served in the fine Bona-
parte Restaurant, which has been done up
in Napoleonic Imperial style. There's also a
pleasant rooftop terrace.

**LES PASSANTS DU
SANS SOUCY B&B** B&B $$
Map p280 (📞514-842-2634; www.lesanssoucy
.com; 171 Rue St-Paul Ouest; d/ste from $165/230;
P ❄ 🛜; M Place-d'Armes) Built in 1723, this
B&B feels more like a classic country inn
straight out of the old country. It's set back
from the road at the rear of a quiet court-
yard in the heart of Old Montréal. Its comfy
rooms are furnished with tasteful antiques
and some have wood-beam ceilings, stone
walls and other original details. The break-
fast room has a stained-glass skylight above
the dining table and the foyer doubles as an
art gallery.

UQAM RESIDENCES APARTMENTS $$
Map p280 (📞514-987-6669; www.residences
-uqam.qc.ca; 303 Blvd René-Lévesque; r from $60;
P @ ❄; M Berri-UQAM) This residence hall at
Université de Québec à Montréal (UQAM)
offers tidy modern studio apartments with
small, fully equipped kitchens in a convenient location not far from the club district
along Blvd St-Laurent. Rooms are available
only during the summer. There's a laundry
and a cafe on-site.

MAISON BRUNET B&B $$
Map p280 (📞514-845-6351; www.maisonbrunet.
ca; 1035 Rue St-Hubert; r from $85; P ❄ 🛜;
M Berri-UQAM) Not far from the Quartier
Latin and the Village, this charming little
guesthouse has a splash of old-fashioned
decor with touches of sugary rococo. Rooms
are spacious with polished-wood floors and
colorful linens, and the congenial owner is
full of local tips.

AUBERGE ALTERNATIVE HOSTEL $
Map p280 (📞514-282-8069; www.auberge-alter
native.qc.ca; 358 Rue St-Pierre; dm $25; ❄ @ 🛜;
M Square-Victoria) This laid-back hostel near
the Old Port has a bohemian vibe with an
inviting cafe/restaurant where you can
mingle with other travelers or enjoy an or

THE B&B CONNECTION

For an overview of the many charming B&Bs across Montréal, visit **B&B Canada** (www.bbcanada.com). It currently has over 110 Montréal B&Bs listed on its network, with photos, room descriptions and reviews.

If you show up in Montréal without a reservation and don't feel like making the rounds, you can always book a place through the city's main tourist office, **Centre Infotouriste** (Map p288; ☑514-873-2015, 877-266-5687; www.tourisme-montreal.org; Sq Dorchester). Keep in mind that it can book you a room only with guesthouses with which it has an affiliation.

ganic breakfast ($5 extra). Guests bunk in trim, colorfully painted dorms that accommodate anywhere from four to 20 people. There's laundry and no curfew.

🛏 Downtown

The city center is the bastion of the business hotel and large, upper-end chains, but there are some interesting independent hotels, B&Bs and budget establishments scattered throughout the area.

TOP CHOICE RITZ-CARLTON MONTRÉAL   LUXURY HOTEL $$$
Map p284 (☑514-842-4212; www.ritzmontreal.com; 1228 Rue Sherbrooke Ouest; d from $425; P❊🛜; MPeel) This classic grande dame of Montréal has been impressing guests ever since Liz Taylor and Richard Burton got married here. For its 2012 centenary, it reopened after a four-year, $200 million renovation, with only half as may rooms as before and a new set of luxury residences. Rooms are ultra-opulent, with classic touches and impeccable service. But you can always splash out in the Royal Suite, the largest in the city, if you don't mind dropping $7000 to $10,000 a night.

TOP CHOICE UNIVERSITY BED & BREAKFAST APARTMENTS   B&B $$
Map p288 (☑514-842-6396; www.universitybedandbreakfast.ca; 623 Rue Prince Arthur Ouest; d with shared bathroom from $80, ste from $135; P🛜; MMcGill) Tucked away on a leafy street near McGill University, this handsome three-story townhouse has abundant charm. Accommodations all vary in size and style, although you'll find wood floors, wrought-iron beds, classy furnishings and exposed brick, while the suites are roomier with modern touches like flat-screen TVs,

kitchenettes and iPod docking stations. Excellent location, too.

FAIRMONT LE REINE ELIZABETH   LUXURY HOTEL $$$
Map p288 (☑514-861-3511; www.fairmont.com/queenelizabeth; 900 Blvd René-Lévesque Ouest; d from $219; P❊@🛜💱; MBonaventure) This is the crème de la crème of Montréal business hotels, with over 1000 tastefully renovated rooms and suites. Its celebrity guest list is longer than a stretch limousine, including Queen Elizabeth, the Dalai Lama and several presidents and prime ministers. The most famous was arguably John Lennon, who wrote the song *Give Peace a Chance* here during his 1969 bed-in – you can stay in the same suite, which contains memorabilia such as the framed seven-inch single.

HILTON MONTRÉAL BONAVENTURE   LUXURY HOTEL $$$
Map p288 (☑514-878-2332; www.hiltonmontreal.com; 900 Rue de La Gauchetière Ouest; d from $254; P❊@🛜💱; MBonaventure) This is your standard business Hilton with deluxe amenities, but the best part is arguably the panoramic view of downtown. All rooms have on-command movies, mahogany furniture, marbled bathrooms and large working areas. The winning highlight is the 1-hectare rooftop garden with a duck pond and heated pool.

LOEW'S HOTEL VOGUE   LUXURY HOTEL $$$
Map p284 (☑514-285-5555; www.loewshotels.com/en/Montreal-Hotel; 1425 Rue de la Montagne; d from $199; P❊🛜; MPeel) This upmarket hotel has managed to blend French-empire style with modern luxury. You'll find flat-screen TVs attached to the oversized marble Jacuzzi bathtubs, an iPod docking station and nicely furnished rooms (though somewhat lacking in individuality). Staff are friendly and efficient, and there's a stylish candlelit restaurant and bar on-site.

HÔTEL LE GERMAIN — BOUTIQUE HOTEL $$$

Map p288 (514-849-2050; www.germainmon treal.com; 2050 Rue Mansfield; d from $210; P ; M Peel) This stylish hotel boasts luxurious rooms with dark wood details (headboard, wood blinds), cream-colored walls, sheer curtains and artful lighting. You'll find all the creature comforts, such as iPod docks and oversized showerheads; the bathrooms have a touch of the eccentric with one big window into the room. (Superior rooms have only a shower.) Service is friendly and professional with the occasional hiccup from time to time. The restaurant receives mixed reviews.

OPUS MONTRÉAL — BOUTIQUE HOTEL $$$

Map p288 (514-380-3899; www.opushotel. com; 10 Rue Sherbrooke Ouest; d/ste from $169/331; P ; M St-Laurent) Set in a minimalist art-nouveau building, this new designer hotel features sleek, ultramodern rooms with all the trappings of luxury. There's plenty of space (rooms are 30 to 50 sq meters), daring color schemes, minimalist bathrooms with rain showers, and atmospheric lighting (which can be a little inadequate at night). The Opus attracts a young, good-looking crowd and its stylish restaurant, Koko (better for drinks than food), becomes a party place on weekend nights. Unless you're a 24-hour party person, be sure to book a room well away from this action. Staff dole out earplugs – a kind but ultimately fruitless gesture.

LE PETIT PRINCE — B&B $$$

Map p284 (514-938-2277; www.montrealbandb. com; 1384 Ave Overdale; d $200-225; @ ; M Lucien-L'Allier) Blessed with four picture-perfect guest rooms, this B&B features handpicked furniture (four-poster beds, sleigh beds, handcrafted bedside tables), wood floors, paintings by local artists and creative but subdued use of color. Two rooms have private balconies. The open-style layout is intriguing, and several rooms have big bathtubs right in the rooms. Breakfast is a full gourmet affair, whipped up in a cool kitchen with fire-engine-red appliances.

SOFITEL — LUXURY HOTEL $$$

Map p288 (514-285-9000; www.sofitel. com; 1155 Rue Sherbrooke Ouest; d from $223; P @ ; M Peel) Yet another solid link in the French luxury chain (and the only Sofitel in Canada), this hotel has stylish, modern rooms and a European feel. Staff hit the right note of sophistication without too much snobbery and the rooms are modern and attractive – featuring either a cool black-and-white color scheme or all-white with blond-wood details. The best rooms are spacious and have separate tub and shower, while the least expensive rooms (the 'superiors') are too small to recommend and have showers only. The usual trappings of luxury are here: fine lobby, excellent French restaurant, fitness center and sauna, and the stylish Le Bar. You can bring your pet.

CHÂTEAU VERSAILLES — HOTEL $$$

Map p284 (514-933-3611, 888-933-8111; www. chateauversaillesmontreal.com; 1659 Rue Sherbrooke Ouest; d/ste from $205/325; P ; M Guy-Concordia) The stately Château Versailles exudes class. Spread among three interconnected townhouses, the best rooms here are elegantly furnished with high-quality fabrics, a light and airy color scheme and handsome decorative details (framed art prints, crown moldings). Less-expensive rooms can be darker and less charmingly furnished. The street in front is a busy one, but traffic noise drops off at night.

CASTEL DUROCHER — APARTMENTS $$$

Map p288 (514-282-1697; www.casteldurocher .com; 3488 Rue Durocher; 1-/2-bedroom $199/249; P @ ; M McGill) This family-run establishment occupies a tall, turreted stone house on a peaceful, tree-lined street near McGill University. Those seeking self-sufficiency will find one- or two-bedroom apartments with kitchen units, homey furnishings and artwork covering the walls (the multitalented Belgian owner is an artist, novelist and chocolate-maker extraordinaire). Discounts for long-term stays.

LES BONS MATINS — B&B $$

Map p284 (514-931-9167; www.bonsmatins .com; 1401 Ave Argyle; d/ste from $119/169; P ; M Lucien L'Allier) Charming and seductive with exposed brick walls and vibrant colors (bed sheets, wall hangings), this classy establishment fills a series of adjoining turn-of-the-century walk-ups. Breakfasts are excellent, with gourmet quiche, homemade waffles and Italian-style espresso.

HÔTEL DU FORT — HOTEL $$

Map p284 (514-938-8333; www.hoteldufort. com; 1390 Rue du Fort; r/ste from $129/169; P ; M Guy-Concordia) This fairly cookie-

GAY STAYS

Any guesthouse located in the Village will be gay-friendly – welcoming gay as well as straight travelers. A few perennial favorites include the following:

➡ **Alexandre Logan** (p217) Splendid 19th-century ambience.
➡ **Atmosphere** (p217) Receives rave reviews from readers.
➡ **Turquoise B&B** (p218) Like stepping into a glossy magazine.
➡ **Alacoque B&B Revolution** (p216) Gorgeous antiques in an 1830s setting.

cutter business hotel has clean, modest rooms done in beige and creams, with carpeting, shiny fabric wallpaper and a few spruce touches like framed botanical prints on the walls. Some also have kitchenettes.

HOTEL PARC SUITES   HOTEL $$

Map p288 (⌖514-985-5656, 800-949-8630; www.parcsuites.com; 3463 Ave du Parc; ste from $169; P✳✿; MPlace-des-Arts) This eight-room all-suites guesthouse is a great place to decamp while exploring Montréal. The accommodations range from small studios to only marginally more expensive one-bedroom suites, with a furnished living/dining area and adjoining kitchenette, and a separate bedroom – all tastefully furnished in a trim, contemporary style. Staff and owner are friendly and helpful and deserve kudos for all the freebies thrown in – wi-fi, parking and long-distance calls to the US and Canada. Mind the steep stairway up to the lobby.

HOTEL MARITIME PLAZA   HOTEL $$

Map p284 (⌖514-932-1411, 800-363-6255; www.hotelmaritime.com, 1155 Rue Guy; r from $99; P✳✿✻; MGuy-Concordia) Inside a magnificently ugly concrete facade, you'll find neat rooms with blue-toned carpeting, striped wallpaper, thick white comforters and trim furnishings (brassy lamps, comfy armchairs). Minuses: overly noisy heating and air-conditioning units, showers that sometimes flood and slow elevators. There is also a bar with pool table.

MANOIR AMBROSE   HOTEL $$

Map p288 (⌖514-288-6922; www.manoirambrose.com; 3422 Rue Stanley; d with/without bathroom from $115/105; ✳✿; MPeel) This hotel consists of two merged Victorian homes in a quiet residential area. Its 22 rooms are comfortably furnished, some with a contemporary minimalist look, and some still with dated floral designs. The economy and standard rooms are cramped, with equally small bathrooms. Upstairs rooms are best (avoid the dank basement quarters). Staff are friendly and the location is decent.

ARMOR MANOIR SHERBROOKE   HOTEL $$

Map p288 (⌖514-845-0915, 800-203-5485; www.armormanoir.com; 157 Rue Sherbrooke Est; d incl breakfast $99-149; ✿; MSherbrooke) This engaging conversion of two fine Victorian houses is replete with atmosphere. Its 30 rooms range from small standards to spacious deluxes. The cheapest rooms have thick carpeting, floral details and en suite showers – but the toilets are outside the room. The best rooms have oversized gilded mirrors, decorative fireplaces and Jacuzzi bathtubs.

HÔTEL CASA BELLA   GUESTHOUSE $$

Map p288 (⌖514-849-2777, 888-453-2777; www.hotelcasabella.com; 264 Rue Sherbrooke Ouest; s/d from $90/99, without bathroom from $75/85, all incl breakfast; P✳✿; MPlace-des-Arts) This intimate greystone along busy Rue Sherbrooke offers humble, simply furnished rooms with frilly touches. Rooms in front are bright but open onto a noisy street. Cleanliness is an issue in some rooms, so have a look before committing. Continental breakfast is served in your room. There's also free wi-fi.

HÔTEL ABRI DU VOYAGEUR   HOTEL $$

Map p288 (⌖514-849-2922; www.abri-voyageur.ca; 9 Rue Ste-Catherine Ouest; r with/without bathroom $89/64; P✳✿; MSt-Laurent) It's on a seedy stretch of Rue Ste-Catherine but if you're not turned off by the nearby sex clubs (no pun intended), you can enjoy clean, cozy rooms with exposed brick walls, wood floors and comfortable furnishings. Some rooms are spacious with tiny kitchenettes, while others could use more natural light. Befitting the neighborhood, there's a funky smell in the stairwell. Free wi-fi.

SLEEPING DOWNTOWN

ZERO 1   HOTEL $$

Map p288 (☑514-871-9696; http://zero1-mtl. com; 1 Blvd René Lévesque Est; d from $139; ⓟ❋@☎; ⓜSt-Laurent) This jazzy updated hotel has contemporary rooms, albeit small, in categories such as Pop and Hip. There's a lounge-like vibe throughout the place, and although it lacks a restaurant, it's steps away from the good eats in Chinatown. Avoid the lower floors due to street noise; the area isn't the best in town and the red-light district isn't far away.

ALACOQUE B&B REVOLUTION   B&B $$

Map p288 (☑514-842-0938; www.bbrevolution. com; 2091 Rue St-Urbain; s/d without bathroom $75/85; ⓟ❋☎; ⓜPlace-des-Arts) This little place offers good rates for its simply furnished rooms. Exposed brick walls and homey touches create a warm ambience, but some beds and furnishings need a refresh. Guests have access to the whole house (kitchen, terrace, garden, dining room, laundry). There's free parking and free wi-fi.

Y DES FEMMES   HOTEL $$

Map p284 (☑514-866-9942; www.ydesfemmes mtl.org; 1355 Blvd René-Lévesque Ouest; s/d $75/85, without bathroom $60/70; ☎; ⓜLucien-L'Allier) The YWCA's hotel welcomes both sexes to rooms that are basic but clean – and decent value for the neighborhood. Each floor has a kitchen with refrigerator and microwave; shared bathrooms are decent for women but not in great shape for men. Unfortunately, the Y no longer lives up to its name – there's no fitness center or pool. The money goes to Y programs.

MCGILL UNIVERSITY RESIDENCE HALLS   HOSTEL $

Map p288 (☑514-398-5200; www.mcgill.ca/ students/housing/summer; s from $30, d $65-110, ste from $149; ☺mid-May–mid-Aug; ⓟ@; ⓜMcGill) Over summer McGill opens its student residence halls to travelers seeking budget accommodations. Lodging is in one of four different buildings, including the uninspiring 1960s New Residence Hall, the greystone Bishop Mountain Hall and the more inviting Solin Hall, near the Atwater market and the Lachine Canal. The latter offers studios and two-, three- and four-bedroom apartments (with no air-conditioning), rented either per room with shared facilities, or for the entire apartment. The other halls are basic student dorms, with a single bed and shared everything else (bathroom, kitchenettes). Bedding is usually not provided. Guests (sometimes for an extra fee) can use the university cafeteria, pool, gym and tennis courts.

HI AUBERGE DE MONTRÉAL   HOSTEL $

Map p284 (☑514-843-3317, 866-843-3317; www .hihostels.com; 1030 Rue Mackay; dm/r from $36/90; ❋@☎; ⓜLucien-L'Allier) This large, well-equipped HI hostel has bright, maintained dorm rooms (all with air-con) with four to 10 beds, and a handful of private en suite rooms. Rooms are small and, depending on your bunkmates, can feel cramped. Energetic staff organize daily activities and outings (pub crawls, bike tours, day trips), plus there's a lively cafe on the ground floor. There's free wi-fi and no curfew. Reservations are strongly recommended in summer.

LE GÎTE DU PLATEAU MONT-ROYAL   HOSTEL $

Map p288 (☑514-284-1276, 877-350-4483; www .hostelmontreal.com; 185 Rue Sherbrooke Est; dm/d without bathroom from $27/60; @; ⓜSherbrooke) This popular youth hostel lies at the southern end of the Plateau (and the western edge of downtown). All the expected hostel features are here (kitchen access, laundry room, lounge), though rooms and facilities are basic. The staff are friendly. There's also bike rental.

HI MONTRÉAL ST-ANTOINE   HOSTEL $

Map p284 (☑514-908-3281, 855-908-3281; www .hihostels.ca/quebec/953/HI-Montreal_St-Anto ine.hostel; 1320 Rue St-Antoine Ouest; dm/r from $36/90; ❋@☎; ⓜLucien-L'Allier) Steps away from the Bell Centre and the home of the Canadiens de Montréal, this spiffy new hostel has simple dorms with metal bunks and no-frills private rooms. Facilities include a laundry room and kitchen, and there are free activities ranging from ice-skating to photography tours of the city.

⌷ Quartier Latin & the Village

You'll find a good mix of options in the nightlife-charged areas of the Quartier Latin and the Village. Delightful, superb-quality B&Bs dominate the choices in this part of town. This is also a good place to base yourself, with excellent

metro connections and walking access to both downtown and Old Montréal – plus the Plateau is just up the hill.

ALEXANDRE LOGAN
B&B $$

Map p290 (☑514-598-0555, 866-895-0555; www.alexandrelogan.com; 1631 Rue Alexandre-de-Sève; s/d from $100/110; P☀@; MBeaudry) The friendly host Alain has an eye for details like original plaster moldings, ornate woodwork and art-deco glass patterns at this award-winning B&B. This splendidly renovated home dates from 1870 and has hardwood floors, high-quality mattresses (some rooms have king-size beds) and big windows, making the rooms bright and cheerful. Common spaces are also beautifully designed, from the breakfast room to the outdoor terrace complete with tiki torches.

ATMOSPHERE
B&B $$

Map p290 (☑514-510-7976; www.atmospherebb.com; 1933 Rue Panet; d with/without bathroom from $180/125; ☎; MBeaudry) Set in a beautifully restored 1875 home, Atmosphere lives up to its name. Rooms here feature exposed brick, polished wood floors, artful lighting and handsome design flourishes. Rooms and common areas are kept meticulously clean, and the friendly host receives rave reviews for the three-course breakfasts (dessert included) he prepares. Our only gripe is that the en suite room (the Sensation) has no door to the bathroom.

AUBERGE LE JARDIN D'ANTOINE
B&B $$

Map p290 (☑514-843-4506; www.hotel-jardin-antoine.qc.ca; 2024 Rue St-Denis; d/ste from $91/137; ☀☎@; MBerri-UQAM) Romantic Victorian decor is the chief selling point at this welcoming four-story hotel, handily located in the thick of the Quartier Latin action. Some rooms sport a classic old-world look with wrought-iron bedsteads, with the florals a bit heavy-handed at times. There's free wi-fi.

LA LOGGIA
B&B $$

Map p290 (☑514-524-2493; www.laloggia.ca; 1637 Rue Amherst; s/d from $125/145, without bathroom from $90/110; P☀☎; MBeaudry) This beautifully maintained B&B has a handful of charming rooms, each with artwork on the walls and attractive furnishings. The best rooms are light and airy with Persian carpets, antique armoires and private bathrooms. Lower-level rooms are a little dark, but still clean. Good firm mattresses and soundproof windows ensure a decent night's rest. The hosts offer a warm and friendly welcome. Buffet-style breakfasts are simple but adequate.

HÔTEL GOUVERNEUR PLACE DUPUIS
HOTEL $$

Map p290 (☑514-842-4881, 888-910-1111; www.gouverneur.com; 1415 Rue St-Hubert; d from $145; P☀☎; MBerri-UQAM) Set in a modern high-rise place in the Village, this clean, well-maintained business hotel offers comfortable, fairly spacious rooms (though bathrooms tend to be small), some with fine views. Friendly staff make up for the somewhat generic feel overall. It's attached to the metro and the Village's Place Dupuis.

LE JAZZ HOSTEL ST-DENIS
HOSTEL $

Map p290 (☑514-448-4848; www.jazzhostels.com; 329 Rue Ontario Est; dm $25, r $65-100; ☎; MBerri-UQAM) This small hostel, which opened in 2008, enjoys a good location near the nightlife action along Rue St-Denis. The amenities are decent (backyard with BBQ, in-room wi fi, guest kitchen), though sometimes the place could use a firmer hand in the cleaning department. The top-floor private room is spacious and boasts its own Jacuzzi, one of the best deals in the city.

LE RELAIS LYONNAIS
GUESTHOUSE $$

Map p290 (☑514-448-2999; www.lerelaislyonnais.com; 1595 Rue St-Denis; r/ste from $145/225; MBerri-UQAM) The small, seven-room Le Relais Lyonnais provides excellent value for money. Exposed brick and dark woods give the rooms an elegant but masculine look, while white goose-down duvets provide a soft complement. High ceilings, oversized windows, rain showers and DVD players add to the allure. Light sleepers beware: front-facing rooms get lots of street noise from lively Rue St-Denis. Suites face the rear and are quieter.

HÔTEL LE ROBERVAL
HOTEL $$

Map p290 (☑514-286-5215; www.leroberval.com; 505 Blvd René-Lévesque Est; d from $92; P☀@☎; MBerri-UQAM) On the southern edge of the Quartier Latin, no-frills Roberval has dated doubles with either carpeting or tile floors and the usual features (coffeemaker, satellite TV, mini-refrigerator). There's also a work desk and free internet access. The suites add a bit more space and also come with kitchenettes.

HOSTEL MONTRÉAL CENTRAL HOSTEL $
Map p290 (🖉514-843-5739; http://hostelmon
trealcentral.com; 1586 Rue St-Hubert; dm/r from
$25/43; 🖳; MBerri-UQAM) An award-winning
hostel, it's just steps away from the local
bus depot and metro station. Four-, six-
and eight-bunk dorms are basic but serv-
iceable, and private rooms are no-frills
but they're a great price for the location.
Deals include getting four-bed dorms for
the price of three beds. Bicycle rental is
also available.

MONTRÉAL ESPACE CONFORT HOTEL $$
Map p290 (🖉514-849-0505; www.montreales
paceconfort.com; 2050 Rue St-Denis; s/d from
$90/120; ✳@🖳; MBerri-UQAM) Back in the
1990s this stretch used to be the stomping
ground for the transient and the confused,
and this address was a notorious flophouse.
Things have changed dramatically since
then, with this new hotel being a shiny ex-
ample of urban renewal in action. Rooms
boast trim Ikea-style furnishings, with
desk and a kitchenette, but are quite small.
Street-facing rooms can be noisy (especially
on weekends). Gay-friendly.

HÔTEL LORD BERRI HOTEL $$
Map p290 (🖉514-845-9236, 888-363-0363;
www.lordberri.com; 1199 Rue Berri; d from $114;
P✳🖳; MBerri-UQAM) This modern high-
rise is a heartbeat away from the nightlife
of Rue St-Denis. Furnishings are tasteful
and contemporary in its 154 rooms, with
big comfy beds and in-room movies. It lies
along busy Rue Berri. Wi-fi costs extra.

AU GÎT'ANN B&B $$
Map p290 (🖉514-523-4494; www.augitann.com;
1806 Rue St-Christophe; d with shared/private
bathroom from $100/180; P✳@🖳; MBerri-
UQAM) This small B&B has just three rooms,
all painted in deep dreamlike hues (laven-
der, canary yellow), with abstract artwork
on the walls and comfortable furnishings.
The best room has a private bathroom and
a balcony. The doting host is extremely
friendly.

HÔTEL ST-DENIS HOTEL $$
Map p290 (🖉514-249-4526; www.hotel-st-denis
.com; 1254 Rue St-Denis; d from $95; P✳🖳;
MBerri-UQAM) In a good location in the Village, this hotel receives positive reviews
for its clean, well-maintained rooms with
wood floors, trim modern furnishings and
comfortable beds. Sizes vary from cramped

to rather spacious – avoid the budget rooms
if you need space. The King Suite has a
Jacuzzi tub tiled right into the living area.
Free wi-fi.

HÔTEL DE PARIS HOTEL $$
Map p290 (🖉514-522-6861, 800-567-7217; www
.hotel-montreal.com; 901 Rue Sherbrooke Est;
dm $16-27, d $90-170, all incl breakfast; P✳🖳;
MSherbrooke) Inside a turreted Victorian
mansion, you'll find a range of rooms and
suites. The most picturesque have balco-
nies overlooking Rue Sherbrooke (though
noise can be a factor). Budget rooms are
small and rather worn, though some travel-
ers find them fair for the price. In the an-
nex across the street are a mix of 'executive
rooms', including several with wood floors,
tall ceilings and wood details. Self-serve
continental breakfast.

TURQUOISE B&B B&B $$
Map p290 (🖉514-523-9943, 877-707-1576; www
.turquoisebb.com; 1576 Rue Alexandre-de-Sève;
s/d without bathroom from $70/80; P🖳;
MBeaudry) The decor in this plush two-
story greystone looks like something out of
Better Homes & Gardens. Each of the five
bedrooms has a queen-size bed, original
moldings, shiny wood floors and carved
faux gables (yes, indoors). Breakfast is
served in the large backyard. Bathrooms
are shared.

LE GÎTE DU PARC LAFONTAINE HOSTEL $
Map p290 (🖉514-522-3910, 877-350-4483; www
.hostelmontreal.com; 1250 Rue Sherbrooke Est;
dm/d without bathroom incl breakfast from
$28/65; @; MSherbrooke) This converted
Victorian house has an atmosphere more
like that of a guesthouse or inn than a hostel. It's located just a 10-minute walk from
the main bus station and close to bar-filled
Rue St-Denis. The continental breakfast is
served on the terrace and guests can use
the kitchen, TV room and laundry. There's
also bike rental available for exploring the
city.

🛏 Plateau Mont-Royal

**Staying in the most fashionable district
of Montréal means being close to some
of the best eateries and nightlife in
town. Like the Village, the Plateau is
packed with B&Bs; hotels are few and
far between.**

AUBERGE DE LA FONTAINE   INN **$$**
Map p292 (✆514-597-0166, 800-597-0597; www
.aubergedelafontaine.com; 1301 Rue Rachel Est; d
from $159; P ✳ 🛜; MMont-Royal) A gem of an
inn on the edge of Parc La Fontaine, this
guesthouse has rooms painted in Provençal
hues, with exposed brick walls (in some
rooms) and cheerful art and furnishings.
Staff are friendly and knowledgeable. The
snack refrigerator with goodies free for the
taking is a nice touch. There's a wheelchair-
accessible room available.

BOB & MARIKO'S BED & BREAKFAST B&B **$$**
Map p292 (✆514-289-9749, 800-267-5180; www
.bbmontreal.ca; 3458 Ave Laval; s/d without bathroom from $75/85; P ✳ 🛜; MSherbrooke) Own-
ers Bob and Mariko Finkelstein receive high
marks for their warm hospitality. Set in a
100-year-old house, this small, cozy B&B
has just four rooms, all with original maple
floors and trim furnishings – some of which
could use an update. Good location.

GINGERBREAD MANOR B&B   B&B **$$**
Map p292 (✆514-597-2804; www.gingerbread
manor.com; 3445 Ave Laval; d from $139, d with-
out bathroom from $109, P 🛜; MSherbrooke) A
warm welcome to visitors is given by the
hosts at this charming B&B near the leafy
Carré St-Louis. The house itself is a stately
three-story townhouse built in 1885 with
bay windows, ornamental details and an at-
tached carriage house. The elegant rooms –
five in all – are uniquely furnished (only one
has a private bathroom, the others share),
and the best have king-size beds and a bay
window. All have decent light. Hot cooked
breakfasts (which may include banana wal-
nut pancakes, French toast and fruit salad,
croissants, etc) are a bonus.

HÔTEL DE L'INSTITUT   HOTEL **$$**
Map p292 (✆514-282-5120; www.ithq.qc.ca;
3535 Rue St-Denis; s/d $129/149; P ✳ 🛜; MSh-
erbrooke) Set in a sleek modern glass cube,
this recently renovated hotel is run as a
training center for the Québec tourism and
hotel board. The 42 rooms are spacious and
comfortable, and all have tiny balconies –
some offering decent views. Bathrooms are
cramped, but otherwise clean and functional. The trim restaurant on-site is a well-kept
secret, with excellent multicourse meals.
Young, attentive staff provide noteworthy
service. Another restaurant next door is
run by students with less experience but

the food is also delicious. Ask the front desk
for details.

KUTUMA HOTEL & SUITES   B&B **$$**
Map p292 (✆514-844-0111; www.kutuma.com;
3708 Rue St-Denis; d/ste from $99/135; P ✳ 🛜;
MSherbrooke) In an excellent location on
lively Rue St-Denis, the Kutuma has the feel
of a boutique hotel. Cozy, well-maintained
rooms feature safari-theme decor, includ-
ing animal-print fabrics, potted palms and
colorful artwork on the walls. Bathrooms
are modern and perhaps overly sleek, but
the two-person tub in some bathrooms is
a nice feature. Negatives: some rooms have
tiny windows, and there's no elevator –
though staff can help you lug your stuff up
the stairs.

À LA BONNE HEURE B&B   B&B **$$**
Map p292 (✆514-529-0179; www.alabonneheure
.ca; 4425 Rue St-Hubert; s/d $105/115, without
bathroom $75/85, P 🛜; MMont-Royal) This is
a typical turn-of-the-century Montréal terrace home with five bright, spacious rooms
that exude an old-fashioned charm. Breakfast is served in the elegant dining room
with high ceiling, French doors and cornice
molding. It's well located, just one block
from the Mont-Royal metro station.

AUX PORTES DE LA NUIT   B&B **$$**
Map p292 (✆514-848-0833; www.auxportesdela
nuit.com; 3496 Ave Laval; d $95-166; P ✳ 🛜;
MSherbrooke) In a lovely location near the
lush Carré St-Louis, this five-room B&B
offers abundant charm. Inside the beauti-
fully maintained 1894 Victorian, you'll find
a mix of elegantly decorated rooms, each
done in a different color scheme, but fea-
turing wood floors, a few antique furnish-
ings and original artwork (painted by the
owner's daughter). The Balcony Room has
lovely views of the park; the Terrace Room
has its own secluded terrace.

ANNE MA SOEUR ANNE   APARTMENTS **$$**
Map p292 (✆514-281-3187; www.annemasoeur
anne.com; 4119 Rue St-Denis; d from $80; ✳ 🛜;
MMont-Royal) These smart, fully equipped
studios fill a valuable niche in the Plateau.
They're suitable for both short- or long-
term stays, with each unit having a 'micro-
kitchen' with a microwave and stove, work
space and Ikea-style furnishings built into
the walls. The cheapest rooms are a little
cramped, while others have private terraces,
with some overlooking the shady backyard.

Croissants are delivered to your door as breakfast.

PIERRE ET DOMINIQUE B&B   B&B $

Map p292 (☑514-286-0307; www.bbcanada .com/928.html; 271 Carré St-Louis; s/d from $75/110; P⟨̂⟩; MSherbrooke) This is one of several inviting B&Bs snuggled in the rows of stone Victorian houses overlooking Carré St-Louis. You'll find just three small, cozy bedrooms, all neatly set with Swedish-style furniture and painted in cheery tones. The best room has a view of the park.

SHÉZELLES   B&B $$

Map p292 (☑514-849-8694; www.shezelles.com; 4272 Rue Berri; d with/without bathroom from $155/90; ⟨̂⟩; MMont-Royal) Shézelles is a bastion of warmth with its paneled walls, wood floors and attractively furnished rooms. The en suite room has a king-size bed and a spacious bathroom with a Jacuzzi. There are smaller but welcoming doubles, as well as a 'love nest' behind a Japanese sliding door (the bed is directly under a skylight).

LE RAYON VERT   B&B $$

Map p292 (☑514-524-6774; www.lerayonvert .ca; 4373 Rue St-Hubert; s/d without bathroom $60/90; P⟨̂⟩; MMont-Royal) This centennial greystone has three comfortable, individual rooms not far from the alternative bustle of Ave du Mont-Royal. Rooms have wood floors and classic wood furnishings (there's even a chandelier and cornice molding in the Victorian room). The breakfast room recalls a French country inn, but the clincher is the idyllic rear terrace – in summer it's as green as the tropics.

AU PIANO BLANC   B&B $$

Map p292 (☑514-845-0315; www.aupianoblanc .com; 4440 Rue Berri; s/d $115/130, without bathroom $80/95, ; P⟨̂⟩; MMont-Royal) The 'colors

of the sun,' as owner Céline – a former singer, puts it – radiate from this delightful B&B a stone's throw from Mont-Royal metro station. Brightly painted rooms, colorful artwork and whimsical bedside lamps add to the good cheer. Some rooms are tiny while others have views of the back terrace.

BIENVENUE B&B   B&B $$

Map p292 (☑514-844-5897, 800-227-5897; www .bienvenuebb.com; 3950 Ave Laval; s/d without bathroom from $80/90; MSherbrooke) On a peaceful backstreet in the Plateau, Bienvenue is a 12-room Victorian B&B set with a range of small, clean rooms with homey furnishings. Decorative touches (artwork here and there and quilted bedspreads in some rooms) add to the appeal, though the carpeting is a little worn. All rooms get decent light and some have high ceilings.

LE GÎTE   B&B $$

Map p292 (☑514-849-4567; www.legite.ca; 3619 Rue de Bullion; s/d from $87/97; ⟨̂⟩; MSherbrooke) In a row house just off restaurant-lined Rue Prince Arthur, Le Gîte is yet another charming Plateau B&B. The four rooms here have polished wood floors, an attractive minimalist design and striking works of art covering the walls (created by the owner's son). Other nice touches are the small shaded terrace, kitchen use and free laundry.

AUBERGE DE JEUNESSE MAEVA   HOSTEL $

Map p292 (☑514-523-0840; www.aubergemaeva .com; 3990 Rue St-Hubert; dm/dm $18/55; @⟨̂⟩; MMont-Royal) This small, quaint, family-run hostel sits in a peaceful residential neighborhood not far from the action on Ave du Mont-Royal. Guests bunk in four- or six-bed dorms, with a bathroom in each. Guests enjoy free wi-fi access and free use of bikes, plus kitchen access and table soccer.

Understand Montréal & Québec City

Montréal Today

Slowly emerging from the effects of the global financial crisis, Montréal has been re-building itself, with the construction of two super-hospitals and the modernization of key highways in progress. While the city was wracked by student protests in 2012, the atmosphere remains as festive as ever, wih a new winter festival inaugurated. And every year the summer party season is always welcome after a long winter.

Best on Film

The Apprenticeship of Duddy Kravitz (1974) Mordecai Richler's timeless story of a Jewish upbringing.

Jesus of Montreal (1989) A prizewinning take on Montreal and Catholicism.

Barney's Version (2010) A touching adaptation of another Richler novel.

Incendies (2010) Two siblings confront the mystery of their mother's past.

Best in Print

Two Solitudes (Hugh MacLennan; 1945) One man's struggles with his English- and French-Canadian background.

The Tin Flute (Gabrielle Roy; 1947) A waitress looks for love in the slums of St-Henri.

The Apprenticeship of Duddy Kravitz (Mordecai Richler; 1959) A boy grows up poor and Jewish in 1940s Montréal.

How to Make Love to a Negro Without Getting Tired (Danny Laferrière; 1985) The sexual exploits of two Africans.

The Red Square Movement

When the provincial government of Premier Jean Charest unveiled plans for a tuition increase for universities, students reacted with vehemence. Beginning in November 2011, tens of thousands of students took to the streets to protest the proposed increase of $325 per year for five years, bringing annual tuition in 2016 to $3793 from $2168. As both sides dug their heels in, and negotiations failed, more students abandoned classes in February 2012. Polls indicated about a 30% public support for the striking students, while some commentators pointed out that Québec students already enjoyed the cheapest tuition in the country. Meanwhile, demonstrators blocked road traffic and access to classrooms and office buildings, prompting police to respond with tear gas and hundreds of arrests. Smoke bombs were set off in the municipal metro system, though no one was hurt. As the nightly protests dragged on into summer and the education minister was replaced, the movement's symbol – a red square – could be seen pinned to jackets in many parts of Montréal.

Rebuilding

After decades of neglect, Montréal's infrastructure is getting a face lift, if not being entirely replaced. The city has had some high-profile accidents, even fatalities, involving crumbling masonry from buildings and tunnels, but residents have greeted plans for rebuilding with mixed emotions. Many argue that construction disruptions to key facilities like the Champlain Bridge and the Turcott, which links the island with the South Shore, will irk drivers no end, especially considering the history of fraud in the local construction industry, as has been widely reported. But the city is also seeing the largest construction project since the

1976 Olympics. The building of two super-hospitals – the MUHC McGill University Health Centre and the CHUM Centre Hospitalier de l'Université de Montréal, expected to be complete around 2016 at a cost of over $3 billion – will be a welcome relief for those who have had to suffer in the city's overcrowded medical centers.

Liveable City

Montréal still remains one of the cheapest cities in Canada to rent an apartment ($720 a month for a three-room in 2011, compared with $1300 in Toronto and Vancouver). In business and industry, Montréal does well for itself, boasting the highest number of research centers in Canada, an impressive high-tech sector and the third-largest fashion industry in North America (after New York and Los Angeles). The global economic downturn, however, has contributed to rising unemployment. Other pressing issues are the city's aging infrastructure and its bloated bureaucracy. Montrealers also complain about paying the highest taxes of any province in Canada. In spite of the city's shortcomings, Montrealers remain proud, citing the city's burgeoning film and music industries, its vibrant multiculturalism and its rich intellectual life. Not surprisingly, Montréal does quite well in quality-of-life surveys (often ranking well ahead of Paris, Barcelona and San Francisco for instance); a 2012 ranking by the Centre for the Study of Living Standards put the province of Québec in 11th place worldwide, on par with Switzerland.

if Montréal were 100 people

47 would be of Canadian origin
26 would be of French origin
2 would be of Québécois origin
25 would be of Other origin

MONTRÉAL TODAY

Language spoken
(% of population)

French 70 English 18 Other 12

population per sq km

CANADA MONTREAL

👤 ≈ 3 people

History

Originally the home of Iroquois people, Montréal has a dynamic history as a small French colony, a fur-trading center and a base for industrialists who laid the foundation of Canada. Later eclipsed by Toronto, it rebranded itself as a powerhouse of French-speaking businesses.

THE EARLY SETTLEMENT

The Island of Montréal was long inhabited by the St Lawrence Iroquois, one of the tribes that formed the Five Nations Confederacy of Iroquois. In 1535 French explorer Jacques Cartier visited the Iroquois village of Hochelaga (Place of the Beaver Dam) on the slopes of Mont-Royal, but by the time Samuel de Champlain founded Québec City in 1608, the settlement had vanished. In 1642 Paul de Chomedey de Maisonneuve founded the first permanent mission, despite fierce resistance by the Iroquois. Intended as a base for converting Aboriginal people to Christianity, this settlement quickly became a major hub of the fur trade. Québec City became the capital of the French colony Nouvelle-France (New France), while Montréal's *voyageurs* (trappers) established a network of trading posts into the hinterland.

As part of the Seven Years' War, Britain clashed with France over its colony in New France. The British victory on the Plains of Abraham outside Québec City heralded the Treaty of Paris (1763), which gave Britain control of New France; it also presaged the creation of Canada itself with Confederation in 1867.

The American army seized Montréal during the American Revolution (1775–83) and set up headquarters at Château Ramezay. But even the formidable negotiating skills of Benjamin Franklin failed to convince French Quebecers to join their cause, and seven months later the revolutionaries decided they'd had enough and left empty-handed.

TIMELINE	1500	1535	1642
	Semi-sedentary Iroquois tribes frequent the island, settling one permanent village, Hochelaga (Place of the Beaver Dam), near present-day McGill University.	French explorer and gold-seeker Jacques Cartier sets foot on the island. He encounters natives, returning home with 'gold' and 'diamonds' – later revealed to be iron pyrite and quartz.	Maisonneuve and a group of 50 settlers found the colony of 'Ville-Marie.' Frenchwomen Jeanne Mance and Marguerite Bourgeoys establish New France's first hospital and school.

INDUSTRY & IMMIGRATION

In the early 19th century Montréal's fortunes dimmed as the fur trade shifted north to the Hudson Bay. However, a new class of international merchants and financiers soon emerged, founding the Bank of Montréal and investing in shipping as well as a new railway network. Tens of thousands of Irish immigrants came to work on the railways and in the factories, mills and breweries that sprang up along the Canal de Lachine. Canada's industrial revolution was born, with the English clearly in control.

The Canadian Confederation of 1867 gave Quebecers a degree of control over their social and economic affairs, and acknowledged French as an official language. French Canadians living in the rural areas flowed into the city to seek work and regained the majority. At this time, Montréal was Canada's premier railway center, financial hub and manufacturing powerhouse. The Canadian Pacific Railway opened its head office there in the 1880s, and Canadian grain bound for Europe was shipped through the port.

In the latter half of the century, a wave of immigrants from Italy, Spain, Germany, Eastern Europe and Russia gave Montréal a cosmopolitan flair that would remain unique in the province. By 1914 the metropolitan population exceeded half a million residents, of whom more than 10% were neither British nor French.

WAR, DEPRESSION & NATIONALISM

The peace that existed between the French and English citizens ran aground after the outbreak of WWI. When Ottawa introduced the draft in 1917, French-Canadian nationalists condemned it as a plot to reduce the francophone population. The conscription issue resurfaced in WWII, with 80% of Francophones rejecting the draft and nearly as many English-speaking Canadians voting for it.

During the Prohibition era Montréal found a new calling as 'Sin City', as hordes of free-spending, pleasure-seeking Americans flooded over the border in search of booze, brothels and betting houses. But with the advent of Great Depression, the economic inferiority of French Canadians became clearer than ever.

Québec's nationalists turned inward, developing proposals to create co-operatives, nationalize the anglophone electricity companies and promote French-Canadian goods. Led by the right-wing, ruralist, ultraconservative Maurice Duplessis, the new Union Nationale party took advantage of the nationalist awakening to win provincial power

So how did the St Lawrence River get its name? The answer is simple: when Jacques Cartier arrived in its estuary around the time of the feast of St Lawrence in 1535, he gave thanks by naming it after the early Christian saint. It has had many other names, such as the River That Walks, the Canada River and the Cod River, but St Lawrence eventually stuck.

A SAINTLY RIVER

1721	1760	1763	1832
After years of on-and-off fighting with the Iroquois, the town erects a stone citadel. The colony continues to grow, fueled by the burgeoning riches of the fur trade.	One year after a resounding victory outside of Québec City, the British seize Montréal.	France officially cedes its territories to Britain, bringing an end to French rule in Canada.	Montréal is incorporated as a city following the prosperous 1820s. The Canal de Lachine dramatically improves commerce and transport.

in the 1936 elections. The party's influence would retard Québec's industrial and social progress until Duplessis died in 1959.

GRAND PROJECTS

By the early 1950s the infrastructure of Montréal, by now with a million-plus inhabitants, badly needed an overhaul. Mayor Jean Drapeau drew up a grand blueprint that would radically alter the face of the city, including the metro, a skyscraper-filled downtown and an underground city (see the boxed text, p84). The harbor was extended for the opening of the St Lawrence Seaway.

Along the way Drapeau set about ridding Montréal of its 'Sin City' image by cleaning up the shadier districts. His most colorful nemesis was Lili St-Cyr, the Minnesota-born stripper whose affairs with high-ranking politicians, sports stars and thugs were as legendary in the postwar era as her bathtub performances.

The face of Montréal changed dramatically during the 1960s as a forest of skyscrapers shot up. Private developers replaced Victorian-era structures with landmark buildings such as Place Bonaventure, a modern hotel-shopping complex, and the Place des Arts performing arts center. The focus of the city shifted from Old Montréal to Ville-Marie, where commerce flourished.

In 1960 the nationalist Liberal Party won control of the Québec assembly and passed sweeping measures that would shake Canada to its very foundations. In the first stage of this so-called Quiet Revolution, the assembly vastly expanded Québec's public sector and nationalized the provincial hydroelectric companies.

Francophones were able to work in French because more corporate managers supported French-language working conditions. For instance, the nationalization of power companies saw the language of construction blueprints change from English to French.

Still, progress wasn't swift enough for radical nationalists (see the boxed text, p229), and by the mid-1960s they were claiming that Québec independence was the only way to ensure francophone rights.

As the Francophones seized power, some of the old established anglophone networks became spooked and resettled outside the province. By 1965 Montréal had lost its status as Canada's economic capital to Toronto. But new expressways were laid out and the metro was finished in time for Expo '67 (the 1967 World's Fair), a runaway success that attracted 50 million visitors. It was the defining moment of Montréal as a metropolis, and would lay the foundations for its successful bid to host the 1976 Olympics – an event that would land the city in serious debt.

In 1940, as Britain struggled against Germany in WWII, Prime Minister Winston Churchill shipped $5 billion in foreign reserves from the Bank of England to Montréal. The fortune was placed in a vault in the third sub-basement of the Sun Life Building, which had been reinforced with metal beams, to fund a British government in exile should the Nazis invade and occupy Britain.

1833

Jacques Viger is elected as Montréal's first mayor.

1840s

Bad times arrive, with violent protests over colonial reform, and a 1847 typhus epidemic that kills thousands.

Jacques Viger plaque, Hôtel de Ville, Montréal

IRISH IN MONTRÉAL

The Irish have been streaming into Montréal since the founding of New France, but they came in floods between 1815 and 1860, driven from Ireland by the Potato Famine. Catholic like the French settlers, the Irish easily assimilated into Québécois society. Names from this period still encountered today include 'Aubrey' or 'Aubry,' 'O'Brinnan' or 'O'Brennan,' and 'Mainguy' from 'McGee'. In Montréal, most of these immigrants settled in Griffintown, then an industrial hub near the Canal de Lachine. The first St Patrick's Day parade in the city was held in 1824 and has run every year since; it's now one of the city's biggest events. For some terrific reads on the Irish community, check out *The Shamrock and the Shield: An Oral History of the Irish in Montreal* by Patricia Burns and *The Untold Story: The Irish in Canada*, edited by Robert O'Driscoll and Lorna Reynolds.

Meanwhile, things continued heating up in the Quiet Revolution. To head off clashes with Québec's increasingly separatist leaders, Prime Minister Pierre Trudeau proposed two key measures in 1969: Canada was to be made fully bilingual to give Francophones equal access to national institutions; and the constitution was to be amended to guarantee francophone rights. Ottawa then pumped cash into French-English projects, which nonetheless failed to convince Francophones that French would become the primary language of work in Québec.

In 1976 this lingering discontent spurred the election of René Lévesque and his Parti Québécois, committed to the goal of independence for the province. The following year the Québec assembly passed Bill 101, which not only made French the sole official language of Québec but also stipulated that all immigrants enroll their children in French-language schools. The trickle of anglophone refugees from the province turned into a flood. Alliance Québec, an English rights group, estimates that between 300,000 and 400,000 Anglos left Québec during this period.

THE NOT-QUIET NATION OF QUÉBEC

The Quiet Revolution heightened tensions not only in Québec but across Canada. After their re-election in 1980, federal Liberals, led by Pierre Trudeau, sold most Quebecers on the idea of greater rights through constitutional change, helping to defeat a referendum on Québec sovereignty the same year by a comfortable margin. Québec premier Robert Bourassa then agreed to a constitution-led solution – but only if Québec was recognized as a 'distinct society' with special rights.

1852	1865	1867	1867
The Great Fire burns much of the city to the ground.	Lured by big industry, immigrants arrive by the thousands; Francophones soon outnumber Anglophones. Over the next 40 years, the population quadruples.	Railways and an active harbor bring wealth to Montréal	Tired of colonial rule, representatives of colonies on the Atlantic coast meet and form a Confederation; modern Canada is born.

In 1987 the federal Conservative Party was in power and Prime Minister Brian Mulroney unveiled an accord that met most of Québec's demands. To take effect, the Meech Lake Accord needed ratification by all 10 provinces and both houses of parliament by 1990. Dissenting premiers in three provinces eventually pledged their support, but incredibly the accord collapsed when a single member of Manitoba's legislature refused to sign.

The failure of the Meech Lake Accord triggered a major political crisis in Québec. The separatists blamed English-speaking Canada for its demise, and Mulroney and Bourassa subsequently drafted the Charlottetown Accord, a new, expanded accord. But the separatists picked it apart, and in October 1992 the second version was trounced in Québec and five other provinces. The rejection sealed the fate of Mulroney, who stepped down as prime minister the following year, and of Bourassa, who left political life a broken man.

REFERENDUM & REBIRTH

When Mayor Camilien Houde was faced with the proposal of building a road over Mount Royal, he famously retorted, 'A road over the mountain? Over my dead body!' After he died, and was duly buried on the side of the mountain, Mayor Jean Drapeau went ahead with the plan and built the aptly named Voie Camilien-Houde.

In the early 1990s Montréal was wracked by political uncertainty and economic decline. No one disputed that the city was ailing as the symptoms were everywhere: corporate offices had closed and moved their headquarters to other parts of Canada, shuttered shops lined downtown streets, and derelict factories and refineries rusted on the perimeter. Relations between Anglophones and Francophones, meanwhile, plumbed new depths after Québec was denied a special status in Canada.

The victory of the separatist Parti Québécois in the 1994 provincial elections signaled the arrival of another crisis. Support for an independent Québec rekindled, and a referendum on sovereignty was called the following year. While it first appeared the referendum would fail by a significant margin, the outcome was a real cliffhanger: Quebecers decided by 52,000 votes – a razor-thin majority of less than 1% – to stay part of Canada. In Montréal, where the bulk of Québec's Anglophones and immigrants live, more than two-thirds voted against sovereignty, causing Parti Québécois leader Jacques Parizeau to infamously declare that 'money and the ethnic vote' had robbed Québec of its independence.

In the aftermath of the vote, the locomotives of the Quiet Revolution (economic inferiority and linguistic insecurity among Francophones) ran out of steam. Exhausted by decades of separatist wrangling, most Montrealers put aside their differences and went back to work.

1917	1959	1959	1967
As war rages in Europe, Quebecers feel no loyalty to France or Britain and resent being conscripted to fight. Tensions seethe between Anglos and French Canadians.	St Lawrence Seaway opens, permitting freighters to bypass Montréal. Toronto slowly overtakes Montréal as Canada's commercial engine.	The strong-arm, anti-labor Duplessis regime ends. Francophone unions and co-operatives are on the rise.	Expo '67 in Montréal marks the centenary of Canadian Confederation, drawing people from across the country and around the world.

THE QUIET REVOLUTION

In the 1960s, the so-called Quiet Revolution began to give French Quebecers more sway in industry and politics, and ultimately established the primacy of the French language.

The 'revolution' itself refers to the sweeping economic and social changes initiated by nationalist Premier Jean Lesage and others that were intended to make Quebecers more in control of their destiny and 'masters at home'. It was an effort to modernize, secularize and Frenchify Québec after years of conservatism under Premier Maurice Duplessis. But this tide of nationalism also had extreme elements.

The Front de Libération du Québec (FLQ), a radical nationalist group committed to overthrowing 'medieval Catholicism and capitalist oppression' through revolution, was founded in 1963. Initially the FLQ attacked military targets and other symbols of federal power, but soon became involved in labor disputes. In the mid-1960s the FLQ claimed responsibility for a spate of bombings. In October 1970 the FLQ kidnapped Québec's labor minister Pierre Laporte and a British trade official in an attempt to force the independence issue. Prime Minister Pierre Trudeau declared a state of emergency and called in the army to protect government officials. The next day Laporte's body was found in the trunk of a car. By December the crisis had passed, but the murder discredited the FLQ in the eyes of many supporters. In the years that followed, the FLQ effectively ceased to exist as a political movement.

While support for Québec independence still hovers around 30% to 45% in the polls, there's little appetite at the moment for another referendum on separation from Canada – the economy is on the upswing these days and real-estate prices surged across the province after Jean Charest of the federalist Liberal Party was elected Québec premier in the spring of 2003 (winning re-election with a majority in 2008). His popularity, however, has since declined sharply amid student protests over tuition costs.

Oddly enough, a natural disaster played a key role in bringing the communities together. In 1998 a freak ice storm – some blamed extra-moist El Niño winds, others cited global warming – snapped power masts like matchsticks across the province, leaving over three million people without power and key services in the middle of a Montréal winter. Some people endured weeks without electricity and heat, but regional and political differences were forgotten as money, clothing and offers of personal help poured into the stricken areas. Montrealers recount memories of those dark days with a touch of mutual respect.

As the political climate brightened, Montréal began to emerge from a fundamental reshaping of the local economy. The city experienced a burst of activity as sectors such as software, aerospace, telecommunications

1970	1976	1976	1980
The separatist-minded Front de Libération du Québec kidnaps labor minister Pierre Laporte (later killing him). Although the FLQ is discredited, separatism gains support.	The Parti Québécois gains power and passes Bill 101, declaring French the official language. Many businesses leave Montréal, taking 15,000 jobs with them.	Montréal stages the Summer Olympics and goes deeply into debt.	The first referendum on independence ends in a comfortable defeat.

and pharmaceuticals replaced rust-belt industries like textiles and refining. Québec's moderate wages became an asset to manufacturers seeking qualified, affordable labor, and foreign investment began to flow more freely. Tax dollars were used to recast Montréal as a new-media hub, encouraging dozens of multimedia firms to settle in the Old Port area.

The upshot is a city transformed and brimming with self-confidence. The Place-des-Arts area teems with new restaurants and entertainment venues; Old Montréal buzzes with designer hotels and trendy restaurants; and once-empty warehouses around town have been converted to lofts and offices.

Montréal's renewed vigor has lured back some of the Anglophones who left in the 1980s and '90s. Language conflicts have slipped into the background because most young Montrealers are at least bilingual, and for the first time there are more homeowners than renters, leading property prices to soar. The impassioned separatists who came of age

HISTORY BOOKS

➧ *A Short History of Quebec* (1993, revised 2008) by John A Dickinson and Brian Young. Social and economic portrait of Québec from the pre-European period to modern constitutional struggles.

➧ *City Unique: Montreal Days and Nights in the 1940s and '50s* (1996) by William Weintraub. Engaging tales of Montréal's twilight period as Sin City and an exploration of its historic districts.

➧ *The Road to Now: A History of Blacks in Montreal* (1997) by Dorothy Williams. A terrific and rare look at a little-known aspect of the city's history and the black experience in New France.

➧ *All Our Yesterdays: A collection of 100 Stories of People, Landmarks and Events From Montreal's Past* (1988) by Edgar Andrew Collard. An insightful look at the city's history, streets and squares, with wonderful illustrations.

➧ *Canadiens Legends: Montreal's Hockey Heroes* (2004) by Mike Leonetti. Wonderful profiles and pics on some of the key players that made this team an NHL legend. Whether you're a sports fan or not, Les Canadiens and the mythology around them is an important part of the city's 20th-century cultural history.

➧ *The Illustrated History of Canada* (2002) edited by Craig Brown. Several historians contributed to this well-crafted work with fascinating prints, maps and sketches.

1993 ❯ **1994**

Prime Minister Brian Mulroney steps down after failing to get support for the revised Charlottetown Accord.

Voters go to the polls again, narrowly defeating Québec gaining sovereignty. Over the next decade the separatist movement slowly fizzles.

Destruction from the 1998 ice storm

SUZANNE TAKES YOUR HAND...

Leonard Cohen, one of the city's most famous sons, grew up in the wealthy Anglo enclave of Westmount, but was drawn to the streets of Downtown and the Old Port. His celebrated 1967 ballad 'Suzanne' was based on his experiences with Suzanne Verdal, then wife of sculptor Armand Vaillancourt. Fans have tried to pinpoint the location of the meeting, and the most likely spot is an old waterfront building along Rue de la Commune in the Old Port. The lyrics refer to 'the lady of the harbor', which is thought to be the statue atop the Chapelle Notre-Dame-de-Bonsecours at 400 Rue St-Paul Est.

during the heady days of the Quiet Revolution are older now, and a critical mass of separatists from the younger generation hasn't emerged to take their place. In the 2007 Québec general election, the Parti Québécois earned its smallest share of the popular vote since 1973, leading some to speculate that the demographic opportunity for separatism may have ended for good.

Jean Charest's Liberals successfully knocked the separatist Parti Québécois out of office in 2003, but the federalist party has had a rocky ride since then and has been the target of dozens of demonstrations after announcing policies to cut public-sector jobs, hike day-care prices and prune Québec's bloated bureaucracy. In 2012, students upset with Charest's plans to end the long freeze on increases to tuition (already the lowest in Canada) staged unprecedented street protests that dragged on for months, resulting in hundreds of arrests. Though it posed the greatest challenge to his administration, a majority of Montrealers supported the hikes as well as a tough new law it passed to curb the protests.

HISTORY REFERENDUM & REBIRTH

1998	2005	2007	2011-12
The Great Ice Storm leaves thousands in Montréal and southern Québec without heat or electricity as power lines are severed by ice.	Canada becomes the fourth country in the world to legalize same-sex marriage. Montrealer Michaëlle Jean is installed as 27th governor general of Canada.	In the Québec general election, the Parti Québécois garners its smallest share of the vote since 1973.	Montreal is wracked by months of street protests by students opposed to government plans to increase tuition. Hundreds are arrested.

People & Culture

Montréal's social scene is nothing if not passionate. Political apathy can turn into fiery protest overnight, while the potent mix of French, English and many other languages bubbles away in a stew that's sometimes tense. But a love of music, festivals and food somehow makes it all work.

POLITICS

For decades Québec politics was dominated by the question: are you separatist or federalist? But since Quebecers voted out the Parti Québécois in the 2003 provincial elections, the entire province has been given a reprieve. These days Québec spends its time clashing with the federal government over gun control and fiscal imbalance rather than language and separation issues.

Québec's premier is Sherbrooke-born Jean Charest, elected on an ambitious platform of better health care, better education, tax cuts and a leaner, less-interventionist government. However, he's had a rocky ride – although his Liberal Party won an unprecedented third consecutive term and a majority government in the December 2008 election, his popularity has since declined dramatically. During the student protests over tuition hikes in the summer of 2012, his support stood at 30%, which was relatively high given levels below 20% seen a year earlier. While this book was being researched, the 'strikes' by students and nightly protests that blocked streets and traffic threatened the city's all-important tourism season, with hundreds of millions of dollars in visitor revenue at stake.

For Charest, the larger question was whether the growing public sympathy for the protestors would translate into a major challenge at the polls. With a slim majority in the provincial legislature and a mandate running through the end of 2013, the premier was faced with a delicate balancing act – maintaining a hard line with students due to the need to bring tuition to national levels, and not alienating the electorate with responses such as Special Law 78, a controversial piece of legislation that placed limits on demonstrations.

Montréal's moderate mayor, Gérald Tremblay, is something of a Teflon man. He has seen widely fluctuating ratings since his 2002 election and was easily re-elected in 2005, obtaining 53% of the vote. He won a third term in 2009, with less than 40% of the vote, and his administration has been plagued by scandals. In 2012, the provincial anti-corruption squad arrested three former members of his political circle over breach of trust charges in connection with a municipal land deal. Authorities also questioned Tremblay in the matter, and he was expected to testify before the Charbonneau commission, which was mandated to examine links between local governments, the construction industry and organized crime.

PAULINE MAROIS

Always unpredictable in provincial politics, the Parti Québécois was rocked by defections of key members over the management of a sports arena in Québec City. But leader Pauline Marois survived the turmoil, earning her the nickname 'the concrete woman'.

LANGUAGE

French is the official language of Québec and French Quebecers are passionate about it, seeing their language as the last line of defense against Anglo-Saxon culture. What makes Montréal unique in the province is the interface of English and French – a mix responsible for the city's dynamism as well as the root of many of its conflicts.

Until the 1970s it was the English minority (few of whom spoke French) who ran the businesses, held positions of power and accumulated wealth in Québec; more often than not a French Quebecer going into a downtown store couldn't get service in his or her own language.

But as Québec's separatist movement arose, the Canadian government passed laws in 1969 that required all federal services and public signs to appear in both languages. The separatists took things further and demanded the primacy of French in Québec, which was affirmed by the Parti Québécois with the passage of Bill 101 in 1977 (see the boxed text p233). Though there was much hand-wringing, the fact is that Bill 101 probably saved the French language from dying out in North America. If you're at a party with five Anglophones and one Francophone these days, the chances are everyone will be speaking French, something that would have been rare 10 years ago.

These days Montrealers with French as their mother tongue number 928,905, and native English speakers 300,580. Fifty-seven per cent of Montrealers from a variety of backgrounds speak both official languages.

Québec settlers were relatively cut off from France once they arrived in the New World, so the French you hear today in the province, known colloquially as Québécois, developed more or less independently from what was going on in France. The result is a rich local vocabulary, with its own idioms and sayings, and words used in everyday speech that haven't been spoken in France since the 1800s.

Accents vary widely across the province, but all are characterized by a twang and rhythmic bounce unique to Québec French, and the addition of the word *lá* at the end of each spoken sentence.

To francophone Quebecers, the French spoken in France sounds desperately posh. To people from France, the French spoken in Québec sounds terribly old-fashioned and at times unintelligible – an attitude that ruffles feathers here in an instant, as it's felt to be condescending.

Quebecers learn standard French in school, hear standard French on newscasts and grow up on movies and music from France, so if you speak French from France, locals will have no difficulty understanding you – it's you understanding them that will be the problem. Remember, even

The French spoken in Québec has swear words centering on objects used in church services. Where an English speaker might yell 'fuck', a Quebecer will unleash 'tabarnac' (from tabernacle). Instead of 'oh, shit!', a Quebecer will cry 'sacrament!' (from sacrament). There are also combos like 'hostie de câlisse de tabarnac!' ('host in the chalice in the tabernacle!').

SIGNS OF PRIDE

Québec's French Language Charter, the (in)famous Bill 101, asserts the primacy of French on public signs across the province. Stop signs in Québec read 'ARRÊT,' a word that actually means a stop for buses or trains (even in France, the red hexagonal signs read 'STOP'), apostrophes had to be removed from storefronts like Ogilvy's in the 1980s to comply with French usage, and English is allowed on signage provided it's no more than half the size of the French lettering. Perhaps most bewildering of all is the acronym PFK (Poulet Frit Kentucky) for a leading fast-food chain.

The law is enforced by language police who, prompted by complaints from French hardliners, roam the province with tape measures (yes – for real!) and hand out fines to shopkeepers if a door says 'Push' more prominently than 'Poussez.' These days, most Quebecers take it all in their stride, and the comical language tussles between businesses and the language police that were such regular features of evening newscasts and phone-in shows have all but disappeared in recent years.

when French-language Québécois movies are shown in France, they are shown with *French* subtitles.

Young Montrealers today are less concerned about language issues, so visitors shouldn't worry too much. Most residents grew up speaking both languages, and people you meet in daily life – store owners, waiters and bus drivers – switch effortlessly between French and English.

MEDIA

English broadcasters

CJAD 800AM *Talk radio*

CBC Radio One 88.5 FM *News and current events*

CHOM 97.7 FM *Classic rock*

Global Montreal *(www.global montreal.com) Television*

CTV Montreal *(http://montreal .ctv.ca) Television*

CBC Montreal *(www.cbc.ca/ montreal) Television*

Montréal is the seat of Québec's French-language media companies and has four big TV networks. New-media firms such as Discreet Logic are renowned for their special effects, and the Cité du Multimédia center in Old Montréal is an incubator for start-ups.

The daily *Montreal Gazette* (www.montrealgazette.com) is the major English-language daily newspaper, with coverage of national affairs, politics and the arts. The big French dailies are the federalist *La Presse* (www.cyberpresse.ca) and the separatist-leaning *Le Devoir* (www.lede voir.com).

Le Journal de Montréal is *the* city's rollicking tabloid, replete with sensational headlines and photos. Though much derided, the *Journal* does the brashest undercover and investigative reporting in town and has the city's biggest daily circulation.

Only one free alternative weekly newspaper remains in Montréal, the French-language *Voir* (www.voir.ca); it covers film, music, books, restaurants, and goings-on about town.

Canada's only truly national papers are the left-leaning Toronto *Globe and Mail* and the right-leaning *National Post*. *The Walrus* is a Canadian *New Yorker/Atlantic Monthly*-style magazine, with in-depth articles and musings from the country's intellectual heavyweights.

Canada's weekly news magazine *Maclean's* is full of high-quality writing and still holds a certain amount of clout with its special issues. *L'actualité* is Québec's monthly news magazine in French. The Canadian Broadcasting Corporation's site (www.cbc.ca) is an excellent source for current affairs. *Maisonneuve* (www.maisonneuve.org) is a sophisticated general-interest magazine with a good e-zine.

FASHION

One of the things visitors first notice here is how well dressed people are – and it's not just the women that stop traffic. The conservative colors prevail in law and banking, but in media, IT and other businesses, local men sometimes sport business suits that merit a double-take; perhaps a chic olive-green with a lavender tie, which their counterparts in Vancouver, Toronto or even New York wouldn't dream of donning.

French-language fashion blogs like Zurbaines (http://zurbaines.com) and English-language counterparts such as Vitamin Daily (http://vitamin daily.com/montreal/fashion-shopping) follow the local fashion scene with breathless excitement, and there is a growing sense of Montréal's importance in the global fashion world.

Whether artists, students or entrepreneurs, it seems like everybody knows the look they're going for and pulls it off well. Label watchers put it down to the perfect fusion of European and American fashion – the daringness and willingness to experiment from Paris coupled with a kind of American practicality that makes people choose what's right for them and not what's just of the moment. Probably most of all, Montrealers have a love of culture and an enjoyment of life that feeds right into their garments. In short, they just have fun with clothes and are happy to flaunt this.

Taking to the snow

SPORTS

No matter the season, Québecers are an active bunch, out jogging, cycling and kayaking on warm summer days, with cold wintry days bringing ice skating, cross-country skiing and pickup hockey games on frozen lakes.

Sporting events – which can essentially be subcategorized as glorious hockey followed by those *other* activities – draw huge numbers of Montrealers. The essential experience – whether you're a fan or not – is to journey into the great hockey hall of the Bell Centre to catch the Canadiens glide to victory (or perhaps shuffle soberly away in defeat).

Other key spectator moments include joining the roaring crowds at Molson Stadium, home to the mighty Alouettes (a Canadian football team with plenty of muscle, despite being named after a songbird). You can also root for the Montréal Impact as it reaches for soccer stardom. Last of all is the Formula One Grand Prix du Canada, which roared back onto the calendar after a hiatus in 2009.

For those who'd rather join the fray than sit and watch, there are plenty of big events where you can channel your inner Armstrong. The Tour de l'Île, for instance, is one of Montréal's best-loved participatory bike rides, when tens of thousands fill the streets for a fun cycle (it's 50km, mind you) around Montréal. There's a palpable energy in the city that even nonpedalers enjoy.

In winter, green spaces become cross-country ski trails, and ponds and lakes transform into outdoor skating rinks at places like the Old Port and Parc La Fontaine.

Other great ways to enjoy the scenery include white-water rafting down the Lachine Rapids (or surfing them if your life insurance policy is in order), kayaking idly down the Canal de Lachine, or simply heading to 'the Mountain' (Parc du Mont-Royal) for a bit of unplanned activity (running, pedal-boating, ice-skating, snowshoeing, bird-watching or – if it's Sunday – gyrating and/or pounding your drums with hippie folk at the free-spirited tam-tam jam). There's much to do in this grand little city.

Music & the Arts

Montréal is both the undisputed center of the French-language enter-tainment universe in North America and the cultural mecca of Québec. It is ground zero for everything from Québec's sizable film and music industries to visual and dramatic arts and publishing.

MUSIC

From Leonard Cohen to Arcade Fire and the Jazz Fest, sometimes it seems Montréal is all about the music. A friend to experimentation of all genres and styles, the city is home to more than 250 active bands, embracing anything and everything from electropop, hip-hop and glam rock to Celtic folk, indie punk and *yéyé* (exuberant 1960s-style French rock) – not to mention roots, ambient, grunge and rockabilly.

Rock & Pop

For better or worse, Québec's best-known recording artist is Céline Dion. Born in Charlemagne some 30km east of downtown Montréal, Dion was a megastar in Québec and France long before she went on to win five Grammys. In 1983 she became the first Canadian to get a gold record in France. After giving birth to twins in 2010, Dion returned to Caesar's Palace in Las Vegas, where her permanent show has earned hundreds of millions of dollars.

On the rock scene, Arcade Fire remains one of Montréal's top indie rock bands. Their eclectic folk/rock/indie sound and manic ensemble of instruments have made them critics' darlings since their first CD *Funeral* was released in 2004 and hit the top 10 lists all over the US and UK. Their 2010 album *The Suburbs* topped charts in several countries and won Album of the Year at the 2011 Grammy Awards.

Rufus Wainwright is another anglophone artist of note who grew up in Montréal. The talented and famously eccentric Grammy-nominated singer and songwriter travels all over the musical map – performing songs of Judy Garland, cutting albums described as 'popera' (pop opera) and recording tracks for big Hollywood films. *Release The Stars* (2007), with elements of pop, melodrama and camp, is a good introduction to his eccentric sound.

In the francophone music industry, the market is crowded with talented artists. A recent hot band is the Lost Fingers, who had one of the top-selling albums in Québec in 2009. Their gypsy-jazz-pop sound (and the group's name) owes much to gypsy guitarist Django Reinhardt. Their fourth album, *La Marquise*, was released in 2011.

Les Colocs is another household name among Québécois rockers. They were known for outrageous and energetic live shows and evocative lyrics, and are still remembered fondly despite the 10-plus years since the band's break-up (following the suicide of lead singer Dédé Fortin).

Up-and-coming bands and singers to keep an eye out for when you're in town are electronica outfit Suuns, hipster collective Honheehonhee and eclectic keyboardist Grimes.

PATRICK WATSON

Voted best singer/ songwriter after Leonard Cohen in a 2011 poll of Montreal *Mirror* readers, up-and-coming cabaret crooner Patrick Watson grew up in Hudson, Québec and is known for singing in English and French, as well as playing unusual instruments, such as a bicycle on his song 'Beijing'.

Jazz

In the 1940s and '50s, Montréal was one of the most important venues for jazz music in North America. It produced a number of major jazz musicians, such as pianist Oscar Peterson and trumpeter Maynard Ferguson. The scene went into decline in the late 1950s but revived after the premiere of the jazz festival in 1979.

Peterson, who grew up in a poor family in a southwestern Montréal suburb, dazzled audiences with his keyboard pyrotechnics for over 60 years until his death in 2007. He was never particularly concerned about fame or commercial success. 'I don't do something because I think it will sell 30 million albums,' Peterson told one reporter. 'I couldn't care less. If it sells one, it sells one.'

The city's other celebrated jazz pianist, Oliver Jones, was already in his fifties when he was discovered by the music world. He had studied with Oscar Peterson's sister Daisy and the influence can be heard in his sound. Since the 1980s he has established himself as a major mainstream player with impressive technique and a hard-swinging style.

Singer and pianist Diana Krall has enjoyed mass appeal without sacrificing her bop and swing roots. In 1993 she launched her career on Montréal's Justin Time record label, and has since gone on to become the top-selling jazz vocalist. Her 1998 album *When I Look Into Your Eyes* earned a Grammy and spent a full year at the top of the Billboard jazz chart.

Originally from New York City, singer Ranee Lee is known for her virtuosity that spans silky ballads, swing standards and raw blues tunes. She has performed with many jazz notables and is a respected teacher in the McGill University music faculty.

Classical

The backbone of Montréal's classical music scene is the Orchestre Symphonique de Montréal (OSM). The OSM was the first Canadian orchestra to achieve platinum (500,000 records sold) on its 1984 recording of Ravel's *Bolero*. Since then it has won a host of awards including two Grammys and 12 Junos, and has made 88 recordings with leading record labels like Decca and CBS.

The smaller Orchestre Métropolitain du Grand Montréal is a showcase of young Québec talent and as such is staffed by graduates from the province's conservatories. The director is Yannick Nézet-Séguin, a Montrealer and among the youngest to lead a major orchestra in Canada. Its regular cycle of Mahler symphonies is a particular treat for classical-music buffs.

Opera

Over the past 25 years the Opéra de Montréal has become a giant on the North American landscape. It has staged over 600 performances of 76 operas and collaborated with numerous international companies. Many great names have graced its stages including Québec's own Leila Chalfoun, Lyne Fortin, Suzie LeBlanc and André Turp, alongside a considerable array of Canadian and international talent. The company stages six new operas every season, including classics like *Le Nozze di Figaro* and *The Magic Flute*.

Locally, new operas are not created, but in 1989 the Opéra de Montréal won a Félix (Québec music award) for the most popular production of the season for *Nelligan,* an opera created in Québec about the life of poet Émile Nelligan by André Gagnon; Michel Tremblay wrote the libretto (see the boxed text, p63).

MUSIC & THE ARTS MUSIC

If you come across a street called Rue Rufus Rockhead near Marché Atwater, don't think it's named after a character from *The Flintstones.* Jamaican-born Rufus Rockhead was the owner of Rockhead's Paradise, the hottest downtown jazz club in the 1930s and '40s. It hosted the likes of Billie Holliday, Sarah Vaughan, and Sammy Davis Jr.

SOUNDS OF MONTRÉAL: THE WORLD-RENOWNED JAZZ FESTIVAL

In a city that loves festivals, the Festival International de Jazz de Montréal is the mother of them all – erupting in late June each year and turning the city into a enormous stage. No longer just about jazz, this is one of the world's biggies, with hundreds of top-name performers bringing reggae, rock, blues, world music, Latin, reggae, Cajun, Dixieland and even pop to audiophiles from across the globe.

It started as the pipe dream of a young local music producer, Alain Simard, who tried to sell his idea to the government and corporate sponsors, with little success. 'I was saying that one day this festival would bring thousands of American tourists to Montréal,' Simard says. 'They really made fun of me.'

Now it's the single biggest tourist event in Québec, attracting nearly two million visitors to 400 concerts – and many say it's the best jazz festival on the planet. Miles Davis, Herbie Hancock, Al Jarreau, Sonny Rollins, Wayne Shorter, Al Dimeola, John Scofield and Jack DeJohnette are but a few of the giants who have graced the podiums over the years.

The festival's success has also prompted the city and corporate backers to overhaul the Place des Arts area into the larger Quartier des Spectacles, opening new venues such as the Maison du Festival Rio Tinto Alcan, a converted heritage building, in 2011.

Practicalities

The festival website (www.montrealjazzfest.com) provides all the details; free festival programs are at kiosks around the Place des Arts. Most concerts are held in the halls or on outdoor stages; several downtown blocks are closed to traffic. The music starts around noon and lasts until late evening when the clubs take over. Tickets go on sale in mid-May.

Folk

English-language folk singers are few and far between in Québec – apart from Leonard Cohen. Best known as a pop icon and novelist of the 1960s, Cohen remains one of the world's most eclectic folk artists. The romantic despair in his compositions recalls the style of Jacques Brel. A second burst of major creativity occurred in the 1980s when Cohen's dry, gravelly baritone could be heard on albums such as *Various Positions* (1984), a treatise on lovers' relationships, and the sleek *I'm Your Man* (1988) and *The Future* (1992), which suddenly made him hip again to younger audiences. And just when you thought he had disappeared from public life for good, Cohen re-emerged in the noughties with another cycle of albums, including 2012's *Old Ideas*, and embarked on a series of wildly successful world tours to rapturous audiences. The aging bard can be heard at the annual Leonard Cohen Event every spring in Montréal.

William Shatner left his native Montreal for *Star Trek* long ago, but the city still loves him. McGill University, his alma mater, awarded him an honorary doctorate in 2011. 'Don't be afraid of making an ass of yourself,' he told students. 'I do it all the time and look what I got.'

Chanson

It's hard to understand music in Québec without understanding what they call chanson, no matter how difficult it may seem to penetrate for non-French speakers at the beginning. While France has a long tradition of this type of French folk music, where a focus on lyric and poetry takes precedence over the music itself, in Québec the chanson has historically been tied in with politics and identity in a profound way. With the Duplessis-era Québec stifling any real creative production, Quebecers were tuned into only what was coming out of France, like Edith Piaf or Charles Aznavour.

The social upheaval of the Quiet Revolution changed all that, when a generation of musicians took up their guitars, started to sing in Québécois and penned deeply personal lyrics about life in Québec and, often, independence.

Gilles Vigneault is synonymous with the chanson *Gens du pays* (People of the Country), a favorite on nationalist occasions. Vigneault has painted a portrait of the province in over 100 chanson recordings. Other leading chansonniers include Félix Leclerc, Raymond Lévesque, Claude Léveillé, Richard Desjardins and veteran Jean-Pierre Ferland. You can hear chanson in *boîtes á chanson,* clubs where this type of music is played.

FILM & TELEVISION

The foundations of Québec cinema were laid in the 1930s when Maurice Proulx, a pioneer documentary filmmaker, charted the colonization of the gold-rich Abitibi region in northwestern Québec. It was only in the 1960s that directors were inspired to experiment by the likes of Federico Fellini or Jean-Luc Godard, though the subject of most films remained the countryside and rural life. The 1970s were another watershed moment when erotically charged movies sent the province a-twitter. The most representative works of this era were Claude Jutra's *Mon Oncle Antoine* and *La Vraie Nature de Bernadette* by Gilles Carle.

Montréal finally burst onto the international scene in the 1980s with a new generation of directors such as Denys Arcand (see the boxed text below), Louis Archambault, Michel Brault and Charles Binamé. Films are produced in French but dubbing and subtitling have made them accessible to a wider audience.

Animation and multimedia technologies became a Montréal specialty following the success of Softimage, a company founded by special-effects guru Daniel Langlois. Creator of some of the first 3-D animation software, Softimage masterminded the special effects used in Hollywood blockbusters like *Jurassic Park, The Mask, Godzilla* and *Titanic.*

Québec on Film

L'Âge des Ténèbres (The Age of Darkness, 2007)

Incendies (2011)

Les Invasions Barbares (2003)

A hit TV show in French is *Tout le Monde en Parle* (Everybody is Talking About It), a rollicking current affairs program hosted by comedian Guy A Lepage. It's controversial, snappy and the first stop for anyone doing anything in Québec's public arena, from politicians and actors to war heroes and wacko psychiatrists.

MUSIC & THE ARTS FILM & TELEVISION

DENIS CORRIVEAU / GETTY IMAGES ©

Cirque du Soleil (p241) performers

THEATER

Founded in 1968, the Centaur Theatre is Québec's premier English-language stage for drama. Initially its programming was contemporary-international, staging plays by playwrights such as Miller, Brecht and Pinter. When a second stage for experimental theater was added in the 1970s, the Centaur set about developing English-speaking playwrights such as David Fennario, whose satirical *On the Job* was considered a breakthrough production for the company. Fennario's award-winning *Balconville* paints a compelling portrait of life among Montréal's working class across the language divide. Though originally performed in 1979, it's remained a classic, and is still revived from time to time.

Québec's fabulously successful Cirque du Soleil set new artistic boundaries by combining dance, theater and circus in a single power-packed show.

One of the most famous playwrights in Québec is Michel Tremblay, whose plays about people speaking in their own dialects changed the way Quebecers felt about their language.

Transatlantique Montréal (www.transatlantique-montreal.com) is a popular two-week contemporary dance festival held at the end of September focusing on new creations by Québécois, Canadian and international performers. This is not to be confused with the Festival TransAmériques (www.fta.qc.ca), an even newer dance fest held from late May to early June.

DANCE

Montréal's dance scene crackles with innovation. Virtually every year a new miniseries, dance festival or performing arts troupe emerges to wow audiences in wild and unpredictable ways. Hundreds of performers and dozens of companies are based in the city and there's an excellent choice of venues for interpreters to strut their stuff.

Several major companies have established the city's reputation as an international dance mecca. Les Grands Ballets Canadiens attracts the biggest audiences with evergreens such as *Carmen* and *The Nutcracker,* while O Vertigo, MC2 Extase, La La La Human Steps, Fondation Jean-Pierre Perraeault and Les Ballets Jazz de Montréal are troupes of international standing.

Montréal resident Margaret Gillis is a modern dancer of international renown and combines performing, teaching and choreography all over the world. She has choreographed solo shows for Cirque du Soleil and usually does at least one performance in Montréal per year. In 2011, she was honored by the Governor General's Performing Arts Award Foundation.

LITERATURE

Montréal proudly calls itself the world's second cradle of French-language writers – after Paris, of course. But the city also boasts intimate links to many English-language writers of repute.

Caustic, quick-witted and prolific, Mordecai Richler was the 'grumpy old man' of Montréal literature in the latter part of the 20th century. Richler grew up in a working-class Jewish district in Mile End and for better or worse remained the most distinctive voice in anglophone

QUÉBEC'S MASTER FILMMAKER

No director portrays modern Québec with a sharper eye than Montréal's own Denys Arcand. His themes are universal enough to strike a chord with international audiences: modern sex in *The Decline of the American Empire* (1986), religion in *Jésus of Montréal* (1989) and death in the brilliant tragicomedy *The Barbarian Invasions* (2003). *Invasions* casts a satirical light on Québec's creaking health-care system, the demise of the sexual revolution and the failed ideologies of the 1960s.

Born in 1941 near Québec City, Arcand studied history in Montréal and landed a job at the National Film Board making movies for Expo '67. The young director was a keen supporter of francophone rights and the Quiet Revolution, but became deeply disillusioned with Québec politics in the 1970s. His latest film is *L'Âge des Ténèbres* (2007), about a government bureaucrat who escapes into a fantasy world; it was the closing film of the Cannes Film Festival that year.

RAGS TO RICHES CIRCUS STYLE: CIRQUE DU SOLEIL

Over the past two decades Cirque du Soleil (literally 'Circus of the Sun') has pushed the boundaries of traditional circus arts with its astounding acts of dexterity, emotional story arcs, ethereal costumery and Vegas-worthy spectacles. While Cirque's touring shows remain the company's bread and butter, Montrealers often enjoy first look at new shows in the Old Port. If you need further proof of the company's visionary approach to arts and life, consider the story of its founder.

The real-life story of Guy Laliberté is one of the great Canadian entertainment stories and almost as dramatic as one of the performances for which his company is so well known.

Born in Québec City in 1959, Laliberté spent his youth basking in the kind of hobbies other people label as weird – stilts, fire breathing and accordion playing. But that all changed when he got together with a group of like-minded friends that became the first incarnation of Cirque du Soleil. Their big break came with the 450th anniversary of Jacques Cartier's arrival in New France in 1984 and has snowballed ever since. Today, the company has 5000 employees worldwide and revenues of over $1 billion. Performances are riots of dance, acrobatics, music and elements that defy categorization but are just mind-blowing to watch.

Though the no-animals, no-speaking rules have remained true to their roots, these days there is no stereotypical Cirque performer who might be hired. Full-time Cirque scouts comb the world including Eastern Europe and remote parts of China, searching for new performers, tricks and skills to add to their shows. Cirque scouts are also regular fixtures at the Olympic Games, where as soon as the competition is over they burn up the phones with offers to gymnasts, swimmers and any other charismatic amateur athlete who catches their eye. Laliberté's productions also regularly include guest performers and artistic contributions.

For more information on current shows, visit www.cirquedusoleil.com.

Montréal until his passing in 2001. Most of his novels focus on Montréal and its wild and wonderful characters.

On the French side, Québec writers who are widely read in English include Anne Hébert, Marie-Claire Blais, Hubert Aquin, Christian Mistral and Dany Laferrière, whose first book *Comment Faire l'Amour avec un Nègre sans se Fatiguer* (the book was released in English as *How to Make Love to a Negro Without Getting Tired*), a wild and witty look at race relations in Canada, was eventually made into a film whose screenplay was nominated for a Genie award. For stories about everyday life on the Plateau, try Michel Tremblay's short stories.

PAINTING & VISUAL ARTS

Québec's lush forests and icy winter landscapes have been inspiring landscape artists since the 19th century. Horatio Walker was known for his sentimental interpretations of Québec farm life such as *Oxen Drinking* (1899). Marc-Aurèle Fortin (1880–1970) is famed for his watercolors of Québec countryside. His portraits of majestic elms along Montréal avenues can be viewed in the Musée des Beaux-Arts, which acquired an extensive collection of Fortin's work in 2007.

The most prolific of the Automatistes was Jean-Paul Riopelle (1923–2002). Though initially a surrealist, Riopelle soon produced softer abstracts called 'grand mosaics' – paintings created with a spatula and featuring colors juxtaposed like a landscape viewed from an airplane. In the 1980s he abandoned conventional painting to work with aerosol sprays. His most renowned paintings are on permanent display at Montréal's Musée d'Art Contemporain and the Musée National des Beaux-Arts du Québec in Québec City.

Roch Carrier's famous short story 'Le chandail de hockey' (The Hockey Sweater), is known by all hockey fans. Due to a mail-order mix-up a child is forced to wear a Toronto Maple Leafs jersey in a small Québec town teeming with Montréal Canadiens fans. It's a parable of the friction between French and English populations of the era.

Architecture

Montréal's split personality is nowhere more obvious than in its architecture, a beguiling mix of European traditionalism and North American modernism. Lovingly preserved Victorian mansions and stately beaux-arts monuments rub shoulders with the sleek lines of modern skyscrapers, lending Montréal's urban landscape a creative, eclectic sophistication all of its own.

OLD-WORLD ICONS

Architectural Montréal is perhaps most easily understood by its neighborhoods and its icons. In Old Montréal, a plethora of 19th-century and some 18th-century buildings crowd in cobblestone streets, where horse-drawn carriages impart a flavor of Europe some 100 years ago; no wonder it's the setting for so many films. The representative structure here is the stunning Basilique Notre-Dame from the mid-19th century. Indeed, for most of its modern history, the city's architecture has been characterized by churches, reflecting the Catholic and Protestant churches' influence on its development. Their innumerable metallic roofs gave Montréal known as the Silver City. When Mark Twain visited in 1881, he famously remarked, 'This is the first time I was ever in a city where you couldn't throw a brick without breaking a church window.'

Today, however, Old Montréal is also home to modern eyesores that clash with the heritage structures: the 500 Place d'Armes building and the Palais de Justice building, relics of the 1960s and 1970s, make no attempt to fit in. Still, Old Montréal is one of the most homogenous neighborhoods of the city. Today's strict building codes require extensive vetting before new construction can begin.

For many visitors, the weathered greystones, such as the old stone buildings along Rue St-Paul, offer the strongest images of Old Montréal. The style emerged under the French regime in Québec (1608–1763), based on Norman and Breton houses with wide, shallow fronts, stuccoed stone and a steep roof punctuated by dormer windows. But the locals soon adapted the blueprint to Montréal's harsh winters, making the roof less steep, adding basements and extending the eaves over the walls for extra snow protection.

From the 19th century, architects tapped any number of retro styles: classical (Bank of Montréal), Gothic (Basilique Notre-Dame) and Italian renaissance (Royal Bank), to name a few. As Montréal boomed in the 1920s, a handful of famous architects such as Edward Maxwell, George Ross and Robert MacDonald left their mark on handsome towers in Old Montréal and Downtown. French Second Empire style continued to be favored for comfortable francophone homes and some public buildings such as the Hôtel de Ville (City Hall).

Must-Sees in Montréal

Basilique Notre-Dame (p52)

Hôtel de Ville (p55)

Biosphère (p75)

Oratoire St-Joseph (p142) Monolithic Renaissance-style monument to a monk's resolve

Stade Olympique (p145)

TRANSFORMING DOWNTOWN

Downtown is a multifaceted jumble of buildings where run-down 20th-century brick buildings abut shiny new multipurpose complexes. Sometimes one building straddles the historical divide: the Centre Canadien d'Architecture integrates a graceful historical greystone right into its contemporary facade. Other important buildings were meant to break with the past. Place Ville-Marie, a multitowered complex built in the late 1950s, revolutionized urban architecture in Montréal and was the starting point for the underground city (see the boxed text, p84).

Since then, architects have explored forms such as Habitat 67, a controversial apartment building designed by Montréal architect Moshe Safdie when he was only 23. Located on a promontory off the Old Port, the structure resembles a child's scattered building blocks. The Biosphère once wore a skin made of spherical mesh, while the Casino de Montréal cleverly merges two of the most far-out pavilions of Expo '67. The 1976 Olympics saw an explosion of large-scale projects, the most notorious of which remains as a reminder of poor planning and the danger of costly white elephants, the Stade Olympique (see box p146). Despite its reputation, many admire the stadium's dramatic tower, which leans at 45 degrees and is home to an observation deck.

Those heady days are back: Montréal's economic revival has sparked a construction boom. One of the largest redevelopment projects in Canada was Montréal's $200 million convention center Palais des Congrès and its adjacent squares. Dubbed the Quartier International, this new minidistrict unites Downtown and Old Montréal by concealing an ugly sunken expressway. Meanwhile, the city is pushing ahead with the multi billion dollar construction of two super-hospitals, while the federal government has announced it will replace the aging Champlain Bridge across the St Lawrence River (see p222).

Montréal also boasts the largest collection of Victorian row houses in all of North America. Numerous examples can be viewed in the Plateau such as along Rue St-Denis north of Rue Cherrier, or Ave Laval north of Carré St-Louis. Visitors are inevitably charmed by their brightly painted wrought-iron staircases, which wind up the outside of duplexes and triplexes. They evolved for three important reasons: taxes (a staircase outside allowed each floor to count as a separate dwelling, so the city could hike property taxes), fuel costs (an internal staircase wastes heat as warm air rises through the stairwell) and space (the 1st and 2nd floors were roomier without an internal staircase).

ICE ARCHITECTURE

In the 1880s, Montréal's winters were all the rage. Why? Enterprising locals took advantage of the frigid temperatures and built a series of castles made of ice. The Winter Carnival of 1883 saw the construction of an Ice Palace designed by AC Hutchinson, who also worked on Canada's Parliament buildings. It had walls fashioned of 500-pound ice blocks cut from the St Lawrence River and a roof of evergreen boughs, which were sprayed with water to form icicles. Built in Dorchester Square, the castles became more and more impressive every year. By 1889 they were more than 10 stories tall made of thousands of ice blocks, as many extant art prints held by the Musée McCord attest. Today, building with ice is back in vogue. In Parc Jean-Drapeau, the new Village des Neiges winter festival centers on the construction of an ice hotel and restaurant. Both are open to the public – just don't lick the walls.

CANADA'S STAR ARCHITECT, MOSHE SAFDIE

Born in Haifa, Israel in 1938, Moshe Safdie graduated from McGill University's architecture program in 1961 and became almost an instant star. He was only 23 when asked to design Habitat '67, which was actually based on his university thesis. Now based in Boston, Safdie has crafted a stellar career gravitating toward high-profile projects where he can unleash innovative buildings with just the right dash of controversy to get people talking about them.

Most notably, Safdie designed the $56 million, 4000-sq-meter Holocaust Memorial in Jerusalem, Israel, which opened in 2005. He also designed Ottawa's National Gallery of Canada, which opened in 1988 with its trademark soaring glass front, and the Vancouver Library Square, which evokes the Roman Colosseum.

Most recently, Safdie's design for the Kauffman Center for the Performing Arts in Kansas City, Missouri, which opened in 2011, features dramatic swooping curves and resembles a giant paper lantern or beehive.

Safdie was made a companion of the Order of Canada in 2005, Canada's highest civilian honor.

URBAN PLANNING & DEVELOPMENT

Since the 1960s the government has spent billions in developing tourist attractions and infrastructure in Montréal. Recently, a number of exciting projects have been realized or are in the works. The 33,000-sq-meter Bibliothèque et Archives Nationale du Québec opened in the Quartier Latin to huge success in 2005, with a record number of Montrealers flocking to the building each day.

The government has invested millions of dollars on the Main (Blvd St-Laurent), with the widening of sidewalks, the planting of trees and the addition of street lights to certain stretches. Rue Notre-Dame, a two-laned nightmare pocked with potholes that's nonetheless an important artery into Old Montréal, is also slated for modernization, including expansion to four lanes.

One of Montréal's most ambitious urban renewal projects in recent years is well under way on the edge of the Quartier Latin and eastern downtown. The project – dubbed the Quartier des Spectacles – aims to bring new life to this culturally rich area (bordered roughly by Rue Berri, Rue Sherbrooke, Blvd René-Lévesque and Rue City Councillors). Currently the 1-sq-km district houses 30 performance halls, numerous galleries and exhibition spaces; it also hosts various big-ticket festivals. The government has pledged $120 million to making the area a more attractive place to live, work and create in hopes of transforming the Quartier into an international destination.

Québec City History & Culture

While Montréal reigns supreme as Québec's largest and most cosmopolitan city, Québec City's cultural identity rests on its dual role as the seat of provincial government and the cradle of French civilization in the Americas. The capital of Nouvelle France still exudes the spirit of days past, revealing deep French roots in everything from its atmospheric 17th- and 18th-century architecture to the overwhelming prevalence of French language and cuisine. Despite its strong historic ties, the city also has a vibrant modern side, with a flourishing arts scene and a jam-packed cultural calendar designed to entertain visitors and locals alike.

HISTORY

The first significant settlement on the site of today's Québec City was an 500-strong Iroquois village called Stadacona. The Iroquois were seminomadic, building longhouses, hunting, fishing and cultivating crops until the land got tired, when they moved on.

French explorer Jacques Cartier traveled to the New World in 1534, making it as far as the Gaspé Peninsula before returning to France. His second trans-Atlantic voyage in 1535 brought him further up the St Lawrence River, where he spent a long and difficult winter encamped at the foot of the cliffs of present-day Québec City; Cartier lost 30 of his men to scurvy (the rest survived in large part thanks to traditional remedies provided by the Iroquois) before beating a retreat back to France in May 1536. Cartier returned in 1541 hoping to start a post upstream in the New World, but again faced a winter of scurvy and disastrous relations with the indigenous population; this last failed attempt set back France's colonial ambitions for 50 years.

Explorer Samuel de Champlain is credited with founding the city in 1608, calling it Kebec, from the Algonquian word meaning 'the river narrows here'. Champlain established forts and dwellings around present-day Place-Royale, laying the groundwork for the thriving capital of Nouvelle-France (New France). The English successfully attacked in 1629, but Québec was returned to the French under a treaty in 1632. As the 17th century progressed, Ursuline and Jesuit missionaries arrived, bolstering Québec City's status as the most important French settlement in the New World.

Great Britain continued to keep its eye on Québec, launching unsuccessful campaigns to take the city in 1690 and 1711. In 1759 General Wolfe finally led the British to victory over Montcalm on the Plains of Abraham. One of North America's most famous battles, it virtually ended the long-running conflict between Britain and France. In 1763 the Treaty of Paris gave Canada to Britain. In 1775 the American revolutionaries tried to capture Québec but were promptly pushed back. In 1864 meetings were held in the city that led to the formation of Canada in 1867. Québec City became the provincial capital.

Hands-on History Hot Spots

....

Parc des Champs de Bataille (Montcalm)

....

Centre d'Interprétation de la Place-Royale (Old Lower Town)

....

La Citadelle (Old Upper Town)

....

Musée de la Civilisation (Old Lower Town)

In the 19th century the city lost its status and importance to Montréal, but when the Great Depression burst Montréal's bubble in 1929, Québec City regained some stature as a government center. Then in the 1950s a group of business-savvy locals launched the now-famous Winter Carnival to incite a tourism boom.

Poor urban planning led to an exodus to the suburbs, leaving downtown depopulated and prone to crime. Things started to turn round in the 1990s, with the rejuvenation of the St-Roch neighborhood and diversification of the economy. Laval University also moved some of its apartments downtown, bringing an influx of young students.

In 2008 Québec City threw a monumental bash in honor of its 400th anniversary, an expression of local pride that drew in tens of thousands of visitors and added several new features to the city's cultural landscape, including public green spaces along the St Lawrence River and ongoing artistic events such as Robert Lepage's *Image Mill* (p182).

Québec City Architectural Gems

Château Frontenac (Old Upper Town)

Gare du Palais (Old Lower Town)

Hôtel du Parlement (Colline Parlementaire)

Église Notre-Dame-des-Victoires (Old Lower Town)

La Maison Henry-Stuart (Montcalm)

ARTS

Visual Arts

Many artists have been bewitched by the beauty of Québec City and its surrounding countryside.

Jean-Paul Lemieux (1904–90) is one of Canada's most accomplished painters. Born in Québec City, he studied at L'École des Beaux-Arts de Montréal and later in Paris. He is famous for his paintings of Québec's vacant and endless landscapes and Quebecers' relation to it. Many of his paintings are influenced by the simple lines of folk art. There's a hall devoted to his art at the Musée National des Beaux-Arts du Québec.

Alfred Pellan (1906–88) was another renowned artist who studied at the local École des Beaux-Arts before moving to Paris. He later became famous for his portraits, still lifes, figures and landscapes, before turning to surrealism in the 1940s.

Amsterdam-born Cornelius Krieghoff (1815–72) was acclaimed for chronicling the customs and clothes of Quebecers in his paintings. He is known especially for the portraits of the Wendats, who lived around Québec City.

Francesco Iacurto (1908–2001) was born in Montréal but moved to Québec City in 1938. His acclaimed works are dominated by the town's streetscapes, landscapes and portrayals of Île d'Orléans).

THE QUÉBÉCOIS ETHOS

Québec City has a reputation for being square and conservative (that is, at least from the Montréal perspective) and locals often refer to Québec City as a 'village' with equal parts affection and derision. Though it has all the big-city trappings, the core downtown population numbers under 200,000.

Québec City locals are very proud, but there's a time in many people's lives, usually after high school or university, when they decide whether they are going to 'try' Montréal or stay put. As the 'everything' capital of French Canada, from arts and business to science, technology and media, Montréal's pull is hard to resist. However, that means that those creative, dynamic people who ultimately choose to stay in Québec City are there because they really love the city and strongly identify with its unique culture.

Québec City is notorious in Montréal and the rest of Canada as a challenging place for outsiders to establish themselves in the long term. With a near-homogenous French-Catholic population, community ties go *way* back. In fact, professional and social networks are often established by the end of high school. Even French-speaking Quebecers from elsewhere in the province say these networks are extremely difficult to penetrate.

Québec City's Place-Royale (p58)

Music

Québec City has plenty to offer music lovers. For classical music fans there's the respected L'Orchestre Symphonique de Québec. Its season runs from September to May and it performs at Le Grand Théâtre de Québec. There's also the terrific Opéra de Québec, which performs at the same venue. Its season runs from October to May.

Some of the province's biggest music stars started out here. Jean Leloup of rock and pop fame was born here, and the politically charged hip-hop trio Loco Locass formed in the city. There's a brash and independent spirit among the eclectic mix of active bands here, but because the scene is so small, most bands and singers eventually relocate to Montréal for its thriving club scene and music industry ties. For the latest developments in local music, ask around at record stores like Sillons and clubs such as Le Cercle or Scanner, or check out the weekly listings in *Voir Québec* every Thursday.

Literary Looks at Québec City

Shadows on the Rock (Willa Cather)

To Quebec and the Stars (HP Lovecraft)

Where the River Narrows (Aimee Laberge)

Bury Your Dead (Louise Penny)

Films

Below are some films in which Québec City gets center stage.

I Confess by Alfred Hitchcock (1953) Québec City has never looked better than when Hitchcock's lens is caressing the city's atmospheric Old World edges. This film-noirish suspense thriller is based on a French play about a priest who hears a murderer's confession that his covenant with God won't let him break, even when he finds himself accused of the murder instead.

Les Plouffe by Gilles Carle (1981) Based on a novel by Roger Lemelin, this film depicts a family's struggles in Depression-era Québec City.

Les Yeux Rouges (The Red Eyes) by Yves Simoneau (1982) A Québec City-set thriller with two cops on the trail of a deranged strangler.

Le Confessionnal (The Confessional) by Robert Lepage (1995) An homage to the above Hitchcock film. Sometimes retracing Hitchcock's steps, Lepage builds a beautiful portrait of Québec City through a man's quest to uncover a family secret.

Ma Vie en Cinémascope (Bittersweet Memories) by Denise Filiatrault (2004) Recounts the life story of singer Alys Robi, Québec's first international superstar,. The brilliant Pascale Bussières plays the adult Alys as she realizes her wildest dreams before mental illness sees her shut up for years in an institution.

Theater

Canada's French-language TV and film industries are firmly based in Montréal, but Québec City's active theater scene still holds its own – though its tight-knit nature cuts both ways. An actor here with a creative or original idea can write a script and have it produced – something that might take years, if it happened at all, in Montréal. On the other hand, plays produced here can't always draw an audience in Montréal; to cite one famous example, the brilliant one-woman show *Gros et Détail* by Québec City actor Anne-Marie Olivier, about people in the St-Roch neighborhood, was a hit in Québec City, France and several countries in francophone Africa, yet when Olivier tried to get it produced in Montréal she was rejected on the basis that it focused too much on Québec City.

In the performing arts realm, Québec City's most famous native son is award-winning playwright and director Robert Lepage. While his best-known films and theater works feature Québec City, he has also achieved major international success, becoming the first North American to direct a Shakespeare play at London's Royal National Theatre (1992's *A Midsummer Night's Dream*), staging two world tours for Peter Gabriel, creating shows for Cirque du Soleil and directing Richard Wagner's Ring Cycle for New York's Metropolitan Opera in 2010–12. In recent years he's also received widespread acclaim for his *Image Mill*, a gigantic video projection against oversized grain silos in the Québec City harbor. The project, which explores his hometown's history, debuted in 2008 during Québec's quadricentennial celebrations but has seen its run extended to 2013 based on popular demand.

CULTURAL EVENTS

Québec City loves a good festival. Warm weather here lasts only a few short months, so locals make the most of it. In midsummer you'll find residents celebrating in city parks and streets packed with performers of every description, including the slew of international musicians that descends on the city every July for the fabulous 11-day Festival d'Été.

Winter, the longest season, holds an equally special place in the hearts of Québec City residents. The annual 17-day Winter Carnival is perhaps the city's most beloved cultural event, but there are other wintry celebrations as well, including ice canoe races across the frozen St Lawrence River and a crazy downhill skating event (the Red Bull race in March), which takes over the entire Old Town with a series of chutes and jumps running from the Château Frontenac down to Place-Royale.

LANGUAGE

Montrealers and Québec City locals can easily recognize each other at parties just by their accents. Linguists consider Québec City's accent to be purer and closer to international French, while Montréal's accent is thicker and more prone to Anglicisms. Although Québec City has far fewer native English speakers than Montréal, children study English from primary school onwards. Even so, if you venture very far outside Québec City's walls or into the surrounding countryside you'll find people who are not used to speaking or hearing much English.

Survival Guide

Transportation

GETTING TO MONTRÉAL

Most travelers arrive in Montréal by air. Located west of downtown on the island of Montréal, Pierre Elliott Trudeau International Airport has frequent connections to cities in the US, Europe, the Caribbean and Latin America, Africa and the rest of Canada. It's easy to drive to Montréal from elsewhere in Canada or the US if you have the time, or take the train or intercity coach in from cities such as Toronto or New York.

Flights, tours and rail tickets can be booked online at lonelyplanet.com/bookings.

Pierre Elliott Trudeau International Airport

Montréal is served by **Pierre Elliott Trudeau International Airport** (www.admtl. com), also known as Montréal Trudeau Airport. It's about 21km west of downtown and is the hub of most domestic, US and overseas flights. Trudeau Airport (still sometimes known by its old name, Dorval airport) has decent connections to the city by car and shuttle bus.

Bus

The cheapest way to get into town takes up to 60 minutes. The $8 fare (coins only, exact change) gives you unlimited travel on the bus and metro network for 24 hours. Outside the arrivals hall at Trudeau Airport, take bus 747 all the way to the **Gare d'Autocars** (Map p290; 505 Blvd Maisonneuve Est), which links to the Berri-UQAM metro station, in the Quartier Latin. Buses run round the clock.

Taxi

It takes at least 20 minutes to get downtown, and the fixed fare is $40. Limousine services are also available.

Car

Driving to or from downtown takes 20 to 30 minutes (allow an hour during peak times). A common route into town is the Autoroute 13 Sud that merges with the Autoroute 20 Est; this in turn takes you into the heart of downtown, along the main Autoroute Ville Marie (the 720).

Shuttles

Several hotels run shuttles from the airport to Downtown or further afield. In addition **Autocars Skyport** (www. skyportinternational.com) runs shuttles to the Mont-Tremblant ski resort area in winter and summer.

Gare d'Autocars

Most long-distance buses arrive at Montréal's **Gare d'Autocars** (Map p290; Ⓜ Berri-UQAM).

If buying tickets here for other destinations in the province, allow about 45 minutes before departure; most advance tickets don't

---

LONG-DISTANCE BUS LINES

Galland Laurentides (www.galland-bus.com) Provides bus service from Montréal to Mont-Tremblant and other destinations in the Laurentians.

Greyhound (www.greyhound.ca) Operates long-distance routes to Ottawa, Toronto, Vancouver and the USA. Greyhound also runs between Montréal and Québec City.

Moose Travel (www.moosenetwork.com) Popular with backpackers, this network operates several circuits around Canada, allowing travelers to jump on and jump off along the way. Pickup points are in Montréal, Québec City, Ottawa and Toronto, among other places.

Orléans Express (www.orleansexpress.com) Makes the three-hour run between Montréal and Québec City.

CLIMATE CHANGE & TRAVEL

Every form of transport that relies on carbon-based fuel generates CO_2, the main cause of human-induced climate change. Modern travel is dependent on airplanes, which might use less fuel per kilometer per person than most cars but travel |much greater distances. The altitude at which aircraft emit gases (including CO_2) and particles also contributes to their climate change impact. Many websites offer 'carbon calculators' that allow people to estimate the carbon emissions generated by their journey and, for those who wish to do so, to offset the impact of the greenhouse gases emitted with contributions to portfolios of climate-friendly initiatives throughout the world. Lonely Planet offsets the carbon footprint of all staff and author travel.

guarantee a seat, so arrive early to line up at the counter.

Greyhound (www.greyhound.com) and its Canadian equivalent **Greyhound Canada** (www.greyhound.ca) provide extensive service across North America. Buses from Boston and New York make regular departures to Montréal. See also the boxed text p250.

Gare Centrale

Canada's trains are arguably the most enjoyable and romantic way to travel the country. Long-distance trips are quite a bit more expensive than those by bus, however, and reservations are crucial for weekend and holiday travel. A few days' notice can cut fares a lot.

Gare Centrale (Map p288) is the local hub of **VIA Rail** (www.viarail.ca), Canada's vast rail network, which links Montréal with cities all across the country.

Amtrak (www.amtrak.com) provides service between New York City and Montréal on its Adirondack line. The trip, though slow (11 hours), passes through lovely scenery.

GETTING TO QUÉBEC CITY

Québec City is a very doable weekend trip from Montreal, and many travelers arrive by car, bus, or rail. The drive is about three hours, and Via Rail's trains take about the same time.

Highway networks connect Québec's capital with the rest of the province, while its airport has frequent connections to Canadian and US destinations, as well as less-frequent flights to and from Paris, Mexico and the Caribbean.

Aéroport International Jean-Lesage de Québec

Québec City's petite **Aéroport International Jean-Lesage de Québec** (www.aeroportdequebec.com) lies about 15km west of the center. It mostly has connections to Montreal, but there are also flights to Canadian cities such as Toronto and US cities including Chicago, Detroit, Philadelphia and Newark. Check the website for other destinations.

Taxi

Options are fairly straightforward going from this public-transit-challenged airport (bus 78 runs infrequently and goes nowhere near the center of town).

A taxi costs a flat fee of $34.25 to go into the city, around $15 if you're only going to the boroughs surrounding the airport. **Les Amis du Transport Roy & Morin** (☑418-622-6566) is a transit service for disabled people. Returning to the airport, you'll pay the metered fare, which should be less than $30.

Car

It takes about 25 minutes to reach the Old Town by car. Among several different routes, you can take Rte 540 South/Autoroute Duplessis, merge onto Rte 175, and follow this as it becomes

TRAVEL & DISABILITY

This nonprofit organization **Kéroul** (www.keroul.qc.ca) is dedicated to making travel more accessible to people with limited mobility. Its guidebook **The Accessible Road** (www.larouteaccessible.com) covers Montréal and 13 other tourism areas in Québec and highlights access facilities in each.

Look out for the **Tourist and Leisure Companion Sticker** (www.vatl-tlcs.org), which indicates free access to facilities for those traveling with people with a disability or mental illness.

Blvd Laurier, then Rue Grand Alleé, before entering the old city on Rue St-Louis.

Gare du Palais: Train

VIA Rail (www.viarail.ca) has several trains daily going between Montréal's Gare Centrale and Québec City's **Gare du Palais** (Map p160). Prices for the 3½-hour journey start at $63/126 for a one-way/return ticket.

Service is good along the so-called Québec City–Windsor corridor that connects Québec City with Montréal and on to Ottawa, Kingston, Toronto and Niagara Falls. Drinks and snacks are served from aisle carts, and some trains have a dining and bar car.

Gare du Palais: Bus

Orléans Express (www.orleansexpress.com) and **Greyhound** (www.greyhound.ca) runs daily services between Montréal's main bus station, **Gare d'Autocars** (Map p290; ⓂBerri-UQAM) and Québec City's **Gare du Palais** (Map p160). Prices for the journey (three to 3½ hours) start at $57/91 for a one-way/return ticket.

If you're coming from Montréal, your bus may first stop at **Ste-Foy-Sillery station** (3001 Chemin des Quatre Bourgeois), so ask before you get off.

Car

Québec City lies about 260km northeast of Montréal, a journey in about three hours. The most common routes are Autoroute 40 along the north shore of the St Lawrence River, and Autoroute 20, on the south shore.

THINGS CHANGE...

The information in this chapter is particularly vulnerable to change. Check directly with the airline or a travel agent to make sure you understand how a fare (and ticket you may buy) works and be aware of the security requirements for international travel. Shop carefully. The details given in this chapter should be regarded as pointers and are not a substitute for your own careful, up-to-date research.

GETTING AROUND MONTRÉAL

Bus & Metro

STM (www.stm.info) is the city's bus and metro (subway) operator. Schedules vary depending on the line, but trains generally run from 5:30am to midnight from Sunday to Friday, slightly later on Saturday night (to 1:30am at the latest).

The fare for bus and metro is $3, but it's cheaper when buying 10 tickets ($24, available in metro stations). Buses take tickets or cash but drivers won't give change. There are also tourist passes for one day ($8) and three days ($16), though a weekly pass ($23.50) may be a better deal. Monthly passes run $75.50.

If you're switching between buses, or between bus and the metro, you should get a free transfer slip, which is called a *correspondance*, from the driver; on the metro take one from the machines just past the turnstiles. A map of the metro network is included on the pull-out map at the back of this book.

Taxi

Flag fall is a standard $3.45 plus another $1.75 per kilometer. Prices are posted on the windows inside taxis. Try **Taxi Champlain** (☑514-273-2435) or **Taxi Co-Op** (☑514-725-9885).

Bicycle

Montréal's bicycle paths are extensive, running over 500km around the city. Useful bike maps are available from the tourist offices and bicycle rental shops.

Top bike paths follow the Canal de Lachine and then up along Lac St-Louis; another popular route goes southwest along the edge of the St Lawrence River, passing the Lachine Rapids and up to the Canal de Lachine, meeting up with the Canal de Lachine path (see the boxed text, p96).

Bixi

One of the best ways to see the city is by the public bike rental service **Bixi** (http://montreal.bixi.com). It's reasonably priced: 24-hour/72-hour subscription fees are $7/15; and bikes are free the first half-hour and $1.75 for the next half-hour. Rental stations are almost ubiquitous in parts of downtown (see the boxed text, p91).

In Montréal, bicycles can be taken on the metro from 10am to 3pm and after 7pm Monday to Friday, as well as throughout the weekend. Officially cyclists are supposed to board only the first two carriages of the train, but if it's not busy no one seems to mind much where you board.

There are also bike paths around the islands of Parc Jean-Drapeau, the Île de Soeurs and Parc du Mont-Royal.

Rental

Ça Roule Montréal (www
.caroulemontreal.com) Bicycle
hire runs $25 per day ($8 per
hour), in-line skates go for $20
per day ($9 per hour).
Le Grand Cycle (www
.legrandcycle.com) Charges
$35 per day ($10 per hour).
My Bicyclette (www.my
bicyclette.com) This is located
along the Canal de Lachine,
across the bridge from the
Marché Atwater. Bicycle hire
per day costs $40 ($10 per
hour).

Boat

Cruise vessels ply the St
Lawrence River for day trips
and longer cruises.
AML Cruises (Map p280;
www.croisieresaml.com) Links
Montréal and Québec City via
multiday cruises during summer. Tickets for adults start
at $339.
**Canadian Connection
Cruises** (www.stlawrence
cruiselines.com) Offers
three- to six-day luxury cruises
between Kingston, Ontario and
Québec City, including meals,
accommodations and on-board
entertainment from $1197.
CTMA Group (www.ctma.
ca) Runs eight day cruises
to the picturesque Îles de la
Madeleine in the Gulf of St
Lawrence.

Calèche

These picturesque horse-
drawn carriages seen
meandering around Old
Montréal and Mont-Royal
charge about $48/80 for
a 30/60-minute tour. They
line up at the Old Port and
at Place d'Armes. Drivers
usually provide running
commentary, which can
serve as a pretty good historical tour.

Train

AMT (www.amt.qc.ca) com-
muter trains serve the suburbs of Montréal. Services
from Gare Centrale are fast
but infrequent, with two-hour
waits between some trains.

GETTING
AROUND
QUÉBEC CITY

Bus

A ride on a white-and-blue
RTC bus (Réseau de Transport de la Capitale; www.
rtcquebec.ca) costs $3 with
transfer privileges, or $7 for
the day. Many buses serving
the Old Town area stop at
Place d'Youville just outside
the wall on Rue St-Jean. Bus
800 goes to the **Gare du
Palais** (Map p160), the central long-distance bus and
train station.

Taxi

Flag fall is a standard $3.45
plus another $1.75 per kilo-
meter. Prices are posted on
the windows inside taxis. Try
Taxi Co-Op (☑418-525-5191).

Bicycle

Québec City also has an
extensive network of bike
paths (some 70km in all),
including a route along the St
Lawrence which connects to
paths along the Rivière St-
Charles. Pick up a free color
map at the tourist office or at
local bike shops.
Cyclo Services (Map
p160; www.cycloservices.
net) charges $35 per day for
hybrid bikes ($15 per hour).

Calèche

In Québec City, calèche
drivers charge $80 for a
45-minute tour. You'll find
them just inside the Porte St-
Louis and near the Chateau
Frontenac.

DRIVING IN
AND AROUND
MONTRÉAL AND
QUÉBEC

Road Rules

Fines for traffic violations,
from speeding to not wearing a seat belt, are stiff in
Québec. You may see few
police cars on the roads but
radar traps are common.
Motorcyclists are required
to wear helmets and to drive
with their lights on.
    Traffic in both directions
must stop when school
buses stop to let children
get off and on. At the white-
striped pedestrian cross-
walks, cars must stop to
allow pedestrians to cross
the road. Turning right on
red lights is legal everywhere in Québec, including
Québec City, but is illegal in
Montréal.
    The blood-alcohol limit
while driving is 0.08%, while
in the rest of Canada is it
0.05%. Driving motorized
vehicles including boats and
snowmobiles under the influence of alcohol is a serious
offense in Canada. You could
land in jail with a court date,
heavy fine and a suspended
license. The minimum drinking age is 18 – this is the
same age as for obtaining a
driver's license.
    Québec also mandates
cars have snow tires on during winter.

Border Crossings

Continental US highways
link directly with their Canadian counterparts along the
border at numerous points.
During the summer and on
holiday weekends, waits of
several hours are common at
major USA–Canada border

crossings. If possible avoid Detroit, Michigan; Windsor, Ontario; Fort Erie, Ontario; Buffalo, New York; Niagara Falls on both sides of the border; and Rouse's Point, New York. Smaller crossings are almost always quiet.

If you have difficulty with the French-only signs in Québec, pick up a decent provincial highway map, sold at service stations and usually free at tourist offices. Visitors with US or British passports are allowed to bring their vehicles into Canada for six months.

Car Rental

Trudeau Airport has many international car-rental firms, and there's a host of smaller operators in Montréal. Whether you're here or in Québec City, rates will swing with demand so it's worth phoning around to see what's on offer. Booking ahead usually gets the best rates, and airport rates are normally better than those in town. A small car might cost around $50 to $65 per day with unlimited mileage, taxes and insurance, or $300 to $400 per week.

To rent a car in Québec you must be at least 21 years old and have had a driver's license for at least a year.

Montréal

Avis (www.avis.ca) At the airport and downtown.

Budget (www.budget.ca) In Gare Centrale.

Discount Car (www.discountcar.com) Good, competitive rates. Canadian owned.

Hertz (www.hertz.ca)

Rent-a-Wreck (www.rentawreck.ca) Often the best rates.

Québec City

Budget (www.budget.ca)

Hertz (www.hertz.ca)

TOURS

Montréal

Amphi Tours (☑514-849-5181; www.montreal-amphibus-tour.com; 75min tour adult/child $32/18; ☺May-Oct) This brightly painted 'amphibus' tootles around Old Montréal before plunging into the St Lawrence for a cruise along the waterfront.

Fitz & Follwell (☑514-840-0739; www.fitzandfollwell.co/bike-tours; 115 Ave du Mont-Royal Ouest; 3hr/4hr tours $69/79; ☺tours 2pm & 10am Apr-Oct) This acclaimed bike shop's tours take in Le Plateau Mont-Royal, the Old Port, the Canal de Lachine and other city highlights. It also offers snow tours and walking tours.

Guidatour (☑514-844-4021, 800-363-4021; www.guidatour.qc.ca; 360 Rue St-François-Xavier; adult/child/student $21/12/19; ☺11am & 1:30pm late Jun-Oct, weekends only late May–mid-Jun) On this walking tour, the experienced bilingual guides of Guidatour paint a picture of Old Montréal's eventful history with anecdotes and legends. Tours depart from Basilique Notre-Dame.

Héritage Montréal (☑514-286-2662; www.heritagemontreal.qc.ca) This independent, nonprofit organization conducts a series of architecture-based tours, focusing on a different neighborhood every week. The departure point varies and reservations are essential.

Les Fantômes du Vieux-Montréal (☑514-844-4021; www.fantommontreal.com; 469 Rue St-François-Xavier; adult/child/student $22/13/19) Gives 90-minute evening tours tracing historic crimes and legends, led by guides in period costume. You'll hear talk of

hangings, sorcery, torture and other light bedtime tales on this good-time evening outing.

Québec City

Ghost Tours of Québec (☑418-692-9770; www.ghosttoursofquebec.com; 4 1/2 Rue d'Auteuil; adult/child/student $19/free/16; ☺English tour 8pm May-Oct) Local actors lead you through the Old Town by lantern recounting the hangings and hauntings of Old Québec. The 90-minute tours are great fun and usually finish with a visit to the city's most haunted building.

La Compagnie des Six Associes (☑418-692-3033; www.sixassocies.com; adult/child/student $16/free/13) Very good walking circuits like the ever-popular 'Lust and Drunkenness,' which illuminates the history of alcohol and prostitution in the city.

Les Tours Voir Québec (☑418-266-0206, 877-266-0206; www.toursvoirquebec.com; 12 Rue Ste-Anne) This group offers excellent tours on the history and architecture of Old Québec City. The popular two-hour 'grand tour' takes in the highlights of the old quarters (adult/child/student $22/11/20). Reserve ahead.

Old Québec tours (☑418-644-0460, 800-267-8687; www.toursvieuxquebec.com) This tour operator has a variety of tours from three-hour walking tours of the Old Port (adult/child $23/11) to 4½-hour tours out of town that take in the Montmorency waterfall and Ste-Anne-de-Beaupré (adult/child $50/26) or Île d'Orléans (adult/child $70/39). There are also adventure excursions, including whale-watching in summer, and dogsledding and visits to the ice hotel in the winter.

Directory
A–Z

Business Hours

Most banks in are open 10am to 3pm Monday to Wednesday and Friday, and 10am to 7pm Thursday. Government offices generally open 9am to 5pm weekdays. Post offices are open 8am to 5pm Monday to Friday.

Hours for museums vary but most open at 10am or 11am and close by 6pm. Most are closed Monday but stay open late one day a week (typically Wednesday or Thursday).

Restaurants generally open 11:30am to 2:30pm and 5:30pm to 11pm, cafés serving breakfast may open at 8am or 9am. Many bars and pubs open from 11:30am until midnight or longer; those that don't serve food may not open until 5pm or later.

Reviews do not list business hours unless they differ from the above standards.

Some attractions in Québec City and outside Montréal shut down or operate sporadic hours outside of the busy summer months (September to May).

Courses

Cooking

Most French cooking courses are offered in French only; courses in Italian and other cuisines are available in English.

Académie Culinaire du Québec (www.academie culinaire.com; 360 Champ de Mars, Montréal; ⓂChamp-de-Mars) This esteemed cooking academy conducts regular cooking workshops and short courses ($95 for a three-hour class). Most are in French, but the school recently began offering some English-language classes.

Mezza Luna Cooking School (www.ecolemezzaluna.ca; 6851 Rue St-Dominique; ⓂDe Castelnau) Known across the country for its Italian cooking classes in French, English and Italian ($70 per class). Elena Faita gives free demonstrations on pasta-making every Saturday at 2pm at Quincaillerie Dante (p139).

Language

Concordia University Centre for Continuing Education (www.concordia.ca; 1600 Rue Ste-Catherine Ouest, Montréal; ⓂGuy-Concordia) Runs eight-week French courses from $320.

McGill University Centre for Continuing Education (www.mcgill.ca; 11th fl, 688 Rue Sherbrooke Ouest, Montréal; ⓂMcGill) Year-round, accredited intensive and part-time courses in French.

Montréal International Language Centre (www.cilm.qc.ca; 2000 Rue Ste-Catherine Ouest, Montréal; ⓂAtwater) Tailor-made language courses at this offshoot of LaSalle University.

YMCA (www.ymcalanguages.ca; 5th fl, 1440 Rue Stanley, Montréal; ⓂPeel) Offers day and evening French courses as well as an intensive summer camp. Seven-week classes cost $235 to $340.

Customs Regulations

For the latest customs information, contact the Canadian embassy or consulate at home. Most fruit, vegetables and plants can be confiscated, so avoid or ask ahead.

Visitors to Canada aged 18 and older can bring up to 1.14L (40oz) of liquor or up to 8.5L of beer or ale, and up to 50 cigars, 200 cigarettes, 200g of tobacco and 200 tobacco sticks into Canada. You can also bring in gifts valued up to $60.

US residents may bring back $800 worth of goods duty-free, plus 1L of alcohol (but you must be age 21 or over), as well as 200 cigarettes and 100 non-Cuban cigars.

Discount Cards

The Montréal Museums Pass allows free access to 38 museums for three days of your choice within a 21-day period

PRACTICALITIES

Weights & Measures

➡ Canada officially uses the metric system, but imperial units still prevail in measurements such as height and weight.

Smoking

➡ Forbidden in all enclosed spaces such as restaurants, bars and clubs. Many people light up on outdoor patios.

($60). For an extra $5, the pass comes with three consecutive days of free access to bus and metro. It's available from the city's tourist offices, or you can buy it online (www.museesmontreal.org).

An International Student Identity Card (ISIC) can pay for itself through half-price admissions, discounted air and ferry tickets and cheap meals in student cafeterias. In Montréal,

ISIC cards are issued by **Voyages Campus** (www.travelcuts.com) and other student travel agencies. The price will depend on what country you buy it in. The **International Student Identity Card** (www.isic.org) is another good source for ISIC cards.

Electricity

120V/60Hz

120V/60Hz

Emergency

When in doubt, call ☎0 and ask the operator for assistance.

Police, ambulance, fire (☎911)
Poison Centre (☎1800-463-5060)

Gay & Lesbian Travelers

Fugues (www.fugues.com) is the free, French-language, authoritative monthly guide to the gay and lesbian scene for the province of Québec. It's an excellent place to find out about the latest clubs and gay-friendly accommodations.

Montréal is a popular getaway for lesbian, gay and bisexual travelers. The gay community is centralized in the Village, and it's huge business. Gay Pride Week attracts hundreds of thousands n early August, and the Black & Blue Festival fills the Olympic Stadium for a mega-fest in early October.

Gays and lesbians are generally well integrated into the community. In the Plateau, for example, two men holding hands in public will get little more than a quick look of curiosity, though in other areas of the city being openly out may attract more attention.

Québec City is a conservative town with more of a village feel to it – open displays of affection between same-sex couples will attract attention.

Montréal Gay & Lesbian Community Centre & Library (Map p290; www.ccglm.org, in French; 2075 Rue Plessis; ◷10am-noon & 1-5pm; Ⓜ Beaudry) has been around since 1988 and provides an extensive library and loads of info on the city's gay and lesbian scene.

Internet Access

If you're traveling with a laptop, a growing number of cafés offer free wi-fi access. Register for free access and then view almost 300 places where you can get online at **Île Sans Fil** (www.ilesansfil.org).

For free wi-fi hot spots in Québec City visit www.zapquebec.org.

Many hotels also provide wi-fi access, though some charge for this service. If you're not traveling with a computer, many hotels have one available for guests (we've labeled these options with the ⓐ icon).

Internet cafés such as the following in Montréal generally charge $4 to $6 to check your *courriel* (email):

Battlenet 24 (1407 Rue du Fort; ◷24hr; Ⓜ Guy-Concordia)

Chapters Bookstore
(1171 Rue Ste-Catherine Ouest; ◉9am-11pm; ⓂPeel)

Net.24 (2157 Rue Mackay; ◉24hr; ⓂMcGill)

In Québec City, internet cafés aren't as prevalent as in Montréal.

Centre Internet (52 Côte-du-Palais; ◉9:30am-9:30pm) Centrally located in the Old Town.

Legal Matters

If you're charged with an offense, you have the right to public counsel if you can't afford a lawyer.

It's an offense to consume alcohol anywhere other than at a residence or licensed premises, which technically puts parks, beaches and the rest of the great outdoors off-limits.

Maps

If you're going to explore Montréal in detail – and you're not using smartphone maps – the best maps are published by **Mapart** (www.mapartmaps. com), available online and at Aux Quatre Points Cardinaux (p108).

Medical Services

Canadian health care is excellent but it's not free to visitors, so be sure to get travel insurance before you leave home.

Canada has no reciprocal health care with other countries and nonresidents will have to pay upfront for treatment and wait for the insurance payback.

Medical treatment is pricey (less so by US comparison), and long waits – particularly in the emergency room – are common. Avoid going to the hospital if possible.

Clinics

For minor ailments, visit the **CLSC** (community health center; ☑514-934-0354; 1801 Blvd de Maisonneuve Ouest, Montréal; ⓂGuy-Concordia) downtown or call ☑514-527-2361 for the address of the closest one.

If you're sick and need some advice, call the **health hotline** (☑811), which is staffed by nurses 24 hours a day.

Expect to pay cash upfront, as checks and credit cards are usually not accepted. You should contact your travel-insurance agency first for referrals, if you intend to make a claim later.

Emergency Rooms

In Montréal:

Montréal General Hospital (☑514-934-1934, ext 42190; 1650 Ave Cedar; ⓂGuy-Concordia)

Royal Victoria Hospital (☑514-934-1934, ext 31557; 687 Ave des Pins Ouest; ⓂMcGill)

In Québec City:

Hôpital Laval (☑418-656-8711; 2725 Chemin Ste-Foy)

Pharmacies

The big pharmacy chains are **Pharmaprix** (www.pharmaprix.ca) and **Jean Coutu** (www.jeancoutu.com). Many stores are large and well stocked, and some branches are open late.

Money

Prices quoted in this book are in Canadian dollars ($) unless stated otherwise. Canadian coins come in 1¢ (penny), 5¢ (nickel), 10¢ (dime), 25¢ (quarter), $1 (loonie) and $2 (toonie) pieces.

Paper currency comes in $5 (blue), $10 (purple), $20 (green) and $50 (red) denominations. The $100

(brown) and larger bills are less common.

Given counterfeiting many stores flat-out refuse to take $100 and even sometimes $50 bills. This is not really legally allowed, unless there is some real reason to believe the bills are fake, but many stores insist on such a policy.

ATMs

Montréal has droves of ATMs linked to the international Cirrus, Plus and Maestro networks, not only in banks but also in pubs, convenience stores and hotels. Many charge a small fee per use, and your own bank may levy an extra fee – it's best to check before leaving home.

Changing Money

The main shopping streets in Montréal, including Rue Ste-Catherine, Blvd St-Laurent and Rue St-Denis, have plenty of banks. There are also foreign-exchange desks at the main tourist office, the airport and the casino.

One option is **Calforex** (1230 Rue Peel; ⓂPeel).

In Québec City there's **Transchange International** (43 Rue de Buade).

Traveler's Checks

This old-school option offers protection against loss or theft. In Canada, many establishments, not just banks, will accept traveler's checks like cash, provided they're in Canadian dollars. They offer good exchange rates but not necessarily better than those from ATMs.

Post

Montréal's **main post office** (1250 Rue University) is the largest but there are many convenient locations around town. Poste restante (general delivery) is available at **Station Place-d'Armes** (435 Rue St-Antoine, Montréal

H2Z 1H0). Mail is kept for two weeks and then returned to the sender. The main **Canada Post/Postes Canada** (☎866-607-6301) provides general information.

In Québec City the **post office** (5 Rue du Fort) in the Upper Town offers the biggest selection of postal services.

Stamps are also available at newspaper shops, convenience stores and some hotels. Standard 1st-class airmail letters or postcards cost 54¢ to Canadian destinations and 98¢ to the USA (both are limited to 30g). Those to other destinations cost $1.65 (their limit is also 30g).

Public Holidays

Banks, schools and government offices close on Canadian public holidays, while museums and other services go on a restricted schedule. This is also a busy time to travel.

Residential leases in Montréal traditionally end on June 30, so the roads are always clogged on July 1 as tenants move to their new homes.

School students break for summer holidays in late June and return to school in early September. University students get even more time off, breaking from May to early or mid-September. Most people take their big annual vacation during this summer period.

The main public holidays:

New Year's Day January 1

Good Friday & Easter Monday Late March to mid-April

Victoria Day May 24 or nearest Monday

National Aboriginal Day June 21 (unofficial)

Saint-Jean-Baptiste Day June 24

Canada Day July 1

Labour Day First Monday in September

Canadian Thanksgiving Second Monday in October

Remembrance Day November 11

Christmas Day December 25

Boxing Day December 26

Safe Travel

Violent crime is rare (especially involving foreigners) but petty theft is more common. Watch out for pickpockets in crowded markets and public transit places, and use hotel safes where available.

Cars with foreign registration are popular targets for smash-and-grab theft. Don't leave valuables in the car, and remove registration and ID papers.

Take special care at pedestrian crosswalks in Montréal: unless there's an *'arrêt'* (stop) sign, drivers largely ignore these crosswalks.

Telephone

Local calls from a pay phone cost 50¢. With the popularity of cell phones, public phones are becoming a rarity. When you do find them they will generally be coin-operated but many also accept phone cards and credit cards.

The area code for the entire island of Montréal is ☎514; Québec City's is ☎418. When you dial, even local numbers, you will need to punch in the area code as well.

Toll-free numbers begin with ☎800, ☎888, ☎877 or ☎777 and must be preceded with 1. Some numbers are good throughout North America, others only within Canada or one particular province.

Dialing the operator (☎0) or the emergency number (☎911) is free of charge from both public and private phones. For directory assistance, dial ☎411. Fees apply.

Cell Phones

The only foreign cell phones that will work in North America are triband models, operating on GSM 1900 and other frequencies. If you don't have one of these, your best bet may be to buy a prepaid one at a consumer electronics store. You can often score an inexpensive phone for around $60 including voicemail, some prepaid minutes and a rechargeable SIM card.

Consumer electronics stores such as **Future Shop** (www.futureshop.ca) sell wireless and prepaid deals of use to travelers. US residents traveling with their phone may have service (though they'll pay roaming fees). Get in touch with your cell-phone provider for details.

Phone Cards

Bell Canada's prepaid cards, in denominations of $5, $10 and $20, work from public and private phones. They're available from post offices, convenience stores and pharmacies.

Many local phone cards offer better rates than Bell's. Sold at convenience stores and newsstands, the cards have catchy names such as Mango, Big Time, Giant and Lucky. See www.thephonecardstore.ca.

Time

Montréal is on Eastern Time (EST/EDT), as is New York City and Toronto – five hours behind Greenwich Mean Time.

Canada switches to daylight-saving time (one hour later than Standard Time) from the second Sunday in March to the first Sunday in November.

Train schedules, film screenings and schedules in French use the 24-hour clock (eg 6:30pm becomes 18:30) while English schedules use the 12-hour clock.

Tourist Information

Montréal and Québec province share a central phone number and website for their **tourist information offices** (⌨877-266-5687; www.tourisme-montreal.org).

The airports have information kiosks that open year-round.

For Québec province info, covering Montréal, Québec City and many other areas, visit **Bonjour Québec** (www.bonjourquebec.com).

In Montréal:

Centre Infotouriste (Map p288; 1255 Rue Peel; ⊙9am-6pm, to 5pm Nov-Apr; Ⓜ Peel) Teems with information on all areas of Montréal and Québec. The center also has independently staffed counters dedicated to national parks, car rental, boat trips, city tours and currency exchange. Hotel reservations are provided free of charge.

Old Montréal Tourist Office (Map p280; 174 Rue Notre-Dame Est; ⊙9am-7pm late Jun-early Oct, to 5pm rest of year; Ⓜ Champ-de-Mars) Just off bustling Pl Jacques-Cartier, this little office is always humming but staff are extremely helpful.

In Québec City:

Centre Infotouriste (Map p160; ⌨418-649-2608, 800-363-7777; 12 Rue Ste-Anne; ⊙9am-7pm late Jun-early Oct, to 5pm rest of year) Central location in Old Town.

Centre Infotouriste (Map p168; ⌨418-641-6290, 800-266-5687, ext 798; 835 Ave Wilfrid-Laurier; ⊙9am-7pm Jun-late Aug, to 5pm rest of year) Located in Battlefields Park.

Travelers with Disabilities

In Montréal, most public buildings – including tourist offices, major museums and attractions – are wheelchair accessible, and many restaurants and hotels also have facilities for the mobility-impaired. Metro stations are not wheelchair accessible; however, almost all major bus routes are now serviced by NOVA LFS buses adapted for wheelchairs. It's recommended that you consult the bus service's website (www.stm.info) to check availability on your route and become familiar with the boarding procedure on the adapted buses.

Access to Travel (www.accesstotravel.gc.ca) Provides details of accessible transportation across Canada.

Kéroul (www.keroul.qc.ca) Has detailed information on its website, and also publishes *Québec Accessible* ($26), listing hotels, restaurants and attractions in the province. It also offers packages for disabled travelers going to Québec and Ontario.

VIA Rail (www.viarail.ca) Accommodates people in wheelchairs with 48 hours' notice. Details are available at VIA Rail offices at Montréal's Gare Centrale and Québec City's Gare du Palais.

Buses in Québec City's public transit system are not wheelchair accessible, though there are other services available for travelers with disabilities.

Transport Accessible du Québec (⌨418-641-8294) Wheelchair-adapted vans available. Make reservations 24 hours in advance.

Transport Adapté du Québec Métro inc (⌨418-687-2641; ⊙7:30am-10:30pm) Has 20 wheelchair-adapted minibuses that zip around Québec. Make reservations at least eight hours in advance of your trip.

Visas

Citizens of dozens of countries – including the USA, most Western European countries, Australia, Israel, Japan and New Zealand – don't need visas to enter Canada for stays of up to 180 days. US permanent residents are also exempt.

Nationals of around 150 other countries, including South Africa and China, need to apply to the Canadian visa office in their home country for a temporary resident visa (TRV). The website maintained by **Citizen and Immigration Canada** (www.cic.gc.ca) has full details.

Single-entry visitor visas ($75) are valid for six months, while multiple-entry visas ($150) can be used over two years, provided that no single stay exceeds six months. Extensions cost the same price as the original and must be applied for at a Canadian Immigration Center one month before the current visa expires. A separate visa is required if you intend to work in Canada.

Women Travelers

It is illegal in Canada to carry pepper spray or mace. Instead, some women recommend carrying a whistle to deal with attackers or potential dangers. If you are sexually assaulted, call ⌨911 or the **Sexual Assault Center** (⌨in Montréal 514-398-8500, in Québec City 418-522-2120) for referrals to hospitals that have sexual-assault care centers.

Language

Canada is officially a bilingual country with the majority of the population speaking English as their first language. In Québec, however, the dominant language is French. The local tongue is essentially the same as what you'd hear in France, and you'll have no problems being understood if you use standard French phrases (provided in this chapter).

Of course, there are some differences between European French and the Québec version (known as 'Québécois' or *joual*). For example, while standard French for 'What time is it?' is *Quelle heure est-il?*, in Québec you're likely to hear *Y'est quelle heure?* instead. Other differences worth remembering are the terms for breakfast, lunch and dinner: rather than *petit déjeuner, déjeuner* and *dîner* you're likely to see and hear *déjeuner, dîner* and *souper*. Québec French also employs a lot of English words; eg English terms are generally used for car parts – even the word *char* (pronounced 'shar') for car may be heard.

The sounds used in spoken French can almost all be found in English. If you read our pronunciation guides as if they were English, you'll be understood. There are a couple of exceptions: nasal vowels (represented in our guides by o or u followed by an almost inaudible nasal consonant sound m, n or ng), the 'funny' *u* (ew in our guides) and the deep-in-the-throat *r*. Syllables in French words are, for the most part, equally stressed. As English speakers tend to stress the first syllable, try adding a light stress on the final syllable of French words to compensate.

WANT MORE?

....

For in-depth language information and handy phrases, check out Lonely Planet's *French phrasebook*. You'll find it at **shop.lonelyplanet.com**, or you can buy Lonely Planet's iPhone phrasebooks at the Apple App Store.

BASICS

Hello.	*Bonjour.*	bon·zhoor
Goodbye.	*Au revoir.*	o·rer·vwa
Excuse me.	*Excusez-moi.*	ek·skew·zay·mwa
Sorry.	*Pardon.*	par·don
Yes./No.	*Oui./Non.*	wee/non
Please.	*S'il vous plaît.*	seel voo play
Thank you.	*Merci.*	mair·see

How are you?
Comment allez-vous?   ko·mon ta·lay·voo

Fine, and you?
Bien, merci. Et vous?   byun mair·see ay voo

What's your name?
Comment vous appelez-vous?   ko·mon voo·za·play voo

My name is ...
Je m'appelle ...   zher ma·pel ...

Do you speak English?
Parlez-vous anglais?   par·lay·voo ong·glay

I don't understand.
Je ne comprends pas.   zher ner kom·pron pa

ACCOMMODATIONS

Do you have any rooms available?
Est-ce que vous avez des chambres libres?   es·ker voo za·vay day shom·brer lee·brer

How much is it per night/person?
Quel est le prix par nuit/personne?   kel ay ler pree par nwee/per·son

Is breakfast included?
Est-ce que le petit déjeuner est inclus?   es·ker ler per·tee day·zher·nay ayt en·klew

dorm	*dortoir*	dor·twar
guesthouse	*pension*	pon·syon
hotel	*hôtel*	o·tel
youth hostel	*auberge de jeunesse*	o·berzh der zher·nes

Signs

Entrée	Entrance
Femmes	Women
Fermé	Closed
Hommes	Men
Interdit	Prohibited
Ouvert	Open
Renseignements	Information
Sortie	Exit
Toilettes/WC	Toilets

a ... room	une chambre ...	ewn shom·brer ...
single	à un lit	a un lee
double	avec un grand lit	a·vek un gron lee

with (a) ...	avec ...	a·vek ...
air-con	climatiseur	klee·ma·tee·zer
bathroom	une salle de bains	ewn sal der bun
window	fenêtre	fer·nay·trer

DIRECTIONS

Where's ...?
Où est ...? — oo ay ...

What's the address?
Quelle est l'adresse? — kel ay la·dres

Can you write down the address, please?
Est-ce que vous pourriez écrire l'adresse, s'il vous plaît? — es·ker voo poo·ryay ay·kreer la·dres seel voo play

Can you show me (on the map)?
Pouvez-vous m'indiquer (sur la carte)? — poo·vay·voo mun·dee·kay (sewr la kart)

EATING & DRINKING

What would you recommend?
Qu'est-ce que vous conseillez? — kes·ker voo kon·say·yay

What's in that dish?
Quels sont les ingrédients? — kel son lay zun·gray·dyon

I'm a vegetarian.
Je suis végétarien/ végétarienne. — zher swee vay·zhay·ta·ryun/ vay·zhay·ta·ryen (m/f)

Cheers!
Santé! — son·tay

That was delicious.
C'était délicieux! — say·tay day·lee·syer

Please bring the bill.
Apportez-moi l'addition, s'il vous plaît. — a·por·tay·mwa la·dee·syon seel voo play

I'd like to reserve a table for ...	Je voudrais réserver une table pour ...	zher voo·dray ray·zair·vay ewn ta·bler poor ...
(eight) o'clock	(vingt) heures	(vungt) er
(two) people	(deux) personnes	(der) pair·son

Key Words

appetiser	entrée	on·tray
bottle	bouteille	boo·tay
breakfast	déjeuner	day·zher·nay
cold	froid	frwa
delicatessen	traiteur	tray·ter
dinner	souper	soo·pay
fork	fourchette	foor·shet
glass	verre	vair
grocery store	épicerie	ay·pees·ree
hot	chaud	sho
knife	couteau	koo·to
lunch	dîner	dee·nay
market	marché	mar·shay
menu	carte	kart
plate	assiette	a·syet
spoon	cuillère	kwee·yair
wine list	carte des vins	kart day vun
with/without	avec/sans	a·vek/son

Meat & Fish

beef	bœuf	berf
chicken	poulet	poo·lay
crab	crabe	krab
lamb	agneau	a·nyo
oyster	huître	wee·trer
pork	porc	por
snail	escargot	es·kar·go
squid	calmar	kal·mar
turkey	dinde	dund
veal	veau	vo

Fruit & Vegetables

apple	pomme	pom
apricot	abricot	ab·ree·ko
asparagus	asperge	a·spairzh
beans	haricots	a·ree·ko
beetroot	betterave	be·trav
cabbage	chou	shoo

celery	*céleri*	sel·ree ·
cherry	*cerise*	ser·reez
corn	*maïs*	ma·ees
cucumber	*concombre*	kong·kom·brer
gherkin (pickle)	*cornichon*	kor·nee·shon
grape	*raisin*	ray·zun
leek	*poireau*	pwa·ro
lemon	*citron*	see·tron
lettuce	*laitue*	lay·tew
mushroom	*champignon*	shom·pee·nyon
peach	*pêche*	pesh
peas	*petit pois*	per·tee pwa
(red/green) pepper	*poivron (rouge/vert)*	pwa·vron (roozh/vair)
pineapple	*ananas*	a·na·nas
plum	*prune*	prewn
potato	*pomme de terre*	pom der tair
prune	*pruneau*	prew·no
pumpkin	*citrouille*	see·troo·yer
shallot	*échalote*	eh·sha·lot
spinach	*épinards*	eh·pee·nar
strawberry	*fraise*	frez
tomato	*tomate*	to·mat
turnip	*navet*	na·vay
vegetable	*légume*	lay·gewm

Other

bread	*pain*	pun
butter	*beurre*	ber
cheese	*fromage*	fro·mazh
egg	*œuf*	erf
honey	*miel*	myel
jam	*confiture*	kon·fee·tewr
oil	*huile*	weel
pepper	*poivre*	pwa·vrer
rice	*riz*	ree
salt	*sel*	sel
sugar	*sucre*	sew·krer
vinegar	*vinaigre*	vee·nay·grer

Drinks

beer	*bière*	bee·yair
coffee	*café*	ka·fay
(orange) juice	*jus (d'orange)*	zhew (do·ronzh)
milk	*lait*	lay
red wine	*vin rouge*	vun roozh

tea	*thé*	tay
(mineral) water	*eau (minérale)*	o (mee·nay·ral)
white wine	*vin blanc*	vun blong

EMERGENCIES

Help!
Au secours! — o skoor

Leave me alone!
Fichez-moi la paix! — fee·shay·mwa la pay

I'm lost.
Je suis perdu/perdue. — zhe swee·pair·dew (m/f)

Call a doctor.
Appelez un médecin. — a·play un mayd·sun

Call the police.
Appelez la police. — a·play la po·lees

I'm ill.
Je suis malade. — zher swee ma·lad

It hurts here.
J'ai une douleur ici. — zhay ewn doo·ler ee·see

I'm allergic (to ...).
Je suis allergique (à ...). — zher swee za·lair·zheek (a...)

SHOPPING & SERVICES

I'd like to buy ...
Je voudrais acheter ... — zher voo·dray ash·tay ...

Can I look at it?
Est-ce que je peux le voir? — es·ker zher per ler vwar

I'm just looking.
Je regarde. — zher rer·gard

I don't like it.
Cela ne me plaît pas. — ser·la ner mer play pa

How much is it?
C'est combien? — say kom·byun

It's too expensive.
C'est trop cher. — say tro shair

There's a mistake in the bill.
Il y a une erreur dans la note. — eel ya ewn ay·rer don la not

bank	*banque*	bonk
internet cafe	*cybercafé*	see·bair·ka·fay
tourist office	*office de tourisme*	o·fees der too·rees·mer

Question Words

What?	*Quoi?*	kwa
When?	*Quand?*	kon
Where?	*Où?*	oo
Who?	*Qui?*	kee
Why?	*Pourquoi?*	poor·kwa

Numbers

1	*un*	un
2	*deux*	der
3	*trois*	trwa
4	*quatre*	ka·trer
5	*cinq*	sungk
6	*six*	sees
7	*sept*	set
8	*huit*	weet
9	*neuf*	nerf
10	*dix*	dees
20	*vingt*	vung
30	*trente*	tront
40	*quarante*	ka·ront
50	*cinquante*	sung·kont
60	*soixante*	swa·sont
70	*soixante-dix*	swa·son·dees
80	*quatre-vingts*	ka·trer·vung
90	*quatre-vingt-dix*	ka·trer·vung·dees
100	*cent*	son
1000	*mille*	meel

TIME & DATES

What time is it?
Y'est quelle heure?   il ay kel er

It's (eight) o'clock.
Il est (huit) heures.   il ay (weet) er

Half past (10).
(Dix) heures et demie.   (deez) er ay day·mee

morning	*matin*	ma·tun
afternoon	*après-midi*	a·pray·mee·dee
evening	*soir*	swar
yesterday	*hier*	yair
today	*aujourd'hui*	o·zhoor·dwee
tomorrow	*demain*	der·mun
Monday	*lundi*	lun·dee
Tuesday	*mardi*	mar·dee
Wednesday	*mercredi*	mair·krer·dee
Thursday	*jeudi*	zher·dee
Friday	*vendredi*	von·drer·dee
Saturday	*samedi*	sam·dee
Sunday	*dimanche*	dee·monsh

TRANSPORTATION

I want to go to ...
Je voudrais   zher voo·dray
aller à ...   a·lay a ...

At what time does it leave/arrive?
À quelle heure est-ce   a kel er es
qu'il part/arrive?   kil par/a·reev

Does it stop at ...?
Est-ce qu'il s'arrête à ...?   es·kil sa·ret a ...

I want to get off here.
Je veux descendre   zher ver day·son·drer
ici.   ee·see

a ... ticket	*un billet ...*	un bee·yay ...
1st-class	*de première classe*	der prem·yair klas
2nd-class	*de deuxième classe*	der der·zyem las
one-way	*simple*	sum·pler
return	*aller et retour*	a·lay ay rer·toor
aisle seat	*côté couloir*	ko·tay kool·war
boat	*bateau*	ba·to
bus	*bus*	bews
cancelled	*annulé*	a·new·lay
delayed	*en retard*	on rer·tar
first	*premier*	prer·myay
last	*dernier*	dair·nyay
plane	*avion*	a·vyon
platform	*quai*	kay
ticket office	*guichet*	gee·shay
timetable	*horaire*	o·rair
train	*train*	trun
window seat	*côté fenêtre*	ko·tay fe·ne·trer

I'd like to hire a ...	*Je voudrais louer ...*	zher voo·dray loo·way ...
car	*une voiture*	ewn vwa·tewr
bicycle	*un vélo*	un vay·lo
motorcycle	*une moto*	ewn mo·to
child seat	*siège-enfant*	syezh·on·fon
helmet	*casque*	kask
mechanic	*mécanicien*	may·ka·nee·syun
petrol/gas	*essence*	ay·sons
service station	*station-service*	sta·syon·ser·vees

Can I park here?
Est-ce que je peux   es·ker zher per
stationner ici?   sta·syo·nay ee·see

I have a flat tyre.
Mon pneu est à plat.   mom pner ay ta pla

I've run out of petrol.
Je suis en panne   zher swee zon pan
d'essence.   day·sons

GLOSSARY

allophone – a person whose mother tongue is neither French nor English

Anglophone – a person whose mother tongue is English

beaux arts – architectural style popular in France and Québec in the late 19th century, incorporating elements that are massive, elaborate and often ostentatious

Bill 101 – law that asserts the primacy of the French language in Québec, notably on signage

boîte à chanson – club devoted to chanson française, folk music from Québec or France

brochette – kebab

cabane à sucre – place where the collected maple sap is distilled in large kettles and boiled as part of the production of maple syrup

calèche – horse-drawn carriage that can be taken around parts of Montréal and Québec City

Cantons de l'Est – Eastern Townships, a former Loyalist region southeast of Montréal toward the US border

cinq à sept – literally means five-to-seven, but refers to happy hours

correspondance – a transfer slip like those used between the métro and bus networks in Montréal

côte – a hill, as in Côte du Beaver Hall

dépanneur – called 'dep' for short, this is a Québec term for a convenience store

Estrie – a more recent term for *Cantons de l'Est*

First Nations – a term used to denote Canada's indigenous peoples, sometime used instead of Native Indians or Amerindians

Francophone – a person whose mother tongue is French

Front de Libération du Québec (FLQ) – a radical, violent political group active in the 1970s that advocated Québec's separation from Canada

gîte (du passant) – French term for B&B or similar lodging

Hochelaga – name of early Iroquois settlement on the site of present-day Montréal

Je me souviens – this Québec motto with a nationalist ring ('I remember') appears on license plates across the province

loonie – Canada's $1 coin, named for the loon stamped on one side

Mounties – Royal Canadian Mounted Police (RCMP)

Québécois – the French spoken in Québec; someone from the province of Québec; someone from Québec City

Refus Global – the radical manifest of a group of Québec artists and intellectuals during the Duplessis era (1944–59)

SAQ – Société des Alcools du Québec, a state-run agency that sells wines, spirits, beer etc

stimés – hotdog in a steamed bun

table d'hôte – fixed-price meal (of the day)

téléroman – a type of Québec TV program that's a cross between soap opera and prime-time drama, in French

toastés – hotdog with a toasted bun

toonie – also spelled 'twonie,' the Canadian $2 coin introduced after the *loonie*

MENU DECODER

ailes wings

allongé watered-down espresso

apportez votre vin or AVV bring your own bottle

boire drink

bouteille bottle

brochette kebab

café café

casse-croûte a snack bar

cretons pork spread with onions and spices

entrée appetizer

escalopes tenderized, boneless meat

foie de veau calf liver

le déjeuner breakfast

le dîner lunch

le souper dinner

maison homemade, by the chef

manger to eat

menu dégustatio a multi-course tasting menu

paté pâté, as in pâté de foie gras

pâtes pasta

plat dish

plat du jour daily special

plat principal main dish

poutine French fries served with gravy and cheese curds

rillettes pastelike preparation of meat

ris de veau veal sweetbreads

service compris service included

stimés hotdog with a steamed bun

table d'hôte fixed-price meal (of the day)

taxes incluses taxes included

toastés hotdog with a toasted bun

tourtière Québec meat pie usually made of pork and beef or veal, sometimes with game meat

verre glass

Behind the Scenes

SEND US YOUR FEEDBACK

We love to hear from travelers – your comments keep us on our toes and help make our books better. Our well-traveled team reads every word on what you loved or loathed about this book. Although we cannot reply individually to postal submissions, we always guarantee that your feedback goes straight to the appropriate authors, in time for the next edition. Each person who sends us information is thanked in the next edition – and the most useful submissions are rewarded with a selection of digital PDF chapters.

Visit **lonelyplanet.com/contact** to submit your updates and suggestions or to ask for help. Our award-winning website also features inspirational travel stories, news and discussions.

Note: We may edit, reproduce and incorporate your comments in Lonely Planet products such as guidebooks, websites and digital products, so let us know if you don't want your comments reproduced or your name acknowledged. For a copy of our privacy policy visit lonelyplanet.com/privacy.

OUR READERS

Many thanks to the travelers who used the last edition and wrote to us with helpful hints, useful advice and interesting anecdotes:

Robert Bingham, Pauline Cordier, Charles-Etienne, Bruno Falardeau, Colin Hulmes, Chris Owens.

AUTHOR THANKS

Timothy N Hornyak

My heartfelt thanks to my foodie friends and family whose restaurant suggestions and companionship made research so delightfully filling: my mother Jennifer Hornyak, stepfather Pierre Boudreault, stepbrother Charles Boudreault, cousin Rebecca Bloom-Geddes, faithful tomodachi Marie Murai, my beloved NSS mates, especially Dimitri Antonopoulos, Felix Gutierrez and Aris Piliguian, and also Yvan Marcoux and Kelly Yee, as well as Marie-Jose Pinsonnault of Tourisme Montréal.

Gregor Clark

Un grand merci to the countless people who shared their love and knowledge of Québec City, the Eastern Townships, Trois-Rivières and the Laurentians with me, especially Nicole O'Connor, Lucien Beaumont, Julien Lapointe, Anne Minnerly, Beth Stanway and Jori Jacobeit. Back home, big hugs and thanks to my wife Gaen and daughters Meigan and Chloe, who helped me immeasurably in researching Québec City's best bakeries and honing my technique on the ice slides at the Ice Hotel.

ACKNOWLEDGMENTS

Cover photograph: Ave St-Denis and Château Frontenac, Québec City; Denis Corriveau/ Getty Images.

THIS BOOK

This 3rd edition of Lonely Planet's *Montréal & Québec City* guidebook was researched and written by Timothy N Hornyak and Gregor Clark. The 2nd edition was written by Regis St Louis and Simona Rabinovitch. The 1st edition was written by Eilís Quinn. This guidebook was commissioned in Lonely Planet's Oakland office, and produced by the following:

Commissioning Editor
Heather Howard

Coordinating Editors Jessica Crouch, Pete Cruttenden

Coordinating Cartographer
Xavier Di Toro

Coordinating Layout Designer Joseph Spanti

Managing Editor Martine Power

Senior Editors Andi Jones, Susan Paterson

Managing Cartographers Shahara Ahmed, Alison Lyall

Managing Layout Designer Chris Girdler

Assisting Editors Samantha Forge, Laura Gibb, Kim Hutchins, Charlotte Orr

Assisting Cartographers Eve Kelly, Alex Leung

Cover Research Naomi Parker

Internal Image Research Nicholas Colicchia

Language Content Branislava Vladisavljevic

Thanks to Lucy Birchley, Melanie Dankel, Frank Diem, Ryan Evans, Jennye Garibaldi, Mark Griffiths, Annelies Mertens, Anna Metcalfe, Kathleen Munnelly, Wayne Murphy, Trent Paton, Jacqui Saunders, Laura Stansfeld, Gerard Walker, Juan Winata, Emily K Wolman, Wendy Wright

Index

See also separate subindexes for:

✖ **EATING P273**

🍷 **DRINKING & NIGHTLIFE P274**

☆ **ENTERTAINMENT P275**

🛍 **SHOPPING P275**

🏃 **SPORTS & ACTIVITIES P276**

🛏 **SLEEPING P276**

Montréal Maps

Map Legend

Sights
- Beach
- Buddhist
- Castle
- Christian
- Hindu
- Islamic
- Jewish
- Monument
- Museum/Gallery
- Ruin
- Winery/Vineyard
- Zoo
- Other Sight

Eating
- Eating

Drinking & Nightlife
- Drinking & Nightlife
- Cafe

Entertainment
- Entertainment

Shopping
- Shopping

Sleeping
- Sleeping
- Camping

Sports & Activities
- Diving/Snorkelling
- Canoeing/Kayaking
- Skiing
- Surfing
- Swimming/Pool
- Walking
- Windsurfing
- Other Sports & Activities

Information
- Post Office
- Tourist Information

Transport
- Airport
- Border Crossing
- Bus
- Cable Car/Funicular
- Cycling
- Ferry
- Monorail
- Parking
- S-Bahn
- Taxi
- Train/Railway
- Tram
- Tube Station
- U-Bahn
- Underground Train Station
- Other Transport

Routes
- Tollway
- Freeway
- Primary
- Secondary
- Tertiary
- Lane
- Unsealed Road
- Plaza/Mall
- Steps
- Tunnel
- Pedestrian Overpass
- Walking Tour
- Walking Tour Detour
- Path

Boundaries
- International
- State/Province
- Disputed
- Regional/Suburb
- Marine Park
- Cliff
- Wall

Geographic
- Hut/Shelter
- Lighthouse
- Lookout
- Mountain/Volcano
- Oasis
- Park
- Pass
- Picnic Area
- Waterfall

Hydrography
- River/Creek
- Intermittent River
- Swamp/Mangrove
- Reef
- Canal
- Water
- Dry/Salt/Intermittent Lake
- Glacier

Areas
- Beach/Desert
- Cemetery (Christian)
- Cemetery (Other)
- Park/Forest
- Sportsground
- Sight (Building)
- Top Sight (Building)

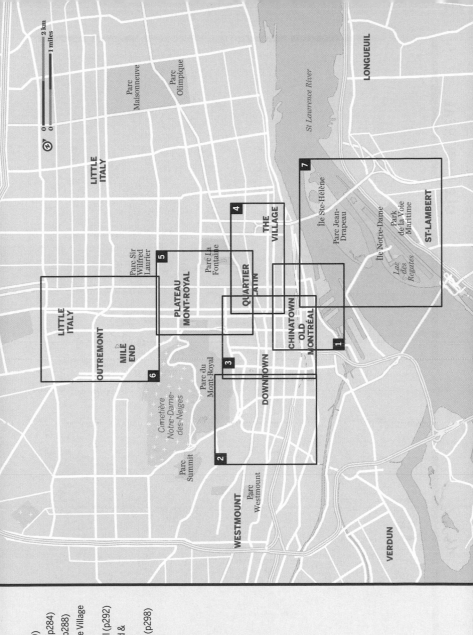

MAP INDEX

LONGUEUIL

LITTLE ITALY

Parc Maisonneuve

Parc Olimpique

St Lawrence River

ST-LAMBERT

Île Ste-Hélène

Parc Jean-Drapeau

Île Notre-Dame

Park de la Voie Maritime

Lac des Régates

THE VILLAGE

QUARTIER LATIN

Parc La Fontaine

Parc Sir Wilfred Laurier

PLATEAU MONT-ROYAL

CHINATOWN

OLD MONTRÉAL

LITTLE ITALY

OUTREMONT

MILE END

Parc du Mont-Royal

Cimetière Notre-Dame-des-Neiges

DOWNTOWN

Parc Summit

Parc Westmount

WESTMOUNT

VERDUN

2 km
1 miles

Key on p282

OLD MONTRÉAL

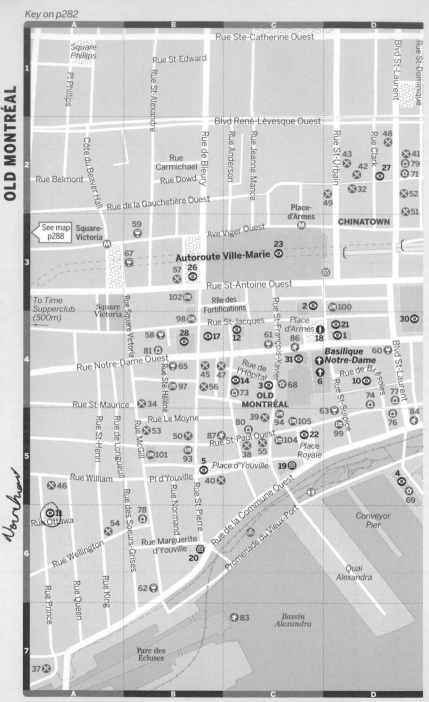

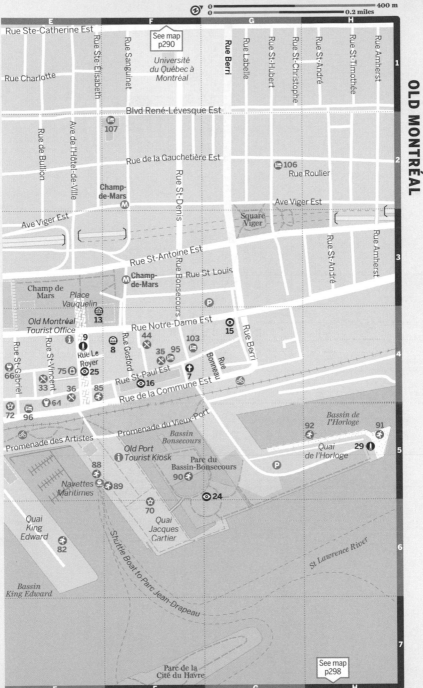

400 m
0.2 miles

Rue Ste-Catherine Est

See map
p290

Université
du Québec à
Montréal

Rue Charlotte

Rue Ste-Élisabeth

Rue Sanguinet

Rue Berri

Rue Labelle

Rue St-Hubert

Rue St-Christophe

Rue St-André

Rue St-Timothée

Rue Amherst

Blvd René-Lévesque Est

Rue de Bullion

Ave de l'Hôtel-de-Ville

107

Rue de la Gauchetière Est

Rue St-Denis

106
Rue Roulier

Champ-
de-Mars
M

Ave Viger Est

Square
Viger

Rue St-André

Rue Amherst

Ave Viger Est

Rue St-Antoine Est

Rue Bonsecours

Rue St-Louis

Champ de
Mars

Place
Vauquelin

Champ-
de-Mars

Old Montréal
Tourist Office

13

P

9

Rue Gosford

Rue Notre-Dame Est

44

103

15

Rue Berri

Rue Bonneau

8

Rue Le
Royer

35 95

Rue St-Vincent

75

25

Rue St-Gabriel

66

Rue St-Paul Est

7

33

36

85

16

Rue de la Commune Est

72

96

64

Promenade du Vieux-Port

Bassin
Bonsecours

92

Bassin de
l'Horloge

91

Promenade des Artistes

Old Port
Tourist Kiosk

Parc du
Bassin-Bonsecours

P

Quai
de l'Horloge

29

88

90

Navettes
Maritimes

89

Quai
King
Edward

70

24

82

Quai
Jacques
Cartier

St Lawrence River

Bassin
King Edward

Shuttle Boat to Parc Jean-Drapeau

Parc de la
Cité du Havre

See map
p298

OLD MONTRÉAL

OLD MONTRÉAL Map on p280

DOWNTOWN (WEST)

Key on p286

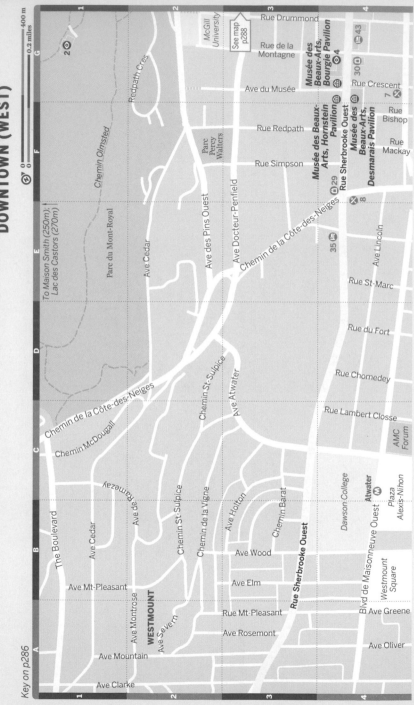

400 m
0.2 miles

McGill University

See map p288

Rue Drummond

Rue de la Montagne

Musée des Beaux-Arts, Bourgie Pavilion

43

Ave du Musée

Rue Crescent

30

Musée des Beaux-Arts, Hornstein Pavilion

Rue Sherbrooke Ouest

Rue Bishop

Rue Redpath

Musée des Beaux-Arts, Desmarais Pavilion

Rue Simpson

29

7

Rue Mackay

8

35

Redpath Cres

Chemin Olmsted

Parc Percy Walters

To Maison Smith (250m); Lac des Castors (270m)

Parc du Mont-Royal

Ave des Pins Ouest

Ave Docteur-Penfield

Ave Cedar

Chemin de la Côte-des-Neiges

Rue St-Marc

Rue du Fort

Ave Lincoln

Chemin de la Côte-des-Neiges

Rue Chomedey

Chemin McDougall

Chemin St-Sulpice

Ave Atwater

Rue Lambert Closse

AMC Forum

Ave de Ramezay

Chemin St-Sulpice

Chemin de la Vigne

Ave Holton

Chemin Barat

Dawson College

Atwater

Plaza Alexis-Nihon

The Boulevard

Ave Cedar

Ave Wood

Rue Sherbrooke Ouest

Blvd de Maisonneuve Ouest

Westmount Square

Ave Mt-Pleasant

Ave Montrose

Ave Severn

WESTMOUNT

Ave Elm

Rue Mt-Pleasant

Ave Greene

Ave Mountain

Ave Rosemont

Ave Oliver

Ave Clarke

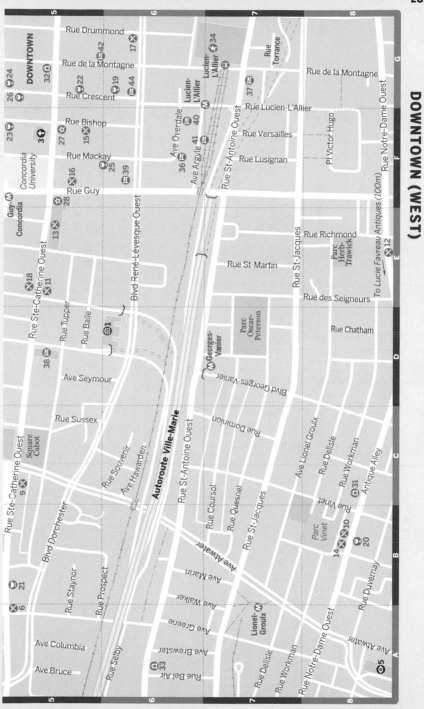

Rue Drummond

DOWNTOWN

42 🍴
17 ❌

32 🛍

24 🍴

Rue de la Montagne

26 🍴

22 🍴

19 🍴
44 ❌

Rue Crescent

23 🍴

27 🔵

15 ❌

Rue Bishop

3 ℹ️

16 ❌

Rue Mackay

25 🔵

39 🍴

28 🌟

Rue Guy

Guy 🅼
Concordia

Concordia
University

13 ❌

Blvd René-Lévesque Ouest

Lucien-
L'Allier 🔵 34

Lucien-
L'Allier 🅼

37 🍴

Rue Torrance

Rue de la Montagne

Rue Lucien-L'Allier

Ave Overdale

40

Rue Versailles

Pl Victor Hugo

Rue Notre-Dame Ouest

Rue Lusignan

Rue St-Antoine Ouest

Ave Argyle 41

36

Rue St-Jacques

Rue Richmond

Parc
Herb-
Trawick

To Lucie Favreau Antiques (100m)

12 ❌ E

Rue St-Martin

Rue des Seigneurs

Rue Chatham

18 ❌

11 ❌

Rue Ste-Catherine Ouest

Rue Tupper

Rue Baile

Parc
Oscar-
Peterson

Georges-
Vanier 🅼

38 🍴

🏛 1

Ave Seymour

Rue Sussex

Rue Ste-Catherine Ouest

Square
Cabot

9 🔵 ❌

Blvd Dorchester

Rue Staynor

Rue Prospect

Rue Souvenir

Ave Hawarden

Autoroute Ville-Marie

Rue St-Antoine Ouest

Rue Coursol

Rue Quesnel

Rue St-Jacques

Rue Dominion

Blvd Georges-Vanier

Ave Lionel Groulx

Rue Delisle

Rue Workman

Antique Alley

31 🛍

Rue Vinet

Parc
Vinet

14 ❌ 10 ❌

20 🔵

21 🍴

6 ❌

Ave Columbia

Ave Bruce

Rue Selby

Rue Bel Air

33 🛍

Ave Brewster

Ave Walker

Ave Greene

Ave Marin

Ave Atwater

Lionel-
Groulx 🅼

Rue Delisle

Rue Workman

Rue Notre-Dame Ouest

Ave Atwater

Rue Duvernay

5 ◎

DOWNTOWN (WEST) Map on p284

DOWNTOWN (EAST) *Map on p288*

288

DOWNTOWN (EAST)

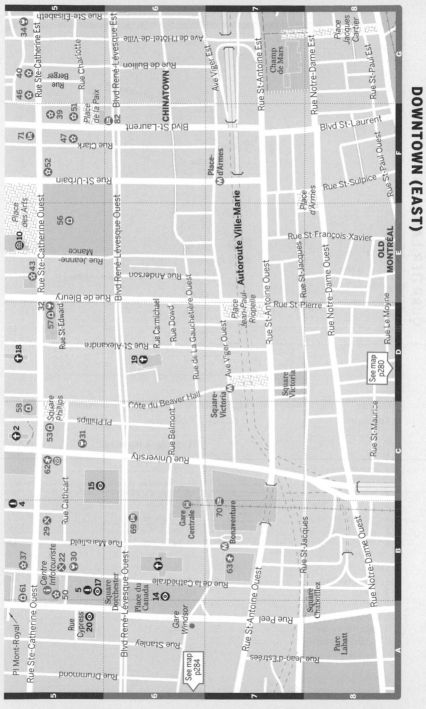

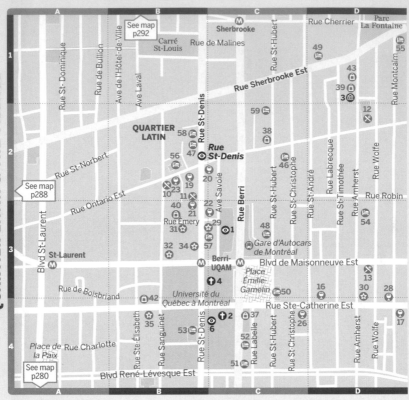

Key on p294

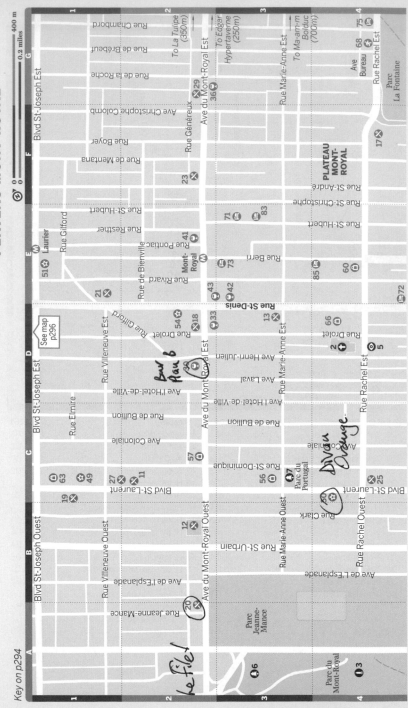

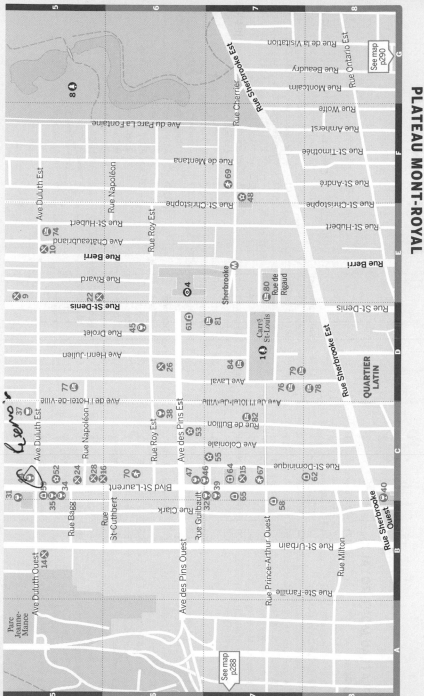

See map p290

See map p288

Rue de la Visitation
Rue Beaudry
Rue Montcalm
Rue Ontario Est
Rue Wolfe
Rue Amherst
Rue St-Timothée
Rue St-André
Rue St-Christophe
Rue St-Hubert
Rue Berri
Rue St-Denis

Rue Sherbrooke Est
Rue Cherrier

QUARTIER
LATIN

Rue de
Rigaud
80

Carré
St-Louis
1

Sherbrooke
Berri

Rue Rigaud
Rue de Menlana
Ave du Parc La Fontaine
8

Ave Duluth Est
Rue Napoléon
Rue St-Hubert
Rue Roy Est
Ave Châteaubriand
Rue Rivard
Rue Drolet
Ave Henri-Julien
Ave Laval
Ave de l'Hôtel-de-Ville
Ave de l'Hôtel-de-Ville
Rue de Bullion
Ave Coloniale
Rue St-Dominique
Blvd St-Laurent
Rue Clark
Rue Guilbault
Rue St-Urbain
Rue Prince-Arthur Ouest
Rue Ste-Famille
Rue Milton

Ave des Pins Est
Rue Roy Est
Ave des Pins Ouest

Rue Sherbrooke
Ouest

Parc
Jeanne-
Mance
Ave Duluth Ouest

Lenoir

LITTLE ITALY, MILE END & OUTREMONT *Map on p296*

LITTLE ITALY, MILE END & OUTREMONT

LITTLE ITALY, MILE END & OUTREMONT

400 m
0.2 miles

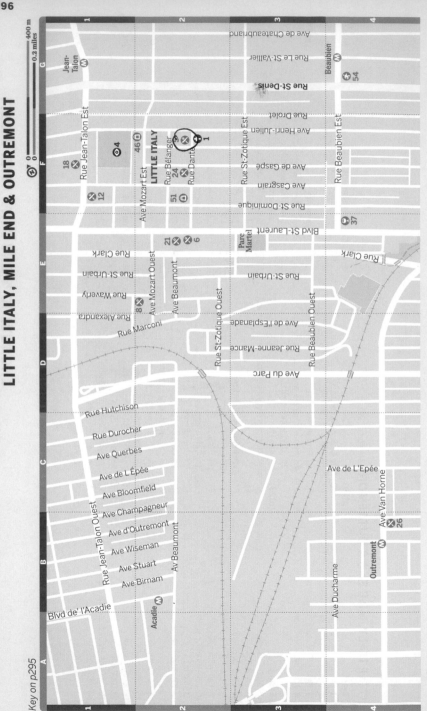

G
Jean-Talon Ⓜ
Rue Jean-Talon Est

F
18 ✗
Rue Jean-Talon Est
⊙ 4
12 ✗
Ave Mozart Est
46 ⊡
LITTLE ITALY
Rue Bélanger
24 ✗
51
⊡
Rue Dante
✗ 3
H 1

E
Rue Clark
Rue St-Urbain
Rue Waverly
Rue Alexandra
Ave Mozart Ouest
Ave Beaumont
Rue Marconi
8 ✗
21 ✗ ✗ 6
Parc Martel
Blvd St-Laurent

Ave de Chateaubriand
Rue Le St-Vallier
Beaubien Ⓜ
Rue St-Denis
⊙ 54
Rue Drolet
Ave Henri-Julien
Ave St-Zotique Est
Ave de Gaspé
Ave Casgrain
Rue St-Dominique
Rue St-Zotique Est
Rue Beaubien Est
37

D
Rue Hutchison
Rue St-Zotique Ouest
Rue St-Urbain
Ave de l'Esplanade
Rue Jeanne-Mance
Rue Beaubien Ouest
Ave du Parc
Rue Clark

C
Rue Durocher
Ave Querbes
Ave de L'Épée
Ave Bloomfield
Ave Champagneur
Ave d'Outremont
Ave Wiseman
Ave Stuart
Ave Birnam
Rue Jean-Talon Ouest
Av Beaumont
Ave de L'Épée
Ave Van Horne
Outremont Ⓜ
26 ✗
Ave Ducharme

A
Blvd de' l'Acadie
Acadie Ⓜ

LITTLE ITALY, MILE END & OUTREMONT

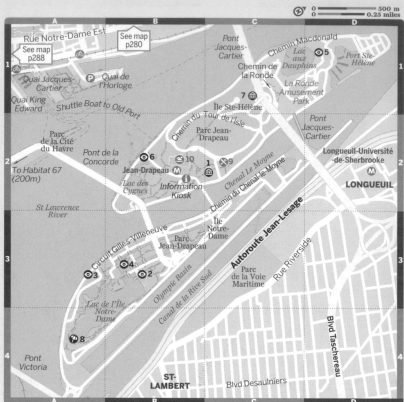

Our Story

A beat-up old car, a few dollars in the pocket and a sense of adventure. In 1972 that's all Tony and Maureen Wheeler needed for the trip of a lifetime – across Europe and Asia overland to Australia. It took several months, and at the end – broke but inspired – they sat at their kitchen table writing and stapling together their first travel guide, *Across Asia on the Cheap*. Within a week they'd sold 1500 copies. Lonely Planet was born.

Today, Lonely Planet has offices in Melbourne, London and Oakland, with more than 600 staff and writers. We share Tony's belief that 'a great guidebook should do three things: inform, educate and amuse'.

Our Writers

Timothy N Hornyak

Coordinating Author, Old Montréal, Parc Jean-Drapeau, Downtown, Quartier Latin & the Village, Plateau Mont-Royal, Little Italy, Mile End & Outremont, Southwest & Outer Montréal A native of Montréal, Tim grew up sledding down Mont-Royal and skiing in the Eastern Townships before his dreams of ninja took him to Japan for 10 years. He has written on Japanese culture, technology and history for CNET News, *Scientific American* and the *New York Times*, and has contributed to eight other Lonely Planet guidebooks. He is also the author of *Loving the Machine: The Art and Science of Japanese Robots*, his favorite robot being Astro Boy. He firmly believes that his hometown's greatest contribution to life on Earth is the perfection of the bagel. He divides his time between Tokyo and Montréal. Timothy also wrote the Plan Montréal, Understand Montréal and Survival Guide sections.

Read more about Timothy at:
lonelyplanet.com/members/timothyhornyak

Gregor Clark

Québec City A lifelong Francophile, Gregor was instantly smitten with Québec City on his first visit in 1981. Now a resident of neighboring Vermont, he regularly hops across the border for doses of French-Canadian culture and still rates Québec City as one of his two favorite North American cities (alongside San Francisco). He's especially fond of Québec's summertime Festival d'Été, but also enjoyed exploring the city's snowier side while researching this edition. Gregor has written more than 20 Lonely Planet guides since 2000, and in this guide also wrote the Day Trips, Visiting Québec City and Québec City History & Culture chapters.

Read more about Gregor at:
lonelyplanet.com/members/gregorclark

[Handwritten notes:]

'Zip'
Café

portugai.
polonai.

Manhatten / Negroni

Pouilly fuisse

(peht) ① Oysters. ← raw / cooked.
② Scallop / avocado / orange salad with beetroot
③ cardeau fish with jap sauce
④ Hommard with pastis + fennel
⑤ Crab rissotto.
⑥ Maple syrup earl grey

Published by Lonely Planet Publications Pty Ltd
ABN 36 005 607 983
3rd edition – Dec 2012
ISBN 978 1 74179 956 9
© Lonely Planet 2012   Photographs © as indicated 2012
10 9 8 7 6 5 4 3 2 1
Printed in China

Although the authors and Lonely Planet have taken all reasonable care in preparing this book, we make no warranty about the accuracy or completeness of its content and, to the maximum extent permitted, disclaim all liability arising from its use.